Contents

Preface

This book was written in the belief that economics is interesting. Many economics texts give the impression that the student needs to memorise lots of facts and complex diagrams. In this book economics is presented as one in which competing schools of thought contend. This reflects the reality of the subject.

Each chapter is organised so that there is a logical development of understanding. Though there are a few variations, each chapter follows a similar pattern:

● A short introduction outlines the area.

● Themes and debates which set the topic in context are then dealt with. Thus the chapter on unemployment begins with a discussion on the measurement and extent of unemployment.

● The competing perspectives which relate to the topic are discussed. At the end of each perspective there is a brief summary.

● The policies which result from a particular analysis follow these summaries, where appropriate.

This book has been written to cover examination syllabuses at A and AS level, professional courses and introductory courses in higher education. It could not have been written without the help of many people. In the first place I would like to thank several of my students for reading various chapters and making helpful suggestions. Several colleagues have also read parts of the manuscript, including John Coates, Paul McKeown, Shaun Lang and Dorothy Coates. Peter Chapman, Fran Smith, Dave Harston and Alan Fletcher commented on an early version, and my wife improved my English. Many of the ideas in the book have been adapted from various chapters in Developments in Economics (published annually by Causeway Press, and which I find is the best way to keep up to date in the subject). I am grateful to all these people, and in particular to my editor, Dave Gray, who has made huge improvements to the book. Despite all this help, there are doubtless errors and omissions; these are my responsibility.

Brian Atkinson, Lancashire Polytechnic.

Introduction and First Principles

Who reads introductions? Reviewers hoping for a quick quotation, insomniacs wanting something to send them to sleep, and the hyper-conscientious who read everything. Sensible people, knowing that time is scarce, often skip to the first chapter. Nevertheless this introduction is probably the most important part of the book because it introduces the basic ideas of economics.

Economics has been called 'the dismal science'. One reason for this (if you think about certain parts of economics syllabuses you may think of another!) is that without scarcity the subject would not exist. If we could all have our wants satisfied there would be no need for economics. A flick of the fingers and a Rolls Royce would appear, another flick and a villa on the Riviera would be mine, another and a machine would do the chores. There would be no need for production or distribution. Money would be irrelevant. Unfortunately the world is not like that.

Every society has to face three basic economic problems since we cannot produce everything that everyone would like:

- What should we produce?
- What methods should be used to produce these goods and services?
- Who should receive the goods and services that are produced?

Economics is the study of how people and societies choose to employ scarce resources which have alternative uses to produce goods and services, and how to distribute them. Economists analyse the costs and benefits of alternative ways of using resources.

By 'resources', economists mean land, labour and capital, such as machines and raw materials, which can be used in production. (These are also known as factors of production.) Resources are used to produce everything from apples to zoos, and it is because resources are scarce relative to wants that the economic problem arises.

Economists make use of concepts, and three in particular underlie much economic thinking: **opportunity cost, marginality** and **efficiency.** Even when these words are not specifically used in the text, the ideas they embody will be relevant to the analysis.

The opportunity cost of any action is the value of the forgone alternative action. All through life, individuals, firms and governments have to make choices. Choosing one alternative means that other alternatives have to be given up. Therefore the real cost of an action is the value of the most attractive alternative. In this sense all costs are opportunity costs. If a child is offered an ice cream or an ice lolly and chooses the latter, its real cost is the ice cream forgone. The real cost to Mary of kissing Peter is that she cannot kiss Paul (at least not at the same time!). If a plot of land could be used for playing fields, but instead the council decides to use it for parking, the real cost of the car park is the playing field forgone.

One view of the opportunity cost of building the Channel tunnel

Source: Flexilink, The Campaign for Cross Channel Choice, 1983.

ECONOMICS

Themes
and
Perspectives

G.B.J. Atkinson

Causeway Press

Cover design and graphics by Susan and Andrew Allen
Cartoons by Ian Traynor

Acknowledgements
The publishers are grateful to the following for permission to reproduce photographs.

Sally and Richard Greenhill p. 103; McDonald's Hamburgers Limited p. 211; Popperfoto pp. 3, 5, 7, 36, 117, 234; Public Relations Office, Liverpool University p. 107; Rex Features Ltd. p. 117; Steve Robertson p. 234; SNCF/CAV p. 110.

All HMSO sources are reproduced with the permission of the Controller of Her Majesty's Stationery Office.

Every effort has been made to locate the copyright owners of material used in the book. Any omissions brought to the notice of the publisher are regretted and will be credited in subsequent printings.

British Library Cataloguing in Publication Data
Atkinson, G.B.J.
    Economics: themes and perspectives.
    I. Title
    330

    ISBN 0-946183-54-6

Causeway Press Limited
PO Box 13, Ormskirk, Lancs, L39 5HP
© G.B.J. Atkinson
1st Impression 1989
Reprinted 1991

Typesetting by Lloyd Williams, Southport.
Printed and bound by The Alden Press, Oxford.

The central assumption underlying opportunity cost is that each act excludes other possible acts at any moment in time. In some cases the opportunity cost can be measured in monetary terms. Often it cannot. Whatever the difficulties of measurement, opportunity cost is probably the most fundamental concept in economics and is applicable in a wide range of circumstances. It explains why some teachers rush off home as soon as school ends (home is preferable to school) - and why some are reluctant to go home. It helps us realise that the real cost of putting up old age pensions may be that child benefit cannot be increased. Similarly, if resources are used to develop a third London airport, provincial airports such as Manchester may suffer restricted growth.

The second fundamental concept is that of the margin.

Marginal analysis is the analysis of the relations between increments or decrements of the total quantity of some economic variable.

The idea of the margin is frequently used in everyday life. A cook deciding to add a little more salt to the soup is undertaking marginal analysis. So too is an athlete who wonders whether or not an extra training session would be beneficial, and the student who considers the (opportunity) costs and benefits of an extra hour's revision.

Marginality is important in economics because the appropriate unit of appraisal is usually the increment. That is because we rarely start from scratch. A business person calculates the consequences of employing extra workers or installing a few more machines. Will the extra costs of production be covered by the extra revenue obtained when the product is sold? Similarly, the Chancellor of the Exchequer starts from the position that the rate of income tax is (say) 30 pence in the pound and therefore calculates the effects of a (marginal) change in the rate of tax to 31 pence in the pound.

Our third basic concept is efficiency. Efficiency means that it is not possible to maintain the present level of output with less input, or that it is impossible to get more output of a good from given inputs.

Efficiency therefore has a fairly specialised meaning in economics. In everyday life it sometimes seems to mean cutting costs, such as wages. For the economist, however, a rise in cost may mean greater efficiency if it causes revenue to rise by a greater amount. Efficiency provides a criterion by which we can judge the success or otherwise of any act. When economic circumstances change, so will efficiency. Thus if people work harder or longer this may increase efficiency, but it may reduce it because output will also change.

In economic analysis these three concepts often interact. Thus in **micro-economics** (the study of individual institutions such as firms), economists analyse such questions as the effect on efficiency if a firm makes a decision to increase output (a marginal decision). This will also involve consideration of the opportunity cost. These three concepts also underlie **macro-economics** (the study of the economy as a whole).

The theoretical framework of economics is one which seeks to improve the allocation of resources. This involves comparing the costs and benefits of actions and drawing appropriate conclusions making use of concepts such as opportunity cost, marginality, and efficiency. The costs and benefits may be measurable in money terms, but they may not; for example, a beautiful view may be lost when a factory is built.

The basic concepts discussed in this introduction underlie the whole economics. They will frequently re-appear in the rest of the book because they are used by economists of all perspectives to develop economic arguments.

For Rachel Atkinson: greatly loved, because greatly loving.

1 Why Economists Disagree

'If all the economists in the world were laid end to end they wouldn't reach a conclusion.' Economists disagree for a very good reason; no one possesses ultimate truth. Like other people, economists tend to associate with those who share their own values and opinions and hence various schools of thought develop. This chapter identifies three main perspectives which are referred to throughout the book:

● One group who, for the moment, will be referred to as supply side or market economists focus their attention on the individuals who provide goods and services, and argue that governments should give more incentives to such individuals. They believe that markets are the best way to allocate resources and that government intervention should be limited.

● Keynesians argue that there is a greater role for government, for example, in combatting unemployment. They are sometimes called interventionists because they believe that, whilst markets are important, they often fail to allocate resources in a satisfactory way.

● Marxists argue that in a capitalist system economic crises are inevitable and so a change in the entire system is needed.

Although many economic debates can be approached through these three perspectives, there are others which can not. Debates about the size of firms, for example, involve other groups. Where appropriate, debates will focus on these other viewpoints.

Reasons for disagreement

It is only in the worlds of dreams or dictators that everyone agrees. In such realms either everything is perfect and all 'truths' are known, so there is nothing to disagree about, or the dictator lays down 'the truth' and everyone is forced to agree. Fortunately there is no dictator of economic theory. Economists believe that they live in the real world and not in the land of dreams. Hence they disagree with each other and occasionally with their own previously expressed opinions. This disagreement is a virtue. Since no economist would claim to have discovered the ultimate truth about the subject, it follows that what is written and spoken by economists is less than the whole truth. Therefore criticism of such untruths or partial truths is necessary, for it is only by rigorous criticism that the subject will progress.

Some economists claim that economics is a science and uses scientific methods of enquiry. There are various ways in which scientific knowledge develops. One which is often fruitful is based on the gradual development of understanding. Scientists build on their knowledge of what has gone before. X puts forward a theory, Y points out a flaw and Z improves the theory. Hence the development of understanding depends on criticising the work of others.

There are several reasons why economists disagree.

Ignorance

Economists disagree because they are ignorant. This statement applies equally to scholars of all disciplines. Until ultimate truth is known, if it ever is, people will make false statements which reflect their ignorance. Consequently economics books, like those of other subjects, are full of half truths. Unfortunately we do not know which half is true and which is not.

Particular difficulties facing social scientists

If all scientists face the problem of ignorance, those working in social sciences, such as economics, face particular difficulties. One reason is that the focus of their attention is people and people's behaviour changes. The same family will save this year, but decide to spend next year. At another time they will

1

want work, but as time passes they may be content to stay at home. If taxes are increased, some people will decide to work more in order to maintain their income after tax, whilst others will work less because they decide work is no longer worthwhile. Moreover, people's behaviour changes over time because they learn from their experiences. An atom of hydrogen will always act like an atom of hydrogen, but people will sometimes change their actions when faced with a similar situation. This makes it very difficult, perhaps even impossible, to derive any general laws of human behaviour. An economic 'law' which seems to operate in one country, or at one period of time, may prove to be quite inadequate elsewhere or at other times. Human beings are complex creatures, so it is not surprising that academics who try to derive laws which will predict their actions are often wrong.

Inadequate methods

Economists also disagree because their methods are not good enough to reveal the whole truth. Economic theory is an attempt to explain and interpret economic data, for example, to determine the causes and effects of economic events. These explanations are often expressed in terms of 'if this, then that'; for example, if the price of fish rises then people will eat less fish, or if the government increases its spending then there will be a fall in unemployment. However, in complex societies such predictions can never be absolute; the demand for fish may not fall, even if its price does rise, if there is a shortage of meat or if there is a successful advertising campaign for fish.

Such predictions depend on the assumption of *ceteris paribus* - that other things remain equal. In real life, however, other things do not remain equal. A prediction that was previously successful may not be so at another time or in another place.

Testing theories

The only way to test economic theories is to match them against the evidence. This may seem obvious, but in practice evidence cannot prove a theory to be true. That is because facts do not speak for themselves, but have to be interpreted. Which facts should be used? There are millions of economic 'facts', so the ones which are chosen will depend, in part, on the purpose of the investigation and also on the values and attitudes of those undertaking the investigation. For example, there may be disputes between economists over whether the people in a particular area are really poor. How do we decide

who is 'poor'? Concentration camp inmates and famine victims are certainly poor, but there is room for considerable disagreement about which people in a country such as Britain can be called poor. Even if this could be agreed, differences of opinion would emerge as to the causes of the poverty.

Some may argue that poverty is caused because:
- people are lazy,
- people are unlucky,
- of ignorance,
- of their family background,
- they are the victims of social forces, such as declining industries,
- of bad government policies.

Evidence could be found to support all these possible causes of poverty. Those researchers who believe that the real reason why some people are poor is that they are lazy or ignorant will certainly be able to find examples to support their case, as will those who favour other causes, such as unsatisfactory government policies.

Values

People tend to seek out evidence to support their beliefs and so substantiate their opinions. We can easily find examples of this in other areas of life. Manchester United football fans often talk to other United supporters and reinforce each other in their belief that theirs is the best team. Similarly, people who believe that poverty is a severe problem in the UK may often associate with others who hold similar beliefs and so strengthen this belief. If such people then decide to research the extent of poverty in the country it is not surprising if they find many examples of people living in poverty.

When Manchester United supporters see their striker fall in the opposing team's penalty area, they interpret this fact to support their belief that the striker was fouled and that a penalty is justified. So it is in economics. People who support or oppose trade unions tend to interpret the facts about unions in ways which will support their beliefs. There is strong disagreement in economics as to whether or not it is possible to develop economic theories which are entirely value free - where the economist's opinions make no difference to the argument or to the evidence which is presented to support or oppose the argument. This 'value free' approach is called **positive economics** and dominated the subject for many years. The positive approach is discussed further in the concluding chapter. Whether or not it is possible for economics to be value free, it is certainly true that in some cases the values and opinions held by economists influence their findings and cause them to disagree with other economists. For example, economists are sometimes paid to investigate a problem and this can influence their findings. A leading American economist, J.K. Galbraith, claimed in his autobiography *A Life in our Times* (1981):

'Economics professors often seek outside income, and one obvious place of resource is the big corporation. This is not good. When an economist argues for lower taxes on the affluent, people should be right in believing that he is speaking out of economic perception or compassion and not because he has been bought.'

A perspectives approach assumes that there are a variety of ways of seeing an economic problem and that the particular approach adopted will depend on the views of the individual economist.

Key ideas

1. The root cause of all disagreement is ignorance. Without ultimate truth, people will disagree.
2. Social scientists face particular difficulties because they study people, and people are inconsistent.
3. Economic theories and models are not adequate for the task they face.
4. Economists' values affect their investigations.

Three schools of thought

There are thousands of economists in the world, so any attempt to divide economists into three groups is bound to be a rough and ready division. Nevertheless, it is possible to divide economists into three such groups, each of which has its own set of beliefs and attendant arguments. However, there are disagreements within each group, just as Christians, Moslems and Hindus each have common underlying beliefs, yet also disagree with others of the same faith.

Economists also share some beliefs with those from other schools of thought, just as some Christians might accept ideas from other religions. Hence the following description of three groups of economists should not be interpreted to mean that there is complete agreement within, or disagreement between, each school of thought. Economists disagree even with those who have quite similar views!

The supply side/free-market perspective

Many of the ideas of this group of economists derive from the work of Adam Smith (1723-90) whose book *An Enquiry into the Nature and Causes of the Wealth of Nations* (1776) is a masterpiece which has stimulated many later economists. Smith was born in Kirkcaldy in Scotland and later attended the universities of Glasgow and Oxford, where he found the teachers scandalously idle and incompetent (how different from teachers today!). The *Wealth of Nations* was an immediate success. It was published at the beginning of the Industrial Revolution and provided a guide to policies in this new world, for example, advocating free trade and less state control.

Adam Smith (1723-1790)

Supply side economists focus their attention on the factors which encourage people to produce and exchange more goods and services. Although this title is relatively new, the approach of these economists represents an updating of **classical economics.** Classical economists, such as Adam Smith, were the first to emphasise the use of markets to allocate resources. Their ideas were refined by **neo-classical** economists who developed important concepts such as demand and supply. In the 1970s,

3

a group of economists worried about inflation built on the ideas of the neo-classical economists and stressed the importance of controlling the money supply. Consequently they are sometimes called **monetarists.** The position is even more complicated because some of these economists advocate **new classical macroeconomics.** This implies that they take the values and approaches of classical economists and apply them to modern macro-economic problems, such as inflation and unemployment. Such a diversity of names is an indication that this is not a single coherent group, but one which contains a variety of views. In this book, we choose not to explore their detailed differences. Instead, where a specific emphasis is required, such as the view of monetarists, then the appropriate name will be used. In most cases, however, we will use the terms 'market economists' or 'supply side economists' to describe this group.

Supply side ideas

Despite the differences, the work of economists within this group has a common focus. Their ideas focus on the beliefs and actions of individuals. They believe that individuals know what is in their own interest and are competent to choose wisely. The only exceptions are those who are not able to look after themselves.

Milton Friedman, one of the leading economists in the group wrote that:

'freedom is a tenable objective for responsible individuals. We do not believe in freedom for madmen or children'.

This may seem a reasonable approach, but its consequences are far reaching. Countries such as Britain have compulsory insurance schemes for illness and old age. Some of the economists in this group believe this should be stopped because it restricts the freedom of the individual. If people want to spend all their money when young and healthy they should be free to choose this option, even if it means that they will be unable to pay for treatment when they are ill and may starve when they become old.

Similarly, it is the responsibility of individuals to seek employment. If people really want work, they can find it. Jobs are always available, but people have to accept lower wages in order to obtain them.

Freedom to choose is a central feature of this approach. Charles Rowley (1978), a leading British supply sider, argues that:

'freedom to choose is an end in itself . . . The freedom is negative and not positive, ensuring an individual of no particular opportunities, but leaving him free to choose among such alternatives as are available to him without restrictions'.

If individuals are to have the maximum freedom, it follows that the state should play a crucial, but smaller, role in society, particularly in economic affairs. At present the state plays a major role in economic life. To give just a few examples, it spends huge amounts of money on social security, health and education. It subsidises certain goods, such as some bus services, and gives mortgage tax relief to those buying their own homes. It also provides money to encourage industries to move to areas of high unemployment. Supply side economists would try to reduce or eliminate many or all of these activities because they limit the freedom of individuals to do what they want.

Put another way, they believe that the best way to allocate resources is to leave it to the market. This is the subject of other chapters. Here it is enough to say that they want to limit the activities of the state to such things as defence, law and order, and the protection of those who are unable to look after themselves because they are children or mentally incompetent. The state should also give top priority in economic policy to the elimination of inflation because this harms individuals.

'In everything we seek to do we must recognise the unique importance of each individual in the scheme of things . . . We shall look to people, not corporate bodies and institutions, to individual flair and drive . . . to spearhead our industrial and commercial recovery'

proclaimed Angus Maude (1977) an early supply sider.

> ### Key ideas - summary of the supply side approach
>
> **1. Economies develop because of the actions of individuals.**
> **2. Individuals are rational and know their own best interests. If individuals are unemployed it is usually because they are not willing to work at prevailing wage rates.**
> **3. The role of the state is important, but it should concentrate on a limited range of activities, such as providing an environment in which individuals can flourish.**
> **4. Market forces are the best way to allocate resources. Trade unions interfere with markets and so are to be discouraged.**

Supply side policies

If this belief in individualism, markets and limited government is accepted, then certain policies follow. Individuals are responsible for their own actions, so state spending on social security should be reduced and targeted on those who are unable to help themselves. If individuals are without jobs this is usually because they choose to be unemployed; they could always get work if they were willing to accept lower wages. State 'interference' in business, such as the need for planning permission before building a new factory, should be cut. Legislation to protect workers' rights should be reduced, so employers can make workers redundant more easily, and trade union power weakened because this interferes with market forces. Taxes should be cut, particularly income tax, because this reduces the incentive to work.

At the heart of these policies is individual motivation and the encouragement of incentives to work, innovate and compete in markets.

'The aim should be to promote free markets throughout the world and maximum reliance by all countries on free enterprise in an environment favourable to competition and to individual initiative'

urges Milton Friedman.

The focus of interest of this group of economists can be illustrated by the titles of the books published by the Institute of Economic Affairs, an organisation specialising in the study of markets:

- *The Fallacy of the Mixed Economy.*
- *Too Much Money.*
- *Experiment with Choice in Education.*
- *Shoppers Choice.*
- *What Right to Strike?*
- *The Birth of Enterprise.*

The Keynesian/interventionist perspective

If supply side economics developed out of the work of Adam Smith and the classical economists of the nineteenth century, Keynesian economics derives from the ideas of the man who challenged that tradition, John Maynard Keynes.

Keynes was born in 1883, the son of a Cambridge University lecturer. He went to a preparatory school and won a scholarship to Eton where he was encouraged by his father's stream of letters which included comments such as 'Why did you let Smith minor beat you in the Maths test last week?' From Eton he went to Kings College Cambridge where he

John Maynard Keynes (1883-1946)

studied Maths. The rest of his life was spent between Cambridge and London. Keynes was one of the few rich economists. In one summer in the 1920s he made £200,000 tax-free by speculating in international currency markets and used the money to finance his passionate interest in the arts. He founded the Cambridge Arts Theatre and later was responsible for the formation of the Arts Council. He was an active member of the Bloomsbury group of writers and artists, which included E.M. Forster, Virginia Woolf and Duncan Grant. Bertrand Russell wrote:

'Keynes' intellect was the sharpest and clearest that I have ever known. When I argued with him I felt that I took my life in my hands and I seldom emerged without feeling something of a fool.'

During the Second World War, Keynes was responsible for British economic policy and was the prime mover in the creation of the International Monetary Fund and the World Bank. He died in 1946.

Keynesian/interventionist ideas

Keynes' ideas were put forward in a huge number of books and articles. Keynes himself believed that although market forces had many virtues, they could also have many undesirable consequences. For example, Keynesian economists believe that without some kind of government intervention market forces may lead to undesirable consequences:

- Persistent unemployment on a large scale, as happened in the 1930s and 1980s.
- Industrialists polluting the atmosphere.
- Too many cars in the cities, leading to congestion and accidents.
- Sick people being unable to afford medical care.
- Young people receiving an inadequate education.
- Some regions of the economy facing long-term decline.
- Poor housing for some people.
- Certain groups in society, for example, the old, those with large families and the handicapped living in unacceptable poverty.

Hence Keynesians argue that the government must intervene in the economy to prevent or remedy the undesirable consequences which can result from unregulated market forces. Roy Hattersley, though not an economist, puts the case clearly in his book *Choose Freedom* (1987). He argues that although markets must determine the allocation of resources for many goods and services, they may have to be regulated in various ways, such as by price controls and subsidies or by regulations to protect workers, consumers and the environment.

He continues:

'The pattern of distribution which unrestricted market forces produce automatically and inevitably creates a hierarchical society in which the needs of the less well-off are neglected in the interest (the immediate financial interest) of the prosperous. A hierarchical society will not create or sustain an adequate health service; nor will it provide all the nation's families with adequate housing or education.'

Note that although Roy Hattersley is a Labour Party politician, people from other political parties would accept Keynesian arguments.

Keynesian policies

Keynesian policies derive from the basic assumption that governments need to intervene in the economy. Keynesian economists argue that if there is large-scale unemployment, then the government should intervene to stimulate the economy by increasing government spending on goods and services. Employers in industries where sales increase will then take on more workers, so reducing unemployment. Similarly, the government should

increase spending in the poorer regions of the country and subsidise industries moving to these areas. They also argue that the government should regulate industry, for example, in order to reduce pollution and protect workers against exploitation. Keynesian economists also tend to favour policies which help disadvantaged groups in society, such as the expansion of the National Health Service, higher social security payments to those in need and greater spending on foreign aid to poorer countries.

Unlike supply siders, interventionists argue that people are sometimes unable to make rational choices and therefore the state must intervene to protect them, for example, by passing laws which stop people selling dubious 'medicines'.

Key ideas - summary of the Keynesian approach

1. **Individuals cannot always be self-reliant and often need the help of the state. The old, the sick and the poor are examples. Similarly, if people are unemployed it is usually not their own fault but the result of the system. If one person gets a job, it may be at the expense of others unless more jobs are created.**
2. **Markets have considerable defects, but are still an important way of allocating resources.**
3. **Governments should play an active role in economic life to remedy these defects, often by increasing government spending to remedy the inability of individuals to afford desirable goods or to regulate the activities of industry.**

The Marxist perspective

Although Marxist economics has never been dominant in countries such as the UK, it does offer valuable insights and acts as a counterweight to the acceptance of more conventional theories.

As with Keynesian economics, Marxist economics derives largely from the work of one person, Karl Marx, who was born in 1818 in Germany and died in 1883 - the year in which Keynes was born. When he was 17 he went to the University of Bonn to study law and took an active part in student life; on one occasion he was imprisoned for a night for drunkenness and on another he was wounded in a duel. He had a long and happy marriage and five children, though three of these died while Marx was still alive. His political views made it difficult for him to obtain work and he was usually hard up. He was forced to leave Germany and spent the last half of his life in Britain. Marx wrote newspaper articles to raise money and was also active in left wing political activities. With Friedrich Engels he wrote *The Communist Manifesto* (1848), but his economic ideas are to be found in the volumes of *Capital* (Vol. 1 1867, Vol. 2 1885, Vol. 3 1894).

Karl Marx (1818-1883)

Marxist ideas

Marx's economic ideas derive from his political/ philosophical analysis. These ideas are very complex, but at the risk of over-simplification it is possible to say that Marx believed he had discovered a universal theory of history. He argued that throughout history societies had been run in the interests of those who owned the dominant means of production. Thus in medieval times the most important means of production was the land and so laws were passed in the interest of the landowners, for example, making poaching punishable by death. He argued that in modern society the dominant means of production is capital, so society is run in the interests of those who own factories and banks. For example, laws are passed attacking trade unions; the media are owned or controlled by the rich and so praise those who make profits and attack those

who threaten the status quo. Marx believed that capitalism could not last.

'Society as a whole is splitting up into two great hostile camps, into two great classes facing each other'

he wrote in *The Communist Manifesto*. He believed competition between capitalists would cause large firms to take over small ones, so the economy would be characterised by a few giant organisations and these would be opposed by a growing number of workers. In this system conflict and crisis would be inevitable. If firms paid high wages then crises would result because profits would be too low. There would also be a crisis if wages were low because then the workers would not be able to buy enough goods and services to maintain full employment.

Key ideas - summary of the Marxist approach

1. Crises are inevitable in capitalist countries. This means that unemployment will be a recurrent feature of such societies.

2. In the long run, economic crises can only be overcome by a complete change in the system - by a revolution.

3. In the short run, appropriate policies can ameliorate the adverse consequences of the system. These involve greater use of state power, either to nationalise privately owned firms or to make them behave in socially desirable ways, such as undertaking functions which are beneficial but not profitable.

4. Markets have a part to play, but these can lead to undesirable consequences, such as unemployment and shortages of desirable goods. Hence the government should intervene to improve the position.

Marxist policies

Marxist economic policies derive from this basic analysis. Economic crises are inevitable and in the long run only a complete change of the system will solve the problems of capitalism. In the short run, however, Marxist economists argue that appropriate policies can improve the economy. These policies usually involve a greater role for the state. Markets have a part to play, but need to be managed so they work in the interests of people and not the capitalists. 'Production for need, not profit' would be accepted as an appropriate slogan by modern Marxists. They also believe that, left to itself, a capitalist system will lead to greater divisions in society. Therefore the government should increase taxes on the rich and improve welfare benefits for the disadvantaged.

Marxists believe that the state needs to own and run the most important industries in the economy, such as banking. Only in this way can the country be sure that there will be high levels of investment, that useful goods and services which are not profitable will be produced and that industries will continue to produce in declining regions. Thus Marxists would tend to keep unprofitable coal mines open in some areas because they serve as a focus for community life and because profit is not a valid way to estimate the contribution of an industry to the community. Marxists also advocate the use of subsidies to persuade privately owned firms to act in socially desirable ways. Firms might be given grants to encourage them to move to areas where unemployment is high or to maintain unprofitable services, such as rural bus routes. To combat unemployment, Marxists argue that the government should increase its spending along the lines which Keynesian economists advocate, but they tend to suggest that greater amounts of money should be spent. Many Marxists would also support controls on imports to protect domestic industries.

Conclusion

No economist possesses ultimate truth. Economists disagree because the world is so complex that we can only hope to understand small parts of how an economy works. Moreover, our inability to understand complex problems is compounded by inadequate methods; complex problems require complicated methods of analysis and all the computers in the world are insufficient to master its economic problems.

People differ in their values and attitudes; this affects the way people see the world and its problems. Often the way economists approach a problem will reflect their underlying beliefs and, because these differ, so will their economic analyses. An economist who believes that contraception is wrong will have a very different approach to the analysis of population to one who favours the use of contraceptives. These differences between economists lead to different schools of thought or perspectives.

Three main perspectives have been outlined in this chapter, each with its own ideas and policies. Others will be examined, where appropriate, in later chapters. It should be noted:

- There is some agreement between economists from different groups, for example, that rising living standards depend on making the economy more efficient.
- There are differences between economists in the same group, for example, about the precise policies needed to bring down the rate of inflation. More dramatically, Trotsky, a leading Marxist, ended up with an axe in his head, put there by another Marxist. Fortunately, few disagreements end up this way or there would be a considerable shortage of economists!

Many of the disagreements between these groups of economists focus on the use of markets to allocate resources and this is the concern of the next two chapters.

Data questions

The profit system

Yet even after the longest and most successful boom in its history (from 1950 to 1970), the system has been unable to provide for everyone a life free from material want. The number of people suffering from starvation and malnutrition around the world, and even in the richest country of all, the USA, certainly grew in absolute numbers and perhaps also relative to the size of the population of the world as well. Even in the advanced countries, with very few exceptions (such as perhaps Sweden and Switzerland), there is evidence to suggest that relative full employment and rapid economic growth did not eliminate widespread poverty.

Part of the reason for this deficiency is the chronically unequal distribution of income, of the power to consume, both within each country and between different countries. Another factor has been the kind of products which the available resources have been used to produce. The most obvious example is the production of armaments and other forms of military expenditure. Not far off one-twentieth of the productive resources of the world in the last thirty years has been used to produce means not of sustaining human life but of producing human death. Many more resources are spent in polluting the natural environment, dirtying the air we breathe, the water we drink and so on, not deliberately but as a by-product of the search for profits.

Much economic effort is also devoted to satisfying socially determined needs intrinsic to capitalism, such as producing drugs to combat stress, or goods and services to counteract the effects of pollution.

There is no way of estimating what proportion of resources are used in these various 'unnecessary' ways, but it must be very substantial. On top of all the unnecessary production is the waste of leaving resources unutilized: the machines, land and other productive equipment which lie idle during periodic depressions, and the masses of unemployed and short-time workers.

The consequences of economic slumps under capitalism are very far-reaching. Their instant result is physical want for a sizeable section of the population, mainly those who already occupy an underprivileged position. Physical want and insecurity result both in material deprivation (even starvation, disease and death) and psychological damage (slumps and recessions produce more stress, fear, mental illness and suicides).

Source: Green, F. and Sutcliffe, B. *The Profit System,* Penguin, 1987.

Unemployment and the unions

The pursuit of gain is thus the only way in which men can serve the requirements of others whom they do not know, and adjust their efforts to circumstances they cannot directly observe. The pursuit of gain is held in bad repute, because it does not have as its aim the visible benefit of others and may be successfully guided by purely selfish motives. Yet the source of the strength of the market order is that it uses the immediate concerns of individuals to make them serve needs that are more important than they can know. It is not because a man's aims are 'selfish' but because they are his own that he can contribute, through his free decisions guided by the signals of prices, more to the welfare of others than if that were his direct goal. His efforts may not be the most beneficial to his immediate neighbours - and for that reason may not make him popular among them - but he will thus serve society at large much better than he could in any other way.

Source: Hayek, F.A. *1980s Unemployment and the Unions,* Institute of Economic Affairs, Second Edition, 1984.

Question 1

1. Identify the perspectives illustrated in the above articles. Justify your choices.
2. Outline the policies that each perspective would advocate for the solution to unemployment.

2 Allocating Resources: Market and Command Economies

There is no such thing as a free school meal. Although the person who eats the meal may not have paid for it, the meal is not free because real resources have been used to prepare it. In other words, free school meals have an opportunity cost because the resources used to make the meal could have been used to make other goods.

This example illustrates the central problem of economics. No society can supply all the goods and services which people would like. That is because resources of land, labour and capital are scarce relative to society's desires for goods and services. Consequently difficult decisions have to be made. Since we cannot produce all the goods and services people would like, we need to decide what should we produce? (the allocation problem), what methods should be used to produce these goods? (the production problem), and who should receive the goods and services which are produced? (the distribution problem):

● There is no perfect way to solve these problems. In command economies the major economic decisions, such as what to produce, are made by the government. Examples of command economies are China, some of the Eastern European countries and the UK during the Second World War.

● However, command economies have a number of limitations - they are often rigid and bureaucratic. Consequently many economists favour market forces as a way of solving the economic problems arising from scarcity.

How should economic systems be judged?

If we want to judge someone's height we have a universally accepted criterion and method. We simply measure the person using a unanimously accepted scale, such as inches or centimetres.

Making judgements on economic systems is a different proposition because there is no generally accepted measure, and because some ways of organising the economy produce good results in one area but not in another. Moreover, there are no generally accepted criteria for deciding what an economic system should achieve. Despite the difficulties, it is probably true to say that for many economists, and perhaps the majority of people in countries such as the UK, the desirable characteristics of an economy are:

● rapid economic growth,
● low levels of unemployment,
● no inflation,
● efficiency,
● equity (fairness),
● a satisfactory composition of output - for example, resources are used to produce those commodities which people want,
● a satisfactory balance of payments.

Note that this list would not be accepted by all economists. For example, some people believe that we put too much emphasis on economic growth and too little on the conservation of natural resources. This would be the view of Green Party supporters in many countries.

Different types of economy attempt to achieve these goals in different ways. In this chapter we will examine two important types - the **command economy** and the **market economy.** In practice these two types of economic system do not exist in a pure form, so that all modern economies are a mixture of the two types.

Nevertheless it is useful to consider these 'ideal types' because they enable us to examine the economic problem in two contrasting contexts.

The command economy

A command economy is one where the allocation of resources is decided by a centralised administrative process.

The command economy is so called because economic decisions are made by commands from authorities who are responsible for planning the economy; consequently this system is sometimes also called a planned economy. This type of system was used in countries such as the UK in the Second World War, when the government took powers to order factories to produce certain goods and the Minister of Labour had power to direct labour - men and women - into particular occupations or into the armed forces. Consumers may have wanted chocolates or bananas, but the country needed weapons of war; central planning ensured that these goods were produced.

However, command economies are more familiar in Eastern European countries today and are closely associated with the Marxist perspective. This is because Marxists advocate the abolition of capitalism, and in existing command economies most of the means of production are owned by the state so that there is only a small capitalist class.

Because of the link between Marxism and command economies, the best examples of command economies are the socialist countries of Eastern Europe and China. As it is the prime example, this section will focus on the Soviet economy, though there are considerable differences between this and some other command economies. The present system dates back to 1928 when Stalin introduced the first Five Year Plan, though there have been changes, particularly in recent years.

Figure 2.1: *Planning in the USSR*

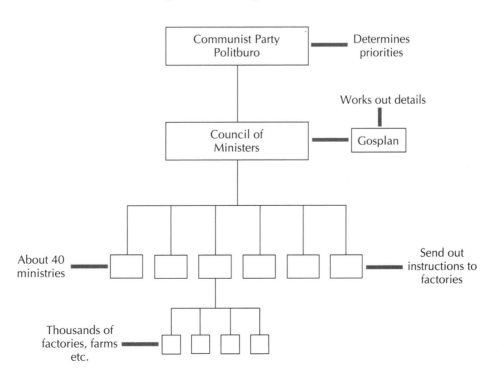

The Soviet system is hierarchical. Every shop, farm and factory is subordinate to a higher level organisation which is, in turn, ultimately subordinate to another organisation. Ultimate power rests in a single central authority, the Politburo of the Central Committee of the Communist Party. The Politburo makes the basic economic decisions, for example, that greater priority should be given to housing or that more resources should be devoted to defence. These decisions are then passed down to the Council of Ministers which clarifies the proposals with the aid of Gosplan, the State Planning Committee. This sets targets for over 20,000 products and groups of products and formulates a plan, usually for five years, though alterations are made each year to reflect changing circumstances. Orders are then passed to particular ministries, of which there are about forty and, in turn, orders are then sent to several hundred thousand factories, farms or other organisations.

In principle the system is simple. The government decides the priorities - what shall be produced - and individual factories are set targets. If these are accomplished, the Plan will be successful. In practice, the system is more complex. The manager of a factory or farm knows the problems and possibilities of the organisation and this information is fed up the hierarchy. If managers think that their target is impossible they will say so and the target will then often be adjusted. Thus to some extent orders are written by those who receive them. Influences such as the weather, which cannot be planned, also affect the system, so that plans cannot be rigid and inflexible but are constantly adjusted in the light of changing circumstances. Moreover, although the authorities can plan production, they cannot really plan consumption. If families do not wish to buy a particular product they cannot be forced to do so.

In this system the authorities make relatively little use of prices to influence production or consumption, though if they wish to discourage consumption of a particular product (such as vodka) they will put up the price. Prices, however, do also play a part in the private sector of the economy. Many people have small plots on which they grow produce to sell and prices do influence what will be grown. High prices for a particular product will persuade people to produce more of it next year. In general, however, the role of the price system is one of the fundamental differences between a planned economy and a market system. The private producers just described are characteristic of the market system rather than the planned economy

because they produce only a small proportion of total output in most planned economic systems.

In the USSR prices are fixed by the state and are usually based on the cost of production, plus a 'profit' margin, though prices for favoured goods such as public transport and housing are kept deliberately low. Once prices have been decided they are then only changed at infrequent intervals.

This section on command economies has focused on the system as it operates in the Soviet Union and may be misleading for two reasons. In the first place, the economic organisation of the Soviet Union is changing in order to give more emphasis to market forces. Secondly, in other socialist countries the practice may be quite different. In Yugoslavia, enterprises are usually controlled by the workers through the election of a workers council and enterprises often compete against each other. In Hungary most enterprises determine their own product mix, find their own markets, and workers' income depends partly on the profits of the enterprise. These variations suggest that the advantages and disadvantages of command economies as described here may depend as much on the history and traditions of the Soviet Union as on the fact that it is a command economy. For example, Russia has always had a tradition of a rather inefficient centralised bureaucracy. It is therefore open to argument whether the strengths and weaknesses of the economy of the USSR are inevitable in all command economies, or whether they reflect the history and traditions of a particular country.

Advantages of a command economy

A command economy can have substantial benefits. If the priorities of the people are those of the planners, then resources can be concentrated to satisfy these priorities. This was the case in the UK in the Second World War. Although people would have liked more consumer goods, it was generally realised that priority had to be given to the war effort and the result of planning was a huge increase in the production of weapons of war. In the USSR priority is given to goods and services such as public transport and housing, classical music, basic foodstuffs and approved books. The prices of these are kept low and most are in abundant supply, though housing, particularly in the big cities, remains a problem area. Education and health are also given priority. In East Germany, sport is given a high priority and the result is that this small country is the most successful in the world in many sports.

Unemployment ceases to be a major problem in command economies. That is because the state planning organisations plan labour as well as production. If the planners decide to expand the motor vehicle industry, for example, they have to ensure that sufficient workers with the right skills are available. Moreover, the managers of individual units try to ensure that they have sufficient workers to fulfil their targets. Although workers can be sacked for breaches of labour discipline, in the USSR at least, they seem to be able to find other jobs quite easily. Although this is an advantage to the individual workers, it can lead to labour inefficiency because idle workers know that other work is available should they be sacked. Full employment does not mean that people always get the job they would like; as in other societies, they have to take what is on offer.

Planning an economy necessitates planning incomes. Since the command economies of Eastern Europe are also socialist countries, people in the West usually expect these societies to have a substantial degree of equality of incomes. This is a misunderstanding. Marx believed that at the socialist stage of development (the present position of the USSR) the right of workers to income should reflect the labour that they supply. Consequently in the USSR, people with desirable skills or high productivity receive high rewards. Such equality as there is in the system lies in **wealth,** not income. That is because there is relatively little private ownership of land or firms, though even in socialist economies some people own more desirable products, such as cars, houses or jewellery. Despite the inequalities which are present in the USSR it would be possible to organise a planned economy where differences in wealth and income were relatively small.

Disadvantages of command economies

Despite its undoubted benefits, the command economy contains many drawbacks. If the planners determine priorities, these may not be what ordinary people would want, so that individual choice is subordinated to that of society. Command economies tend to restrict consumer choice by providing only a limited range of goods and services. People who like chewing gum, drinking genuine champagne, wearing jeans or driving their own car would tend to be frustrated in the USSR because these goods are in limited supply and difficult to obtain. That is because society, as represented by the planners, has rejected the values which these goods embody.

Moreover, many products are of low quality. In a command economy an organisation which produces goods where quality is low cannot go bankrupt, so that the consequences of producing faulty products are less drastic than in a market economy. Whilst it is possible for the planners to specify that goods should be produced up to a certain standard, it is difficult to ensure that they do meet these standards. Planning services is particularly difficult. It is hard to plan how many lifts will need repairs, how many pipes will burst, or how many cars will break down, or to ensure that the quality of such repairs will be satisfactory. Consequently services such as these are often undertaken through a 'black market' which operates outside the official system.

Shortages occur and are difficult to eliminate. The Soviet press often points out these deficiencies. In 1982 a Soviet weekly, the *Literaturnaya Gazeta* sent a correspondent to the city of Krosnodo which has a population of half a million and told him to buy items in everyday use - soap, razors, socks and underwear. He reported that in a day's shopping he had failed to buy any of these items, but that all were available on the black market.

One reason for these deficiencies is that the planners suffer from information overload. This makes them slow to respond to deficiencies. Detailed plans have to be drawn up for thousands of factories and farms and then co-ordinated. If it is decided to produce more cars, then the economy must also produce more steel; to do this more coal and electricity will be needed and, in turn, more buildings and so more bricks and cement. More workers will have to be trained with the requisite skills. The co-ordination of such plans for an entire economy is clearly an immense task and the bureaucracy is frequently overwhelmed.

At the level of the individual plant there are often considerable inefficiencies. Managers want to ensure that their part of the plan will be fulfilled. This means that they try to negotiate easy targets so that these can be achieved. In turn, Ministers go along with this so that their Ministry can achieve its targets. This means that even when targets are achieved or surpassed there may still be a considerable amount of inefficiency in the system. Moreover, in order to achieve their targets managers often try to ensure that they have hidden reserves of labour and raw materials. Since shortfalls and delays in supplies will occur, the careful manager will try to keep spare supplies knowing that these can always be used to bargain with other units if shortages do occur. A unit with a shortage of buttons

but a surplus of cloth may be able to arrange a swop. The existence of these excess supplies means that the system is inefficient; the ratio of inputs to outputs is higher than it need be.

Some incentives can easily be incorporated into the working of a command economy. Higher productivity can be rewarded by higher wages. It is much more difficult to introduce incentives for new products. Bacon flavoured crisps or video recorders would probably never be invented in a planned economy because there are no rewards for doing so and because goods such as these would receive a low priority. Production units are often slow to introduce new technologies because improved performance may lead to higher targets in the next period and to different requirements for raw materials, which might not be available. Consequently Soviet technology has tended to follow that in the West.

Key ideas - command economies

1. Command economies are sometimes called planned economies because the crucial economic decisions are planned by a central authority.

2. They are often associated with a Marxist approach because they often feature public ownership of the means of production.
3. Supporters of command economies say that they can ensure resources are used to produce the most desirable goods and that unemployment can be reduced or eliminated.
4. Disadvantages of command economies can include lack of incentives for producers and choice for consumers, poor quality of goods, bureaucracy and shortages.

The market economy

Opposing the ideas of the command economy is the market economy, sometimes also called the free enterprise system. In a market economy resources are allocated by the operation of market forces of demand and supply working through the price system. In this system no individual or organisation consciously seeks to solve the basic economic problem of what to produce, how to produce, or for whom should production be organised. Instead economic agents such as families or firms seek to promote their own self-interest. This system was first analysed by Adam Smith (1776) in *The Wealth of Nations:*

'It is not from benevolence of the butcher, the brewer or the baker that we expect our dinner but from their regard to their own self-interest.'

In other words, all the participants in the system - workers, employers, consumers - try to maximise their own utility. Consumers will try to buy goods and services as cheaply as they can. Producers will try to charge high prices and pay low wages so that they maximise their profits. Workers will aim to obtain high wages. Through all this self-seeking develops a system which needs no planning, but which works as if an 'invisible hand' was guiding the economy.

How a market system works

Let us take a few examples to show how such a system might work. We can start with an increase in demand. Assume that for some reason there is an increase in the birth rate. Other things being equal, this will mean that producers of products used by babies such as nappies, cots, push chairs and baby foods, will find that they sell more products. If production does not rise then shortages will develop. Rational producers and shopkeepers seeking to maximise their incomes will respond to these shortages by putting up prices in order to increase profits. Manufacturers of similar products will note these higher profits and diversify into the market for childcare products. Some shops which sold cycles will now sell push chairs; some which traded in teenage clothes will change to maternity wear. In this way resources - labour, land and capital - will be re-allocated to produce the goods and services which consumers want. The wishes of consumers will have led to changes which help satisfy these wishes. Indeed, the extra supplies may force down prices so that consumers not only benefit because they have increased supplies of goods which they want, but also because these may cost less.

Resources are also re-allocated if consumers choose less of a product. If men want fewer hats, ties, or suits, the market responds by producing fewer of these commodities. Shops which sell these commodities will have to cut their prices to clear their stocks and either go bankrupt or else diversify into selling clothes that people want. Producers will similarly be forced to respond to the dictates of market forces. If they continue to produce clothes which consumers are unwilling to buy they will

Figure 2.2: *Consumer sovereignty*

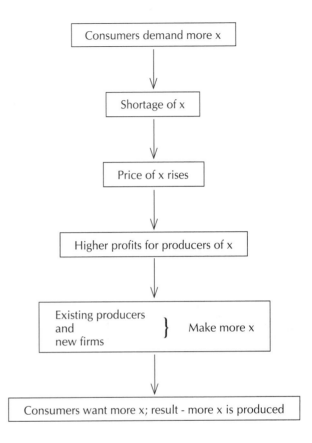

soon go out of business. Their factories and workers will become available to make products which consumers wish to buy.

These changes in consumer demand will also affect wages. Workers in industries where there is a rising demand for the products that they make will be able to benefit by negotiating higher wages. Those in declining industries will find that their wages fall relative to those in other sections of the economy. Some workers will respond to this by changing jobs. In this way consumer preferences for particular products will encourage labour to be re-allocated, so that workers are available to produce the goods that people want.

The system also responds to changes in the supply of goods. For example, if bad weather in Brazil cuts the supply of coffee, this will lead to a shortage. Producers and shopkeepers, being rational, will respond by putting up the price. In the long run this may stimulate producers in other countries to increase production. The rise in coffee prices may also encourage some consumers to switch to other drinks such as tea. If tea producers believe that the switch is likely to be long lasting they will increase production.

Thus the system works to allocate resources whether the impetus for change is a movement in demand or in the supply of goods. Markets are able to function in this way because of the operation of the price system.

The price system

A price system enables people to co-operate in attempting to solve economic problems even though they do not know each other. Millions of economic transactions take place each day and the prices that result from these voluntary transactions co-ordinate the activities of producers and consumers in such a way that everyone benefits - if the system works well. In order to do this the price system must perform three functions.

Information

It must transmit information to the people who need to know. If there is a boom in one sector of the economy, shopkeepers selling these products will increase their orders to the manufacturers and, in order to persuade manufacturers to supply more goods, they will probably have to pay higher prices. This will induce the suppliers to increase their workforce - or make it possible for them to pay overtime rates of pay. All the people involved in this market will be aware of the change in prices. The information will be of no interest to those in different markets and will be ignored by them.

Incentives

The price system must provide incentives to people to act in certain ways. If the price of a product is rising it will pay producers to increase output because this will cause their profits to rise. If wages in one occupation are rising it will pay some workers to shift jobs. If one shop sells a product at a lower price than its competitors then it will pay consumers to buy at that shop (though there are costs involved in changing jobs and in shopping around, particularly the time involved). To give a real example, in 1973/74 the price of oil doubled and then doubled again. This had many effects on the world economy. It provided an incentive for producers to explore potential oil fields and for consumers to use less oil. People stopped buying oil fired central heating. Electricity producers used more coal fired stations and decided to build

nuclear powered generating plants. Consumers bought fewer large cars, whilst sales of cars giving more miles per gallon increased, so encouraging producers to introduce new models which used less petrol. All these changes occurred without central direction because of the information and the incentives provided by fluctuations in price.

Income distribution

The price system must also influence the distribution of income. People's earnings depend on the price they receive for their services. In the case of employed workers, wages will depend largely on the success of their employer's business and on the demand and supply of people with their particular skills. A 'striker' for Glasgow Rangers will receive very high earnings because he has very scarce skills which are needed by a wealthy employer. People with skills that are not required by employers receive low earnings. Someone who is good at sweeping the streets will receive low earnings because there are many people with this ability relative to the demand for them.

Advantages of markets

The central belief of many economists is that markets offer the best way of allocating resources. In the first place, they give consumers enormous choice. Whether we want to buy a radio, a pen, or a haircut, the market will provide a wide range of alternatives. The goods will vary in quality, in design, and in price, so that knowledgeable consumers can maximise their satisfaction by buying goods and services that suit their particular purposes. The choices offered by a modern market economy are so familiar that we tend to take them for granted, but no society in history has offered so many alternatives to consumers as does the modern market economy.

Moreover, the discipline of the market works to ensure a high quality of goods. A producer who makes shoddy products may be able to sell them once, but the rational consumer will not succumb twice. Good products drive out bad ones and therefore business people who produce poor products go out of business. Firms making quality goods will be rewarded with high profits.

Another feature of markets is that they provide incentives to desirable behaviour. If a firm can organise so that it makes its product at less cost than its competitors, it will be rewarded by higher profits. Thus built into the system are features that encourage efficiency. Business people are therefore constantly searching for ways to cut costs by introducing new techniques of production and better management of resources. The firm benefits because profits rise, but consumers also benefit because competing firms become more efficient and competition keeps down prices.

The market rewards those who provide what consumers want. Hence it encourages innovation. People who make new or better products desired by consumers benefit from larger sales and profits. Every year thousands of new products are marketed. Many are rejected by consumers, but others increase consumer choice and satisfaction.

All this takes place without any great bureaucracy to organise it. The system is decentralised. Decisions are made by millions of consumers and thousands of producers and co-ordinated through the invisible hand of the price system. The mass of civil servants and government planners required by the command economy are not needed in a market economy. This not only makes available the services of thousands of workers who can produce goods for the consumer rather than spending their time passing paper, it also means that the system is very flexible and responds quickly to changes. A bad harvest, a strike, a new discovery - those interested will be made aware by changes in prices and will take appropriate action without any need for government action.

Some supporters of markets believe the system has close affinities with democracy; Enoch Powell, (1969) in *Freedom and Reality,* claims:

'The free enterprise economy is the true counterpart of democracy; it is the only system which gives everyone a say. Everyone who goes into a shop and chooses one article rather than another is casting a vote in the economic ballot with thousands or millions of others. That choice is signalled to production and investment and helps to mold the world just a tiny fraction nearer to people's desire. In this great and continuous general election of the free economy, nobody, not even the poorest is disenfranchised; we are voting all the time.'

Thus its supporters claim that a market system is characterised by **consumer sovereignty,** where the wishes of consumers are translated into actions by producers.

The case against markets

Criticisms of the pro-market argument

Those economists who believe that markets have only a limited part to play in allocating resources advance a number of arguments. In the first place they claim the analogy with democracy is misleading. In a democracy each person has only one vote; each person's wishes carry equal weight. In a market economy the reverse is true. The system does not provide what the majority of people would choose, but what the people with money would choose. A millionaire has far more preferences satisfied than does a pauper. Put another way, the argument for markets assumes that the existing distribution of income is satisfactory. To this criticism, some pro-marketeers would respond that if the distribution of income is not satisfactory it should be corrected by tax and social security changes and not by government interference in the goods market.

Some critics argue that the apparent choice provided by markets is largely an illusion. Choice depends on knowledge. Unless consumers are well informed, they may choose poor quality products at a high price. Many competing consumer goods are complex and technical so that only a few people are really competent enough to understand the differences between them. In addition, better goods may be available elsewhere, but nobody has complete knowledge of what products are available in every shop.

Choice is limited in another way. Advertisers spend large amounts of money to influence consumers. If this is successful then spending represents not consumer choice, but the influence of the advertising agency. Rather than consumer sovereignty we would have producer sovereignty. Instead of the sequence:

Consumers choose → Producers respond

which is supposed to happen in a market system, we would have:

Firms plan production and marketing → Consumers respond

Supporters of this line of argument point to the huge size of firms in the modern economy and claim it is naive to expect giants of industry to respond passively to the whims of consumers. Instead they plan their production, often years in advance, and then carefully market their products to try to ensure that their plans are successful.

Weaknesses of markets

Critics of markets point out that unemployment is common in such systems. Whilst the level of unemployment varies over time, it is never totally absent and sometimes reaches very high levels. It is therefore necessary for governments to intervene in order to reduce the level of unemployment. The existence of unemployment is a specific example of a more general argument; that there seems to be a tendency for markets to break down in disorder. Marxists would argue that this is an inherent tendency. The sequence of events depicted earlier in Figure 2.2 can break down in various ways:

- There can be volatile swings caused by over-shooting. The traditional example is the 'pig cycle'. If there is an increased demand for pork or bacon the price of pigs will rise. This will cause more farmers to breed pigs and in time these will come on to the market. This excess supply will force down the price and cause many farmers to switch to other products. Eventually a shortage will occur causing the price to rise and encourage more farmers to breed pigs. So the cycle can continue without demand and supply ever reaching a stable equilibrium.
- All markets are related - some more closely than others - so that instability in one market will affect others. Thus large changes in the foreign exchange market will affect domestic prices, cause firms to postpone investment and create unemployment.
- Markets depend on money. Because people may at one time choose to spend and at another to save, markets are often subject to disruption.
- Markets are not always competitive. They are often dominated by a few firms so that competition may be limited. If this is so, consumers will not receive the full benefits of choice and low price which markets are supposed to confer. This is discussed in more detail in Chapter 6.

Public goods

A specific limitation of markets is that they are not able to supply the most desirable quantity of **public goods.** These have two characteristics. They are non-rivalry in consumption. This means that any individual can consume the good without reducing the quantity available for others - if I listen to the radio, it does not prevent anyone else from listening to the same programme. The other characteristic of public goods is that they are non-excludable. This means that they cannot be withheld from one person without withholding them from everyone. A lighthouse is a good example. Once it is built the owner cannot stop passing ships from seeing it and being warned away from any danger. Other examples of public goods include defence, street lighting and flood defence systems.

Since public goods are available to all, they are not provided in the right quantities by markets because businesses cannot charge all those who benefit. Some people would have a free ride - that is benefit without paying. In the case of a private good, such as ice cream, this does not happen. The producer can ensure that only those who pay get the goods. Consequently whilst private goods are provided by markets, public goods are usually provided by the state because otherwise too few of these goods would be produced. A complication of this argument is that the distinction between private and public goods is not always clear, particularly in areas such as health and education. The existence of these semi-public goods means that economists who believe most strongly in market forces argue that services such as education, health and housing are not pure public goods and so should be left largely to market forces, whilst other economists believe the state should intervene on a substantial scale to ensure that an appropriate level of services is supplied.

Merit goods

Merit goods pose a similar dilemma. These are goods which the community believes would be consumed in too small a quantity if left to market forces. If people had to pay an economic price for goods such as classical music concerts, using swimming pools, education or roof insulation, the quantity demanded would be much smaller than at present. Consequently the state intervenes in these markets, either to provide the goods or to pay or subsidise provision by others.

The state also intervenes to discourage or prohibit economic 'bads' such as the consumption of cigarettes or heroin. Some extreme proponents of market forces would argue that the state should not intervene in this way because it restricts the choice of rational consumers who desire such goods.

Externalities

Another reason why markets may fail is that externalities are present. These occur when the activities of producers or consumers affect third parties other than through the normal working of the price system. Externalities are sometimes known as spillovers because the effects of an action spill over on to others. There are lots of examples:

- Throwing take away containers into the street.
- Releasing industrial waste into the river or air.
- Night flights by aeroplanes.
- Commuters or lorries causing congestion.

These are all negative externalities. There are also some positive ones:

- Beekeepers whose bees pollinate nearby flowers.
- An attractive garden which gives pleasure to others.
- Clearing a rubbish-filled site to build a well-designed factory.

Because people usually only take account of their own costs and benefits, these spillover effects are usually ignored. If these effects are negative, it is argued that society ought to intervene to restrict the freedom of those undertaking the activity (for example, to force firms to reduce pollution) or to take other appropriate action, such as subsidising public transport in order to reduce congestion on the roads.

Key ideas - summary of the case for and against markets

1. Market systems allocate resources through the interplay of consumer demand and producer supply, with consumer sovereignty being the driving force.
Supporters of markets would claim:
2. The system provides a huge range of consumer choice.

3. It rewards efficient producers and penalises inefficient ones.
4. Markets provide incentives to innovate and to improve existing products.
5. The system adapts quickly to changing circumstances and requires no bureaucracy to administer it.
Critics of unrestricted markets would claim:
6. Whilst choice is important, it is often more apparent than real because producers manipulate consumers, for example, through advertising.
7. Markets often fail to ensure desirable results; for example, unemployment is common.
8. Markets also fail because consumers and producers have imperfect knowledge and because some producers have monopoly power.
9. Instability in one sector (for example, the money market) often spreads to affect others.
10. Markets often do not provide the optimum amount of public and merit goods.
11. Governments should intervene to correct for externalities.

Conclusion

At the heart of economics is the problem of scarcity. No society can produce all the goods and services which its citizens would like. Hence disagreements arise about how to choose what goods and service to produce.

Some economists favour command economies where the most important economic decisions are made by the government and orders are sent to factories and farms telling them what to produce. This system has advantages - it concentrates resources on producing the goods which are thought desirable. However, such systems are often inefficient and bureaucratic. An alternative way to allocate resources is to use markets. Some economists believe these are a marvellous way to allocating resources because they are efficient and reflect the wishes of consumers. Critics - often Keynesians or Marxists - believe markets often fail to allocate resources in a satisfactory way and that therefore the government should intervene on a substantial scale to correct these failures. Both command and market systems have limitations. Modern economies are, in practice, mixed economies containing elements of both systems and argument centres on the composition of the mixture. Most Western economies have a market system with some government intervention in order to deal with the criticisms made of markets. The extent of such intervention will depend on the extent to which the market is seen to fail. This is the subject of the next chapter which concentrates on the market mechanism and the consequences of intervention.

The argument about markets also reflects differing values and political positions. Left wing economists have usually favoured intervention because they believe markets tend to favour the better off sections of society. Those on the right dispute this, or else argue that incentives are necessary and that markets spur the poor to improve their position. In judging this argument, the reader should be aware that writing about markets reflects not only economic judgements but also political beliefs.

Data questions

The cost of shaving

The people of Burma live under a state planned economy. Unfortunately the plans do not succeed in producing the goods which people want. Consequently goods as diverse as cement and deodorants are smuggled into Burma from Thailand. Since there is a long chain of dealers on this supply route, these smuggled goods are expensive.

In Rangoon, I needed to replace my shaving kit. On a market stall I found a British deodorant which in Boots would have cost about 75 pence. At the official Burmese rate of exchange, the cost on the Rangoon market would have been £75.

Source: Adapted from *The Times*, November 19, 1985.

Question 1

1. Explain what is meant by a 'state planned economy'.
2. What reasons can be given to explain the high cost of the aerosol?
3. What other disadvantages might result from a command economy? Do you think any advantages that may occur would outweigh the disadvantages? Give reasons for your answer.

THE FORGOTTEN GENERATION.

Of the 1.1 million dwellings unfit for
human habitation in the UK
half are inhabited by elderly people.

One household in seven is an old
person living alone.

1800 old people were victims of
violent crime.

Half a million have no living relatives.

1.5 million have no regular visitors.

Nearly 2 million depend entirely on
supplementary benefit.

In 1985, 571 old people died in
their homes from the cold.

These facts paint a grim picture of what it can mean to be old in Britain today. Help the Aged is dedicated
to improving this situation by campaigning for better pensions and heating allowances. Funding Day
Centres, Day Hospitals and Hospices. Providing emergency alarm systems and minibuses.
To find out more about our work, or if you would like to make a donation, please write to:
John Mayo OBE, Director-General, Help the Aged, St. James's Walk, London EC1R 0BE.

Help the Aged
THE TIME TO CARE IS NOW

Source: Help the Aged.

Question 2

1. To what extent are the problems listed in the
   advertisement caused by the operation of the
   market system?

2. Should governments intervene to solve these
   problems? If so how?

3. How would a command economy deal with such
   problems?

3 Demand, Supply and the Market

The previous chapter discussed the relative merits and problems of market and planned economies. This chapter focuses on the market economy and particularly on the working of the market mechanism. This is one of the key areas of economics; perhaps the key area. In modern Western economies, markets are used to allocate most resources and to decide what goods and services are produced. The forces of demand and supply interact through the price system in order to allocate these resources. There are, however, instances where government intervention in markets is necessary:

● Supporters of markets would argue that, left to itself, the market will usually allocate resources efficiently. Government intervention should be restricted, for example, to the provision of services such as defence.

● Critics would suggest, as outlined in the previous chapter, that governments need to intervene in order to deal with the consequences of market failure. Intervention can take many forms, including levying taxes, giving subsidies, and fixing maximum and minimum prices. The Common Agricultural Policy of the European Community is another example of government intervention.

In order to examine the role of governments and markets we need first to consider the factors which determine demand and supply, and to show how these interact to bring about market equilibrium, where demand equals supply.

Market equilibrium

A market exists when buyers wishing to exchange money for a good or service are in contact with sellers wishing to exchange goods or services for money.

Markets need not be confined to a single place. They can occur without the buyer and seller actually meeting. This can happen, for example, when people buy and sell shares, or when they buy goods by post or telephone. In a market economy, prices are determined by the interaction of demand and supply.

Demand

By 'demand' economists mean the willingness and ability to pay money for some amount of a particular good or service.

'Demand' in economics has a precise meaning. It is a **desired** quantity, how much of a commodity or service households would wish to purchase at differing prices if the commodity were available. It does not necessarily measure how much they are actually able to purchase. If there were a strike or a crop failure, consumers may wish to buy but not be able to do so. Note that economists distinguish between 'demand' and 'quantity demanded'. 'Demand' describes the behaviour of consumers at every price - so much will be demanded at one price, rather less if the price is higher. 'Quantity demanded' refers to a particular price: 'At a price of £50 consumers will demand a thousand units a week.'

There are several factors which influence how much of a good consumers will demand. The level of consumers' incomes, an advertising campaign and the price of competing products are just three of these factors. In order to analyse the effect of changes in these variables we will make use of a technique much used by economists, namely to assume *ceteris paribus* - that all factors except one remain unchanged. This enables us to estimate the effect of a change in one variable.

We will first examine the relationships between price and demand. The other influences will be examined later. For most items the relationship is clear; demand will rise as price falls. The promoter of an LP may sell a million if the price is £1; at £10 sales may fall to a few thousand. Similarly, a chip shop which charged a penny a portion would have queues outside the door; at £5 trade would be zero. This inverse relationship between price and demand applies to almost all products, though there are a few exceptions. For example, firms selling goods with a 'snob value' sometimes find they sell more when they put up the price. Another exception from the general rule is a 'Giffen good', where demand varies directly with price. The classic example is that of the potato famine in Ireland. At that time, potatoes were the staple food, and so when their price rose people could not afford other foods and so bought more potatoes.

Supply

The comparable concept to demand is supply. Supply is the quantity of a good or service which sellers will wish to sell at various prices.

As with demand, 'supply' measures not how much firms actually sell, but how much they would like to sell at a range of prices. There are a number of influences on supply; for example, the price of raw materials, the state of technology, the availability and cost of labour, and, for particular products, the weather. Again we will make use of *ceteris paribus* and consider only the most important determinant of supply, that is price. The relationship will differ for particular products, but in general we may expect that the higher the price the more profitable it will be to make the good or provide the service.

At high prices firms will be able and willing to put workers on overtime rates and so increase output whilst still making a good profit. When prices are low, some firms may be unable to cover their costs and therefore supply may be zero. In the case of fish and chips, if a customer walked into a shop and asked 'How many portions of fish and chips will you sell me at £5 a portion?' the proprietor would presumably be willing to supply all that it was physically able to produce; at 5 pence a portion the supply may be zero. Consequently we may expect supply to rise with price.

Equilibrium

Table 3.1 shows hypothetical demand and supply schedules for jeans. In both cases we assume that factors other than price remain unchanged. The Table shows that firms will be willing to supply more jeans at high prices than when the price is low. Conversely consumers will be willing to buy more when the price is low. Thus at low prices demand will exceed supply. For example, at a price of £16 per pair, consumers would like to buy 60,000 pairs a month but firms are only willing to supply 25,000. At a high price, such as £26, firms are willing to supply 80,000 pairs but consumer demand is only 20,000 per month. It follows that at some price between these two the quantity demanded will just equal the quantity supplied. This is the equilibrium price (£20).

Table 3.1: Demand for, and supply of, jeans

Price (£ per pair)	Demand (Thousand pairs per month)	Supply (Thousand pairs per month)
12	100	15
14	80	20
16	60	25
18	50	30
20	40	40
22	30	50
24	25	60
26	20	80

A market is in equilibrium when the quantity of the product which consumers wish to buy at the prevailing price exactly matches the quantity consumers wish to sell.

At the equilibrium price the market will **clear.** This means that there will be no scarcity and no surplus. At prices higher than equilibrium, firms will have unsold stocks; a sign of excess supply. When the price is below equilibrium, shortages will occur; a sign of excess demand.

An alternative presentation of the data in Table 3.1 is given in Figure 3.1. This shows the equilibrium price of £20 and the excess demand which exists at a price of £16. At the low price demand will exceed supply by A - B, that is 60,000 - 25,000 = 35,000 pairs of jeans a month.

The forces of demand and supply usually cause markets to move towards equilibrium. In the case just described, where demand is greater than supply, shortages will occur. Shopkeepers will be faced by consumers wanting jeans but be unable to supply them. They will pass on extra orders to manufacturers. The response of rational firms in this situation will be to raise prices and hence profits. The increase in price will cause some consumers to leave the market and it will also induce firms to supply more. This will continue until the equilibrium price is reached and the market clears.

Figure 3.1: Equilibrium in the market for jeans

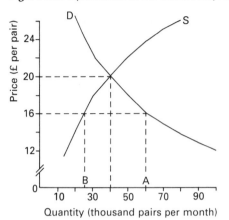

In the opposite case, where price is higher than equilibrium, firms will be left with rising stocks which they cannot sell at the prevailing price.

Sometimes they may store the excess in the hope of better times, but unless some other factors change, at some point of time they will be forced to cut prices in order to clear stocks. The process of adjustment will be quicker for perishable goods, such as strawberries, than for goods which can be easily stored, such as diamonds or spoons. The cut in price will induce more consumers into the market and it will also cut supply; at lower prices manufacturers will be unwilling to pay overtime rates. Eventually demand will equal supply, other factors remaining unchanged.

Note that at any particular time the market may not be in equilibrium. Moreover, in the real world other factors are constantly changing so that equilibrium may never be reached.

Key ideas

1. Markets exist whenever buyers wishing to exchange money for goods and services interact with sellers wishing to exchange goods and services for money.
2. By 'demand', economists mean the willingness and ability of consumers to pay for a good. Consumers will usually demand more when price falls.

3. 'Supply' is the quantity of a good which firms wish to sell at various prices. They will usually be willing to sell more when price rises.
4. When demand equals supply the market is in equilibrium. At the equilibrium price the market will clear.

Shifts in demand and supply

So far we have held constant all factors except price and considered what happens when this changes. As we have seen, when the price fo a good rises or falls there is movement along the demand or supply curve. However, when there is a change in factors other than price there is a movement of the whole curve. It is now time to explore what factors will cause the demand and supply curves to shift.

Other factors affecting demand

There are many factors, other than price, which could affect demand, but we will consider four: advertising and fashion, complementary goods, substitute goods and income. The relationship between demand and these other factors can be shown in a demand function:

Demand = f (Price, Advertising, Complementary goods, Substitute goods, Income . . .)

(The dots in this equation indicate that some other unlisted variable may affect demand.)

Demand for some goods is hardly affected by advertising or fashion. The amount of chalk teachers use is not affected by adverts on TV, and film stars do not try to persuade us to use more blotting paper. Nevertheless, for many goods and services advertising does have a considerable effect; if it did not firms would not spend large sums of money on it. Similarly, fashions change, particularly for products such as records or clothes. If a manufacturer decides to have an advertising campaign for jeans and this is successful (or jeans become more fashionable), what effect will this have on the price and quantity of jeans bought and sold?

The result of a successful advertising campaign is shown in Table 3.2 and Figure 3.2. Consumers are willing to buy more jeans at every price. This is represented graphically as a **shift** in the demand curve from D$_1$ to D$_2$. The supply curve is not affected; this continues to show how many pairs of jeans firms are willing to supply at each price and is not affected by an advertising campaign.

Table 3.2: The effect of a successful advertising campaign for jeans

Price (£ per pair)	Original demand (Thousand pairs per month)	Demand after advertising (Thousand pairs per month)
12	100	120
14	80	100
16	60	80
18	50	70
20	40	60
22	30	50
24	25	45
26	20	40

Figure 3.2: A shift in demand

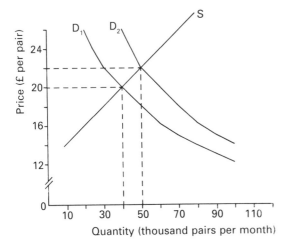

Quantity (thousand pairs per month)

The effect of a shift in the demand curve is that a new equilibrium is reached where the supply curve intersects with the new demand curve D_2. The price of jeans has risen from £20 to £22 and the quantity has also risen, from 40,000 pairs a month to 50,000. At any other price there will be excess demand or supply. At the original price, for example, demand will be 60,000, supply 40,000, and shortages would occur forcing up price.

A second factor which affects demand is what happens to **complementary goods.** These are goods which 'go together'. Examples are cars and petrol, fish and chips, squash courts and squash balls. The relationship is significant because if a factor changes which influences one good, the complementary good will also be affected. For example, if there is a rise in the price of potatoes fewer people will go to

chip shops and hence the demand for fish will fall. This is illustrated in Figure 3.3 which shows that the demand curve for the complementary good - in this case fish - moves to the left, resulting in a price fall from p_1 to p_2. The quantity bought and sold also falls from q_1 to q_2. A fall in the price of potatoes would have the opposite effect, leading to an increase in demand for fish and hence a rise in price and quantity.

Figure 3.3: Effect of a rise in the price of a complementary good

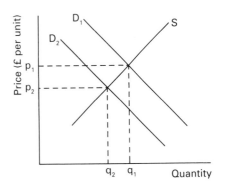

As their name implies, **substitute goods** offer an alternative to the consumer. If we want a cold drink we may not mind if it is lemonade or a cola; nor whether we drive a car made by Ford or Vauxhall, or whether we eat beef or pork. In all these cases a rise in the price of one will lead to an increase in demand for the other. Thus if the price of beef rises, some shoppers in the butchers or supermarkets will choose to buy pork instead. The amount of substitution will vary according to the particular alternative and the preferences of the consumer; some people would not buy pork whatever happened to the price of beef. When substitution does occur, a rise in the price of beef will cause the demand curve for pork to shift to the right, the extent of the shift depending on the amount of substitution. This shift will lead to an increase in the price of pork and in the quantity bought and sold.

Changes in income also affect demand. As incomes rise we tend to buy more of some goods, such as records or clothes. This will also cause a shift in the demand curve leading to a rise in price and quantity. However, for some goods such as salt or nails, a rise in income will have little or no influence on demand. The effect of a change in income is important and is discussed further in a later part of this chapter.

This discussion of the factors which affect demand is far from complete and particular products may be affected by specific influences. Sales of flowers and cards rise before Mother's Day; the demand for toys rises before Christmas, and we buy more ice cream in August than in January. Similarly, the weather ensures that we buy more winter coats in November than in May. Changes in the birth rate would cause changes in the demand for baby care products such as nappies. These factors all cause a shift in the demand curve.

Shifts of a curve and movements along a curve

It is important to understand the difference between a shift in the demand curve and a movement along the demand curve. The two are very different as can be seen in Figure 3.4. Other things being equal a change in price from p_1 to p_2 leads to a movement along a curve, for example from A to B.

This is quite different from an increase in demand which occurs, for example, when there is a favourable change in fashion or tastes. This causes the whole demand curve to shift so that more is demanded at each price, for example, at price p_1 demand will rise from A to C. If the change in tastes is unfavourable then less will be demanded at each price.

Figure 3.4: Shifts in demand curves and movements along a curve

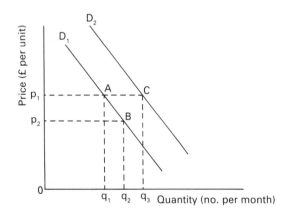

Other factors affecting supply

The supply curves we have drawn so far have been based on the assumption that factors other than price remain constant. It is now time to relax that assumption and to examine what will occur when these other factors change.

Changes in the price of inputs will affect the quantity of goods which firms are willing to supply.

If raw material prices fall, then manufacturers will be willing to supply more at each price and the supply curve will move to the right as shown in Figure 3.5. The result is a fall in price from p_1 to p_2 and a rise in quantity bought and sold from q_1 to q_2. A rise in the price of inputs would have the opposite effect. If wages go up or there is an increase in the cost of raw materials then business people (often called entrepreneurs or decision makers in economics) will then wish to supply less at each price and the supply curve will shift to the left, leading to a rise in price and a fall in quantity.

Technology affects the position of the supply curve. An entrepreneur who was willing to supply (say) a thousand telephones per week at a certain price may be willing to supply more at that price if new techniques of production mean less labour or raw materials are needed to produce each telephone.

Figure 3.5: Shifts in the supply curve

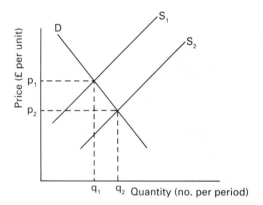

A firm's goals will also affect the extent to which it is willing to supply goods at particular prices. A change in management may make the firm more aggressive, for example, making it eager to capture a larger slice of the market. This would shift the supply curve to the right. Conversely, an ageing management may be less willing to compete and be content to supply less.

The actions of governments also have a considerable effect on supply. If a government imposes regulations on an industry this will affect the amount of goods which firms are willing to supply at particular prices. A notable example is car manufacturing. Governments in many countries have imposed detailed regulations about safety and pollution control and these have the effect of shifting the supply curve to the left.

The government also influences supply when it imposes taxes on a good. For the manufacturer this has the same effect as a rise in the price of inputs. If the government imposed a tax of £10 on each micro computer, manufacturers would be forced to hand over this amount to the government and its effect would be exactly the same as if the manufacturer had to pay component suppliers an extra £10. The result will be that the supply curve moves to the left. Similarly, the imposition of VAT on hot food take away meals caused a fall in the supply of fish and chips.

A subsidy has the opposite effect. If the government decides to improve house insulation and give a subsidy to the producers of such material, then firms will be willing to supply more at each price because they will receive a hand-out from the government as well as receiving money from the consumer. The supply curve will shift to the right.

Key ideas

1. The demand curve for a good will shift when there is a change in variables such as advertising, consumer incomes, complementary or substitute goods. For particular goods, other influences, such as the weather, will shift the demand curve. A shift in the demand curve means that more or less is demanded at each price.

2. The supply curve for a good will shift when there is a change in variables such as the cost of raw materials or in wages. Changes in technology and the weather will also move the supply curve causing more, or less, to be supplied at each price.

Elasticity

So far we have considered movements along curves and why curves shift. It is now time to discuss the shape of demand and supply curves, because this has a considerable affect on the price and quantity of goods bought and sold.

Imagine that you are in charge of a business and have to decide what price to charge. Will the firm benefit if you cut the price, keep it unchanged, or raise it? The answer will largely depend on how consumers respond to changes in price.

Price elasticity of demand

For some goods a change in price will make little difference to demand. If manufacturers doubled the

price of paper clips, halved the price of candles, or trebled that of toilet paper, demand for the products would hardly change. For other goods the position would be very different and consumers would be very sensitive to changes in price. The responsiveness of the quantity demanded to price changes is measured by the price elasticity of demand, often abbreviated to just the elasticity of demand:

The price elasticity of demand

$$= \frac{\% \text{ change in quantity demanded}}{\% \text{ change in price}}$$

We can examine elasticity both arithmetically and graphically. If the price of a good falls from £100 to £50 and demand rises from 10 to 30 items then:

$$\text{Price elasticity} = \frac{+200\%}{-50\%} = -4$$

For another good the same fall in price may lead to a much smaller rise in demand, say from 10 to 12 items. In this case:

$$\text{Price elasticity} = \frac{+20\%}{-50\%} = -0.4$$

Although price elasticity is negative (since a rise in price leads to a fall in demand and vice versa), the minus sign is often omitted for the sake of brevity.

When the price elasticity of demand for a good is higher than one we say that it is **elastic.** This indicates that demand for the good is very sensitive to changes in price. Demand is **inelastic** when its price elasticity is less than one, showing that changes in price have relatively little effect on consumer purchases. When the elasticity of demand equals one we say that it is **unitary.**

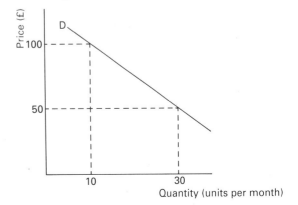

Figure 3.6: *Price elasticity of demand*

(ii) Unitary

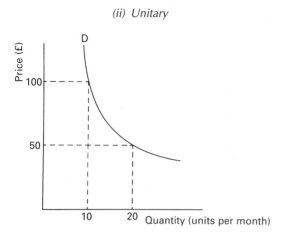

(iii) Inelastic

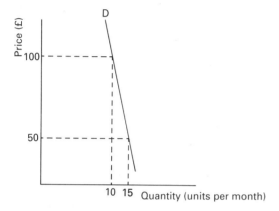

The three conditions are shown in Figure 3.6. This shows that when demand is elastic, a small fall in price leads to a large rise in quantity. Since the total revenue received by a firm is price x quantity, the total revenue will rise when the price is cut. In the case of Figure 3.6(i), a total revenue at the higher price of £100 is £100 x 10 = £1,000. When the price is cut to £50 total revenue rises to £50 x 30 = £1,500. It is therefore not surprising that firms in this position try to keep their prices below those of their competitors. A good example is a petrol station along a road where there are several other petrol stations; if it sells its petrol for a penny a litre less than its competitors sales will rise substantially. That is why pricing is so keen that prices are signposted in fractions of a penny.

When demand is unitary the firm's revenue is the same at all prices. This is shown in Figure 3.6(ii) where the firm's revenue is always £1,000. This is clearly a statistical freak. Of more importance is the case where demand is inelastic. A large cut in price will only lead to a few more sales so that total revenue falls. In the case of Figure 3.6(iii), total

revenue falls from £1,000 to £750 when price is cut from £100 to £50. Consequently markets for products where demand is inelastic will not be characterised by price cutting. Indeed, firms will seize every chance to put up prices because total revenue will also rise.

At the two extremes demand can be perfectly elastic or perfectly inelastic. These are shown in Figure 3.7. When demand is perfectly inelastic a rise or fall in price will make no difference to sales. When demand is perfectly elastic demand would fall to zero if price was raised by even a penny. These are theoretical extremes and do not exist in everyday life.

Figure 3.7: *Perfectly inelastic and perfectly elastic demand*

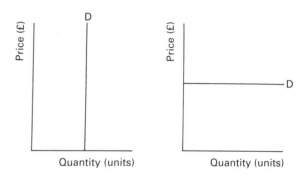

What determines price elasticity of demand?

The most important determinant of price elasticity of demand is the extent to which consumers can find acceptable substitutes. Goods such as salt, light bulbs, cigarettes or drawing pins have no close substitutes. Consequently it is not difficult to predict that if the price of these products were raised by say 10% then sales might fall as a result, but probably by much less than 10%. In other words, these goods are characterised by inelastic demand. Other examples of goods in this category are alcoholic drinks, toilet paper and rulers - goods with no close substitutes and which are either habit forming, or where expenditure on the good is only a small part of total spending.

Where goods have close substitutes demand becomes elastic. This occurs where the term 'good' is narrowly defined. Demand for oil is inelastic, demand for Esso or Shell is elastic because there are close substitutes.

Table 3.3: *Estimates of price elasticity of demand in the UK*

Dairy produce	-0.05
Bread	-0.22
Entertainment	-1.40
Expenditure abroad	-1.63
Catering	-2.61
Pork	-2.01
Mutton and Lamb	-1.86
All carcass meats	-1.46

Source: Adapted from Deaton, A. 'The Measurement of Income and Price Elasticity', *European Economic Review*, vol. 6, 1975; *Household Food Consumption and Expenditure*, Ministry of Agriculture, 1986.

Price elasticities of selected UK goods are given in Table 3.3. The table shows that demand for dairy produce is clearly less likely to respond to a change in price than entertainment, for example.

Estimates of price elasticity are of considerable interest to firms because they make it possible to calculate what will happen to sales and total revenue if prices are raised or cut. For example, if the manager of a firm calculates that the price elasticity of demand for a product is -0.5, it is possible to calculate that if prices are raised by 10% then sales will fall by only 5%:

Price elasticity of demand

$$= \frac{\% \text{ change in quantity demanded}}{\% \text{ change in price}}$$

$$-0.5 = \frac{\% \text{ change in quantity demanded}}{10\%}$$

therefore change in quantity = -5%

Since total revenue is price x quantity, the firm's total revenue will rise as a result of the price increase.

It is difficult to make accurate estimates of price elasticities. The most usual approach is to use experience; that is to look back on what happened to sales of the product when prices were altered in the past. Of course, since then other factors will have changed; new products may have appeared, existing products been redesigned and advertising campaigns undertaken. All of these factors may have affected the price elasticity of demand. Textbook analysis is easier than real life application!

Table 3.4: *Price, elasticity and total revenue*

Price	Elasticity	Total revenue
Rises	Inelastic	Rises
	Elastic	Falls
Falls	Inelastic	Falls
	Elastic	Rises

When demand is unitary, total revenue is unchanged.

Cross-elasticity of demand

The cross-elasticity of demand is a measure of the effect on one good when the price of another changes:

Cross-elasticity of demand

$$= \frac{\% \text{ change in quantity demanded of good X}}{\% \text{ change in the price of good Y}}$$

For substitute goods the cross elasticity will be positive. A rise in the price of tea will lead to an increase in the quantity of coffee which consumers demand. Similarly, an increase in the price of bitter will lead to a rise in demand for lager.

For complementary goods the cross-elasticity will be negative. Thus we may expect a rise in the price of fountain pens to lead to a fall in the demand for ink. Similarly, a fall in the price of video recorders would be expected to lead to a rise in the demand for video cassettes.

Income elasticity of demand

It is now time to examine in more detail the relationship between income and demand. Earlier we suggested that as incomes rise more will be demanded. That is true for many goods, but not for all. Again we make the usual assumption that factors other than income remain unchanged:

Income elasticity of demand

$$= \frac{\% \text{ change in quantity demanded}}{\% \text{ change in income}}$$

For most goods income elasticity will be positive, showing that a rise in consumers' income will lead to a rise in quantity demanded. For example, if incomes rise by 5% and as a result spending on meals in restaurants rises by 10% we can calculate that the income elasticity of demand is +2. This is an example of a **normal good.**

A normal good has a positive income elasticity of demand whilst an **inferior good** has a negative income elasticity of demand.

For a few goods the quantity demanded will fall as incomes rise. Examples are coal, journeys by bus, cheap clothes and cuts of meat. As their incomes rise consumers will buy less of these goods and substitute others; for example, spending on coal will fall as consumers install central heating and instead of travelling by bus people will buy cars. Table 3.5 illustrates the close link between income and the ownership of various consumer durables. In all cases except one, households with higher incomes own more consumer durables. The exception is that the number of families owning black and white TVs falls as incomes rise (though of course families with high incomes may purchase a black and white TV as a second set).

Table 3.5: *Income and % of households owning particular consumer goods*

| | Usual gross weekly income (£) | | |
	0-60	100-120	350 or more
Deep-freezer	39	65	91
Washing machine	53	79	95
Microwave oven	5	14	39
Dishwasher	1	1	22
Telephone	63	74	98
Video	7	21	65
Black and White TV only	26	9	2

Source: *Social Trends*, HMSO, 1989.

The difference between normal and inferior goods is shown in Figure 3.8. When the good is normal, as incomes rise more will be demanded at each price; in other words the demand curve will shift from D_1 to D_2. When the good is inferior less will be demanded at each price and the curve will shift from D_1 to D_3.

Figure 3.8: *Normal and inferior goods*

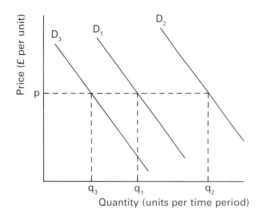

The Importance of income elasticity

Income elasticity of demand is an important concept. Over a number of years incomes tend to rise. When the income elasticity of demand is positive and also greater than one (sometimes used as a definition of luxury goods) spending will rise considerably and the industry will expand. Examples are holidays abroad, microwave ovens, detached

houses, wine and various recreational activities, such as squash, surfboarding and sailing.

For some industries income elasticity will be positive but less than one (sometimes used as a definition of necessities). Most food is in this category. Such industries will not be substantially affected by changes in incomes. Shoe laces, toothpaste, washing up liquid and light bulbs are other examples. When the income elasticity of demand is negative (inferior goods) then spending will fall as incomes rise and producers will see their industries decline. This is what has happened to coal and also to bus travel and is the reason why governments have had to subsidise this form of transport in order to ensure that services continue.

One of the problems of the UK economy is that it exports goods which have a low or even negative income elasticity of demand and imports goods with a high income elasticity. That means that as world incomes rise UK exports of manufactured goods tend to be static whilst imports to the UK rise. This leads to balance of payments problems, to industrial decline and to high unemployment. The problem is easy to recognise, but it is less easy to devise a strategy which would lead to such a substantial change in the structure of the British economy that the position would be reversed.

Elasticity of supply

Just as the elasticity of demand measures the responsiveness of demand to changes in price, so the elasticity of supply shows how the supply of a particular good or service will be affected by changes in price:

Elasticity of supply

$$= \frac{\text{\% change in quantity supplied}}{\text{\% change in price}}$$

Because the supply curve (almost) always slopes upwards the elasticity of supply is positive; higher price leads to a rise in quantity supplied.

When elasticity is greater than one, we say supply is **elastic.** When the change in quantity is less than one we say that it is **inelastic.**

In a few cases supply will be perfectly inelastic showing that whatever happens to price the supply will not vary. That is the case for new paintings by Leonardo, new songs by John Lennon, seats at the F.A. Cup Final or commercial flights to the moon this year. This position is illustrated by a vertical supply curve. At the opposite extreme we can imagine a horizontal supply curve showing perfectly elastic supply; in this case a slight fall in price would cause supply to fall to zero and a slight rise in price would lead to an infinitely large supply. These are extreme cases.

The crucial factor influencing the elasticity of supply is **time.** We can distinguish between two periods:

● The short run. This is when firms can produce more with existing plant. Workers can be put on overtime, or shift work introduced, but no major reconstructions take place. In this case it may be impossible to produce much more however high the price rises. This is the case with most agricultural products; during any one season, little can be done to increase the quantity of produce which can be grown. In the case of coconuts, the 'short run' can be a very long period of time. By the same reasoning, the supply of rubber is inelastic!

● The long run. Existing firms can build new factories and new firms can enter the industry. In the long run a rise in price will tend to call forth proportionately greater quantities so supply is elastic.

Figure 3.9: *The effects of an increase in demand under different supply conditions*

(i) Perfectly inelastic supply

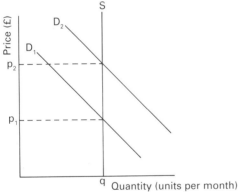

(ii) Inelastic supply

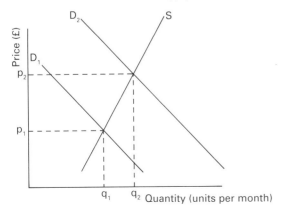

(iii) Elastic supply

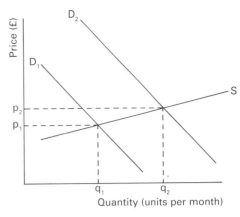

The shape of the supply curve will determine how much a change in demand will have on price.

Three possible cases are shown in Figure 3.9. In each, an increase in demand leads to a rise in price, but this is much less when the supply curve is elastic. This is the usual long-run equilibrium condition.

Key ideas

1. Price elasticity of demand measures the responsiveness of demand to changes in price.
2. When demand is responsive to price changes we say that it is elastic. When it is not responsive to price changes, demand is said to be inelastic.
3. The main determinants of price elasticity of demand are the existence of substitutes, whether goods are habit forming and the proportion of total expenditure which is spent on the good.
4. When demand is elastic, producers will attempt to cut prices because this will increase total revenue.
5. Income elasticity of demand measures the responsiveness of demand to changes in income. For normal goods a rise in income will lead to an increase in demand and the demand curve will move to the right.
6. Elasticity of supply measures the responsiveness of supply to changes in price. Time is the crucial factor influencing elasticity of supply. In the long run, firms can increase supply by building new factories; hence in the long run, supply tends to be elastic.

The need for government intervention

The previous chapter discussed the reasons why markets might fail. These included the existence of public and merit goods, externalities and unsatisfactory distribution of income. Consequently governments intervene in order to correct these failures, and it is possible to use the analysis we have developed to investigate the consequences of various forms of intervention.

The imposition of a tax

Governments impose taxes for a number of reasons. One is to raise revenue, but taxes on goods such as cigarettes can be used to discourage consumption. The effects of a tax on a particular product are shown in Figure 3.10.

Figure 3.10: *Effect of an indirect tax on price and quantity*

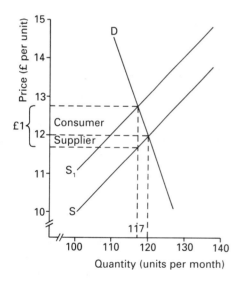

This shows the effect of a tax on price and quantity. Original equilibrium is at a price of £12 and a quantity of 120. When a tax of £1 per item is imposed, firms will supply fewer goods at the original price (so far as firms are concerned, a tax is equivalent to a rise in the price of labour or raw materials) so the supply curve shifts to the left giving a new equilibrium price of £12.75 - a rise of 75p, and a fall in quantity to 117 items.

In this way, the producer has managed to shift most of the burden to the customer. As a result of the tax, the consumer pays £0.75 x 117 = £87.75 to the government, whilst the supplier pays £0.25 x 117 = £29.25. Note that only 75% of the tax rise has been passed on to the consumer, so that the price does not rise by the full amount of the tax. The ability of the producer to shift the burden depends on the elasticity of demand. When demand is inelastic, the producer will be able to shift most of the burden because people will continue to buy the product even at a higher price. When demand is elastic, the imposition of a tax will lead to a large fall in quantity demanded, the price will not rise by much, and the producer will be forced to pay most of the tax (to check this try drawing Figure 3.10 with a very elastic demand curve). Consequently governments usually tax goods with inelastic demand because this has relatively little effect on the quantity of goods bought.

Thus we can conclude that a tax on a product raises the price and cuts the quantity, the extent depending on the price elasticity of demand.

Because habit forming goods, such as cigarettes, are assumed to have inelastic demand they have been subjected to relatively high taxes on the grounds that most of the burden would be carried by the consumer and that the industry would not suffer unduly.

Subsidies

There are various reasons why a government may wish to subsidise a particular product:

- To help the producer. Before Britain joined the EEC, farm incomes were lower than non-farm incomes and governments helped farmers by paying a subsidy so that, in addition to money received from the consumer, farmers received money from the government.
- To increase consumption of a particular good. For example, the government may wish to encourage house insulation in order to reduce energy consumption. A subsidy will increase the quantity bought and sold, the extent depending on the price elasticity of demand.
- To help customers, particularly the poor. In many countries governments subsidise basic foodstuffs in order to help those with low incomes. A subsidy will bring down the price, the extent depending on the price elasticity of demand.

The analysis of the effects of a subsidy is similar to that showing the effects of a tax, except that the subsidy causes producers to supply more at each price causing the supply curve to shift to the right. Consequently we can conclude that a subsidy on a product cuts the price and increases the quantity, the extent depending on the price elasticity of demand.

Economists often argue against subsidies for two main reasons. In the first place, they interfere with the working of the price system. The equilibrium price of a good measures the extent to which consumers are willing to pay; if they are not prepared to pay this price then it follows that they would rather spend their money on something else. Consequently it is argued by some economists that subsidies lead to the misallocation of resources because they lead to an increase in the consumption of the subsidised goods and a fall in demand for other goods (since consumers cannot spend the same money twice).

Secondly, someone has to pay the subsidy; in most cases this is the taxpayer. Consequently those who pay taxes face additional costs whilst those who receive the goods benefit. Depending on the circumstances, this may or may not be fair.

Fixing a maximum price

Another way in which governments intervene in markets is to fix the maximum price at which particular products can be sold. This is often done to help poorer sections of the community who may not be able to afford basic foodstuffs. Governments intervene in this way in many Third World countries and it was the practice in the Second World War in Britain.

Figure 3.11: *The impact of maximum price legislation*

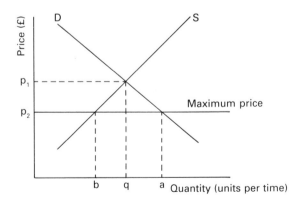

Figure 3.11 shows how maximum price legislation operates. Original equilibrium is at price p_1 and quantity q_1. The government believes this price is too high - perhaps unscrupulous merchants are exploiting the poor. They therefore pass a law which fixes the maximum price at which the product can be sold at p_2. At this price the quantity demanded

rises to a, but supply falls to b. The result is a shortage equal to a - b. This may lead to a black market because, as the demand curve shows, some people are willing to pay much higher prices than p2. Hence some shopkeepers hide stock, tell ordinary customers that they have sold out, and then secretly sell at much higher prices to special customers.

There are various possible government responses to this position. Shooting a few shopkeepers has been tried in some countries, but is undesirable! The solution in the Second World War in the UK was to introduce a rationing system which divided up the available supply fairly among the population. The price system 'rations' a given supply by using price, and a rationing system does this more fairly - or so it can be argued. Against this a rationing system can be very bureaucratic and expensive to operate and the maximum price may cut down the quantity which is available for purchase.

Note that Figure 3.11 may exaggerate the problem. If demand and supply are both inelastic the quantity demanded will not rise much when price is cut and the quantity supplied will only fall slightly. Consequently the shortage may be very small and the black market problem insignificant.

Minimum wage legislation

Similar analysis can be used to study the effect of legislation to fix a minimum wage. Many workers are low paid; poverty is a social problem which society should alleviate. Therefore it is argued that laws should be passed forcing employers to pay all their workers at least a minimum wage.

The result is shown in Figure 3.12(i). Original equilibrium is at wage w_1 and the quantity of labour employed is q_1. The government believes that this wage is too low and fixes a minimum wage of w_2. The diagram shows that the higher wage will increase the supply of labour to point a - some existing workers will want to work longer hours and new workers will enter the labour market. However, the higher wage will force some employers to cut down on the quantity of labour they wish to employ, so the quantity of labour in employment falls to point b. Thus, it is argued, minimum wage legislation will lead to a rise in unemployment equal to a - b.

However, a note of caution needs to be sounded. Firstly the diagram has been drawn with fairly elastic demand and supply curves; the rise in unemployment would be much less if these were inelastic. This would be the position if higher wages did not cause many more workers to seek jobs and if

Figure 3.12: The effects of minimum wage legislation

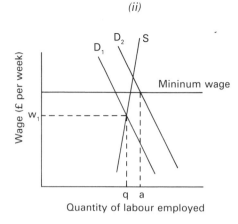

(i)   (ii)

only a few employers laid off workers at the higher wage level.

Secondly, the workers receiving higher wages will spend some of their extra money. This will lead to higher demand for some products and to more jobs in these industries; that is the demand curve for labour will move to the right as shown in Figure 3.12(ii). Whilst the extra spending by workers with higher incomes may not be sufficient to move the demand curve by much, changes in other factors may do this. For example, if the government were to increase its spending (on say education, health and construction) this would increase the demand for labour in certain industries causing the demand curve to move to the right so that the quantity of labour employed was a. Thus whilst minimum wage legislation will tend to increase unemployment if **other things remain equal,** appropriate measures by government may be able to override this effect.

The Common Agricultural Policy of the EC

Article 39 of the Treaty of Rome sets out the objectives of the CAP. These are to increase agricultural efficiency, stabilise markets, secure food supplies, increase farm incomes and ensure reasonable prices for consumers. There are various methods used to achieve these goals, but the main one is shown in Figure 3.13. The free market price within the Common Market is given by the intersection of the demand and supply curves. However, world prices are much lower than this at op_1. If foreign supplies were able to enter freely, Community farmers would only supply oa at this price, but Community demand would be ob and imports would fill the gap ab.

Figure 3.13: The CAP price support system

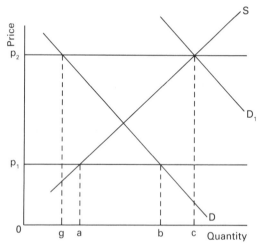

Source: Adapted from Swann, D. 'The Economics of the European Community' in Atkinson, G.B.J. ed, *Developments in Economics,* Causeway Press, 1986.

In order to achieve its objectives the Community imposes a levy on imports equal to price p_1-p_2. The high price stimulates Community farmers to supply quantity oc, but the high price also cuts demand down to og. The problem is 'resolved' by community administrators entering the market and buying up the surplus gc, in effect shifting the demand curve to D_1.

Of course this creates a new problem - what to do with all the produce that has been purchased? They can put it into store, thus creating the famous butter mountains and wine lakes. Alternatively they can sell the surplus at very low prices in world markets, or seek new uses for particular products. None of these solutions is very satisfactory. An alternative suggestion is that European surpluses should be given away to help people in poor countries. However, this may cause greater poverty, because the increase in supply will force down the local price for food, making it uneconomic for local farmers to grow food so that more shortages occur.

In recent years the size of some surpluses has been reduced by imposing a quota on farmers, so limiting supply. This is unpopular with farmers and rather bureaucratic. Whilst the agricultural policy enables some of the Community objectives to be realised, it is expensive and inefficient. The obvious solution is to bring down prices closer to the market equilibrium, but this is politically very difficult since farm lobbies are very powerful in all EC countries.

Key ideas

1. Governments intervene in the economy in various ways to correct market failure.
2. A tax on goods raises the price and reduces the quantity bought and sold, the extent depending on the price elasticity of demand.
3. A subsidy may be imposed to help producers or consumers. Subsidies lead to falls in price and to increases in the quantity of goods bought.

4. Governments sometimes fix the maximum price at which a product can be sold in order to help poor consumers. However, this may lead to shortages.
5. Governments sometimes fix minimum wage levels in order to help low paid workers. Critics say this causes unemployment.
6. The CAP aims to help farmers and stabilise prices. However, price guarantee schemes like CAP can lead to surplus production.

Conclusion

Markets, operating through the forces of demand and supply, have many advantages as a way of allocating resources. But as the last chapter showed, markets also have disadvantages. Consequently governments sometimes intervene. Some of these interventions, such as the imposition of taxes, are accepted as necessary by all economists. Other interventions, such as government action to fix prices or wages, are more controversial. Demand and supply analysis allows the effects of such intervention to be studied, but the results of the analysis often reflect the values of the researcher. For example, different assumptions about elasticity can lead to very different conclusions about the effect of any intervention.

Data questions

According to the system of natural liberty, the sovereign has only three duties to attend to: three duties of great importance, indeed, but plain and intelligible to common understandings: first, the duty of protecting the society from violence and invasion of other independent societies; secondly, the duty of protecting, as far as possible, every member of the society from the injustice or oppression of every other member of it, or the duty of establishing an exact administration of justice; and thirdly, the duty of erecting and maintaining certain public works and certain public institutions which it can never be for the interest of any individual, or small number of individuals, to erect and maintain; because the profit could never repay the expense to any individual or small number of individuals, though it may frequently do much more than repay it to a great society.

Source: Smith, A. *The Wealth of Nations*, Book 4, Chapter 9. First published 1776.

Question 1

1. What additional duties of government would:
  (i)   supporters of market forces and
  (ii) interventionists
  advocate to those outlined in the section from *The Wealth of Nations*?

2. What reasons can be given for the increase in the role of government since Smith's time?

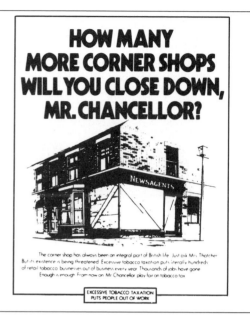

Source: The Tobacco Advisory Council.

Question 2

1. Using demand and supply diagrams, explain the effect of a tax on cigarettes on the price charged and the quantity demanded and supplied.

2. To what extent does the price elasticity of demand affect the answer to question 1?
3. Discuss the arguments for and against a large rise in the tax on cigarettes.

Tickets for sale

International tickets are like gold dust. For next Saturday's England-Wales match Twickenham could have been sold out three times over. All national unions distribute tickets to their clubs and constituent bodies, but there are nowhere near enough to go round. For example, London Welsh received only 139. They applied for 1,500.

Because of the potential for profiteering, the Rugby Football Union warned clubs that tickets are for individual members, strictly not for commercial organisations marketing lavish days out at Twickenham comprising lunch, drinks, entertainment and match tickets.

'I have discovered that tickets were misused last season, and we decided to put the boot in', said Bob Weighill, RFU secretary. The result is that some clubs have had their allocation stopped for the season. In letters to offenders, the RFU said: 'We have evidence that a number of tickets allocated to your club were . . . included in a package deal . . . to provide corporate entertainment in marquee complexes adjacent to the Rugby Football Union ground.'

The punishment was summary, and there was no appeal. The RFU would not reveal the number of tickets involved, or the numbers on them, so no club could trace their miscreants.

Source: *The Sunday Times,* January 12, 1986.
© Times Newspapers Ltd., 1986.

Rugby at Twickenham

Question 3

1. Is the price of international tickets fixed above or below the equilibrium price? What impact would this have on demand and supply?
2. How would the price system solve the problem of disequilibrium suggested in question 1?
3. Why do you think that the Rugby Football Union use this method to distribute tickets? Make use of demand and supply diagrams in your answer.

4 Behind the Demand Curve: The Theory of Consumer Choice

The demand curve is so crucial in economics that it is useful to analyse the reasoning which explains the slope of the curve. Consumer theory attempts to explain why the curve slopes down from left to right and also the situation where, when faced with a choice of goods, a consumer will maximise satisfaction (utility).

There are several ways in which the theory of consumer choice can be analysed. This chapter looks at two alternatives, which both fall within the neo-classical approach:

● The marginal utility approach uses a cardinal measure of utility to explain consumers' behaviour. This theoretical model assumes that a numerical value can be placed on the amount of utility gained from the consumption of a good.

● Indifference curve analysis rejects this idea and attempts to explain consumer behaviour using an ordinal measure of satisfaction. In this theory, consumers state that they prefer one quantity of goods to another rather than placing an actual value on the amount of satisfaction gained.

Marginal utility analysis

Diminishing marginal utility

Consumers buy goods and services because of the utility (satisfaction) which they receive from the goods. A bag of fish and chips or a bottle of cola will give a certain amount of satisfaction to someone who is hungry or thirsty. A second helping may also increase utility, but perhaps not by very much. A third helping may not increase utility at all and indeed may make the consumer sick - an example of negative utility. This is an example of the law of diminishing marginal utility.

Marginal utility can be defined as the extra utility obtained from the consumption of one more unit of a good. The law of diminishing marginal utility states that as the amount of a good consumed increases, the marginal utility tends to decrease, though total utility may continue to rise.

A simple example of the law of diminishing marginal utility is given in Table 4.1. In this case, marginal utility at first rises, but then the fall sets in after the consumption of the second good. Note that this example assumes that utility can be given a numerical value.

Table 4.1: Diminishing marginal utility

Quantity of the good consumed	Total utility	Marginal utility
0	0	—
1	5	5
2	12	7
3	16	4
4	18	2
5	17	-1
6	16	-2

The law of diminishing marginal utility can be used to explain the slope of an individual's demand for a single good. As more units are consumed, marginal utility falls, hence the price which consumers are willing to pay will also fall to compensate for this loss of satisfaction. An alternative way to look at the slope of a demand curve is to say that when only a small quantity of a good is consumed, an extra unit gives a relatively high marginal utility; hence consumers are willing to pay a high price. When a number of units have been bought, an extra unit yields only a small amount of satisfaction, hence only a low price will be paid.

A rational consumer, when faced with deciding what quantity of this good to consume, will aim to maximise total satisfaction. In the example illustrated in Table 4.1, the consumer will buy 4 goods. At this point, total satisfaction is maximised. However, in practice, consumers are faced with the choice from a number of goods and are constrained by a limited income, and by the price of the goods.

The equi-marginal principle

In order to maximise satisfaction a consumer should arrange expenditure so that the marginal utility of a particular purchase is proportional to its price. Let us examine this idea. Assume that the satisfaction a person obtains from going to a disco is greater than that resulting from a visit to a cinema. If the satisfaction obtained from the disco is five times that obtained from the cinema, it is reasonable that the person should spend five times as much on discos as on films. If the person had been spending ten times as much on discos as on visiting the cinema, it would be rational to switch some expenditure from discos to cinemas since discos only give five times the satisfaction (assuming that the cost of the two is the same).

We can generalise from this example. If a particular good gives less marginal utility than goods as a whole, we should switch expenditure away from that product, until the marginal utility of a good relative to its price rises to equal that of other goods. In the example in Table 4.1, it would be foolish to buy 4 items of that particular good when this has a marginal utility of only 2 if purchases of other goods had a higher marginal utility - say 4 (again assuming that the price of each good is the same). If that was the case we should buy three items of the good to equalise marginal utility between this good and others.

The fundamental condition of consumer equilibrium can be expressed as:

$$\frac{MUx}{Px} = \frac{MUy}{Py} = \frac{MUz}{Pz}$$

where MU = marginal utility, P = price and x, y and z are goods.

When the price of a good such as x falls the value of $\frac{MUx}{Px}$ will rise and more should be spent on x. In other words, when the price falls the ratio of marginal utility to price will rise. More will be bought, causing the demand curve to slope downwards. Since more money is spent on x, less can be spent on y and z. Given the law of diminishing marginal utility, the reduced consumption of these goods will raise their marginal utilities until the ratio of marginal utility to price is equal for all goods. This is the equilibrium condition which maximises consumer satisfaction.

This equilibrium will be disturbed if there is a change in income. A rise in income will allow more goods to be bought, though consumers will not buy more of all goods. The way a particular good is affected will depend on how consumer preferences change as a result of income.

Substitution and income effects

An alternative way of analysing the downward sloping demand curve makes use of substitution and income effects. We can use these effects to show how, when the price of a good rises, the quantity demanded falls, or how, when the price of a good falls, the quantity demanded rises. If the price of beef rises whilst other prices do not, then beef has become relatively more expensive and its marginal utility will fall compared to other goods. It will therefore pay consumers to substitute other products for beef. Similarly, if train fares rise, rational consumers will substitute other services for this form of travel. The substitution effect will be large when a product has close competitors.

When incomes are fixed and the price of a product rises, the effect is the same as a cut in real incomes. With a lower real income, consumers will cut their expenditure on many products, including the good whose price has risen. (The exception to the general rule occurs with **inferior goods** when a fall in income will cause consumers to buy more of that product.) The income effect will be large when spending on the product takes a high proportion of income. It will have little or no effect for products such as pencils, calendars or plastic bags, where expenditure takes only a minute part of total spending.

The substitution and income effects together explain why some goods have elastic and some inelastic demand. When both income and substitution effects are strong, a rise in price will have a considerable effect on consumer spending and demand will be elastic. When the effects are small, demand will be inelastic.

Consumer surplus

On hot days people are thirsty and would be willing to pay much more for a cool drink than the price actually charged. The difference between the price paid and the utility obtained by the consumer is a measure of consumer surplus. Because of the law of diminishing marginal utility, the surplus will diminish as more drinks are bought, and it will eventually disappear.

Consumer surplus can be defined as the difference between the total amount of money a person would be prepared to pay for some quantity of a good and the amount actually paid.

Figure 4.1: Consumer surplus

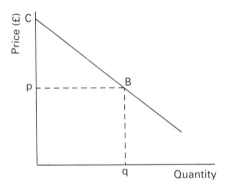

In Figure 4.1 equilibrium is at price p and quantity q. However, some consumers are willing to pay much higher prices - even as high as C. Consumers' surplus is measured by pBC. This is the area above the price, but below the demand curve.

Cardinal and ordinal utility

So far this analysis has implicitly assumed that utility can be measured. The term used for this is cardinal utility. A cardinal measure of utility assumes the consumer can compare the increase in utility obtained from (say) consuming two apples instead of one, with the increase in utility obtained from increasing the consumption of pears from two to three.

This assumption that utility can be measured has been criticised on the grounds that such measurement is not possible in practice. Centimetres

can be used to measure length, but there is no scale to measure changes in the satisfaction obtained by consuming different goods. Despite this disadvantage, the marginal utility approach can still be used to make useful predictions about consumer choice.

An alternative approach is to use ordinal utility. This assumes a person can say that he or she prefers three pears to two pears, but not by how much more. An approach based on ordinal utility is used in indifference curve analysis.

Key ideas - summary of marginal utility

1. Marginal utility is the extra utility obtained from the consumption of an additional good. The law of diminishing marginal utility states that as more of a good is consumed, marginal utility will eventually decrease.

2. Since marginal utility falls as consumption increases, consumers will be unwilling to pay as much for more of the good, i.e. the demand curve will slope down to the right.

3. Consumers will maximise satisfaction when the marginal utility obtained from buying a good is proportional to its price.

Indifference curve analysis

Indifference curve analysis offers an alternative approach to the analysis of consumer choice.

An indifference curve joins together all the combinations of two goods which yield the same utility.

Assume a consumer buys only two commodities: bread and apples, and that their relative value is as shown in Table 4.2. The Table shows that the consumer is indifferent if offered the choice between 1 loaf of bread and 6 apples, or between 2 loaves and 3 apples. 'Indifferent' in this context means that it does not matter on way or another; the alternatives have equal value. These points can be linked up to form an indifference curve as shown in Figure 4.2. In the example illustrated in this figure, the consumer is indifferent between combinations A and B, but would prefer A (with 6 apples and 1 loaf) to another alternative such as 3 apples and 1 loaf.

Table 4.2: *Indifference combinations*

Bread	Apples	
1	6	A
2	3	
3	2	B
4	1.5	

Figure 4.2: *An indifference curve*

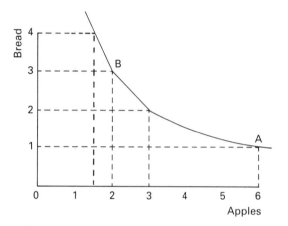

The curve illustrates the law of substitution; that the scarcer the good the greater its relative value. In other words as a good becomes scarcer its marginal utility rises relative to the marginal utility of the other good. Thus at point A the consumer would be willing to give up three apples in order to obtain an extra loaf of bread because bread is relatively scarce. However, at B the consumer would only be willing to give up half an apple to obtain a loaf of bread because bread is plentiful. If we compare two points on an indifference curve in this way, we obtain the **marginal rate of substitution.** This shows the amount of one commodity a consumer would be willing to give up in order to obtain one more unit of another commodity, leaving the overall level of satisfaction unchanged. Indifference theory assumes the marginal rate of substitution is negative and diminishing. This means that to gain an increase in the consumption of one good, a consumer is prepared to reduce consumption of another commodity. It also means that if there are two goods, x and y, as consumers obtain relatively large quantities of good x they will only be willing to give up smaller and smaller amounts of y to obtain more x.

If more resources become available the consumer may be able to choose more of each good as shown in Figure 4.3. Here I_3 offers a higher level of utility

than I_2 and I_2 than I_1, because they offer a greater quantity of either or both goods. Indifference curves never cross because each offers a combination of more goods or fewer goods, depending on the distance from the origin.

Figure 4.3: *Indifference curves*

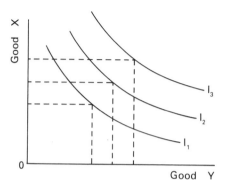

The budget line

A budget line indicates what combination of goods a consumer can buy when resources are limited. Assume that our imaginary consumer has £5 a week to spend and can choose whether to spend this money on apples or on bread. In Figure 4.4(i) the budget line shows the alternatives; at X all the money goes on apples, at Y all goes on bread. The position between these extremes shows various combinations of possible expenditure, such as £3 on bread and £2 on apples. The consumer cannot choose a position such as C because this would require £8, more money than is available.

Figure 4.4: *The budget line and indifference curves*
(i) Budget line

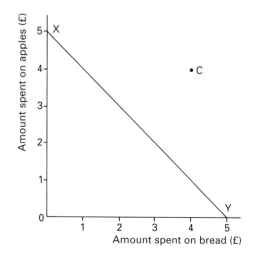

(ii) Consumer's optimal equilibrium

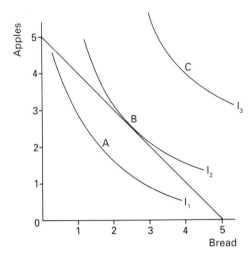

Consumer's equilibrium

The consumer's optimal equilibrium position will be at B in Figure 4.4(ii) where the indifference curve touches the budget line. This is the point where the consumer's substitution ratio is just equal to the ratio of bread prices to apple prices, and where the marginal utilities of both goods are equal.

Points such as A and C do not give optimal equilibrium. A is not acceptable, because although the ratio of apples to bread is acceptable, more of both goods are available on higher indifference curves. C is not possible because the money available does not permit the purchase of this quantity of goods.

Here position B gives the highest combination of goods which the budget will allow the consumer to buy. This is usually explained as being the position where the ratio of marginal utilities is equal to the ratio of prices.

A rise in income

A rise in income will change the position as shown in Figure 4.5. When income rises, a new budget line is drawn and makes possible a position on a higher indifference curve parallel to the original. This is because, with a higher income, the consumer can buy more of both goods (assuming that the price of the goods is unchanged). In this particular example income rises to £8 so that the consumer could spend this amount on various combinations of apples and bread. The rise in income will cause more of each good to be bought (unless one is an inferior good), but the exact proportion of the income will depend

on the relative income elasticities. In the example of Figure 4.5 the new equilibrium is at C. The points A, B and C show the **income expansion path.**

Figure 4.5: Effect of a change in income on equilibrium

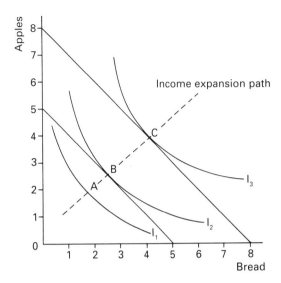

A change in price

A fall in the price of pears, while the price of apples is unchanged, will cause the budget line to shift as shown in Figure 4.6. The line shifts in this way because with an unchanged income the consumer will be able to buy as many apples as before, and more pears. Initially consumer satisfaction would be maximised at point Z on indifference curve I_1. The fall in pear prices shifts the budget line from AB to AC so that the consumer will be able to choose a point on indifference curve I_2.

Figure 4.6: The effect of a change in price

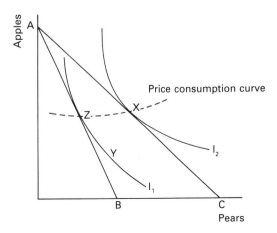

The final result will depend on the sum of two effects - a substitution effect, and an income effect. The substitution effect will mean a move along the indifference curve from point Z to say point Y, showing an increase in consumption of pears and a reduction in the consumption of apples. The income effect will mean a move from indifference curve I_1 to curve I_2 and a final position at X. A line joining points such as X and Z is called a price consumption curve. This analysis shows that a fall in price leads to an increase in the quantity demanded - the demand curve will slope down.

Indifference curve analysis and the demand curve

Indifference curve analysis can be used to show why the demand curve usually slopes down. To do this, we will analyse one commodity, beer, and assume that consumer income and the price of all other goods remains constant.

Figure 4.7: Indifference curve analysis and the demand curve

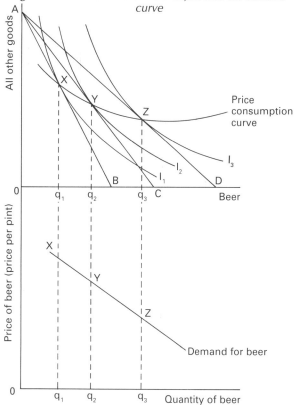

The top part of Figure 4.7 is a conventional indifference curve diagram. The budget line AB shows that the consumer can buy B pints of beer, or

quantity A of all other goods. When the price of beer falls, the budget line will move to OC and then OD. Originally, the consumer would be at position X on indifference curve I_1, but as the price of beer falls the consumer will be able to move to higher indifference curves I_2 and I_3. Points X, Y and Z show successive places on the price consumption curve corresponding to changes in the price of beer.

The bottom part of the Figure is derived from the top part. In both parts, the horizontal axis shows the quantity of beer which will be bought, but in the bottom part of the diagram, the vertical axis shows the price of beer. As you can see, this part of the diagram is a conventional demand curve diagram. At the original price of beer, the consumer's preference for this drink will be at point X, and quantity q_1 will be consumed. This is shown in both parts of the Figure. The budget line AB also corresponds to a particular price of beer, and is shown in the bottom part as point X.

If the price of beer then falls to that shown by budget line OC, the consumer will maximise satisfaction at point Y, and this corresponds to point Y in the bottom part of the Figure. If we move along the price consumption curve to position Z, we will find the quantity of beer which will be consumed when the price falls to OD. This gives us point Z in the bottom part of the Figure. Joining together these points gives us the demand curve for beer, which slopes down to the right. The slope of the curve - the elasticity - will depend on the consumer's preferences as shown in the top part of the diagram. If a fall in the price of beer caused very little more to be consumed, then OB, OC and OD would be closer together, giving a steeper demand curve.

Key ideas - summary of indifference analysis

1. **An indifference curve joins together all the combinations of a good which yield the same utility. The slope of the curve shows the marginal rate of substitution.**
2. **Indifference curves can never intersect.**
3. **A consumer's optimum equilibrium position will be where an indifference curve touches the budget line.**
4. **A rise in income will make possible a position on a higher indifference curve.**
5. **A price rise will involve both substitution and income effects.**

Conclusion

The theory of consumer choice is a rather technical way to analyse the demand curve. An approach using marginal utility is useful, but sometimes criticised because it assumes utility can be measured in a cardinal way. Indifference curve analysis does not have this disadvantage and can be used to show the effects of changes in prices and in incomes.

Data questions

Spending on food

Unfortunately for food producers, the human stomach has a limited capacity for food. The world being what it is, farmers throughout the world try to produce more, but the more they produce the lower the price that they receive for their produce. There are exceptions, of course. At one end of the spectrum, in poor countries where food is scarce, the population is rising, and where people are hungry, the price of food may rise. This is also the position at the other end of the spectrum, where in rich countries such as Britain people are willing to spend more money on exotic foods such as tropical fruits and vegetables. However, these exceptions are relatively unimportant. The overall picture is clear; without government intervention the price of basic foods will fall. The position is made worse because as incomes rise people spend proportionately less of their income on food, and more on other goods.

Question 1

1. Using either of the two approaches to consumer theory outlined in this chapter, explain the effect on consumers' equilibrium of:
   (i) the change in the price of food and
   (ii) the change in income
   as discussed in the article.

2. Explain what is meant by income and substitution effects and relate these concepts to the changes in the price of food.

5 Size of Firm: Big is Best - or is Small Beautiful?

Two hundred years ago production was organised on a small scale. Whilst a few merchants and manufacturers employed comparatively large numbers of people, most production was organised round the home. Moreover, the public sector was tiny and composed largely of the armed forces and a minute civil service. Today the position is very different. Millions of people work in the public sector and many large firms employ thousands of people. There are two conflicting opinions on these changes:

● On the one hand some economists believe that large-scale production is more efficient because it allows firms to take advantage of economies of scale.

● On the other hand critics of this view believe that these economies can be exaggerated and argue that large-scale organisation breeds bureaucratic inefficiency and often dehumanises the workers. Moreover, it is held that if economic power is concentrated in the hands of a few large firms, they will also have a great deal of political power and that this would weaken the democratic rights of ordinary people.

Consequently there is considerable debate about the most desirable size of firm. However, before we can participate fully in that debate, we need to discuss the relative importance of small and large firms in the UK, and also how firms grow.

How important are large and small firms in the UK?

Is the UK economy dominated by a few large firms or is economic power evenly spread throughout the economy? One way to examine this question is to see what proportion of total manufacturing output is produced by a certain number - usually 100 - of the largest firms and the extent to which this has changed over the years. This is shown in Figure 5.1. As can be seen, the degree of concentration rose until the depression of the 1930s and then fell until the end of the Second World War. Then there was a huge rise in concentration which seems to have levelled out in recent years. Ignoring short-term variations, there is no doubt that over the long period there has been a great increase in the economic importance of large manufacturing firms. Table 5.1 gives a specific example of this increasing concentration. At the beginning of the century there

were nearly 1,500 brewing companies in the UK; now the number is down to just over 60, though the total production of beer has hardly changed.

This evidence is supported by looking at what has happened to small firms. In the forty years following 1930 the number of small firms (in this case those employing less than 10 people) fell by a half, though in the last few years there appears to have been a recovery in the importance of these firms. One reason for this is the fall in the size of some large firms as they laid off workers in response to the decline in economic activity after 1979.

In recent decades the service sector has grown in importance and this has had an important effect on the overall picture. However, data for this sector is not easily available. What is clear is that in the service sector there is great disparity in size, often depending on the particular industry. In banking and air transport, for example, the industry is dominated by a few large firms, whilst in hairdressing and shoe repairs the typical firm is very small.

Figure 5.1: *Share of 100 largely privately owned manufacturing enterprises in manufacturing net output 1909-1980*

%
50
40
30
20
10
0
1920
1940
1960
1980

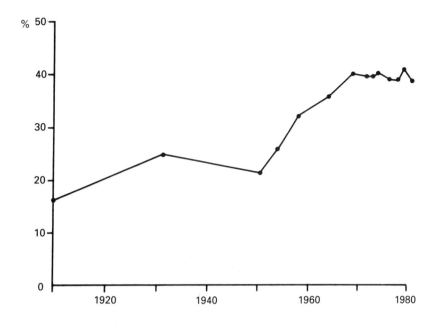

Sources: Adapted from Department of Industry, 1976; Census of Production 1980, 1983; Prais, J. *The Evolution of Giant Firms in Britain*, CUP, 1976.

Table 5.1:

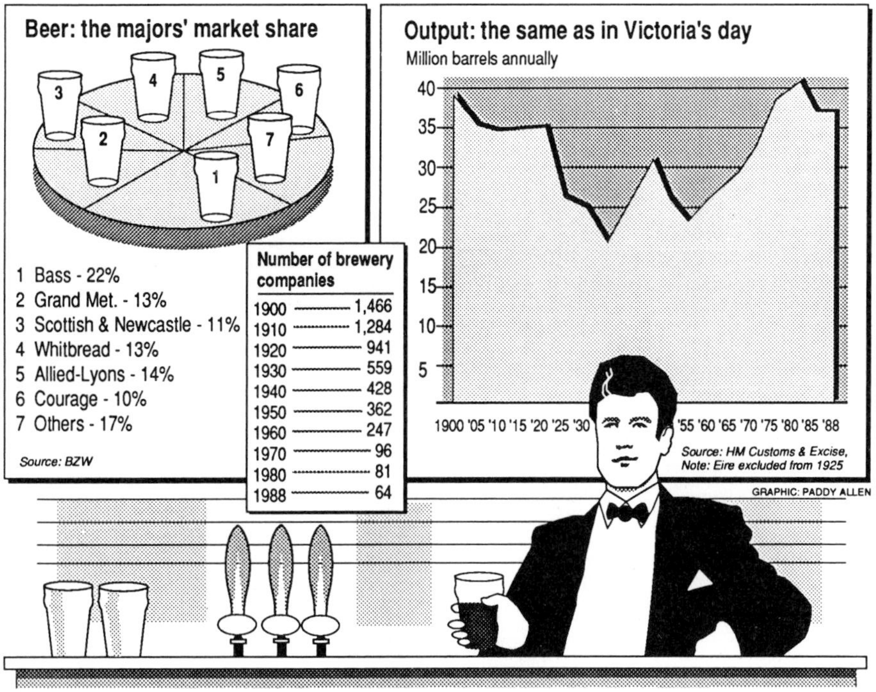

Beer: the majors' market share
1 Bass - 22%
2 Grand Met. - 13%
3 Scottish & Newcastle - 11%
4 Whitbread - 13%
5 Allied-Lyons - 14%
6 Courage - 10%
7 Others - 17%
Source: BZW
Number of brewery companies
1900 1,466
1910 1,284
1920 941
1930 559
1940 428
1950 362
1960 247
1970 96
1980 81
1988 64
Output: the same as in Victoria's day
Million barrels annually
40
35
30
25
20
15
10
5
1900 '05 '10 '15 '20 '25 '30
'55 '60 '65 '70 '75 '80 '85 '88
Source: HM Customs & Excise,
Note: Eire excluded from 1925
GRAPHIC: PADDY ALLEN

Source: *The Guardian*, February 27, 1989.

The size of firms in manufacturing

Measurement

There are a number of ways in which the size of firms can be measured. Perhaps the most common is to use the number of people employed by the firm, but some economists prefer to use the value of the output produced or the level of profits. Each method has its problems. For example, the number of people employed by a firm may vary considerably over a year, so that arbitrary decisions have to be made about which figure to use. Moreover, most firms employ part time workers and it is not always obvious how many part timers equal a full time worker. Similar problems arise if output or profitability are used. Should these be measured inclusive or exclusive of taxes such as VAT or corporation tax? There are problems which arise whatever the method. Many large firms have overseas subsidiaries. Should these be included when estimating the size of UK firms? There is no correct answer to questions such as these. What is clear, is that different methods will give different results. Using the value of output will increase the relative importance of firms making products such as tobacco or petrol where the retail price includes a large tax element. Using the number of workers will increase the relative importance of labour intensive firms. Table 5.2 illustrates this point. What order would you put the firms in if you were arranging them in order of size?

Evidence

Whichever method is used the same pattern emerges when manufacturing industry is analysed; there are a large number of small firms and a very small number of large firms. However, these large firms are economically very important in the UK. This is also true in most other advanced industrial countries.

Table 5.3 shows the total number of manufacturing firms, the number of people they employ and the value of their output. As the Table shows, there are a huge number of firms which employ less than 100 people, but they only account for just over 28% of total employment and about 22.5% of sales. At the other extreme there are 315 giant firms employing over 1,500 people. These firms account for nearly 23% of employment in manufacturing and 28% of sales. The figures only relate to activity in the UK. If foreign sales and employment were included, then the importance of these giants would be even more marked. Table 5.3 gives the picture for UK manufacturing as a whole, but this general picture conceals considerable variations between industries. For example, Figure 5.2 looks at the variation in three industries. In vehicle manufacture the five largest firms are responsible for nearly 90% of total sales. Whilst small firms produce hand built cars they do not contribute much to total output. By contrast, in brewing the five largest firms produce just over 70% of British beer, and small local breweries remain important, though their importance is diminishing over time. A different picture is found in the leather goods industry where small firms dominate.

Table 5.3: *Size distribution of employment and sales in UK manufacturing*

Size (No. of people employed)	No. of establishments	Employment (thousands)	Total sales (£ million)
1 - 9	101,981	323.4	
10 - 19	17,328	241.3	52,260
20 - 49	12,602	400.0	
50 - 99	5,939	416.5	
100 - 199	3,767	532.3	23,724
200 - 499	2,850	874.6	41,715
500 - 999	945	642.9	32,250
1000 - 1499	262	314.9	17,033
1500 and over	315	1,132.2	64,700
Total	145,989	4,878.1	231,682

Source: Census of Production, 1986; *Business Monitor*, HMSO, PA 1002.

Table 5.2: *Which firm is biggest?*

	Turnover (£ million)	Capital employed (£ million)	Employees (thousands)	Profit before tax (£ million)
British Petroleum	27000	212000	127	958
BAT Industries	16600	5259	350	1393
Unilever	17140	6496	300	1143
British Gas	7610	18135	93	1062

Source: *Kompass*, Reed Information Services, 1988.

Figure 5.2: Share of sales of the 5 largest firms in the UK in three industries

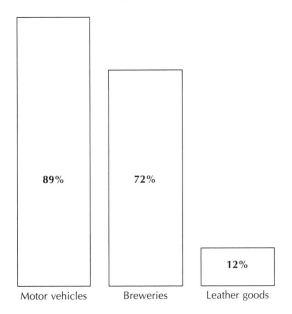

| Motor vehicles | Breweries | Leather goods |
| 89% | 72% | 12% |

The public sector

Most of this chapter will focus on the private sector, but the picture would not be complete without giving a brief survey of the position in the public sector. This includes a very wide range of activities including the work of teachers, soldiers, police officers and civil servants as well as those working in nationalised industries such as coal, British Rail, or the Post Office. In some cases the employers are responsible for thousands of workers, yet the individual operates in a small environment. An example of this would be teachers working in small village schools. This example illustrates an important point to be made when discussing the scale of operations. In some cases people work in small units even though they are part of a large organisation. The size of the unit in the public sector is often determined by the nature of the job. If the town is small, then the library and the local sports centre will also be small.

For nationalised industries, the factors governing their size are often the same as those affecting private sector firms, for they are influenced by similar - though not identical - economic factors.

> **Key ideas**
>
> 1. Over the long period, there has been an increase in the importance of very large firms.
> 2. In manufacturing there are only a few large firms, but they have considerable economic importance.
> 3. In some industries the typical firm is very large, in others small firms are more common.
> 4. In the public sector organisations tend to be large, but individual work units may be small.

Revenue and costs

How do firms decide how much to produce? One major influence in making this decision will be the profit that they expect to make at various levels of output. In order to examine the effects of firm size we need to examine in some detail two important economic concepts: revenue and costs.

Total revenue and total costs

Profit = Total revenue - Total cost

The total revenue received by a firm depends on two factors: the number of items sold and their

Table 5.4: Total revenue, total cost and profit

(1) Output (units per month)	(2) Price (£ per unit)	(3) Total revenue (QxP) (£ per month)	(4) Total cost (£ per month)	(5) Profit (TR-TC)
10	50	500	450	50
11	49	539	486	53
12	48	576	516	60
13	47	611	541	70
14	45	630	550	80
15	43	645	560	85
16	40	640	575	65
17	36	612	620	-8
18	32	576	680	-104

price. In most cases the demand curve slopes down, showing that firms which wish to sell more have to cut the price. In the hypothetical example given in Table 5.4, ten items can be sold at a price of £50, but to sell eighteen the price has to be cut to £32. Multiplying price by quantity gives total revenue as shown in column 3. Total cost also depends in part on the number of items produced. It costs more to produce eighteen items than ten because more raw materials and more labour are needed. However, costs may not rise proportionally with quantity because at some point the firm will have to pay overtime rates and perhaps hire extra machines which will push up costs. For this reason costs in the Table are shown as rising faster than output.

Column 5 shows profits. In this hypothetical example they rise with output, reaching a maximum when fifteen items are produced. Profits then start to fall, and the firm would make a loss if it produced seventeen or more items. The fall in profits at high levels of output reflects the high cost of producing this number of goods and also that the price has to be cut if large numbers are to be sold.

Average and marginal revenue and costs

Marginal cost is the cost of increasing output by one extra unit. Average cost is found by dividing total cost by the quantity produced.

Table 5.5: Total, average and marginal costs

(1) Output (Units per month)	(2) Total cost (£ per month)	(3) Average costs (TC ÷ Q) (£)	(4) Marginal cost (£)
10	450	45.0	-
11	486	44.2	36
12	516	43.0	30
13	541	41.6	25
14	550	39.3	9
15	560	37.3	10
16	575	35.9	15
17	620	36.5	45
18	680	37.8	60

In the example given in Table 5.5, when ten items are produced the total cost is £450 and consequently the average cost is £45. If output is increased to eleven items the total cost rises from £450 to £486, an increase of £36. This figure of £36 is the marginal cost of producing the eleventh item. Similarly, the marginal cost of producing the twelfth item is £516 - £486 = £30.

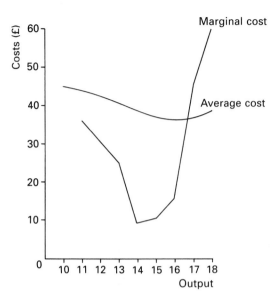

Figure 5.3: Average and marginal costs

The average cost curve is usually drawn with a 'U' shape. That is because it is influenced by what is happening to marginal cost. When marginal costs are falling it pulls down the average (just as when a cricketer with a batting average of 50 is out for 10 in his next innings). In the example illustrated in Table 5.5 and Figure 5.3, marginal cost at first falls as output expands. The reason for this is explored in more detail later; for the present we can say it is because the firm can use more specialised techniques as output expands and this brings down the cost. However, at higher levels of output the marginal cost may rise quickly, perhaps because the firm is forced to take on untrained labour or pay overtime rates. This rise in marginal cost will pull up average cost (just as a batsman's average will rise if he has a big score in his next innings).

Table 5.6

(1) Quantity	(2) Price (£ per unit)	(3) Total revenue (£ per month)	(4) Marginal revenue (£)
10	50	500	-
11	49	539	39
12	48	576	37
13	47	611	35

Marginal revenue is the extra revenue generated by the sale of an extra unit. In Table 5.6 total revenue is £500 when the quantity sold is ten; when this rises to eleven total revenue rises to £539. Consequently the marginal revenue is £539 - £500 = £39.

Table 5.7: *Marginal cost and marginal revenue*

(1) Quantity	(2) Marginal cost (£)	(3) Marginal revenue (£)
10	-	-
11	36	39
12	30	37
13	25	35
14	9	19
15	10	15
16	15	-5
17	45	-28
18	60	-36

Figure 5.4: *Marginal cost and marginal revenue*

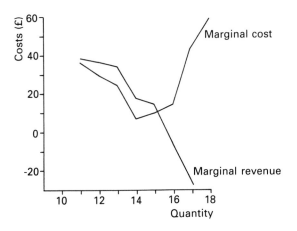

As Table 5.7 and Figure 5.4 show, if the firm increases its output from thirteen to fourteen, its costs rise by £9 and its revenue by £19. Clearly it will pay the firm to expand its output from thirteen to fourteen items. Similarly, when output rises from fourteen to fifteen, costs rise by £10 and revenue by £15. Again it will be profitable to increase output. However, if output was increased

to sixteen, costs would rise by £15 whilst revenue would actually fall by £5. Hence if the firm wishes to maximise profits it will produce 15 items. This marginal analysis has confirmed the result we obtained by looking at total costs and revenue. In marginal analysis the general rule, of which this is a contrived example, is that a firm will maximise profit if it expands output up to the point at which **marginal revenue (MR) equals marginal cost (MC).**

Normal profit

This rule can only be explained in full if we bring in a slight complication. You may wonder why the firm should expand output until marginal revenue equals marginal cost. If increasing production raises both revenue and costs by the same amount, why bother to increase output? The answer is that the economist's concept of cost differs from that of the accountant and also from that used in everyday life. Economists include in 'costs' a notional element of profit needed to keep the firm in business. If the firm received less than this notional amount, it would be rational for the firm to close down the business and invest the money somewhere else. Hence if the firm produces at the level of output where marginal revenue equals marginal cost it will be making just enough profit to stay in business. This notional amount of money needed to keep a firm in business is called 'normal profit'. Any profit greater than this is called excess or abnormal profit.

Fixed and variable costs

An alternative way to analyse costs is to distinguish between fixed and variable costs. 'Fixed' costs are those which the firm has to pay whether or not it produces any goods. Examples of fixed costs are rent, rates, bank charges, security costs and some salaries.

'Variable' costs do vary with output. Examples are wages, raw materials and the power used for machinery. These costs will normally rise as output expands:

Table 5.8: *Costs of a firm in the short run*

(1) Output (units)	(2) Total fixed costs (£)	(3) Total variable costs (£)	(4) Total costs (£)	(5) Average fixed costs (£)	(6) Average variable costs (£)	(7) Average costs (£)	(8) Marginal costs (£)
0	100	0	100	00	-		
1	100	10	110	100	10	110	10
2	100	15	115	50	7.5	57.5	5
3	100	19	119	33.3	6.3	39.6	4

Total costs = Fixed costs + Variable costs

In Table 5.8, column 2 gives total fixed costs; these do not vary with the level of output. Column 3 shows total variable costs; these do increase as output rises. Column 4 shows that total costs are the sum of fixed and variable costs. Columns 5 and 6 give average fixed and average variable costs. In the case of average fixed costs, these are obtained by dividing total fixed costs by output. Average variable costs are obtained in the same way, by dividing total variable costs by output. The last two columns in the Table show average costs and marginal costs. These are calculated as shown in the last section.

These relationships can be shown diagrammatically and Figure 5.5 does this for marginal cost (MC), average fixed costs (AFC), and average variable costs (AVC).

Figure 5.5

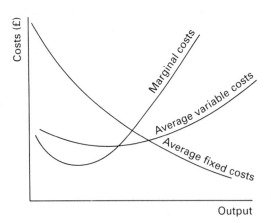

Average fixed costs fall as output rises, because at low levels of output these costs are very large for each item produced, but as output expands the fixed costs can be spread over more items. If a factory produced a hundred thousand tins of baked beans a week, the rent bill would only add a minute cost to each tin.

Diminishing returns

In Figure 5.5 the average variable cost curve and the marginal cost curve are drawn sloping down and then rising up again. One explanation of this rise derives from the law of diminishing returns. This says that if all factors of production except one are held constant, then increases in the variable factor will eventually lead to declining average and marginal products.

An example will clarify this law. If we have fixed inputs of land (say 100 acres) and capital (say 2 tractors and a given amount of seed), but can vary the quantity of labour, what will happen to output as the number of workers increases? At some point the marginal product of labour will start to fall. Workers will start to get in each others way, and some will have no tools. If more workers are added there will be growing management problems and at some point the amount produced may actually fall as the number of workers increases.

Two points about the law of diminishing returns should be noted. Firstly, the word 'eventually' makes it clear that at first output may rise as additional units of the variable factor are added. Two people building a house may be more than twice as productive as one because they can specialise and also help each other with heavy jobs. Time is also important. In the short run firms cannot build new factories and so we may expect the law of diminishing returns to operate. This will mean that at some point output per worker will fall, thus explaining why marginal costs eventually rise.

Figure 5.6: *Long-run average cost*

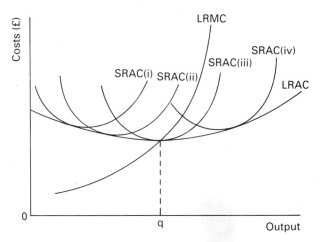

In the long run the position is different because firms can vary all the factors of production. In particular they can build new factories. This means that the firm's long-run average cost curve will be made up of a series of short-run curves as shown in Figure 5.6. In the long run the firm can choose to produce anywhere on this long-run curve. The most efficient place will be at q where average cost is lowest. (This is also the place where the long-run marginal cost curve intersects the long-run average cost curve.)

A word of caution is needed here. The analysis of costs presented here is very theoretical. This has advantages; it enables us to develop a framework of analysis. However, real life is often more complicated. Two examples will illustrate this. Firstly, firms may not seek to maximise profits, instead they may be content to make reasonable profits. If this is so, they may produce at a range of places on the cost curve. This issue is examined in more detail in Chapter 6. Secondly, in practice cost curves may not always rise and fall in the 'U' shape shown in most diagrams. For example, costs may not rise when output expands (this is illustrated in Figure 5.9). Their actual shape will vary considerably between firms because some will have lower costs than others.

Key ideas

1. Marginal cost is the cost of increasing output by an extra unit. Marginal revenue is the extra revenue obtained when output is increased by one unit.
2. Profits will be maximised when a firm produces where marginal revenue equals marginal cost.
3. Fixed costs do not vary with output; variable costs do.
4. The law of diminishing returns says that if all factors of production except one are held constant, then increases in the variable factor will eventually lead to declining average and marginal products.

How do firms grow?

Firms grow in two ways: by internal growth and by merging with others.

Internal growth

Many firms become large by generating internal growth. Marks and Spencer is an example. It started as a market stall selling clothes and still does this, though it has also diversified into other products. Other firms have also grown by diversifying within the same industry. The Ford Motor Company started by producing only one car model; now it produces not only a wide range of cars, but also trucks and

other related products. Such diversification makes it possible for firms to become large whilst still remaining in the same business.

One reason why firms grow large is that, in some cases, their costs fall in the long run as the firm produces more. This was illustrated in Figure 5.6. When the cost curve is this shape, any firm producing only a few goods will be at a disadvantage compared to its competitors because its costs will be higher. Where costs vary with output in this way, firms tend to grow until they produce a level of output where costs are low.

Mergers

Some firms are content to remain small. Their owners are satisfied with reasonable profits and are not willing to deal with the problems which may arise if the firm is to grow. On the other hand some entrepreneurs want to be big. They are constantly seeking new opportunities for growth and are willing to struggle in order to take over other firms, even though these may resist. For this group big is beautiful.

Figure 5.7: Types of integration

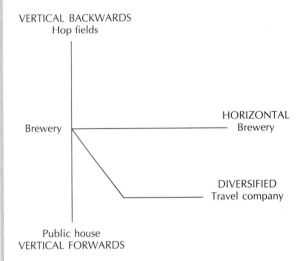

Mergers can take several forms. Sometimes firms take over their suppliers or their customers. This is called **vertical integration.** Examples would include a brewing company which bought hop fields or took over a firm owning pubs. Vertical integration can be either forward or backward. Firms integrate backwards to obtain control over the raw materials and components they need. Forward integration gives them control over marketing the products they make. Another reason for vertical integration is that it reduces transactions costs. As the phrase implies, these are the costs involved in buying and selling goods. Uncertainties over demand and supply conditions can lead to costly haggling over the terms of a contract between firms. This haggling can be eliminated if one firm merges with the other. For example, Stuckley (1983) examined vertical integration in the American aluminium industry. The basic raw material used in this industry is bauxite, which varies in quality. This leads to uncertainty, haggling and high transactions costs when trade takes place. Consequently aluminium producers seek to reduce these costs by backward vertical integration.

Horizontal integration occurs when a firm buys another at the same stage of production. Examples include a brewer buying another brewer or one publisher taking over another. One reason firms do this is that it gives them an element of monopoly power. This may allow them to put up prices. It can also increase their bargaining power with suppliers who may be forced to cut the price they charge a large customer.

The other form of merger is sometimes called **diversified integration** and occurs when a firm merges with another in a completely different industry as, for example, when a tobacco company buys an insurance company or an engineering firm joins a company building houses. Mergers between very different firms lead to the formation of **conglomerates.** For example, what have the following in common?

Galliford (housebuilders), William Hill (betting shops), Mappin and Webb (jewellers), Adams (children's wear), In-Time (watch shops), Freeman Hardy and Willis, Truform, Saxone, Skinner, Curtis and Dolcis (shoe shops).

The answer is that all are part of a conglomerate called Sears. This example illustrates horizontal integration (the shoe shops) and also diversified integration - all the rest.

One reason for diversified integration is that it reduces risk. If one product or firm within the conglomerate fails, profits from the others will allow the firm to continue in business. Another reason is that diversified firms within a conglomerate possess assets which can be shared. One may have technological know-how, another spare physical capacity and a third may have marketing or managerial expertise. Sharing such assets can bring substantial benefits to the group. Moreover, diversification can reduce transactions costs if quick managerial decisions within a firm replace expensive negotiations with other firms.

> **Key ideas**
>
> **1. Many firms grow through internal growth. One reason is that costs may fall in the long run as the firm grows.**
> **2. Alternatively firms grow through mergers. These can take the form of vertical, horizontal or diversified integration.**

Big is best

No one believes that in every case large firms are better than small ones; but many economists do argue that in numerous industries large firms will have a significant advantage. They therefore advocate that government policies should recognise this advantage, for example, by encouraging firms to merge or at least refraining from restricting firms' growth. One reason for this belief is the existence of economies of scale.

Economies of scale

Economies of scale exist when long-run average costs fall as output expands. Sometimes these occur as the **firm** grows, sometimes they result from growth in the individual **factory or plant.**

Plant economies of scale

As the name implies technical economies arise out of the techniques of production. Some occur because of specialisation of both labour and machines. When plants operate on a large scale they can make use of specialised equipment which would be too expensive for small operations. A good example is the robots used on car production lines.

Specialised machinery often goes hand in hand with the use of specialised labour, that is with the division of labour. Over two hundred years ago Adam Smith described the spectacular results which could be achieved in a pin factory when each worker concentrated on one task. In modern factories, as in those described by Smith, workers who concentrate on one task become expert and highly productive.

Another related economy of size arises from increased dimensions. A large truck and a small van can both be driven by one person, but the larger vehicle can carry far more goods. Moreover, as units are built on a larger scale the construction costs may

Figure 5.8: Economies of scale

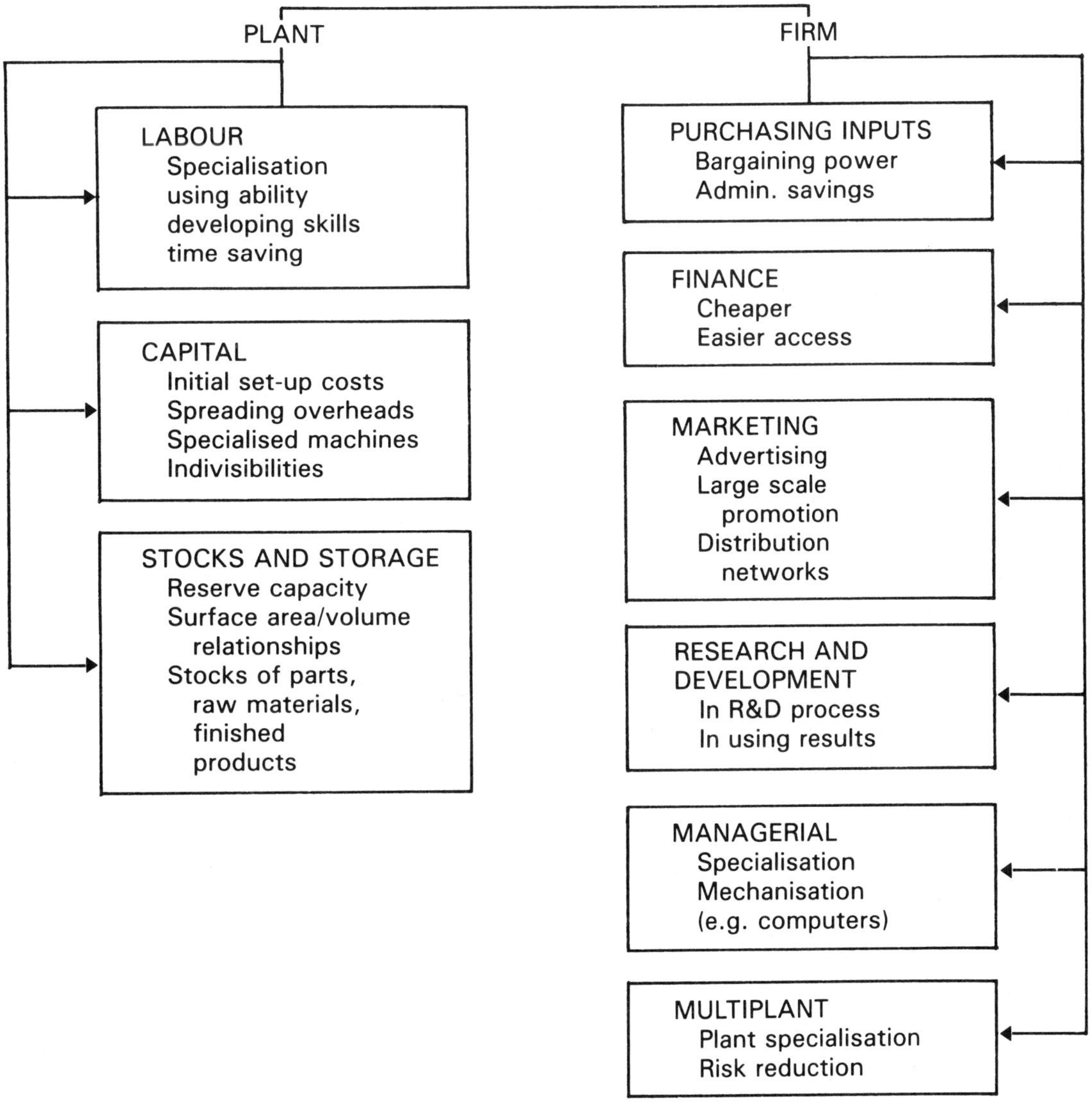

rise proportionally less than the building size. Engineers have a rule of thumb which suggests that the cost of a building increases by only two-thirds of the increase in the size of the building. Some machines and techniques of production are indivisible. It is not possible to build a small nuclear power station or a tiny plant making jet engines for aeroplanes. Another economy accruing to large-scale plants sometimes arises in the use of stocks. Small workshops need spare parts for all the processes; a much larger plant may also require only the same quantity of spares.

The existence of plant economies of scale means that factories are inefficient if they do not reach a certain size. Table 5.9 gives estimates of this minimum efficient size for a number of products.

Table 5.9: Some estimates of minimum efficient plant size

Product	Minimum efficient plant size
Beer	1 million barrels per annum
Commercial vehicles	30,000 units per annum
Electric cookers	30,000 units per annum
Sugar refining	45,0000 tonnes
Diesel engines	10,0000 units

Source: Adapted from *A Review of Monopolies and Mergers Policy*, HMSO, 1978.
Note: This is a simplified extract; the original contains several estimates for some items.

Firm economies of scale

Risk bearing economies arise because a large firm which produces many products can stand the loss if one product does not sell. This is an economic version of the adage: 'Don't put all your eggs in one basket'. Hence B.A.T., which makes many of the cigarettes sold outside the UK, bought an insurance company in order to reduce the risks associated with the production of only one commodity. This is an example of diversified integration discussed earlier.

Table 5.10: *Multi-plant and firm economies*

Industry	Source of economies
Beer brewing	Advertising, co-ordination of new plant investments
Cement	Risk spreading and raising finance
Refrigerators	Long production runs, advertising, transplantation
Cigarettes	Advertising and product differentiation

Source: Scherer, F.M., *Industrial Market Structure and Economic Performance*, 2nd ed. Rand McNally, 1980.

Large firms can have **financial advantages** compared to small ones. They can afford to employ financial specialists. In addition, financial institutions often prefer to lend to large organisations, so these find it easier to borrow money. Moreover, they can often borrow more cheaply. Thus a firm such as Sainsburys can borrow money more easily and cheaply than could a village shop.

Large firms may also have advantages in both **buying and selling.** Big firms can buy in bulk and hence buy at lower cost. Often they can also sell more cheaply because they can spread their marketing costs over a larger output. A firm with a hundred shops can advertise them all on television for the same price that a small firm can advertise one shop. **Research and development** can be expensive. To introduce a new medicine, for example, can involve large teams of highly trained - and expensive - people, and even when the drug has been created it needs expensive testing. Small firms cannot afford such costs.

Some evidence on economies of scale

The supporters of large-scale production can produce evidence to support their claims. Pratten (1971) investigated the minimum efficient scale of

plants and concluded that in some industries, such as aircraft production, electronic data processing equipment, steel rolling mills and electric motors, there were significant advantages in producing in large plants. Put another way, the slope of the long-run cost curve in Figure 5.6 was steep so that firms producing quantities less than q in that diagram would face much higher costs. Other evidence was provided by Scherer (1980) who investigated the minimum efficient size of plants in the USA. His evidence is presented in Table 5.11.

Table 5.11

Industry	Minimum optimal scale
Cigarettes	36 billion cigarettes a year, 2,275 employees
Glass bottles	133,000 tons per year, 1,000 employees
Refrigerators	800,000 units a year
Shoes	1 million pairs a year
Paints	10 million gallons a year

Source: Scherer, F.M. *Industrial Market Structure and Economic Performance*, Rand McNally, 1980.

These are only examples and changes in technology over time alter the precise point at which plants reach their greatest efficiency.

Another example of the efficiency of large-scale production occurs in the steel industry. In the mid-1950s, half the plants in Japan had a capacity of less than half a million tons. By the end of the decade almost all these plants had been closed and replaced by larger ones so that nearly half of the plants had a capacity of five million tons or more. This development enabled Japan to dominate the world steel market and by the early 1980s one Japanese plant was so large that it could produce more than the entire British Steel Corporation whilst using far fewer workers.

Experience curves

Another argument in favour of large-scale operation derives from the notion of experience curves. The long-run average cost curve shows how costs behave at a particular moment in time; but there is some evidence which suggests that costs can fall over time as the volume of output increases over the life of a product. It is suggested in management literature that costs will decline by a constant percentage each time the accumulated production or experience of the firm doubles. Such a curve is called an 'experience curve' and one example taken from the government Green Paper on mergers and monopolies suggested that as Pilkington Glass increased their experience of producing float glass

on a large scale, total cost per square foot fell by over 40%. If falls in real costs are common they are a good reason why firms should try to increase the volume of production.

Key ideas - summary of the argument in favour of large-scale production

1. **As living standards have increased over the years, firms have grown larger. This suggests that further increases in size will lead to greater rises in living standards.**
2. **As factories grow in size they can make use of specialised machinery and extend the division of labour.**
3. **As firms grow in size they can enjoy other economies of scale in areas such as finance, marketing, purchasing, and in risk bearing.**
4. **Experience curve arguments suggest that costs fall as the volume of production rises.**

Small is beautiful

It is clear that there is a powerful set of arguments to suggest considerable advantages from large-scale production. Yet there are strong competing arguments which emphasise the advantages of small organisations.

Criticisms of the economies of scale argument

In the earlier section we emphasised the economies to be gained from large-scale production. Many of these arguments are open to criticism.

In the first place, in many industries there may be either no economies of scale, or these may be of negligible importance. This is the case in many service industries where personal attention is needed. That is why there are no enormous hairdressing shops employing hundreds of assistants. Similarly, there are few economies of scale in other jobs that require individual attention, such as roof repairs, plumbing, or painting and decorating. In all these cases firms tend to be small; indeed, they are often owned and operated by only one person.

Even in manufacturing, economies of scale are often small. In industries as diverse as the production of shoes, bricks, bread, beer, cotton spinning and weaving, and book printing, it is possible to produce economically on a small scale. Put another way, the minimum efficient size of plant is relatively small and once this is reached there are few economies to be obtained in growing bigger. Hence the long-run average cost curve quickly becomes flat as shown in Figure 5.9. This line of argument is supported by the work of Pratten (1971), who estimated that only in a few cases would costs rise by more than 10% if the firm operated at half the optimal capacity. Similarly, Scherer (1980) analysed American industries and concluded that the long-run cost curve was similar to that shown in Figure 5.9 and that:

'the minimal optimal plant scale revealed in studies of American manufacturing industries has been small relative to industry size'.

Figure 5.9: *Few economies of scale*

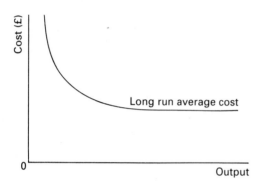

Similar arguments can be used to suggest that there are few economies accruing to large-scale firms. Profits are one possible measure of efficiency. Whittington (1976) examined the rate of return on assets of a large number of firms over a twelve year period and found that small firms had a mean rate of return of 17%, whilst for large firms it was only 15.8%.

Even where firms do benefit from being large, this may not be in the interest of the consumer. In some cases large firms may use their large size to dominate the market and reap monopoly profits by exploiting the consumer. Similarly, where there are economies in size these may not benefit the consumer. Advertising may protect the positions of established firms and reduce competition. Firms which borrow money more cheaply may not pass the benefits on to the consumer and, if the supply of funds is scarce, then large firms may obtain loans at the expense of small ones, who may be unable to borrow.

Diseconomies of scale

Even where economies of scale do exist, they have to be balanced against the possibility that

diseconomies of scale may also exist. The main reason for this is that management is more difficult in large firms. Managers spend lots of time in meetings and much effort goes into ensuring satisfactory communications. Decision making may be slow, so that the firm takes time to adapt to change. In addition, one characteristic of large-scale organisations is that parts of the whole develop their own goals which may be at variance with the needs of the whole. The managing director may wish to maximise profits, but the manager of a particular department may be more concerned to increase the size and influence of that department.

Moreover, large firms may have poorer labour relations than small ones. Workers may feel that they they are just tiny cogs in a huge wheel and be more likely to strike or to take other forms of industrial action than workers in small firms.

Advantages of small firms

Small firms sometimes have positive advantages over large ones or else devise methods which minimise their disadvantages. For example, they sometimes buy in expertise and so take advantage of other firms' specialities. This is common in the building industry, where the main contractor for a development may hire specialists, such as architects or scaffolders. They sometimes buy in semi-finished products and so take advantage of the economies of scale enjoyed by their suppliers. Above all, small firms can offer personal service and can react quickly to changing opportunities in the market.

Small is beautiful

A rather different line of argument in support of smallness is taken by a group inspired by the writings of E.F. Schumacher, whose book *Small is Beautiful (1974)* is subtitled 'a study of economics as if people mattered'. He argues that large-scale methods often de-humanise workers and quotes Gandhi:

'I want the dumb millions of our land to be healthy and happy, and I want them to grow spiritually . . . If we feel the need for machines, we will certainly have them. Every machine that helps every individual has a place, but there should be no place for machines that concentrate power in a few hands and turn the masses into mere machine minders.'

Schumaker argues in favour of 'technology with a human face' - small-scale machines that give workers a feeling of satisfaction. He argues that:

'the technology of mass production is inherently violent, ecologically damaging, self-defeating in terms of non-renewable resources, and stultifying for the human person'.

What is needed is **intermediate technology**, superior to the primitive technology of old, but without the destructive qualities of super-technology. This intermediate technology should be located in small-scale organisations which promote individual dignity. Critics of this approach suggest that international competition forces firms to search for ways to cut costs so that they are 'locked into' particular methods of production and cannot adopt a more humane approach because the risks would be too great.

Key ideas - summary of the argument in favour of small size

**1. In many industries there may be few - if any - economies of scale.
2. Large firms may use their size to exploit the consumer.
3. There are diseconomies of scale, such as bureaucracy.**

**4. Small firms have positive advantages, such as personal service and flexibility.
5. Schumacher argues that large organisations de-humanise people, while small ones using intermediate technology can promote health and happiness.**

Conclusion

In a modern industrial economy there is a huge diversity in the size of firms and factories. That is because, in some cases, economic forces encourage the growth of large units, whilst in others these forces are weak or non-existent. On one side of the argument there are good examples to show that costs sometimes fall as the scale of organisation increases. Large firms can undoubtedly benefit from economies of scale.

On the other hand, it is argued that these economies may be exaggerated and that small-scale organisations have positive advantages.

The balance of the argument seems to depend on the particular circumstances; there is no overall ideal size of firm or factory.

Data questions

Why did Mr Hamlyn sell?

Paul Hamlyn's sale of Octopus to Reed last Thursday, after only five days of intense talks, is by a long shot the biggest UK book publishing takeover deal so far. The price put on Octopus' head is £535m, and Paul Hamlyn's own share, together with Hamlyn Trust's and including a £50m donation by Mr Hamlyn to his own charitable trust, is well over £180m. The scale of the deal has been acknowledged by extensive reports in the financial press, and most of the commentators have been impressed by and supportive of the deal.

Mr Hamlyn set up Octopus in 1971 with £10,000 capital. Its 17-year growth has been spectacular. In 1986 it had a £159m turnover and a £26m pretax profit. It bought Heinemann in 1985 for £100m, and its most recent acquisition was that of Mitchell Beazley in May for £4.9m.

There is the unarguable benefit of scale - the companies have between them a turnover of over £1bn in the publishing of books and magazines. There is synergy (a current vogue word which seems to mean little more than a good fit):

Company	The Takeover Trend Purchaser	Date	Price
Thomson Books	Penguin	Mar 85	£21m
Routledge	ABP	Mar 85	£4.5m
Pitman	Longman	May 85	£18m
Bowker	Reed	June 85	$90m
Heinemann	Octopus	July 85	£100m
Hamlyn	Octopus	Mar 86	£10m
Doubleday	Bertelsmann	Sept 86	£330m
NAL	Penguin	Oct 86	£46m
CVBC	R House	May 87	£17.5m (est)
M Beazley	Octopus	May 87	£4.9m
ABP	ITOL	June 87	£210m
Octopus	Reed	July 87	£535m

particularly noted is the potential of linking Octopus books with Reed consumer magazines, of books spun off mags. There is internationality and - although Mr Hamlyn does not put the highest priority on this - there can be no doubt that Octopus, which has little North American strength, will benefit from Reed's substantial presence there. There are the opportunities for rationalisation, with Ian Irvine already thinking aloud on the possibilities of merging Reed's Butterworth subsidiary with Octopus in Australia and New Zealand.

High cost of buying

And there are two specially important factors. Mr Hamlyn was an involved spectator in the auction for ABP and realised more keenly than ever the current cost of major acquisitions in both the US and the UK. Now that he is in bed with Reed, desirable acquisitions - purchases even bigger than Doubleday, which he reckons Octopus could have afforded - become affordable. Secondly, Octopus has an entrepreneurial and marketing flair which is extremely rare and hard to overvalue; it will add a further dimension to Reed's operations.

Source: *The Bookseller*, July 10, 1987.

Question 1

1. Describe the trend shown in the table. What explaination can you give for this trend?

2. What economies of scale do you think might operate in the publishing industry?

3. Why do you think small-scale publishing firms still exist?

Private contractors in the construction industry (Great Britain)

Size of firm (by number employed)	Number of firms	Number employed	Value of work done (£ million)
1	79,354	77,700	527.8
2-3	54,712	129,400	698.4
4-7	24,838	115,600	744.3
8-24	11,559	151,500	1,104.0
25-114	3,876	179,200	1,529.4
115-599	650	150,700	1,428.0
600-1199	71	60,000	592.2
1200 and over	35	97,800	918.8
All firms	175,095	961,900	7,542.9

Source: *Housing and Construction Statistics 1977-88*, HMSO, 1988.

Question 2

1. What percentage of firms employ less than 25 people? What percentage of total employment and output are these firms responsible for?
2. Calculate the value of work done per person employed in these small firms and compare this with the value of work done per person in very large firms employing over 1200 people. Comment on your results.

3. Why do you think this industry has such a wide variation in the size of firms?

6 Monopoly, Competition and the Theory of the Firm

This chapter has two themes. The first is concerned with the advantages and disadvantages of competition compared to those which arise when competition is limited. The second theme is concerned with the merits of the neo-classical approach to the theory of the firm compared to those which have developed more recently.

Neo-classical theory has largely been concerned with explaining the price a firm should charge and the output it should produce. A prime determinant of firms' behaviour will be the market structure in which it operates:

● At one extreme is perfect competition. This is a hypothetical situation where firms face vigorous competition and individual firms have little influence. 'Market' economists agree that competition has considerable benefits for the consumer, so that any restriction of competition is undesirable.

● At the other extreme is monopoly - where the firm is the industry. In between these two extremes there are other forms of market structure, such as monopolistic competition and oligopoly, where some market control exists. It can be argued that these market structures do bring benefits to the consumer.

A further debate concerns the extent to which these theories give a realistic account of the way firms operate. Other developments in the theory of the firm have attempted to give a more true to life explanation.

Defining and measuring market structure

A major theme in the economic analysis of markets is that the structure of an industry affects the conduct and performance of firms in terms of the price they charge, the level of output produced and the amount of profit made. Several aspects of market structure have a particular effect on the way firms operate:

● Seller concentration - the number of firms in an industry and their relative size.

● Buyer concentration - the number of customers for a product. For many consumer goods there are potentially millions of customers, but for products such as telephone exchanges or tanks the market is limited. Similarly, most coal in the UK goes to the electricity industry.

● Barriers to entry - how easy it is for new firms to enter the industry.

● Product differentiation - whether or not products in the same market are regarded as perfect substitutes.

Here we will focus on two of these, seller concentration and barriers to entry.

Seller concentration

At one extreme an industry may be made up of thousands of small firms - hairdressing and roof repairs are examples. At the other extreme a single firm may dominate the industry - British Telecom is an example. Between these two extremes lies a huge range of differing degrees of **concentration.** By this term we mean the proportion of a market which is supplied by a small number of firms. If only a few firms supply most of the market, then the industry

Table 6.1: *Types of industrial structure*

Structure	Number of producers	Product differentiation	Firm's control over price	Example
Perfect competition	Many	Identical products	None	Wholesale market
Monopolistic competition	Many	Products differ	Some	Hairdressers
Oligopoly (i)	Few	Little or no differentiation	Some	Petrol
Oligopoly (ii)	Few	Some differentiation	Some	Cars
Monopoly	One	Unique product	Considerable	British Telecom

has a high degree of concentration. The extent of concentration is usually measured by using a **concentration ratio** which shows the proportion of the market supplied by a specified number of firms.

Table 6.2: *Five firm concentration ratios for certain industries, UK*

Industry	1963	1977
Beer	50.5	62.2
Bread	71.4	81.2
Cars	91.2	98.4
Flour	51.0	85.7
Refrigerators	71.9	98.8
Washing machines	85.2	96.2

Source: 'Stabilisation of Product Concentration of UK Manufacturing', *Business Monitor*, HMSO, PO 1006, 1978.

Usually three or five firms are chosen according to the circumstances. A five firm concentration ratio of 70% means that the five largest firms possess 70% of the total sales (or employment or assets) in the industry.

As Table 6.2 shows, in some industries a few firms dominate the market. Moreover, there is some evidence that the degree of concentration is increasing. Curry and George (1983) analysed UK industry over a long period (1935 - 1968) and concluded that, on average, the level of concentration had increased. As Table 6.2 shows, this trend seems to have continued, at least in some industries, in more recent times.

Barriers to entry

The level of competition in an industry does not only depend on the number of firms operating in an industry at any one time, but also on the ease with which new firms can enter the market. If barriers to entry are high, then existing firms may be able to exploit their position; if these barriers are low, then firms in the industry may modify their behaviour -

for example, by keeping down prices and profits - in order not to attract new firms. Barriers to entry are costs which any new firm entering an industry will have to bear. They were first analysed in depth by Joseph Bain (1958) who distinguished three types.

Economies of scale barriers

In some industries firms have to be big to survive. Only a huge firm could construct a nuclear energy plant or build a commercial aeroplane. Sometimes existing firms try to create barriers; the advertising costs needed to get a substantial share of the detergent market are so large that they deter possible new entrants.

Absolute cost barriers

These barriers are often related to knowledge. New entrants may lack experience so that their costs are higher than those of existing firms. Moreover, these firms may protect their position by patents which prevent new entrants using existing methods. Thus Polaroid patented methods of taking instant photographs which prevented potential competitors such as Kodak from entering this market. Finally, firms already in the industry may have control of sources of raw materials and this makes it difficult for new firms to join the industry.

Product differentiation

This occurs when a firm makes several products which appear to the customer to be competing against each other. If a single firm makes ten varieties of soap powder, then any potential entrant would be faced by this range of competing products and, on average, would only be likely to capture one tenth of the market. This may not be enough for the product to be viable and so potential entrants are deterred. Where barriers to entry are high, we may expect competition to be at a low level; if these barriers are low then new firms will tend to be drawn to profitable markets and so increase competition. However, it remains to be seen if competition is necessarily desirable.

61

The case for competition

Perfect competition

The argument for competition is most clearly approached by using theoretical models of differing market structures. These may not exist in 'real life', but they set out various assumptions and show what the results will be if these assumptions are satisfied. This is the case with perfect competition.

In order for a market to be perfectly competitive, several conditions have to be met. There have to be large numbers of buyers and sellers so that even if one firm increased production considerably or one customer bought many more goods, it would have no effect on total supply or on the price at which the product sold. In addition, all the firms in the industry are assumed to make an identical product so that customers do not mind from which firm they buy. Moreover, the model assumes perfect knowledge so that everyone - buyers and sellers alike - knows what is going on. This means that if one firm attempted to put up its price no one would buy its product because an identical product could be bought from many other firms. Hence firms are **price takers** - they charge the same price as everyone else.

Figure 6.1 shows the position of the industry and the firm in perfect competition. For the industry as a whole, the forces of demand and supply lead to an equilibrium price for the product. This is shown in the left part of the diagram. At this price the market clears - there is no shortage and no surplus; every consumer willing to pay this price will be able to purchase goods and every firm willing to supply will sell all its products. The individual firm takes this price as given and is unable to influence the price it charges for its goods. Consequently, this is the price at which every firm has to sell its product. Since there are many firms in the industry, each can sell as much as it likes at this price because none is large enough to have significant influence on total sales. Because firms can sell all they produce at the same price, the demand curve will be perfectly elastic and the average revenue received from sales will equal the marginal revenue - the price received from selling an additional unit. The figure also shows the costs of the firm. The average cost curve is the familiar 'U' shape shown in the last chapter and the marginal cost curve has also been included. This is the cost of producing an extra unit. The marginal cost curve falls for a while as the output increases, but then rises as diseconomies of scale set in. As the last chapter showed, the firm will maximise its profits if it produces where marginal cost equals marginal revenue. In Figure 6.1 the firm will maximise profits when it produces quantity q. If it makes more or less than this quantity, costs will exceed revenue. Only at q will the firm cover its costs. This is an efficient quantity to produce, because average costs are at a minimum. Moreover, the consumer benefits from the lowest possible price - firms are charging a price which only just

Figure 6.1: *The industry and firm in perfect competition*

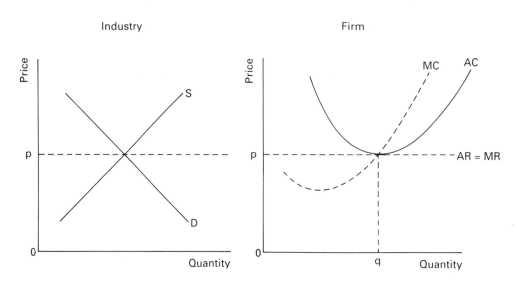

covers their costs. These characteristics of low cost, low price and no excess profits suggest that competition is desirable in an economy.

The short and long run

Figure 6.1 shows the long-run equilibrium position. In the short run, however, firms can make excess profits as shown in Figure 6.2. In this Figure, profits are shown by the difference between the average revenue and average cost curves multiplied by the quantity of goods. This is only a short-run position and cannot last in perfect competition. That is

Figure 6.2: Perfect competition - possible short-run position

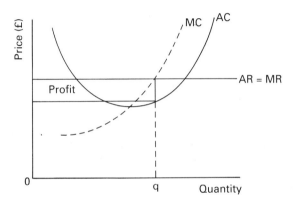

because the model assumes perfect knowledge so everyone knows about these profits. The model also assumes that it is easy to enter the industry. Hence new firms will move in and this will force down the price until it reaches the long-run equilibrium position shown in Figure 6.1. Here the firm is making just enough profit to stay in business and is not making excess profits as described in the last chapter.

Table 6.3: Perfect competition

1	Assumptions	Many buyers and sellers
		Identical product
		Easy entry and exit
		Perfect knowledge
2	How firm is affected	Firm is price taker
		Demand curve is horizontal (AR=MR)
		Firm attempts to maximise profit and produces where MR = MC
3	Result	Low price
		Firm produces at minimum average cost
		Firm makes only normal profit

Monopoly

Monopoly is at the opposite end of the spectrum from perfect competition. In economic theory it exists when there is only one firm in the industry. Pure monopoly is very rare. British Telecom and British Coal come close, but both face competition in some parts of their activities. Because there is only one firm in the industry the firm's demand curve is also the industry demand curve. This will normally slope down to the right, showing that if the monopolist wants to sell more it has to cut its price. Hence the monopoly has a choice; it can sell more - but at a lower price. Alternatively it can charge a higher price, but then will only be able to sell a smaller quantity. Consequently the monopolist is a **price maker**; unlike the firm in perfect competition it can choose its price.

Figure 6.3: Monopoly equilibrium

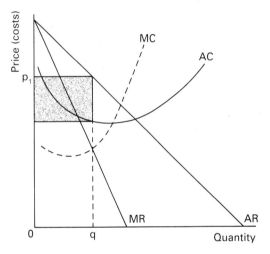

Critics of monopoly argue that this means that monopolists often choose to fix a high price. Figure 6.3 shows the equilibrium position of a monopolist. The marginal cost and average cost curves are the usual shape. The demand curve (which is also the average revenue curve) slopes down because to sell an extra good the firm will have to cut its price, and the marginal revenue curve slopes more steeply because to sell an extra good the firm will have to cut its price still more.

The firm will maximise profits when marginal revenue equals marginal cost, that is at quantity q. At this level of output the firm will be making excess profits. These are shown by the difference between average cost and average revenue multiplied by the quantity and are shaded in the diagram. Note that at output q the firm will not be producing as efficiently

63

as it could (at the lowest point on the average cost curve) - average cost would fall if it produced more goods. This would also benefit consumers because they would gain both from lower costs and from the availability of a greater quantity of goods. The firm does not expand output to this level because to sell these extra goods it would have to cut prices to such an extent that profits would fall. Hence supporters of competition oppose monopoly because they associate it with inefficiency, low output and high prices.

Table 6.4: Monopoly

1	Assumptions	Only one firm in the industry Barriers to entry prevent competition
2	How firm is affected	Firm is price maker Demand curve slopes down Firm attempts to maximise profit and produces where MR = MC
3	Result	High price Firm makes excess profit Inefficient firm does not produce where average cost is lowest Excess capacity - firm could produce more at lower cost

Discriminating monopoly

In some cases a monopolist can charge consumers different prices for what is essentially the same service. Consider a British Rail train. Some of the passengers will be travelling first-class and paying a high fare. Some will be paying full standard class fare. Sitting next to them may be someone with a saver ticket and paying a much lower price. There may also be someone with a railcard paying an even lower fare. Under what circumstances can a producer charge different prices for the same service?

In the first place, the producer must be a monopolist, otherwise another producer might offer a cheaper service. The other essential characteristic is that different groups of people must have different elasticities of demand. Those travelling first-class have a very inelastic demand. Either they are 'rich', or the firm is paying. In either case, the price makes little difference to their decision to travel. At the other extreme, someone with a Young Person's Railcard has a very elastic demand curve. This is because there are other close alternatives, in particular travel by bus - or not making the journey at all. A high price would deter such travellers. The third characteristic is that it must be possible to

separate these different groups. This can be done on a train. Some seats can be limited to first-class passengers and some trains forbidden to people with savers.

Other examples of discriminating monopoly are first and second-class letters which can be treated differently by the Post Office, telephone calls at different times of day, and aeroplane flights. Where these conditions apply, a firm will maximise its profits when it charges different prices to the different groups. The highest price will be charged to those with inelastic demand, the lowest to those whose demand is elastic.

Since discriminating monopolies charge different prices for essentially the same service, they are criticised for being unfair. However, they do offer advantages. Since the essence of a discriminating monopoly is that it splits up the market, this means that if one group of people stop buying the service, the firm can still continue in business, supported by the other groups. Moreover, people with low incomes can benefit since they can obtain essentially the same service as richer people, but at a lower price.

Perfect competition and monopoly are theoretical models at opposite ends of a spectrum. In between are two forms of imperfect competition which are much more common. One is called monopolistic competition, the other, oligopoly. Supporters of competition criticise both these forms of market, suggesting they result in an unsatisfactory allocation of resources.

Monopolistic competition

Monopolistic competition is so called because it combines some features characteristic of monopoly and some which resemble competitive industry. It has monopolistic features in that its products are not identical. Company X and company Y make **similar** products, but they do differ, for example, in design, quality, after sales service, or as a result of advertising. This **product differentiation** means the firm is faced with a downward sloping demand curve; if it wants to sell more goods it will have to cut its price.

However, other characteristics are similar to those found in competitive industry. There are many firms in the industry and it is relatively easy for new ones to enter.

Monopolistic competition is frequently found in a modern economy. Public houses, hairdressers, roof repairers and pop records are examples.

This combination of competition and monopoly leads to some results which are desirable and some which are not in the public interest. The competitive elements, such as freedom of entry, mean that firms do not make excess profits - if they did new firms would enter the industry and force down the price. Consequently monopolistic competition is characterised by normal profit. However, the fact that firms are faced by a downward sloping demand curve means that some firms will choose to sell smaller quantities at a higher price; hence some consumers who would like the product will not be able to afford the goods. This restriction in quantity is undesirable. It means that, as in monopoly, firms in this kind of industry will have substantial excess capacity; they could produce more and if they did so their average costs would be lower. Firms do not follow this desirable path because they would have to cut their price to sell these extra goods and this would result in a fall in profits.

Oligopoly

Oligopoly is also a form of imperfect competition and is usually defined as an industry with many buyers but only a few sellers. Examples are the manufacture of a wide range of products as diverse as cigarettes, cars, newspapers and detergents. The distinguishing characteristic of all these industries is that there are only a few firms in the industry because there are significant barriers to entry; for example, enormous building and machinery costs for a firm wishing to mass produce cars and high expenditure on advertising in the cigarette industry.

Because there are only a few firms in the industry, all firms have to consider the response of competitors to any change in price or output. In some cases firms will collude - act as if they were a single firm. This is what happened in 1973/4 when the oil producing countries in OPEC doubled the price of oil. This was successful, so a few months later they doubled the price again. In some cases the collusion may be explicit, as with OPEC, but in others it may be less formal - for example, small firms may follow the market leader in putting up prices. In this case the analysis is similar to that of monopoly and critics say the result will be high prices, excess profits, a reduction in the quantity of goods produced, and excess capacity, with the typical firm not producing at minimum average cost.

In other cases of oligopoly the firms may not collude; indeed they compete vigorously. This competition may take the form of **non-price** competition. Firms spend a lot of money on product differentiation - a glance at the local supermarket will show a huge variety of crisps, for example, and car manufacturers try to build in features which cause customers to prefer their cars to those of competitors. They also spend large sums of money on advertising and special offers.

The kinked demand curve

Where oligopolistic firms may not compete is on price. Some firms may fear that if they cut their price their competitors will follow suit so that all the firms may be worse off. If they put up prices, competitors may not change theirs so that the firm making the change will lose sales and be worse off. This line of argument has led to the suggestion that oligopoly will be characterised by stable prices, shown in Figure 6.4 by a kinked demand curve. If the firm moves from the price at the kink its revenue will fall. If the firm puts up its prices, competitors may not follow suit so its sales revenue will fall. On the other hand, if it cuts prices, competitors may also cut their prices so that the original price-cutting firm does not sell much more. Consequently firms may prefer to keep prices stable.

However, research evidence tends to suggest that most oligopolies are not characterised by stable prices, showing that persuasive arguments are not always correct. For example, oil companies frequently change the prices that they charge for petrol and banks often vary the interest they charge borrowers.

Critics of oligopoly argue that its results are unsatisfactory. It can lead to collusion, high prices and lower quantities of goods being put on the market than would be the case in perfect competition. Even where firms do not collude, there may be undesirable results since competition may take forms which do not really benefit the consumer, such as advertising, trivial product differences and 'free' gifts which the consumer would not choose to buy.

Figure 6.4: A kinked demand curve

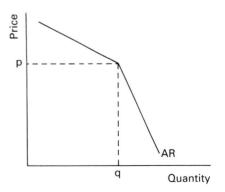

Key ideas - summary of the pro-competition argument

1. **Perfect competition leads to low prices, low profits, no excess capacity, and production is efficient, in that firms produce at minimum average cost. Hence competition is the most desirable form of market structure and any deviation from this is to be deplored.**
2. **Monopoly is characterised by high prices, excess capacity and high profits, the extent depending largely on the strength of barriers which prevent new firms entering the industry.**
3. **Monopolistic competition is characterised by many firms which practice product differentiation. The result is normal profits, but excess capacity.**
4. **An oligopolistic industry is one with few sellers. The consequences will depend on whether firms collude.**

Policy recommendations

The group of economists who emphasise competition put forward policies which they believe will strengthen competition and weaken monopolistic elements in the economy. They argue that nationalised industries should be split into separate competing firms. Thus they suggest that the coal industry should be privatised and its assets split up into several competing firms. In the private sector they want policies which would reduce the number of mergers because these restrict competition. Also they would like tough policies on monopolies. They support the breaking up of monopolies and, where a degree of monopoly is unavoidable (as with British Telecom, for example), they want strong controls to prevent such firms exploiting their monopoly position. Similarly, in industries characterised by oligopoly they want firms to be punished when they collude.

The argument against competition

Few economists would deny that there can be considerable merits in competition. However, some economists argue that there are limits to these benefits and that monopolies can sometimes be beneficial.

Criticism of the case for competition

The case for competition is often derived from the theoretical analysis of the benefits of perfect competition or the disadvantages of monopoly. However, these theoretical results depend on the assumptions underlying the analysis; if these assumptions do not hold, then neither do the results. Since the assumptions underlying the perfect competition model are so stringent that they are not found in the real world, it is argued that the supposed benefits are also unlikely to be realised. For example, perfect competition assumes perfect knowledge, but since this does not exist, firms may be unaware of profitable opportunities and may not move in to new markets, thus allowing existing firms to continue to charge high prices and make excess profits.

How firms really operate

Economists who are critical of the case for competition argue that theoretical analysis ignores the way in which firms really operate. For example, they argue that the theoretical analysis assumes firms attempt to maximise their profits, whereas in real life firms may have different objectives. If this is so, then the theoretical analysis given earlier is invalidated.

Surveys of how firms fix their prices suggest they do not attempt to maximise profits by producing at the level of output where marginal revenue equals marginal cost. Instead they tend to adopt a strategy of cost-plus pricing, sometimes called full cost pricing. To give just one example, Skinner (1970) surveyed 170 firms on Merseyside and found that 70% used cost-plus pricing. There are a number of varieties of cost-plus pricing, but typically price is decided by adding a percentage profit margin to unit costs. In some cases firms vary the profit margin to take account of demand conditions. Where this is done, the results would be similar to those predicted by the marginal analysis discussed earlier. However, overall the evidence is sufficient to cast doubt on the view that firms will attempt to maximise profits.

One reason for this is that decisions in firms are taken by managers rather than shareholders. Although the legal position is that shareholders own the firm, there are often so many shareholders that individually they hold little power and only a tiny minority attend the annual general meeting of their company. Consequently the relationship between owners and managers is like that of principals and agents. The principals - the shareholders - do not have full information so managers are often free to pursue their own interests, which may be different from those of the shareholders. Different groups within the firm will have their own objectives; some managers, for example, may be more interested in enlarging their own department than in maximising profits. This line of argument suggests that conflicts are inevitable inside firms and that these are often resolved by 'satisficing' - compromises within the firm so that different groups get something of what they want. This is an 'organisational' approach to the firm and, to the extent that it represents reality, it weakens the theoretical arguments which suggest that competition is better than monopoly.

An alternative critique reinforces this conclusion. The disadvantages of monopoly depend on the assumption that monopolies attempt to maximise profits. However, there are various reasons which suggest that they may not do this. For example, Baumol (1958) suggested that firms do not attempt to maximise profits, but instead try to maximise sales revenue, even though this means that profits are not as high as they could be. These arguments suggest that firms may be content with 'reasonable' profits, that is a level of profits which gives shareholders a satisfactory return on their capital. One reason for this, pointed out earlier in the chapter, is that high prices and profits may encourage competitors to enter the market. If the barriers to entry are not impenetrable, then the lure of high profits may give an incentive to new firms to breach these barriers. Lower profits may reduce this incentive. Moreover, the managers would then benefit from a quiet life; they would be able to get on with the job of running the firm without worrying about the actions of rivals. Hence the high prices predicted by the assumption that firms attempt to maximise profits may not be realised in practice. Instead firms may cut prices and increase production in order to reduce the likelihood of new firms entering the market.

Another defence of monopoly was put forward by Galbraith (1952) when he introduced the concept of 'countervailing power'. This suggested that monopolists were often prevented from exploiting their position because they were faced by a countervailing power - other firms which had the power to resist them. Thus a large monopoly such as British Coal sells most of its output to the Central Electricity Generating Board, which is also a large monopoly and can resist any attempt by British Coal to exploit it.

Positive advantages of monopoly

In addition to criticising the theoretical case for competition, there are some positive points to be made in favour of monopoly. In the first place, some monopolies are 'natural' in the sense that huge quantities of capital are needed to start the business. Hence it is logical that there should only be one organisation responsible for the national grid distributing electricity, and only one organisation laying water pipes down any particular street. In cases such as these competition would be wasteful.

Moreover, monopolies are often (but not necessarily) large and can take advantage of the economies of scale discussed in the last chapter. If this is so their costs will be lower than would be the case if there were several small competing firms in the industry. In particular, large firms may be able to spend more on research and development than could small firms. This line of argument was developed by one of the great Austrian economists, Joseph Schumpeter. (Like many economists Schumpeter was not noted for his modesty. He once remarked that in his youth he had had three ambitions - to be the greatest lover in Austria, the greatest horseman in Europe and the greatest economist in the world. He regretted that he had failed in his second ambition.) In his book *Capitalism, Socialism and Democracy* (1943) he wrote:

'"Restraints of trade" of the cartel type, as well as those which merely consist in tacit understandings about price competition, may be effective remedies under conditions of depression . . . they may in the end produce not only steadier but also greater expansion of total output than could be secured by an entirely uncontrolled onward rush that cannot fail to be studded with catastrophes.'

In Schumpeter's view there are two reasons for this. One is the belief that market forces, depending on competition, do not always represent a satisfactory way to allocate resources. Secondly, Schumpeter introduced the concept of 'creative destruction'. By this phrase he meant that innovation led to the destruction of traditional techniques and their replacement by more efficient ones. He argued that monopolists were more likely to undertake creative destruction, partly because they had the resources needed and partly because innovation - helped by patents - would help them maintain barriers to entry.

Since Schumpeter's time there has been a good deal of research into innovation. However, this evidence has proved to be inconclusive. On the one hand many inventions originated with small-scale operators, while some monopolies were lazy. On the other hand there have been dynamic monopolies and many innovations have originated within large firms.

Transactions costs

An alternative line of support for large organisations such as monopolies is that they are efficient because they reduce transactions costs. Traditional textbooks focus on the market as the way in which resources are allocated. However, some economists believe that in markets substantial costs arise in buying and selling raw materials and equipment used in the manufacture of goods, and that these costs can be minimised if organisation takes place inside firms rather than through the market. Consequently a large firm, such as Ford, will allocate capital and labour within the firm in several countries in order to produce cars efficiently. If large firms do reduce transactions costs, consumers may benefit, even though the firm is a monopoly.

Benefits of oligopoly

Oligopoly has its merits. Cynics may sneer at the 'special offers' which characterise this type of industry, but firms would not offer them if they were not attractive to customers. Moreover, it is possible to argue that oligopolists can only keep out competitors because they offer their customers a good service. These satisfied customers are the best indication of the merits of oligopoly. In addition, oligopolies also keep out competitors because they are efficient. If they were not, new firms would enter the market.

Key ideas - summary of the case against competition

1. The theoretical case for competition depends on unrealistic assumptions; if these are not met then the conclusion that competition is best also fails.
2. Monopolies may not exploit their position and may choose to make only reasonable profits.
3. Monopolies may be more efficient because, if large, they can enjoy economies of scale, spend more on research and development, and incur lower transactions costs.
4. Similarly, oligopolies can often only restrict entry by satisfying customers and by being efficient.

Policy recommendations

The line of argument followed here leads to policies based on the assumption that whilst competition may have its virtues, so do less competitive forms of market structure. Whilst in some cases monopolies may exploit their position, in others they may be beneficial and policies should reflect this. They therefore advocate that each case should be judged on its merits with an independent body considering the advantages and disadvantages of a particular monopoly or proposed merger. This approach lies behind UK policy on monopoly.

These arguments about competition and monopoly overlap with those about markets and also those concerned with size. Those economists who favour markets as a way of allocating resources tend to be critical of monopolies which they believe hamper the efficient allocation of resources. Similarly, those economists who favour small-scale production are critical of monopolies because they argue that these tend to be large-scale bureaucratic organisations.

As we have seen, some economists would suggest that the case against monopolies is overwhelming, and that the law should seek to prevent them. This is the case in the USA where for a hundred years Congress has passed laws to reduce the extent of monopoly power. However, other economists believe that monopolies can have benefits and that each case should be judged on its merits. This is the assumption taken by British legislation concerning mergers and monopolies. The 1973 Fair Trading Act said that the Monopolies and Mergers Commission - an independent body appointed by the government - should investigate mergers bearing in mind 'the public interest'. This is defined to mean that the Commission should have regard to points such as promoting competition, the interests of consumers, reduction of costs and promotion of exports. A similar approach is taken by the EC. Article 85 of the Treaty of Rome, which set up the Community, gives the European Commission power to prosecute firms which make collusive agreements that distort competition. Article 86 gives it power to take action against dominant firms which exploit their power, for example, by imposing unfair prices or trading conditions on their trading partners.

When considering monopolies, British law defines monopoly as existing when a company or group of companies supplies one quarter of all the goods or services of a particular kind in the UK. There is no presumption in the legislation that it is wrong to be a monopolist; each case is investigated on its merits. Thus in 1989 the Monopolies and Mergers Commission reported on its investigation into the brewing industry. It came to the conclusion that a few brewing firms had too much power because they owned too many public houses, and that this was to the detriment of consumers. Among other recommendations they made to remedy this position was one which would have prevented any firm from owning more than 2,000 public houses. The Commission believed that this would increase consumer choice. The brewers retorted that their size enabled them to spend large sums of money improving pubs, and to keep open pubs which would otherwise close. Consequently the Commission's proposals were not accepted by the government.

Monopoly legislation illustrates the link between economic analysis and policy. Economists who believe that there are often advantages to be derived from monopoly are, by and large, content with the legislation; those who favour more competition would like to see the law revised to discourage mergers and to do more to weaken monopolistic elements in the economy.

Developments in the theory of the firm

So far this chapter has been mainly using what might be called 'neo-classical theory', though some more modern concepts have been used. Neo-classical theory assumes firms try to maximise profits and uses marginal techniques to analyse firms' decisions. The theory treats the firm as an individual decision maker, as if a single person in a firm made all the decisions.

In recent years there have been a number of developments in the way that economists analyse firms, and some of these are considered here.

Managerial models

Although managerial models are not really new, they do represent a development in the traditional model of the firm. These models start with the recognition that in most modern firms shares are owned by very many people who have little real power. Consequently decisions are made, not by owners, but by managers. This means that decisions are not aimed at maximising profits. Instead they try to maximise the utility of managers. This may involve maximising other objectives such as sales, or the firm's growth. One conclusion of this line of

approach suggests managerial desire for growth will encourage firms to merge, since this will increase promotion opportunities and give managers increased status. The model also explains the existence of extensive managerial 'perks' such as company cars. These often reduce profits, but benefit managers.

Why do firms exist?

One answer to this question was given in 1937 by R.H. Coase. He suggested that in some circumstances there are costs involved in using markets which make it cheaper to organise production within a firm. To use his own words:

'Firms arise voluntarily because they represent a more efficient method of organising production.'

One reason for this is the existence of transactions costs which were explained earlier in this chapter. Coase suggested that in some circumstances markets will be used to allocate resources. In others, these will be allocated within firms because this will reduce costs. The crucial factor will be the extent of transactions costs. When these are high, resources will be allocated within firms. The same principle can be used to explain the size of firms. Firms will grow until the costs of organising an extra transaction within the firm are equal to the costs of using the market. Thus a firm such as Ford will constantly ask if it should produce this new component itself, or if it should buy it in the market?

Principal-agent theory

Another recent development in the theory of the firm is principal-agent theory. This does not draw a sharp distinction between 'market' and 'firm' ways of organising resources. Instead it suggests that inside firms people must often be left to decide for themselves how to behave. The same is true outside firms in relationships, such as those between an estate agent (the agent) and a principal selling a house. In principal-agent relationships, agents choose their own behaviour within the terms of a contract.

In a principal (P)-agent (A) relationship, P's welfare depends on what A does. P wants A to do what is best for (P), but A will be self-interested and do what is best for A. This causes problems, particularly as A often has hidden information since P cannot always supervise A. Within firms this leads to principals, i.e. the owners, giving share incentive schemes to their agents, the managers, in order to encourage them to take risks. Without such schemes, managers would be too cautious since their reputations would suffer if things went wrong, and they would not benefit much from success.

Performance-related pay schemes are another example of P-A relationships. Workers often have scope to make their own decisions, and performance-related pay schemes provide an incentive for effort, especially in cases where the workers' actions cannot be closely supervised.

Key ideas - summary of recent developments

1. The new approach is more realistic and aims to give better explanations of how firms really operate.

2. One emphasis in this approach is to recognise that managers may run firms in their own interest, which is not necessarily the same as that of the owners.

3. Firms exist because it is more efficient to organise production within firms than through markets.

4. Firms grow to reduce transactions costs.

5. Principal-agent theory offers explanations of behaviour both inside and outside firms where one person is contracted to carry out actions for another.

Conclusion

The traditional theory of the firm is concerned with questions such as the consequences of different forms of market structure. If certain rigorous assumptions are fulfilled, then perfect competition will have desirable consequences, such as low price. However, these conditions are not found in the real world and there is a vigorous debate about the advantages and disadvantages of competition. More recently, economists have asked more basic questions such as: 'Why do firms exist?; What causes them to grow?'. This new approach offers the potential for greater understanding of the nature of large firms which organise resources within the firm and not through the market. Similarly, work on transactions costs and on principal-agent theories can offer ideas to improve organisational relationships, for example, by providing appropriate incentives.

Data questions

Firm	Number of holidays (millions)
Thompson	3.24
ICG Travel *	2.44
Horizon	0.88
BA Holidays	0.64
Sky Tours	0.50
Wings	0.44
Best Travel	0.40
Airtours	0.36
Others	4.70
Total	13.60

Note: ICG Travel includes Intasun, Skyworld and Club 18-30*.
Source: Adapted from *The Observer*, December 27, 1987.

Question 1

1. What are the economic characteristics of this market?

2. What would economic theory predict about the price and output in this type of market?

3. Compare and contrast the benefits of this market to the consumer and the firms in the industry with the benefits of a perfectly competitive market.

British Posters

The canvas makers to the country's innumerable graffitists will awake this morning to find 'competition rules. OK' stir large across their own patch-grace of the Government's official spraycan.

Following almost three years of investigation into the operation of Britain's 170,000-odd roadside poster sites, the Monopolies and Mergers Commission has declared British Posters Limited a neau-geau area as one of its own clients might put it.

Its inquiry found that the marketing company, which controls almost 80 per cent of all roadside sites, has been forcing up prices, limiting competition and inhibiting the flexibility of advertisers wishing to promote their wares to passing motorists and marathon runners.

The overriding recommendation of the commission, couched in unusually unequivocal terms, is therefore that British Posters 'should cease to exist and not be reformed'. But it would still like advertisers to be provided with some sort of marketing operation which would enable them to paint their kerbside murals on a grand scale.

The problem is that posters have long been one of advertising's more maverick media, liable to frustrate even the best laid marketing plans. Selecting poster sites from which to blazon the merits of a new product is a far more haphazard process than, say, choosing a night-time slot on ITV or a newspaper or magazine whose readers are likely to be sympathetic.

Even with the development of organisations like British Posters, advertising agencies are never wholly sure what sort of site they are getting.

Another client grievance highlighted by the investigation is the lack of flexibility of the poster organisations and the long lead-in times they require for a new campaign. At the other end of the scale, lengthy contracts can mean that posters are still on display when their relevance has faded: Now! magazine was being promoted in London long after it had been relegated to a 'Then!'

But the main grudge of clients and the Monopolies Commission alike is that the poster contractors have been making a killing in recent years, pushing up their prices far more dramatically than the independent TV stations or publishers.

Although poster advertising accounts for only about 4 per cent of all advertising expenditure at just over £100 million (which includes the myriad sites on British Rail stations, London Underground stops and other off roadside locations) its operators tend to be among the fatter cats of the industry.

The commission concluded that British Posters' monopolies 'have led to a higher level of prices than would have obtained in a more competitive market'. Advertisers comparing notes would also point to the discrepancies - sometimes running into hundreds of pounds - between the prices they pay for adjacent sites in city centres.

The Monopolies Commission ruling comes at a time when the poster industry is already reeling from the blow of new cutbacks in cigarette advertising on its hoardings, which will lead to less gold and silk linings next summer. But the contractors argue that the advertising industry actually needs national poster facilities and will now take their case to the Director General of Fair Trading. Watch this space.

Source: *The Guardian,* July 2, 1981.

Question 2

1. What criticism has the Monopolies and Mergers Commission made of British Posters?

2. Use diagrams to illustrate the effect of the break up of British Posters.

People of the same trade seldom meet together, even for merriment and diversion, but the conversation ends in a conspiracy against the public, or in some contrivance to raise prices. It is impossible indeed to prevent such meetings, by any law which either could be executed or would be consistent with liberty and justice. But though the law cannot hinder people of the same trade from sometimes assembling together, it ought to do nothing to facilitate such assemblies; much less to render them necessary.

Source: Adam Smith, *Wealth of Nations,* First published 1776.

The introduction of new methods of production and new commodities is hardly conceivable with perfect - and perfectly prompt - competition from the start. And this means that the bulk of what we call economic progress is incompatible with it. As a matter of fact, perfect competition is and always has been temporarily suspended whenever anything new is being introduced - automatically or by measures devised for the purpose - even in otherwise perfectly competitive conditions.

Source: Schumpeter, J. *Capitalism, Socialism and Democracy,* Allen and Unwin, 1943.

Question 3

1. Summarise the economic arguments which lie behind the quotations.

2. What types of economic policy would follow from the views expressed in these articles?

7 Nationalisation and Privatisation

The role of government in the economic life of the country is a topic which occurs in several parts of this book, most obviously in the chapter on markets. This chapter is concerned with a particular aspect of that debate; the activities of government in the production of goods and services. Over recent decades there have been great changes in some industries, from private to public and then back to private ownership. These changes are the consequence, in part, of changes in political control of government, but they also result from changes in the relative power of competing economic arguments:

● On the one hand, some economists are sceptical about the value of market forces and favour public ownership and control of particular industries or firms. Some Keynesians and most Marxist economists would be included in this group.

● Opposing this are supply side economists who believe that government run industries are often inefficient and that wherever possible the private sector should take over.

Public ownership and privatisation

This chapter will focus particularly on the nationalised industries, but it should be noted that there are other forms of public ownership. There are, for example, local authority enterprises which are part of the public sector, but which are not nationalised. Thus local authorities run swimming pools and sports centres, and Hull even runs its own telephone service. Those industries which are nationalised are legally Public Corporations and are run by boards of directors appointed by the Secretary of State. In principle, the government sets out appropriate policies - such as a requirement to charge prices which will cover costs - and then the directors execute these policies.

The idea of publicly owned industries is not limited to Britain. In France, for example, there are a considerable number of nationalised industries including Renault cars and the match and tobacco industries. The idea of public ownership is an old one and not the preserve of any particular political party. As early as 1912 a nationwide public service of telephones was added to the Post Office and in 1912 a Liberal government passed an act setting up the Port of London Authority, which in many ways provided a model for future Public Corporations. Between the two World Wars, Conservative governments set up the British Broadcasting Corporation, the London Passenger Transport Board, the British Overseas Airways Corporation (later British Airways) and the Central Electricity Generating Board, which was responsible for the distribution of electricity through a national grid. Although both Liberal and Conservative governments have thus been responsible for setting up publicly owned organisations, the greatest thrust towards nationalisation came with the post-war Labour government. Between 1945 and 1951, the government nationalised coal, steel, railways, the Bank of England and road transport, together with a number of smaller organisations. By the early 1980s, the nationalised industries accounted for approximately 10% of national output, employed 7% of the nation's workers and were responsible for about 17% of total investment. However, in recent years there has been a reversal of policy and a move towards privatisation. 'Privatisation' is a relatively new word and describes the transfer of industrial and other assets from the public sector to the private sector. Previously the transfer of assets from public to private ownership was called 'de-nationalisation' and was carried out on an ad hoc basis; for example, road haulage was partially de-nationalised in the 1950s.

'Privatisation' can take a number of forms. One view is that of Kay and Silberston (1984) who distinguish three aspects. In the first place it can mean the liberalisation of entry into areas previously dominated by the state; for example, competitors were allowed to compete in certain areas with British Telecom and National Express, even before they were privatised. This is sometimes referred to as deregulation. A second meaning refers to private provision of services, such as hospital cleaning and refuse disposal; activities which were formerly undertaken by publicly employed personnel. The final meaning of privatisation refers to a change in ownership when state owned industries are sold off. This is the most common use of the term and the focus of most of this chapter. Table 7.1 shows the extent of these sales.

Table 7.1: Transfer of ownership

i)   British Petroleum

ii)   British Aerospace

iii)   British Sugar Corporation

iv)   Cable and Wireless

v)   Thomas Cook

vi)   Amersham International (high-technology development)

vii)   Britoil

viii)   Sealink (British Rail ferries)

ix)   Associated British Ports

x)   National Freight Corporation

xi)   British Transport Hotels (British Rail group)

xii)   Enterprise Oil (North Sea oil interests of British Gas)

xiii)   Jaguar

xiv)   British Telecom

xv)   British Gas

xvi)   Rolls Royce

xvii)   British Airways

xviii) British Airports Authority

xix)   National Bus Company

xx)   Vickers Shipyard

xxi)   British Steel

Key ideas

1. Nationalised industries are just one form of public sector production.

2. In the past, Conservative and Liberal governments have taken firms into the public sector; now this policy is most closely associated with the Labour Party.

3. Privatisation can be defined in various ways. Three aspects are examined here: liberalising entry into areas previously dominated by the state, private provision of services and selling off state owned industries.

The case for public ownership

'Public ownership' has been used in this sub-heading rather than nationalisation because some economists who favour public ownership do not like the particular form of ownership and control which characterises nationalised industries. They believe that nationalised industries are often cumbersome and bureaucratic; responsive neither to the needs of consumers nor of their workers. Despite this they believe that there are strong arguments for public ownership, but with more democratic forms of control than those currently used for nationalised industries. For example, some writers suggest that the workers in a firm should control it. This line of argument would be supported by Marxists and also by many non-Marxists who support a mixed economy.

The natural monopoly argument

Natural monopolies were discussed in the previous chapter. These are industries where the initial costs are high, but where there are large economies of scale so that the marginal cost of production is very low. A good example of a natural monopoly is the supply of clean water to houses. The start up costs of constructing reservoirs and laying pipes to every house are enormous. However, once constructed, the costs of supplying an extra gallon of water are very low. These characteristics mean that it would be difficult, if not impossible, for a competitor to challenge an existing supplier. Hence there is a 'natural' monopoly. Other examples are the construction of railway or telephone lines. In such cases there is a possibility that a privately owned firm would exploit its position and charge high prices in the knowledge that it is safe from competition. One answer to this problem is to take the industry into public ownership. Then 'fair' prices can be charged and consumers protected from exploitation.

Economists opposed to public ownership recognise the problem, but argue that a better solution is to allow private ownership and then to regulate the monopoly. This was the procedure adopted when British Telecom was privatised. The firm was only allowed to raise its prices by X-3%, where X was the average rise in prices in the economy as measured by the Retail Price Index.

Externalities and merit goods

Externalities occur when the actions of a firm or individual spill over on to others. Thus if a firm decides to transport its goods by road there will be an increase in congestion, more pollution and a greater likelihood of accidents. These disadvantages are not borne by the firm, but fall on others. Hence there is a case for keeping open railway lines which would not otherwise be profitable in order to prevent an increase in road traffic.

Merit goods are those which society believes should be provided in greater quantities than would be provided by market forces. For example, closing rural railway lines may mean that local industries close or that people are forced to move homes to be near their work. Similar arguments apply to the provision of telephone and electricity lines and the delivery of mail in rural areas. If these activities are unprofitable they will not be undertaken by privately owned industry. Public ownership can solve the problem because it can take into consideration the social consequences of decisions and not be ruled solely by questions of profitability.

The 'lame duck' argument

Sometimes vitally important industries run into trouble. This happened to Rolls Royce and to British Leyland (now Rover Group). Some economists believed that the government should not have interfered; that it should have let market forces take their course. This would have meant that both companies would have gone bankrupt. However, the government took both companies into public ownership. The reason for this was that it believed that there would have been considerable negative externalities if the firms had closed down. In the case of British Leyland, a collapse would have

affected a large number of the company's suppliers and the result of non-intervention would have been many bankruptcies and a significant rise in unemployment. The Rolls Royce argument was similar, but there was an additional point. Rolls Royce was an important supplier of defence material to the British government, so there were strategic reasons for intervention. Consequently both companies were taken into public ownership, though they were not formally nationalised - the government bought shares and put in money to ensure that the companies survived. This 'lame duck' argument was also one reason for the nationalisation of the coal and rail industries. After the Second World War these industries were extremely run down and needed massive new investment. Public ownership was seen as the best way to achieve their regeneration.

Equity

There are also equity arguments for public ownership. Some of these have already been mentioned. Private industries seeking to maximise profits would not provide services such as electricity to poorer regions; a nationalised industry would have different criteria for decision making and could supply such services.

However, the main equity argument concerns the distribution of wealth and involves people's values. Those economists who would like a more equal society see public ownership as one way in which this goal can be reached. In 1956 Hugh Gaitskell, then leader of the Labour Party, published a pamphlet called *Socialism and Nationalisation* in which he suggested several arguments in favour of public ownership:

'The first is in essence a Marxist argument . . . The flow of unearned income - of rent, interest and profits - is the root evil of capitalism; it represents the toll laid upon the workers by the owners of capitalism, who therefore deprive them of their rightful earnings . . .'

Gaitskell's second main argument relates to the working of the capitalist system. Both in the light of experience and on theoretical grounds, he claimed that the free individualist economy led perpetually to the unnatural result of 'poverty in the midst of plenty'.

Thirdly, he argued that the private possession of capital inevitably gave too much power to those who own it. This line of argument develops from a belief in a more equal society. It suggests that private ownership leads to greater inequality, and that one way to combat this is for the state to take over industries so that the benefits accrue to the people as a whole and not to a few owners. Counter arguments are put forward by those who do not share the value of greater equality and also by those who think that this is an inefficient way to achieve the goal. This latter group believes that other measures, such as higher taxes on the rich, would be more successful and that, in any case, if the owners of firms taken into the public sector were paid compensation the effect on the distribution of wealth would be trivial.

Arguments about the equity aspects of public ownership are bound up in the debate about the prices which these firms should charge. Since they are often monopolies, they could charge high prices and make huge profits. This would penalise consumers. On the other hand, it has been suggested that prices should be kept low in order to help poor consumers. However, this may lead to excessive consumption and to a waste of resources. Many economists suggest that public sector firms should adopt 'marginal cost pricing'; that is they should charge consumers the marginal cost of producing the product. However, this may be difficult to calculate and it can lead to the firms making losses.

Market failure

Another line of argument in favour of public ownership derives from the belief that market systems of allocating resources are likely to fail and that the state should intervene. In particular it is argued that market systems are characterised by unemployment and that, left to themselves, private enterprise firms would not invest enough to ensure a high rate of economic growth. The solution is for the state to take over 'the commanding heights of the economy', i.e. the most important firms in the economy, impose its political will on these, and so ensure high levels of investment. This was one reason why the post-war Labour government nationalised the Bank of England and such industries as coal and steel.

Marxist arguments

Marxists would accept many of the arguments given above in favour of public ownership, but they would add others. Since they believe that crisis and conflict are inevitable in a capitalist economy, they advocate a large scale extension in order to reduce such conflicts. Only in this way can problems such as unemployment be solved, since public sector firms can take on more workers, even though this may lead to a fall in profits.

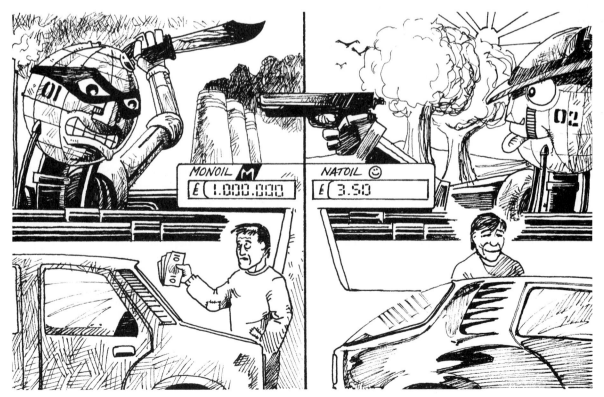

Key ideas - summary of the argument for public ownership

1. **Natural monopolies exist in a number of industries and these should be in the public sector to prevent exploitation of consumers.**
2. **Since they do not have to be guided by the profit motive, public sector firms can allow for the existence of externalities and supply merit goods.**
3. **If important industries run into difficulties, the public sector can save these firms, thus maintaining employment and output.**
4. **Private ownership leads to huge divisions between rich and poor; public ownership can reduce these divisions.**
5. **The state needs to own and control the 'commanding heights' of the economy in order to ensure full employment and steady growth.**
6. **Private ownership means that profits go to shareholders who usually take no part in the running of firms. Public ownership allows the workers to receive the full fruits of their labour.**
7. **Marxists would argue that only a large scale extension of public ownership can solve economic problems such as unemployment.**

Policies

In the first place, measures to privatise publicly owned industries should be resisted. Secondly, some firms should be taken into public ownership. For some Marxists, this would be a large number, sufficient to change the nature of capitalist society. Others would only support a much more modest policy of public ownership and many of these would oppose nationalisation because they regard this particular form of public ownership as unnecessarily bureaucratic. Instead they advocate alternative forms of public ownership, for example, workers' co-operatives. These could take many forms, but the essence of such organisations is that the workers in a firm own the company, receive all the profits, and are responsible for decision making.

The case for privatisation

Critics of public ownership frequently begin by arguing that privatisation should take place because publicly owned firms are not efficient. They focus on two forms of efficiency, allocative efficiency and X-efficiency, and they also point out the benefits of wider share ownership.

Allocative efficiency

As its name implies, allocative efficiency is concerned with the allocation of resources. A system is efficient in this sense when it produces the 'best' combination of goods and services - usually this means those desired by consumers - by means of the most efficient combination of inputs. The argument is that privatised firms would be more responsive to consumers' needs. Since profits accrue to the owners - and sometimes to the managers in the form of incentive bonuses - the people who run private sector firms have a direct incentive to provide the goods and services which consumers want. This means that privatised firms would be more innovative in producing new products in response to changes in public taste and be more concerned to ensure the goods which they produced were of a high quality.

X-efficiency

X-efficiency is a rather pompous term used to describe a simple concept. A firm is X-efficient if it produces a given output at the lowest possible cost. The argument is that without the spur of competition, nationalised industries will be able to have a quiet life, content to produce in traditional ways without worrying too much about improving efficiency. On the other hand, privatised industries will face the disciplines imposed by the market. If they are not efficient they may be forced into bankruptcy. Even if that does not occur, poor performance will mean it is difficult to raise money for expansion. Moreover, the price of the shares will fall, penalising not only shareholders, but also those managers who receive financial incentives related either to profits or to the price of shares. To this argument the critics of privatisation retort that profits and share prices depend far more on external factors, such as the state of the economy or changes in the general level of prices, than on a firm's efficiency. Further, they maintain there is little hard evidence that large companies find it difficult to raise money to finance developments, so that the 'discipline' of the stock market is more myth than reality. A further claim is that privatised industries will be more efficient because they will face competition. However, merely privatising an industry does not increase the amount of competition, which depends on other factors such as the presence or absence of competing firms, rather than the form of ownership of one firm. Hence privatised firms, such as British Gas and British Steel, face little more competition now than they did when nationalised.

Empirical evidence about efficiency

The arguments about efficiency are hard to judge because the empirical evidence is difficult to evaluate. In competitive industries the level of profits is a good measure of efficiency, but in publicly owned industries it would be more likely to measure the extent of price increases. If the Post Office put up its prices, then its profits would also rise; but this would say nothing about its efficiency.

A better criterion is whether private or public sector industries would attain the lowest cost curve. This is difficult to judge. The last chapter showed that in industries where competition was not perfect, a lot of firms would not produce at the lowest point of the average cost curve. An evaluation of 30 studies in different countries undertaken by Yarrow (1985) concluded that private sector firms tended to be more efficient than public sector firms if both operated in very competitive markets. When the market was not very competitive there was no clear difference between the two types of organisation.

Figure 7.1: Productivity$_1$

— Whole economy (excl. North Sea oil and non-trading public sector)

- - - - Manufacturing

- - - - - - Nationalised industries$_2$

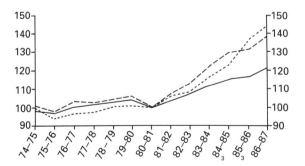

Source: Treasury.

Note:
1. Output per person employed.
2. Industries in public sector at end 1987-88, excl. Girobank and British Shipbuilders (Merchant).
3. Figures for nationalised industries output and whole economy have been adjusted to exclude the effect of the coal strike.

An alternative approach is to look at productivity. Figure 7.1 shows that productivity in nationalised industries has increased more quickly than in manufacturing and much more quickly than in the economy as a whole. However, this is far from conclusive as it may have been at a lower level at the start so that there was greater room for improvement. Hence it is not possible to arrive at a definite conclusion concerning the efficiency of nationalised industries.

Wider share ownership

Another argument in favour of privatisation is that selling nationalised industries increases share ownership, and that this is desirable because it gives people a stake in the wealth of the nation. It therefore contributes to political stability. This argument would be attacked by Marxists and others on the grounds that individual rewards from owning a few shares are so trivial that they do not really give people a stake in the wealth of society.

Another argument in this context is that, since the workers in privatised firms often receive shares on a preferential basis, they will have an increased motivation to work hard. Consequently efficiency will improve in privatised firms.

Criticisms of privatisation

Privately owned firms which have some monopoly power, particularly those that are natural monopolies, must be regulated and this is difficult to achieve. Sometimes the regulatory board has too little power and even when it has sufficient power it often fails to use it. This is called 'regulatory capture' and occurs because the firm and those who are supposed to regulate it become very close, so that the regulators become sympathetic to the firm.

Critics of privatisation make a number of other points. Thus the Trades Union Congress makes the following claims:
- People will only buy shares in successful businesses so it is only the profitable public enterprises which are 'sold off'. Hence the government is penalising successful public enterprise.
- Privatised companies have been sold too cheaply. Moreover, the Exchequer loses the income from the profitable nationalised industries which it formerly received and is left to fund unprofitable industries.
- De-nationalisation is likely to break up an industry's network of services and its ability to cross-subsidise loss making activities, such as

rural postal deliveries, with the profits made from delivering business mail in the cities. To this argument the supporters of privatisation retort that cross-subsidisation is undesirable - the price which is charged for a good should reflect its cost of production. If rural postal deliveries are thought to be desirable, then the cost should not be borne by other consumers, but by the community as a whole.

The claim is also made that the government is taking a very short-term approach and is selling off the country's assets to finance tax cuts - 'selling off the family silver' as Harold Macmillan, a former Conservative Prime Minister put it.

Deregulation

So far, this chapter has focused on privatisation in the sense of selling off public sector firms. However, allowing private sector firms to provide services previously restricted to public sector organisations is an important aspect of privatisation. It is argued that this benefits consumers by giving them lower prices. Thus in 1981 a Telecommunications Act was passed which allowed new operators to compete in certain areas with British Telecom, and subsequently a licence was given to Mercury, a recent entry to the telecommunications business. The result was that British Telecom cut prices on its 100 highest density routes - most of which would also be Mercury routes. Those who dislike privatisation point out that this kind of result can be achieved whether or not a firm is in private or public ownership. Moreover, they point out that although British Telecom cut these particular prices, it subsequently raised prices in areas not facing competition from Mercury. Thus domestic users found their British Telecom charges rising faster than large business users.

Private provision

This is the third aspect of privatisation. It is concerned with the private provision of services, such as hospital catering or cleaning. This is sometimes called 'contracting out' and a number of claims are made in its favour by writers such as E.V. Savas (1983) in a pamphlet published by the Adam Smith Institute:

'Contracting out permits a lesser intrusion of purely political factors into the process (of providing services). It means that there are fewer patronage positions to dispense . . . I believe that it is politically attractive to be an efficient deliverer of

public services, even if it takes contracting out and foregoing patronage positions.'

Contracting out services makes it possible for the government to take advantage of specialised skills which may be lacking in its own workforce. It also permits firms to take advantage of economies of scale which may arise when they specialise in the provision of particular services.

Supporters of the privatisation of services also claim that putting out services for tender increases competition and means that the public gets the service at the lowest possible cost. One reason for this is that it is claimed the public sector unions whose members provide these services have had too much power and have insisted on conditions of service and inefficient work practices which are advantageous to their members, but which penalise the public.

Against this, a number of arguments are put forward. In the first place it is suggested that the only reason privatised services save money is that the firms cut the pay and work conditions of their employees. Since the workers in these services are already often low paid, this is objectionable on grounds of equity. Furthermore, the quality of service will deteriorate because contractors will have an incentive to cut corners. The less that is spent on the service, the larger will be the profits of the contractor. And finally, although the service may cost less in the short run, as time passes the firms involved will have an incentive to collude to put up prices, so the community will be the loser.

Key ideas - summary of the argument for privatisation

1. **Nationalised industry is inefficient because it lacks incentives to cut costs.**
2. **Privatised industry will have the incentive of private gain to become more efficient. This incentive will encourage people to cut costs and also to introduce new products.**
3. **The discipline of the market will penalise inefficient private firms, while no such discipline affects nationalised industry.**
4. **Contracting out services will save public money.**
5. **Private enterprise is better than public because public ownership brings in political considerations which reduce efficiency.**

Policies

Since public ownership is to be deplored, publicly owned firms should be sold off and returned to the private sector. Whilst this may not be possible in the short run because the industry is making losses, it should be done as soon as possible. In the meantime, nationalised industries should be pruned of loss-making activities to facilitate privatisation. Many more services should be contracted out. In addition to refuse collection, hospital cleaning and laundry, many other activities could be privatised. Examples are cleaning schools, running swimming pools, building and running prisons. In addition, schools should be encouraged to opt out of local government control and private medicine encouraged.

Conclusion

The nationalised industries remain an important part of the economy. In 1987 they accounted for 5.5% of UK output and employed 800,000 people. Other public sector activities would greatly increase this total.

The public sector has its supporters and its critics. Its supporters are sceptical of the argument that market forces are the best way to allocate resources. Instead they believe that government intervention is necessary to prevent market failure and that public ownership brings positive benefits to society. Its critics believe the public sector is less efficient than the private and for this reason the government should take all possible measures to reduce the size of the public sector. The economic evidence is inconclusive. What is certain is that people's values in this argument affect the way in which they interpret the evidence.

Data questions

Hurd claims TV reforms will give viewers more choice

Douglas Hurd, the Home Secretary, yesterday outlined proposals for the *deregulation* of commercial television in Britain. The proposals aim to increase consumer choice and competition between companies.

This will be the biggest change in British television for more than a quarter of a century. If the proposals are carried out, television franchises will be sold to the highest bidder using competitive tenders. In addition, new TV channels will be introduced, and the Independent Broadcasting Authority will be replaced by a new body called the Independent Television Commission.

In announcing the changes, Mr Hurd said the changes would do away with a great deal of regulation and would give viewers and listeners much more choice.

The main points in the White Paper *Broadcasting in the '90s: Competition, Choice and Quality* were:
● ITV would become Channel 3, and regional ten year licences would go to the highest bidder. Like other companies, they could be taken over on the stock exchange.
● A new service, Channel 5, would be launched in 1993. This would reach 70% of the population.
● An Independent Television Commission would replace the IBA and Cable Authority. This new body would licence all commercial television.
● Separate licences would be granted to independent companies to encourage more night time television.
● The BBC would face a financial squeeze after 1991. This would encourage a move to subscription television.
● Two new DBS channels were likely to start as early as 1990 in addition to those already on the way.
● Cable and microwave transmissions would make it possible to set up new local television franchises from 1991.
● Radio would benefit from three national commercial radio channels and there would be several hundred local and community stations. These would be monitored by a Radio Authority.

Source: Adapted from the *Financial Times*, November 8, 1988.

New TV channels herald move towards privatisation

A government White Paper published yesterday put forward proposals which included the abolition of the Independent Broadcasting Authority and a move towards the *privatisation* of broadcasting transmission. The White Paper also suggested that subscriptions should help pay for television. Douglas Hurd, the Home Secretary, worked for two years preparing the proposals. Introducing the White Paper he said 'The proposals are necessarily radical to enable broadcasters to make the most of opportunities offered by the new technology.'

The Home Secretary said that he wanted to preserve what was best in what was often regarded as the finest broadcasting service in the world. He claimed 'I think we have got the balance right. I believe that British broadcasting will go on to even greater strengths.' Mr Hurd said that the proposals would give viewers and listeners a much wider choice and at the same time maintain and build on quality broadcasting. In the future there could be several dozen television channels and hundreds of commercial radio stations. The government's aim was to make sure that there were no unnecessary limits on increasing the number of programmes. At the same time, people should be given the opportunity to pay for the TV they wanted to watch by direct payments to a channel on a pay-per-programme basis.

In order to reduce the barriers which limited new entrants to the industry 'there should be a greater separation between the various functions which make up broadcasting and have in the past been carried out by one organisation. These include programme production, channel packaging and retailing and transmission of delivery'.

Source: Adapted from the *Financial Times*, November 8, 1988.

Question 1

1. Explain what is meant by 'deregulation' and 'privatisation' as outlined in the passages.

2. What potential benefits and problems of deregulation can you envisage?

3. What economic justification would supply siders put forward for the future privatisation of the IBA?

Re-acquiring public assets
Joint statement by the Labour Party and the TUC

Selling off public assets is the worst possible policy as far as the British people are concerned. It means that assets which have been built up with public money are handed to private interests, while public funds continue to support loss makers. No thought has been given to industrial or strategic issues by the Government in its privatisation measures. Only a Government guided by dogma could be considering selling-off our North Sea oil assets, when these are bound to become increasingly valuable and strategically crucial.

Not only have vital public assets been disposed of, they have been sold off cheaply. Very large profits were immediately taken by private speculators when the denationalised shares reached the Stock Exchange. Immediate windfall profits of 14 per cent - compared with the price paid for shares by investors - were made in the case of British Aerospace; 17 per cent with Cable and Wireless; and 32 per cent with Amersham International. The all-party House of Commons Committee on Public Accounts in a recent report on the share sales said that it hoped that in future there would not be 'such large windfall profits' from privatisation.

The Labour Party and the TUC have repeatedly made it clear that they are not prepared to see private speculators benefit from the loss of public funds as a result of the Government's unnecessary and disruptive privatisation measures.

The next Labour Government will therefore re-acquire at the earliest opportunity the shares of denationalised concerns by paying for them exactly what the Government received for them when they were denationalised. No allowance will be made for inflation, though the private shareholders will keep dividends received. Separate consideration may be needed, however, for assets split up or re-sold while in private hands.

We believe that the approach set out in this statement is fair to the nation as a whole.

Source: The Labour Party, September, 1982.

Question 2

The article relates to the policy of the Labour Party in 1982.

1. According to this article from 1982, who has benefited from privatisation? Who has lost?

2. What other arguments could be put forward against privatisation?

3. How would you counter such arguments?

8 Regional Policy

In the nineteenth century certain regions specialised in a limited range of industries which subsequently experienced massive declines in employment. Localised job losses in industries such as coal mining, iron and steel and shipbuilding were responsible for high rates of unemployment in particular areas.

The first significant policy response came in 1928 when the Minister of Labour set up a Board 'for the purpose of facilitating the transfer of workers, and in particular of miners, for whom opportunities of employment in their own district or occupation are no longer available'. Since then the details of regional policy have varied, but the general approach has been remarkably consistent.

● State intervention has attempted to provide incentives for new industries to move to disadvantaged regions by giving grants or loans and by encouraging the retraining and relocation of workers. Behind the specific details of these policies lies the belief that unrestricted market forces will not reduce regional differences.

● This view is opposed by some supply side economists who argue that government intervention to help particular regions leads to a misallocation of resources - for example, inefficient industries are kept in business. This group suggests that policies should focus on encouraging market forces to operate more effectively.

Before we can examine these views, we must first examine the nature and extent of regional differences in Britain.

How serious are regional differences in modern Britain?

Regional differences in Britain are sometimes summarised as 'the North - South divide'. Whilst this is an over-simplification - there are areas of poverty in the South and prosperity in the North - it does focus attention on the geographical dimension. In the South we find prosperous regions; in the North decline and decay are common. Each of these 'regions' has certain characteristics.

Prosperous regions

Prosperous regions tend to be located in the South of the UK, close to the centre of population and the large EC market. It is in these regions that government departments and large companies have their headquarters, so that the most important economic decisions are made here. The head offices of the majority of the leading financial institutions are also found in these regions. Consequently raising money for expansion is easier and so most new investment is found in these parts of the country. These regions typically have a smaller manufacturing base than their northern equivalents; more importantly, there is no excessive concentration on one or two heavy industries. Instead, there is a well-developed service sector. This mixture of economic activity contributes to a higher level of GDP per head. Moreover, GDP is rising more quickly than in other regions. These areas are characterised by an inflow of population and those people who move in tend to be young, healthy and well educated.

Depressed regions

In many ways the depressed regions of the UK are the converse of the prosperous regions. They tend to be on the periphery of the country, have relatively low GDP per head and have unemployment rates above the national average. For many years they were characterised by declining industries, such as coal, steel, shipbuilding and textiles. Few large companies locate their headquarters there. Young, active people often move out, so that the population tends to be older and less skilled. People in these regions have more illnesses and lower life expectancy than those in more prosperous areas.

Another feature of these depressed areas is that they tend to have relatively large numbers of cities which grew rapidly at the time of the Industrial Revolution. Liverpool is a classic example. Such cities face multiple problems; unsatisfactory housing, high rates of crime and unemployment are common features.

This comparison of two types of region is exaggerated. There are prosperous areas in the North and depressed parts of the South. Nevertheless, as the next section shows, there is a great deal of evidence to affirm the existence of a substantial regional problem and to suggest that this is, in large part, a North-South divide.

Evidence on the UK regions

Unemployment and employment

In considering the relative prosperity of an area, the most easily available evidence, and perhaps also the most telling, is to look at figures for unemployment. Figure 8.1 shows that over half a century ago there were significant regional differences in unemployment. What is also obvious is that the regions which were prosperous then are also those which are doing well today. Those which were depressed then are still characterised by high rates of unemployment, as can be seen from Figure 8.2.

Figure 8.2: Regional unemployment, percentages, 1989

Source: Adapted from *Employment Gazette*, February, 1989.

Figure 8.1: Rates of unemployment in selected UK regions, 1927-39 (June each year)

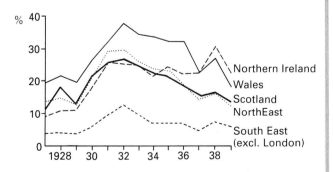

Source: *British Labour Statistics*, Historical Abstract, 1886-1968.

Precise comparisons between these two periods are difficult to make because, over the last half century, there have been changes in the measurement of unemployment as well as in the way the regions are defined. Nevertheless, the pattern is clear. In both periods the highest levels of unemployment are to be found in the North, whilst the South and East have had low levels of unemployment. However, this is not the whole story. In the peripheral regions, not only are people more likely to be unemployed, but they are more likely to have been unemployed for long periods.

There is also considerable disparity between the kind of jobs which are to be found in the regions. Table 8.1 analyses the type of manufacturing employment to be found in each region. As it shows, compared to the average region, the South East has 41% more professional and managerial jobs in manufacturing. At the other extreme the North has 28% less than the average. When unskilled and semi-skilled jobs are compared, the South East has 20% less than the average whilst Wales has 18% more of these type of jobs.

Table 8.1: *Share of manufacturing employment in each region, 1981 (GB = 100)*

	Professional, managerial	Unskilled, semi-skilled
South East	141	80
East Anglia	107	91
South West	101	104
East Midlands	92	102
West Midlands	90	106
Yorks/Humberside	84	111
North West	88	112
North	72	108
Wales	74	118
Scotland	78	105
GB	100	100

Note: The figure for the South East excludes London.

Source: Martin, R. *The New Economics and Politics of Regional Restructuring: The British Experience*, Department of Geography, University of Cambridge.

Migration

Another indicator of regional inequality is migration. As Figure 8.3 shows, there is a tendency for people to move out of the northern regions and into those in the South. The Figure can be misleading, because

Figure 8.3: *Migration in and out of G.B. regions (thousands), 1980-81*

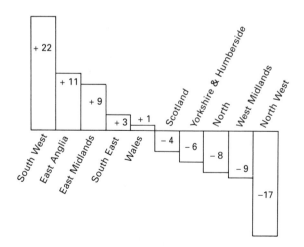

Note: The figures refer to migrants only between GB regions and exclude migrants to and from N. Ireland and the rest of the world.

Source: Adapted from *Census of Population*, OPCS, 1981.

some people have moved only short distances, for example, out of the cities and into small towns. This may involve crossing regional boundaries and give a false impression. Moreover, some of the movement is of older people moving to retirement homes. This is one explanation of the net migration into Wales, an area of high unemployment. What the Figure does not show is the character of the people who move. Excluding those retiring, most movement is of young, educated and qualified people moving to find work or to obtain better jobs.

Incomes

Regions also differ in the incomes of their inhabitants. Table 8.2 shows that, in the southern regions, the income per week per person is significantly higher than it is in the rest of the country. Moreover, in the South, households receive less of their incomes in the form of social security benefits than do those in the North.

Table 8.2: *Variations in income*

Region	Income per week per person (£)	Social security benefits as % of total income
North	74.9	16.2
Yorkshire & Humberside	76.3	15.9
East Midlands	82.1	11.8
East Anglia	87.5	12.4
South East	106.3	9.5
South West	90.1	14.2
West Midlands	77.4	12.0
North West	80.0	13.7
Wales	77.7	16.6
Scotland	81.7	13.9
Northern Ireland	66.4	22.0

Source: *Regional Trends*, HMSO, 1988.

Thus the evidence is conclusive. Although there are substantial pockets of poverty in the South and of prosperity in the North, people in the North are more likely to be unemployed, to have been unemployed for long periods, to have lower incomes and to be receiving social security benefits. The question therefore arises; what should be done to correct these disparities?

The supply side/market forces approach

Economists who favour this approach tend to argue that there is not really a 'regional problem' in the UK. Instead they argue that there is a **national** economic problem which affects all regions but which is particularly acute in some of them. They argue further that this problem arises because market forces have not been allowed to operate freely in the economy.

In considering what is called 'the regional problem', supply siders focus more on the labour market than the goods market. If the labour market functions perfectly, then workers will try to maximise their wages while employers will attempt to hire labour as cheaply as possible. The result will be an equilibrium wage at which there is no shortage or surplus of labour. In other words, the labour market will clear.

In terms of the regions, what should happen when market forces operate freely is that in areas of high unemployment wages will fall, leading to an increase in the demand for labour by firms in the region. Moreover, some firms in places where wages are high because there is little unemployment will be attracted by the possibility of reducing their labour costs; consequently they will move to areas of high unemployment. This will increase demand for labour in the depressed areas and lead to the labour market clearing - no unemployment and no shortage of labour at prevailing wage rates.

One other movement needs to be noted. If the labour market is operating freely, then some people in areas of high unemployment will be attracted by the possibility of earning higher wages elsewhere and will therefore migrate. This will reduce the unemployment problem in areas of high unemployment and increase the supply of labour in places where wages are high, thus pulling down wages in these areas. According to this group of economists, a freely operating market mechanism would eliminate regional differences in unemployment. These differences only persist because markets are unable to operate freely.

Market imperfections

There are three reasons in particular which prevent the labour market from working to remove regional imbalances in unemployment.

Inflexible wages

Wages tend not to fall in areas where unemployment is high. A government White Paper in 1983 claimed:

'Imbalances between areas in employment opportunities should in principle be corrected by the natural adjustment of labour markets. In the first place, this should be through lower wages and unit costs than comparable work commands elsewhere. Wage flexibility . . . would increase the attractiveness to industry of areas with high unemployment.'

The White Paper goes on to point out:

'There is, however, little evidence that regional wage rates respond readily to variations in regional unemployment.'

In part this is because in many industries wages are negotiated nationally, so that (with the possible exception of a London allowance) workers in an industry doing the same job receive the same wage whatever the local level of unemployment. In the view of supply side economists, this prevents the labour market from cutting unemployment in depressed areas.

Labour immobility

Only a few unemployed workers move out of areas with high unemployment. The reasons for this are well known. In the first place, they may find it difficult to obtain jobs even in areas where unemployment is much lower. This may be because of personal characteristics, such as low levels of education, or because they are ignorant about the jobs on offer in other areas. In addition, the costs of moving may be greater than the prospective benefits obtainable from a new job. The cost of living may also prove to be too high, especially when faced with the prospect of finding accommodation in areas where houses are very expensive. However, the main reasons preventing people from migrating are linked to family responsibilities. Children's education, or the need to care for older relatives, may prevent some people from even attempting to find work in other areas. The need to house families can make moving to other areas impossible. Those living in council houses will find it impossible to get similar accommodation in areas of low unemployment and those who own their own house would be likely to receive a much lower price for the house they sell than for a similar one in a prosperous area. Hence the people who are most likely to move are young people without family responsibilities who are willing to live in bed-sits or similar accommodation for a year or two until they can afford a better place to live.

Firms are immobile

Only a few firms move into areas of high unemployment. This is not surprising. Once settled, most firms stay where they are; there are not many **footloose** firms looking to relocate. If they want to expand into new premises they will be tempted to look at sites close to their present location and will need strong reasons to look further afield. The possibility of taking on workers at lower wage rates may be such an incentive - as will the possibility of cheap premises - but the costs of relocating are high, and new labour will need to be trained which can be expensive.

In the view of supply side economists, these imperfections do not weaken the case for the use of markets to solve regional problems; instead they call for action to remove or reduce these imperfections.

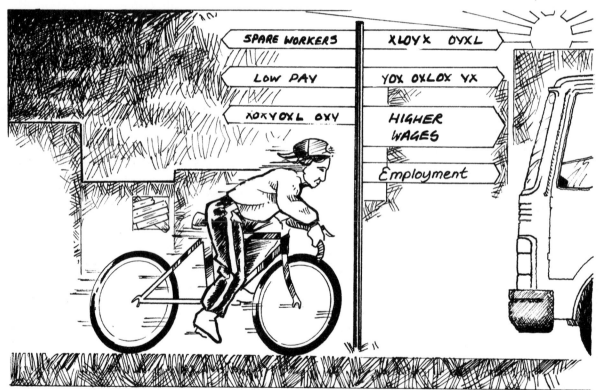

Key ideas - summary of the supply side argument

1. The so-called 'regional problem' is only one aspect of a national problem which occurs because market forces are not allowed to operate as they should.

2. If market forces are allowed to operate, then wages will fall in areas where unemployment is high. This will give workers an incentive to move out of these areas and firms an incentive to move, in order to take advantage of abundant labour at low cost.

3. Governments and trade unions prevent these forces from operating freely.

Supply side policies

The points discussed above suggest that market imperfections limit the extent of firms' and workers' mobility. Those economists who support the use of market forces to allocate resources believe that policies should be adopted which would improve the workings of the market mechanism.

Housing

In the first place, they argue that the housing market should be radically reformed - in particular the system of rent controls and guaranteed tenure which keeps down rents so that it does not pay entrepreneurs to build houses to let. If there was no government interference, the market would eliminate the shortage of houses to rent and so facilitate mobility. Without controls, rents would rise, people with empty rooms or houses would make them available for rent and investors would start to build houses, not only for sale, but also to rent. This would increase the supply of places to rent in prosperous areas and, in the long run, might even bring down the level of rents. The process would be accelerated if planning controls on building new houses were relaxed or abandoned. This would also increase the supply of houses to buy. The housing market would be further invigorated if more council houses were sold, since sitting tenants have an asset - their tenure - which makes it difficult to move.

Wages

Supply siders also believe that policies are needed to make wages more responsive to changes in the demand for labour. At present many wages are decided by national wage negotiations, which ensure that people in different parts of the country receive the same wage for the same job, irrespective of the level of unemployment. If wages were negotiated locally - or better still a matter for individuals to negotiate with their employers - then wages would fall in areas where unemployment was high and perhaps rise in prosperous places. This would increase the incentives for workers to move and encourage firms to locate in low wage areas.

This policy is difficult to implement. A start could be made if the government and the nationalised industries stopped agreeing to common levels of wages across the country. Measures to weaken the power of trade unions would also improve wage flexibility so, for example, the law could be changed to make strikes more difficult and penalise unions for losses which their actions may cause to employers.

Re-training

One reason for regional unemployment is that many workers in depressed regions have obsolete skills and therefore find it difficult to obtain work. Consequently, one policy which should be adopted is that workers should be encouraged to retrain. This policy would also be supported by interventionists. The difference is that supply siders would limit the role of government to providing incentives to firms and individuals. Interventionists would give a greater role to the government, suggesting, for example, that the government should subsidise or provide training courses.

Planning

Supply siders also argue that planning requirements should be relaxed. The need to get planning permission deters firms from moving because of the time and expense involved. Instead, market forces should determine land use, except where there are substantial spillover effects (such as extensive pollution), when intervention might be needed to correct this distortion. These policies are criticised by those economists who are sceptical of the benefits of unrestricted market forces.

Enterprise zones

One supply side approach to the urban problem is to encourage the formation of enterprise zones. These are areas where there are few planning restrictions and where firms are given exemptions from paying rates for a period. They are one way of reducing government interference in the economic life of cities.

The first enterprise zones were designated in 1981 in areas such as Hartlepool, Clydebank and Belfast. By 1988, twenty nine areas had been designated and the Department of the Environment estimated that there had been an increase of 3,300 in the number of people employed in these areas. Critics of the policy claim that this required a large amount of public spending on the infrastructure, loss of rate income, and that many of the jobs would have been created in any case, or were merely transferred from areas outside enterprise zones.

The case for government intervention

Critique of the supply side argument

Supporters of government intervention begin by criticising the market forces argument on a number of grounds. In the first place, cutting wages in areas of high unemployment would be penalising the poorer sections of society and be morally unacceptable. Further, the fall in wages would depress the demand for goods and services in these regions and would therefore make unemployment worse. It would also have a negative effect on worker morale and hence on productivity. Taylor and Armstrong (1988), two economists who have researched the regional problem, give other reasons why the supply side approach is unsatisfactory. They point out that the unemployed are the least likely group to move to other areas because they often cannot afford the costs involved in moving and may also be poorly informed about jobs available in other areas. It is young, highly educated and ambitious people who are most likely to leave, thus depriving depressed areas of their talents. In addition, because of inertia, firms are unlikely to relocate or to start subsidiaries in other areas unless they receive substantial financial incentives, for example, those provided by government grants.

The aims of regional policy

Whilst it is possible to argue about the precise objectives of regional policy, aims that would be supported by some economists include:
- The reduction of unemployment in areas where it is excessively high.
- An increase in the utilisation rate of resources.
- The reduction of population pressure in congested areas.
- The preservation of regional cultures.
- The encouragement of national unity (which may be threatened if some regions are dissatisfied).

Note that these objectives spill over from the purely 'economic' and depend in part on the values of those determining the objectives. Thus it is possible to disagree about which regional cultures should be encouraged - or even to deny that this should be a policy concern at all. The case for government intervention in regional policy rests on the assumption that these objectives are worthwhile and that they will not be achieved by market forces.

Unemployment

Persistent high levels of unemployment in particular regions suggest to economists who favour intervention that market forces can do little to reduce the differences between prosperous and depressed regions. Figure 8.1 showed the rates of unemployment in selected regions of the UK in the 1920s and 1930s. The same pattern persists today. If market forces were going to eliminate such differences, they would have done so in over half a century. Instruments of regional policy have helped to reduce regional differences, but such policies have been inadequate and need strengthening. The main cause of high unemployment in the regions is high unemployment nationally. Therefore policies should be adopted which will bring down the national rate. Most economists who favour an interventionist regional policy would probably argue that Keynesian policies to stimulate aggregate demand are the best method to achieve this goal. They would also suggest that what is needed is not indiscriminate increases in government spending, but spending which is targeted on depressed areas. This is discussed in more detail in Chapter 16.

One reason why unemployment is concentrated in particular regions is that these regions have a high proportion of declining industries, such as coal, cotton, shipbuilding and steel. Such industries should be helped to adjust, new industries should be given financial inducements to locate in these areas and workers in declining industries should benefit from government-funded training courses.

Utilisation rate

Regional policy can also help to achieve the second objective listed above - an increase in the utilisation rate of resources. Indeed, this is closely linked to the reduction of unemployment. But land, capital and entrepreneurship can also be under-utilised in depressed areas. (This is not to suggest that all resources should be fully used all the time. Workers need time for leisure and it is inefficient to try to make full use of all resources. Farming in the Arctic and the Sahara would be a waste of time and effort and, even in countries such as the UK, some land is not worth exploiting.) Nevertheless, many resources are underused and intervention offers the possibility of obtaining a better use of scarce resources, for example, by enabling unemployed workers to produce goods for which there is a demand and by making use of empty buildings.

Population density

Population densities vary considerably throughout the country and there is often good reason for this - people like to live near their work and it would be idiotic to try to resettle millions of people in the Highlands of Scotland. However, regional imbalance can lead to excessive concentration of economic activity in some urban areas and can cause costs to society in the form of congestion, pollution and noise. This is particularly apparent in developing countries, where some urban areas may be growing exceptionally quickly, but it can also affect industrialised countries, for example, in the form of traffic congestion especially in large cities such as London. People driving cars or lorries in urban areas cause disagreeable external effects which reduce the welfare of other people. The existence of these externalities leads to a misallocation of resources which can only be reduced by government intervention. This can take the form of regional policy, though it is doubtful if regional policy on its own can solve this problem.

Culture and unity

The goals of encouraging regional culture and preserving national unity are also beyond the scope of regional policy on its own. People in depressed areas, such as Northern Ireland, are more likely to threaten national unity than those in prosperous places. If regional policy is successful it will offer opportunities to the dissatisfied and reduce discontent. But more than economic policy is needed to achieve unity. Similarly, regional policy can stimulate cultural activities in the regions, but cannot ensure that these reach a high standard.

There is another point which needs to be considered when deciding whether governments should intervene in economic life in order to help particular regions. The expansion and development of the European Community and the construction of a tunnel between Britain and the Continent will encourage footloose industries to locate in the south east corner of England. Industries in this location will be close to a rich and rapidly growing market and will have an advantage over industries in other parts of the country. Unless the government intervenes, regional differences in employment and income will grow.

Supply side critique of the interventionist approach

Those who oppose government intervention make both theoretical and operational criticisms of the interventionist approach. The theoretical case for the use of markets was discussed in Chapters 2 and 3. Underlying this argument is the belief that intervention by governments leads to a misallocation of resources unless the intervention can be justified on specific grounds, such as the existence of public goods. In the case of the regions, the argument is that these reasons do not arise and that the government should leave economic decision making to the markets. If, for example, governments intervene by giving grants to industry, the result will be greater inefficiency. This is because the best people to decide the location of a factory are the entrepreneurs whose money is at risk from the decision. If the government offers them money to locate in a place other than that which they would have chosen, the result will be a factory in a less than optimum situation, resulting in higher costs for the firm. Thus Lord Stokes, when in charge of the British Leyland Motor Corporation (later the Rover Group) argued that government intervention in regional policy increased business risk:

'You have cost us a fortune by making us set up factories in places which are quite unsuitable to have factories. You ruin our business; we try to make it survive.'

Figure 8.4: GB assisted areas in July 1984

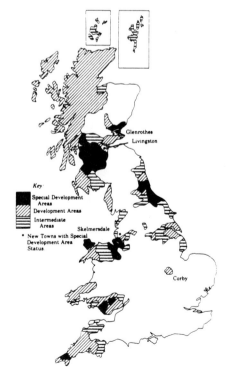

Source: Department of Trade and Industry.

Moreover, the grants given to firms have not always been cost-effective. Sometimes these have been given to firms which would have located in depressed areas even without a grant, and the cost has been high - figures of £35,000 cost to public funds per job created have been quoted in a few extreme cases. In 1988 the government announced that, in future, grants would no longer be automatic but would be subject to prior investigation, to try to ensure value for money. However, people who emphasise market forces believe that governments are not equipped to make business decisions and giving power to civil servants to judge applications for investment grants is counter-productive.

Key ideas - summary of the argument for government intervention

1. Market forces do not work towards the elimination of regional inequalities.
2. Without government intervention companies would tend to locate in the prosperous areas, thus reinforcing regional differences.

3. Depressed regions suffer from a number of disadvantages - low levels of investment, less education and poorer health, for example.
4. Government intervention is therefore required in order to help achieve the objectives of regional policy.

Interventionist policies

The alternative to a free market is intervention by central and local government. Figures 8.4 and 8.5 show the assisted areas before and after 1984. Taylor and Armstrong (1988) suggest a number of improvements to present policy. In the first place, there needs to be a substantial increase in the level of investment grants to stimulate the development of new products and new techniques in depressed areas. More spending is also needed on the infrastructure of the less prosperous areas. If these areas had good communications, excellent training facilities and attractive environments, companies would be encouraged to locate in these areas.

Agencies with a wide range of powers need to be set up in the regions to stimulate development. Initiatives by local authorities have been on a

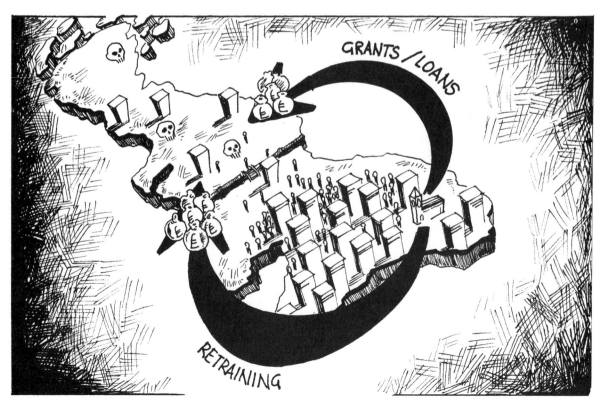

limited scale and could be extended if the central government introduced a regionally-discriminating policy towards new and small firms.

Similarly, a more active policy needs to be taken to encourage a more equitable distribution of venture capital. Since most large firms have their headquarters in the South, locations in other areas tend to be neglected when new initiatives are being developed. Another policy which would help the regions would be for the government to relocate more of its own activities in the regions.

Figure 8.5: *GB assisted areas in November 1984*

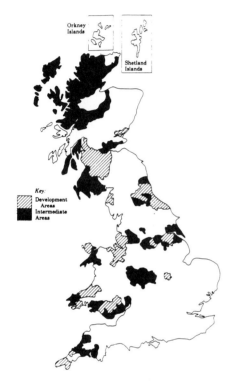

Source: Department of Trade and Industry.

Conclusion

The evidence is clear; there are substantial differences between regions in the UK and these differences persist over long periods of time. People who live in regions that have high levels of unemployment also tend to have lower incomes, lower educational levels, higher rates of infant mortality and are more likely to live in decaying towns.

However, arguments develop about what should be done to rectify this position. One school of economists favours more emphasis on market forces, believing these will encourage labour mobility and also persuade firms to move into depressed regions in order to benefit from lower wage rates. This group favours policies which will weaken trade unions and encourage local wage negotiations. They also advocate the removal of many planning restrictions and the removal of government controls on housing.

Their opponents believe market forces would exacerbate the problem; that firms which were mobile would tend to locate in the richer areas of the country. Hence the government needs to intervene in order to give firms incentives to locate in the depressed areas. There is no universal agreement about the precise nature of such incentives, but the consensus would favour more generous grants, government spending on infrastructure in poor regions and greater concentration of the government's own expenditure in depressed areas.

Data questions

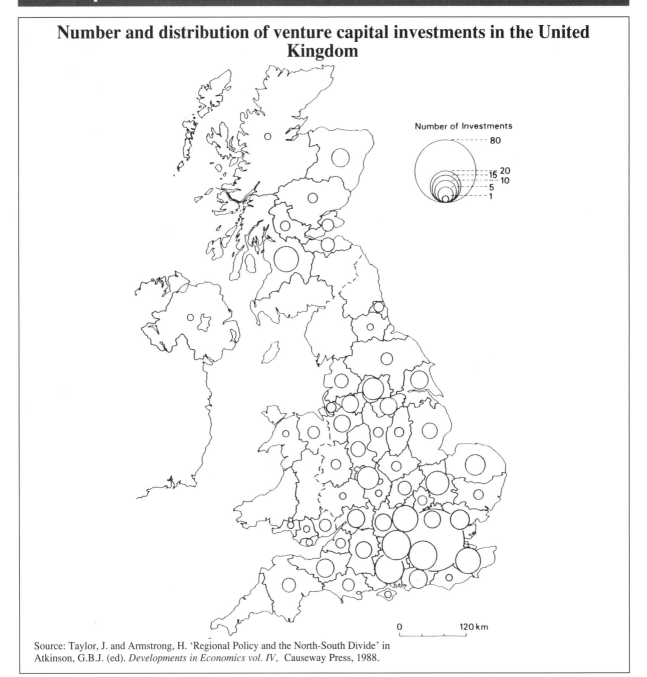

Number and distribution of venture capital investments in the United Kingdom

Number of Investments

80
20
15
10
5
1

0   120 km

Source: Taylor, J. and Armstrong, H. 'Regional Policy and the North-South Divide' in Atkinson, G.B.J. (ed). *Developments in Economics vol. IV,* Causeway Press, 1988.

Question 1

1. What factors do you think explain the distribution of venture capital investments in the UK?

2. What consequences for the regions will follow from the distribution?

3. Which policies could be advocated to mitigate these effects?

The North-Region profile

The population of the North declined by 1.2% between 1981 and 1986.

The average household expenditure in the North of £145 per week in 1985-86 was lower than in any other region. Households allocated a higher proportion of this expenditure on alcohol than in any other region, 5.9%, but they also allocated an above average proportion of expenditure on food and in fact consumed more meat, fish, vegetables (other than potatoes) and cakes and biscuits per head than households elsewhere.

Compared with the other regions of Great Britain, households in the North were more likely to have washing machines in 1984-85, but were among the least likely to have a deep freezer, dishwasher, tumble drier or telephone.

Adjusted for age, the mortality rate for males in the North was the third highest in the UK in 1986. The North had a higher death rate for cancer for males than any other part of the UK (366 deaths per 100,000) and that for females (273 per 100,000) was exceeded only in Scotland.

Social and economic characteristics

Between 1981 and 1986 the illegitimacy rate for the North rose by 85% to 244 illegitimate births per 1,000 live births. This was the second highest regional rate in the United Kingdom.

The North had one of the highest regional rates in the UK of notifiable offences recorded by the police in 1986 at 9648 offences per 100,000 population, second only to the North West. The region had the highest recorded rate for theft and handling stolen goods.

In 1986 the North had the lowest private sector dwelling completion rates of all the UK regions, at 1.8 dwellings per 1,000 population. Only 56% of dwellings in the North were owner-occupied, less than for any other region in the UK apart from Scotland. 56% of pupils aged 16 in the North were staying on at maintained schools or were in non-advanced further education, the lowest proportion in the UK. The North also had the lowest proportion of school leavers who intended to enter full-time further education (21%) among the regions of Great Britain.

Next to Wales, the North had the highest proportion of heads of households who were economically inactive in 1986 at 41%. In 1987 it continued to have the second highest unemployment rate in the UK at 15%.

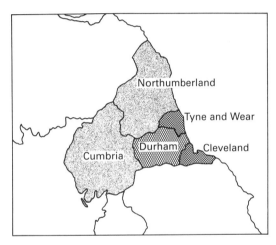

Source: *Regional Trends,* HMSO 1988.

Question 2

1. What factors do you think explain the characteristics of the northern region?
2. What policies would:
   (i)   supply siders or
   (ii) interventionists
   advocate to remedy the position? What criticisms could be made of their approaches?

Why does Paul McCartney earn more than the Prime Minister? Why do some people who work hard earn very little money? How do firms decide how many workers to employ? Questions such as these are the province of distribution theory which analyses how the factors of production (land, labour, capital and entrepreneurship) are rewarded. This chapter will focus on the labour market, though the method of analysis is applicable to the other factors.

Two questions dominate the chapter. The first is the debate concerning what determines the rewards received by the factors of production. One group emphasises demand and supply; another suggests that the labour market may often not reach equilibrium.The other question discussed in this chapter concerns the extent to which government intervention in the labour market is necessary:

● One approach to such questions is to say that these markets are like any other market and that the forces of demand and supply should determine issues such as the number of people to be employed and how much they should earn. Just as these forces allocate resources efficiently in markets for goods and services, so it is argued that demand and supply will lead to an efficient allocation of resources in factor markets.

● On the other hand, some economists believe that factor markets are different to other markets. Take labour as an example. People are less mobile than goods, such as potatoes or pins, and therefore what might be a satisfactory system for allocating other resources will not be so for labour. Moreover, people are not inanimate objects and so the assumptions made about goods cannot be made about labour. Consequently problems such as poverty would result if the market was left to its own devices.

How are the rewards to the factors of production determined?

One approach to the economic analysis of factors of production is to analyse these markets as we would any other. Supply siders would tend to take this approach. Their emphasis focuses on the way that the forces of demand and supply determine the quantity of a factor which is employed, and the rewards that factor will receive. Other economists accept that demand and supply analysis can explain a great deal, but they emphasise the limitations of markets; for example, some economists would argue that labour markets may never reach equilibrium because labour is immobile and slow to respond to change.

The supply of labour

Not everyone participates in the labour market, in fact as Figure 9.1 shows, just under half of the UK population can be described as 'economically active'. Those who are inactive include the young, the old and women with young children - which explains the much lower participation rates for women shown in the Table.

There are other influences on the participation rate. As with the market for goods, the prime determinant of supply is the price which will be received for the product. A rise in price will usually lead to an extension in supply, i.e. a move up the supply curve, and a fall in price will lead to a reduction in the quantity supplied. In the labour market, the 'price' is the amount which will be earned in wages, and it seems reasonable to assume that an increase in this price will encourage people to supply more labour. To take an absurd example,

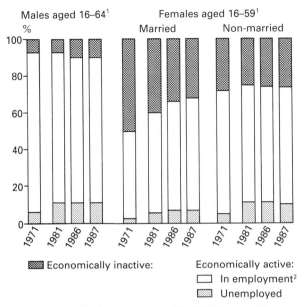

Figure 9.1: *Population of working age: by economic status*

Economically inactive: ▨

Economically active:
☐ In employment[2]
▨ Unemployed

1 Figures for 1971 relate to persons aged 15–59/64 (the school-leaving age was raised in 1972)

2 Includes those on government schemes

Source: *Social Trends*, HMSO, 1989.

at a wage of £10 a week not many people would wish to work; at £10,000 a week there would be no lack of applicants.

However, the labour market is rather different from other markets because people can analyse their position, whilst goods such as carrots or lipsticks cannot. Even at a high wage some people may be reluctant to take a particular job because they do not like it. Some nurses would not like to work in an abortion clinic whatever the pay, and many of us would be reluctant to work as a steeplejack or boxer. Hence high rates of pay may not necessarily be associated with a high supply of labour. Moreover, in some cases rises in pay may actually lead to a fall in the supply of labour. A rational person will want to work so long as the marginal utility produced by an extra hour's work exceeds the utility obtained from an hour's leisure. A higher real wage increases the quantity of goods which can be bought for an extra hour's work and therefore induces the individual to work longer. On the other hand, a higher real wage would permit people to maintain their income and at the same time enjoy more leisure. Hence when pay increases, some people would choose not to work longer hours and indeed may choose to work less whilst maintaining their level of income. This means that the supply curve of labour may slope backwards, as shown in

Figure 9.2. In this Figure, an increase in wages causes the quantity of labour supplied to increase until the wage reaches W_2. Then as the wage rises further the quantity of labour supplied will fall, and at wage W_3 the quantity of labour will only be q_3.

Figure 9.2: *A backward sloping supply curve for labour*

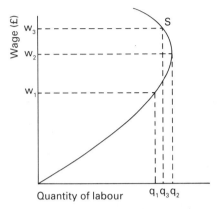

The demand for labour

A firm's demand for labour is a **derived** demand. Firms employ workers not for the pleasure of employing them, but because they want people to produce goods and services. If demand for a product rises, then demand for the labour making the product will also tend to rise. However, this does not explain what factors determine the demand for labour in the first place.

Just as the rational worker considers the wage that is offered and then decides whether to work, so the rational employer considers whether an additional worker will bring in more money than the increased cost in wages. The argument is shown in Table 9.1. As this shows, the eleventh worker increases output by 9 items (to use the jargon, the **marginal physical productivity** of the eleventh worker is nine). If these items sell for £10 each, then the firm's income will rise by £90 as a result of employing this person. (Again to use the jargon, the **marginal revenue product** of this worker is £90.)

Since the wage of this worker is £60, it will pay the firm to employ this eleventh worker (for simplicity we are ignoring other costs, such as raw materials). However, as the number of workers rises the marginal revenue product falls (because diminishing returns occur as discussed in Chapter 5). If the thirteenth worker was employed revenue would rise by only £40 whilst the cost in wages would be £60. It would be unprofitable to employ this worker.

Table 9.1: *Marginal revenue product and wage rate*

Number of workers	Total output per week	Marginal physical product	Marginal revenue product (£10 per item)	Wage rate per week (£)
10	100	—	—	—
11	109	9	90	60
12	116	7	70	60
13	120	4	40	60

The approach illustrated in this example is called the marginal productivity theory and represents a neo-classical approach to the labour market. It suggests that a firm seeking to maximise profits will employ extra units of a factor of production, such as labour, until the cost of employing that factor equals the extra income it generates. The theory thus predicts that, other things remaining unchanged, a rise in wages will lead to a fall in the number of workers employed whilst a rise in labour productivity will have the opposite effect and lead to firms taking on extra workers.

Criticisms of this approach

Critics argue that the labour market frequently fails to clear. That is because the number of workers, the hours they work, and the wages they receive are often determined more by negotiation and by custom and practice than by the results of marginal analysis. Hence changes in wages and employment levels are unlikely to bring the market into equilibrium. If this is so, then the neo-classical theory of wage determination is unrealistic.

Even if the overall approach is accepted, there are complications in practice. Firms may not try to **maximise** profits and instead may be satisfied with **reasonable** profits.

If this is the case, then firms may not cut the number of workers as wages rise. This will be the result if the firm takes a paternalist attitude to its workers and is reluctant to make them redundant. Above all, if the firm is not operating in a competitive market for its goods, it may respond to a rise in wage costs by exploiting its monopolistic position and putting up the price of its products.

The neo-classical theory predicts that people with scarce skills which are needed to produce desirable products will earn more than those without such skills. Figure 9.3 gives some figures for incomes in Britain. Non-manual workers tend to earn more than manual workers and one explanation for this is that they have more educational qualifications and are

more productive than manual workers. However, an alternative explanation also fits this data - that non-manual workers earn more because they are more likely to be promoted even though they are no more productive.

Figure 9.3: *Earnings in Great Britain (£ per week)*

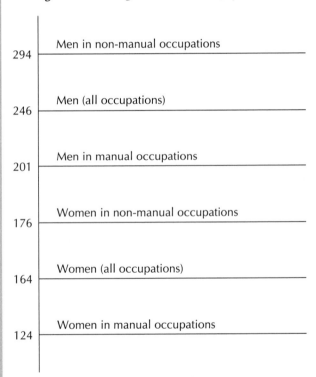

294	Men in non-manual occupations
246	Men (all occupations)
201	Men in manual occupations
176	Women in non-manual occupations
164	Women (all occupations)
124	Women in manual occupations

Source: Adapted from *Employment Gazette*, HMSO, 1989

Similarly, one explanation of men earning more than women is that men are more productive - they are more mobile, more likely to go on training courses and to work overtime than women and hence produce more goods than their female colleagues. This would cause men to have a higher marginal revenue product than women and so earn more. An alternative explanation is that women earn less because of discrimination at work which limits their choice of jobs and chances of promotion.

Economic rent

The concept of economic rent is an important part of the neo-classical theory of distribution. The analysis begins by dividing the total earnings of a factor of production, such as labour, into two. One part, called **transfer earnings,** is the amount that a factor must earn in order to stop it transferring to another use. Transfer earnings are the opportunity cost of employing a factor. The other part of a factor's earnings is called **economic rent** and is the excess which a factor earns over what is needed to keep that factor in a particular employment. Note that this is a different definition of rent to the one used by the 'man or woman in the street' who associates the word rent with payment for the use of a house or flat. Economic rent can be illustrated by taking the example of a professional footballer who may earn £20,000 a year, but who in any other occupation could only earn £5,000. This £5,000 is his transfer earnings and the other £15,000 he earns is economic rent:

Total earnings = Transfer earnings + Economic rent.

Economic rent arises when the demand for a factor of production is greater than its supply, which is relatively scarce.

Figure 9.4 illustrates the concept. The curve OS shows the supply of labour - how much each worker needs to be paid to stay in a particular employment. In this case equilibrium occurs when three workers are employed at a wage of w_3. However, the first worker would have been willing to work at a wage

of only w_1. Hence this worker's transfer earnings are ow_1 and the rest of the wage, $w_3 - w_1$, is economic rent. At the other extreme the third worker does need to be paid a wage of w_3 in order to work in this occupation. Hence all this worker's earnings are transfer earnings.

Looking at all three workers, total factor earnings are ow_3 aq_3. Transfer earnings are the area under the supply curve oaq_3. Economic rent is oaw_3, the area between the supply curve and the actual wage.

Economic rent and the price of land

The notion of economic rent was developed by the British economist David Ricardo, who used it to analyse a particular question. In the Napoleonic wars there were large rises in corn and land prices. Did the rise in land prices force up the price of corn, or did the high price of corn increase the demand for land and so push up land prices?

Figure 9.5: Earnings of a factor in fixed supply

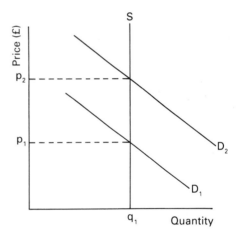

Ricardo assumed that land had only one use, to grow corn. This meant that its supply was fixed, as shown in Figure 9.5. Hence the price of land was totally determined by the demand for land. In other words, all the price of a factor of production in perfectly inelastic supply is economic rent - it has no transfer earnings. Thus it was the high price of corn which caused an increase in the demand for land and a rise in its price, rather than the price of land pushing up the price of corn. Note that this analysis depends on the assumption that land has only one use. In the real world a particular piece of land can be put to many different uses. This means its supply for any one use is elastic so that it has transfer earnings.

Figure 9.4: Economic rent

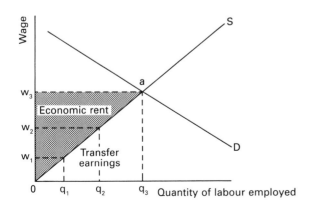

In principle it would be a good idea to tax economic rent since this would not reduce the supply of the factor. In practice, however, this has proved impossible because it is too complicated to differentiate economic rent from transfer earnings. Thus it would not be possible to find out how much every professional footballer could earn in another occupation and then impose a tax on any earnings above this.

Key ideas

1. Distribution theory analyses how much of a factor of production will be employed and the rewards it will receive.

2. The supply of labour will depend on factors such as the level of wages, but increases in wages will not always cause an increase in the supply of labour.

3. Marginal productivity theory suggests that more of a factor of production will be employed until its marginal revenue product equals its price.

4. Marginal productivity theory is criticised on a number of grounds. Markets may not clear, for example, if firms are paternalistic and do not reduce the quantity of labour employed when wages rise.

5. Economic rent is the excess which a factor earns, which is more than is needed to keep the factor in a particular employment.

The market forces approach

In *1980s Unemployment and the Unions* (1984), the Nobel Prize winner F.A. Hayek claims:

'Nobody is morally entitled to claim a share in the wealth which such a society produces unless he is prepared to obey the discipline of other people's wants or other countries' production methods that are ultimately the sources of our wealth . . . the size of the national product will depend not on individuals "working hard" but on making the "right" (desired) things in the "right" (most economic) manner and at the "right" time (required by the consumer in the market).'

Hayek goes on to argue that it is only through the prices that people find in the market that they can learn what to do and how to do it. High standards of living depend on the division of labour, and the specialisation which this implies is only made possible by the flow of information provided by the price system.

Another key feature of the price system is that it provides incentives to people to become more productive, for example, by changing jobs or by undertaking training. In this way the economy benefits from higher levels of production. For this group of economists, profit - the difference between costs and returns - is the true measure of the social usefulness of people's efforts. And production at a loss is an offence against the best use of resources. The market thus induces firms to obtain, from a given input of resources, as large a profit as possible.

This efficient use of resources depends on competition, and anything which restricts competition is to be deplored. Some of these restrictions were discussed in the last chapter. If people cannot move to alternative employment because housing is short, then the labour market will not be able to operate efficiently. Similarly, if the government, the largest employer in the country, does not respond to the signals given by the price system, then the whole labour market will be affected. For example, the approach suggests that in areas where the price of labour is low, the government should pay lower wages than it does where labour is in short supply. If it does not do this, the labour market will be distorted.

Trade unions

However, for these supply side economists, the prime reason why labour markets do not work efficiently is because of the actions of trade unions. They see trade unions as a monopolistic element in the market which distorts the efficient allocation of resources. They do this by restricting the supply of labour, as shown in Figure 9.6. In a market without trade unions equilibrium would be at A, where the demand for labour equals the supply. The wage rate would be w_1 with q_1 units of labour employed. If a trade union could restrict the supply of labour (for instance by insisting on a 'closed shop' where everyone has to join a union) then the new equilibrium would be at B; the union has succeeded in pushing up wages, but at the cost of reducing employment from q_1 to q_2.

This line of argument is criticised by supporters of unions who argue that few unions have the strength to move the equilibrium wage far from the level that would be obtained by market forces, and that in most cases the demand for labour is inelastic; in other words the demand curve in Figure 9.6 should

Figure 9.6:

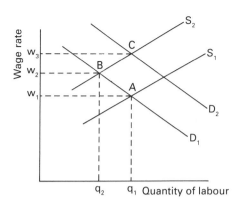

be drawn much more vertically because the firm's demand for labour is not much affected by changes in wage rates. If a union negotiates a 5% increase in wages, few firms are going to reduce their labour force significantly. If this is so, then the movement from q_1 to q_2 would be much smaller than is shown in the Figure. Moreover, critics of the supply side approach argue that the market for the products made by most firms is not perfectly competitive. This means that it is possible to put up prices for the firm's products and so increase the demand for labour to make the product. In the diagram this is shown by the second demand curve D_2. In this case, equilibrium will be at C - the actions of the unions have had little effect on the quantity of labour employed, but have succeeded in obtaining higher wages for their members.

Empirical evidence

There has been a good deal of empirical research into the activities of unions. Some of this is concerned with their effect on employment and is presented in Chapter 16. As that chapter shows, there is considerable disagreement amongst those who have undertaken research; some economists, such as Minford, Professor of Economics at Liverpool University, believe that unions are a prime cause of unemployment, whilst others believe their effect on employment is minimal. Similarly, there is disagreement about their effect on wages. This is not surprising, because the research usually involves comparing what has happened in unionised industries with what would have happened if there had been no unions - something that is very difficult to do. A typical piece of research in this area is that of Stewart in *Economica* (1981), who calculates that in manufacturing industry union members earn 7-8% more than non-union members with similar

characteristics. The reason may be that they have reduced the supply of labour, but an alternative explanation is that unions co-operate with management to increase productivity so both employers and workers benefit.

Key ideas - summary of the market forces approach

1. Whilst the labour market has certain characteristics which make it unique, the most efficient way of allocating resources in this market, as in others, is through the forces of demand and supply. Anything which distorts market forces reduces efficiency.
2. When the market works well, those with scarce, desirable skills will earn high wages, those without will have an incentive to re-train. Similarly, firms will move to locations where labour is relatively cheap.
3. The government distorts the labour market by paying similar salaries to people across the country irrespective of the scarcity of labour.
4. The trade unions distort the labour market by forcing up wages and causing rigidities in the market.

Supply side policies

Supply side policies are designed to make the labour market work more effectively. Since the government is the largest employer it can do most to improve the position. In the first place, some of its activities can be privatised so that firms can compete to supply goods and services, such as cleaning services to schools and hospitals. Where services cannot be privatised, the government should take greater account of the labour market. It should consider moving some of its activities to areas where labour is cheap and it should pay the 'going rate' for labour. This means that in areas of high unemployment wages should be lower than they are elsewhere. This implies an end to national wage bargaining.

Similarly, the position of trade unions should be weakened. There are various suggestions for achieving this, but they tend to concentrate on weakening the legal status of unions, for example, by making them liable for any losses suffered by firms where unions have called strikes. There are also suggestions for making it more difficult to call strikes or to instigate other industrial action.

The interventionist approach

Markets may sometimes be marvellous, but they are not without fault. This is the central argument of those who dispute the supply side approach. In particular they argue that, without government intervention, there will be undesirable inequalities. These are manifested in several ways, but particularly in the form of low pay, inequality for women and discrimination against ethnic minorities.

Low pay

The arguments against trade union intervention in the labour market have been given in the section above, but there are strong arguments in their favour. In the markets for goods and services both buyers and sellers usually have more or less equal power. If a customer does not like a particular product, an alternative can be bought. Similarly, a producer will usually find it easy to find a substitute customer. The position in the labour market is very different. In the first place, a person with particular skills may find it difficult to find an alternative purchaser for specialised skills. A firefighter will not easily find employment outside the fire service and most social workers are forced to find employment within local government. Hence employers are in a much stronger position than workers, because workers often find it difficult to sell their specialist skills to alternative employers. Similarly, in any dispute the employer can usually call upon the services of many lawyers and has the financial resources to withstand a dispute much better than could an individual worker. Trade unions can help to redress this balance. If the workers are united they can put pressure on the employer to provide higher wages, better working conditions (such as longer holidays and shorter hours) and greater safety at work than would be offered without union power. Moreover, unions help to mitigate the extent of low pay. If market forces are allowed to operat without any government intervention, then people with certain characteristics will tend to earn much less than others.

Factors associated with low pay are:
- Low levels of education and training. For various reasons some children do badly at school. Low levels of intelligence, poor teaching, parents having low educational qualifications, low social class, poor health - all these factors are associated with low educational achievement. In turn there is a close link between the level of education and the subsequent level of earnings. Those people with high educational qualifications tend to earn more than those with poor qualifications. The position is exacerbated because, once at work, those people with a good education tend to be selected for further training and this leads on to higher incomes. Of course, there are many exceptions to this generalisation. Teachers are an example of a group with high qualifications but relatively low levels of pay, and there are many examples - pop singers and sportsmen are notable - who have high incomes despite low qualifications.
- Particular occupations or industries. Some jobs and some industries are associated with low pay. Cleaners, shop assistants and hairdressers are examples. Such workers are often employed by small employers and are not in trade unions. Left to the mercy of market forces, it is argued that their position will deteriorate.

Women workers

As Figure 9.7 shows, women earn less than men. One reason for this is that women are concentrated in the 'caring occupations', such as nursing, which are traditionally low paid. However, even within the same occupation women earn on average less than men. Teaching is an example. Occasionally lower pay for women may be due to prejudice; but probably other reasons are more important. Until recently women on average have had lower educational qualifications than men. Now the achievements of both sexes are about equal at GCE A level, and girls do better than boys at GCSE. It

Figure 9.7: *Relative earnings of men and women, £ per week, all occupations*

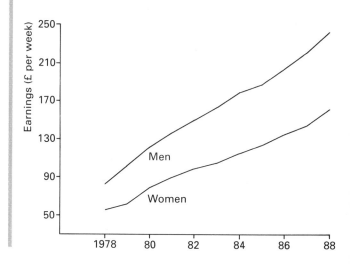

remains true that women undergo less training than men once they are employed and are less likely to be promoted. This reflects a deep-seated view in society about the role of women; that it is the role of women to look after the children. Hence, once children are born it will usually be the job of women to look after them and this career break reduces the likelihood of promotion. Similarly, when children are ill it is usually the women who have to stay off work to care for them. This makes employers more reluctant to employ women in responsible posts. Moreover, women frequently have to follow their husband's careers. If the man is offered promotion in another area, his wife may have to give up her job and follow. All this means that, left to market forces, employers will prefer to take on men rather than women and hence men will earn more than women. Consequently interventionists argue that this is unfair and that it devalues the contribution which women could make to the economy. Hence they advocate state intervention in order to remedy the position.

Ethnic status

People from ethnic minorities tend to earn less than those from the majority culture. In part this is because they may have many of the characteristics discussed above which are linked to low pay. Thus, while there are many exceptions, people from ethnic minorities in the UK tend to have lower levels of education, receive less training and when in work to be employed in jobs associated with low pay. Moreover, as Table 9.2 shows, they are more likely to be unemployed. The reasons for this are too complex to be explored here, but there is no doubt that prejudice also plays a part. Sometimes this is overt - employers refuse to consider black applicants or are reluctant to promote them. More often the discrimination is hidden - employers fail to select suitable black applicants because subconsciously they think they are inferior, or because they think white workers will be reluctant to work for a black boss. Hence interventionists argue that, without government intervention, this discrimination will continue.

Table 9.2: *Unemployment rates by ethnic group*

	%
White	11
Indian	16
Other	17
West Indian	21
Pakistan/Bangladesh	29

Note: 'Other' includes African, Chinese and Arabs.
Source: *Social Trends*, HMSO, 1989.

Key ideas - summary of the interventionist approach

1. Unrestricted market forces lead to an unsatisfactory allocation of resources in the labour market.
2. Employers are much more powerful than individual workers; left to themselves workers would be exploited. Trade unions and government action can protect workers' rights.
3. Those who do badly in such a system include women, ethnic minorities and those with low educational qualifications or in particular occupations.
4. The state needs to intervene in order to achieve a more equitable distribution of income and also to improve the allocation of resources - if women and black people are not allowed to make a full contribution to the economy, then the country will be poorer.

Interventionist policies

Where specific groups can be identified which suffer from discrimination, this approach suggests that statutory bodies, such as the Equal Opportunities Commission, should be set up to help remedy the position. These can help employers establish procedures which reduce the likelihood of indirect discrimination and can take legal action when the laws against discrimination are broken, so helping workers who feel that they are not receiving their due. For example, the law says that women should receive equal pay when they undertake work of equal value to that of men, but this can be difficult to prove. The Commission can offer help to people in this position. In the case of disabled people, employers are supposed to employ a quota, but this requirement is often ignored. It is therefore suggested that the law should be tightened. For some industries such as catering which are associated with low pay, there are Wages Councils which have the power to lay down statutory minimum levels of pay, but these only apply to a few occupations and are frequently ignored by employers.

An important proposal made by this group of economists is that a law should be passed which lays down a legal minimum rate of pay. This was discussed in Chapter 3. Such a law would say that all adults working above a certain number of hours a week would be legally entitled to receive a wage of, say, £70 a week. Its proponents say that this is the only way in which the low paid can be guaranteed a reasonable income. Its opponents argue that this would cause employers to employ fewer workers, causing a rise in unemployment. This is accepted by many supporters of the proposal, but they suggest that the rise would be very small and that, in any case, the level of employment can be increased by government intervention to stimulate the economy.

Conclusion

Most economists would probably agree that the forces of demand and supply should play an important part in the labour market. When the market works well it provides incentives for individuals and firms to change their behaviour - for instance, to learn new or scarce skills - in ways which will improve the allocation of resources. However, there is considerable disagreement about the extent to which the market has limitations and hence about the extent to which government intervention is necessary to remedy any defects. Supply siders believe very little intervention is needed and that the government should be primarily concerned with improving the working of the market, for example, by paying different wage rates in different regions of the country and restricting the powers of trade unions. This line of argument is strongly opposed by economists who believe that unrestricted markets will lead to an unsatisfactory position which will penalise many of the weaker elements in society, and that the government should therefore intervene in order to protect groups against discrimination and to help the low paid.

Data questions

UK distribution of income before and after tax

United Kingdom						Percentages
			Quintile groups of households			
	Bottom fifth	Next fifth	Middle fifth	Next fifth	Top fifth	Total
Original income						
1976	0.8	9.4	18.8	26.6	44.4	100.0
1981	0.6	8.1	18.0	26.9	46.4	100.0
1985	0.3	6.0	17.2	27.3	49.2	100.0
1986	0.3	5.7	16.4	26.9	50.7	100.0
Disposable income						
1976	7.0	12.6	18.2	24.1	38.1	100.0
1981	6.7	12.1	17.7	24.1	39.4	100.0
1985	6.5	11.3	17.3	24.3	40.6	100.0
1986	5.9	11.0	16.9	24.1	42.2	100.0

Source: *Social Trends*, HMSO, 1989.

Question 1

1. Describe the trends taking place in the table.
2. Comment on the trends, and suggest economic reasons for them.

3. Should the government take action to ensure a more equal distribution of income?

Too many black staff still on lowest rates

A survey by the Commission for Racial Equality of eight local authorities has found that teachers from ethnic minorities accounted for less than 2% of the teaching staff. Yet in these areas people from ethnic minorities make up between 2.4% and 33.5% of the total population.

The Commission also found that black teachers tended to be on the lowest pay scales, and that they were often concentrated in units specially concerned with the needs of black pupils. Black teachers found it more difficult to obtain work since they had to make twice as many applications as whites in order to secure employment.

The Commission's chief executive, Dr. Aaron Haynes, said 'We have no reason to think that the situation of ethnic minorities in the teaching profession is any better than that in other areas.'

Source: Adapted from *Times Educational Supplement,* March 25, 1988.

Question 2

1. What reasons can be given to explain the findings in the article?

2. To what extent would the use of market forces be more effective in helping 'black' teachers gain promotion?

10 Cost-Benefit Analysis

Firms and governments need to have some way of deciding whether a particular investment would be a good idea. Would it pay a firm to build a particular factory or should the resources be used in another way? Should the government build a new road? Cost-benefit analysis is a sophisticated way of answering such questions. In essence it involves adding together all the costs and then comparing these with all the benefits which would follow if an investment went ahead. If the expected benefits are greater than the costs, the investment should proceed. The debate centres around the following arguments:

- Supporters of the technique argue that it provides the best way of appraising potential investments and should be used extensively in both private and public sectors.
- Critics suggest that it gives a spurious accuracy. They argue that it ignores political and social factors, which are particularly important in the public sector and which are the focus of this chapter.

How accurate is the technique of cost-benefit analysis?

Over twenty years ago Prest and Turvey (1965) defined cost-benefit analysis as:

'a practical way of assessing the desirability of projects, where it is important to take a long view (in the sense of looking at repercussions in the further, as well as the nearer, future) and a wide view (in the sense of allowing for side effects of many kinds on many persons, industries, regions, etc.), i.e. it implies the enumeration and evaluation of all the relevant costs and benefits'.

Hence the basic idea is simple. A firm wondering whether or not to invest in a new factory will add up all the costs - land, building, machinery and so on - and then try to estimate all the benefits, chiefly the extra output multiplied by the expected price of the product. If the benefits exceed the costs, then the project should go ahead. Similarly, a government deciding whether or not to build a new road or an airport will also enumerate (place a money value on) all the costs and benefits which would accrue to society if the project proceeded.

However, there are a number of complications and these will be considered in turn.

Discounting the future

'A bird in the hand is worth two in the bush.' Put another way, a certain sum of money now is worth more than the same sum in the future.

There are several reasons for this, one being inflation. Money loses its value over time, so waiting means that the recipient will receive less in real terms if forced to accept money at a later date. Secondly, having the money now gives a choice - the recipient can spend the money immediately or wait. If the money is received now, it can be invested and interest received. Finally, there is a risk involved in waiting. The giver or the recipient may die, or the giver may go bankrupt and be unable to pay any money owed.

For all these reasons, people prefer money now to money in the future and so **discount** future earnings. The amount of the discount depends on the circumstances. If a ninety-year-old offers to pay a debt in a year's time, the wise person asks for earlier payment! If the government issues a National Savings Certificate, the owner is sure of payment in the future, but will require some interest to compensate for losing the use of the money in the meantime.

All this is relevant to investment appraisal because investments involve costs in the near future, whilst the benefits are often spread over a much longer period of time. Since the investor has to wait for the benefits, these have to be discounted. This is shown in Table 10.1.

Table 10.1: *Net present value at discount rate of 10%*

Year	Actual cost	Net present value of costs	Actual benefits	Net present value of benefits
0	500	500	0	0
1			100	90
2			100	81
3			100	72.9
4			100	65.6
5			100	59.1
6			100	53.1
7			100	47.8
8			100	43.0
9			100	38.7
10			100	34.9
Total	500	500	1000	586.1

Net present value

Table 10.1 shows a hypothetical example of a cost-benefit analysis using a technique called **net present value**. In this example a person makes an investment of £500 in year 0. The returns start one year later and amount to £100 a year for ten years. These are discounted at a rate of 10% a year; the £100 which is due to be received after one year is discounted so that it is only worth £90 today. Returns which are not expected for two years have to be discounted twice, so that they are worth only £81. As all the costs in this example are incurred during the present year they do not need to be discounted.

In the example, the net present value of the costs is £500 and the net present value of the benefits is £586. Since the benefits exceed the costs, the project should succeed.

Internal rate of return

A variation of this technique involves calculating the internal rate of return. In the example given in Table 10.1 the discount rate was 10%. If the discount rate was higher, say 15%, then the net present value of the benefits would have been lower since £100 discounted at 15% would give rise to a lower stream of net present values - £85, £72, £61 etc. The total net present value would be only £455, which is less than the value of the costs and therefore the project

should not proceed.

At a discount rate of 10% the benefits exceed the costs and at a rate of 15% the costs exceed the benefits. It therefore follows that at some rate between 10% and 15% the benefits will equal the costs. This rate (just under 13% in this example) is called the **internal rate of return.** The project should proceed if this internal rate of return exceeds the desired discount rate.

These two techniques - comparing net present value of costs with net present value of benefits and calculating the internal rate of return - will give the same results in almost all cases. Purists seem to prefer the net present value method, but to most people it is more meaningful to talk about an internal rate of return of 13% than to imagine a figure for net present value.

What rate of discount?

A crucial element in cost-benefit analysis is the choice of discount rate. High discount rates will greatly reduce the number of projects given approval. Private firms will vary their chosen discount rate according to the rate of interest and the amount of risk involved in the project. Risky projects financed by money borrowed at high interest rates will have their expected returns discounted at a high rate, while safe ones undertaken when interest rates are low will be discounted at lower rates.

The choice of discount rate for public sector projects is controversial. Some writers believe that the correct rate for public sector projects is the rate of interest that the government has to pay when it borrows money. Others suggest that this is too low a rate because lending to the government is safe and that the public sector should evaluate its projects at the higher rate used by private sector firms. The argument is important because a higher rate of discount would reduce the number of public sector projects.

Correcting for externalities

In some cases, people can push part of the costs on to other people. If a firm dumps its rubbish into a river it will reduce its costs, but these will fall on to other people in the form of pollution. In this example the private costs to the individual are less than the social costs to the community as a whole. Pollution is one example of an **externality** or **spillover.** When external costs, such as pollution, are added to private costs we obtain social cost - the real cost to society as a whole. In some cases, externalities can be beneficial. It is argued that educating an individual not only benefits that person but also benefits others in various ways, such as improved behaviour from the person who has been educated. In this case, private benefits plus externalities gives us social benefit - the real benefit to society. 'Social' cost-benefit analysis means an analysis considered from the viewpoint of society as a whole as opposed to a private analysis which considers only the costs and benefits accruing to some participant, such as a firm. Indeed, one difference between cost-benefit analysis undertaken by firms and by government is that private firms usually ignore all externalities and just consider their own private costs and benefits, whilst public sector investments should take account of externalities.

Whilst, in principle, social cost-benefit analysis should take into account all the costs and benefits of a decision, including the externalities, this is often difficult in practice, as the following examples show.

Cost-benefit analysis of building a new road

Before building a new road the government calculates the costs and benefits. Some of the costs are obvious and relatively easy to calculate. For example, the money to be paid to the contractor will be known when firms put in estimates for building the road. What is harder to calculate are the costs which fall on to others, for example, those who suffer from noise and dirt during construction. These are real costs, but they do not come in the form of bills and so their size is difficult to estimate.

The benefits are even more difficult to estimate. One benefit is the time saved by people using the new road. This is hard to calculate because it depends on accurate estimates of the amount of traffic which will use the road and then also on calculations of the value of the time saved. A further benefit accrues to people using other roads who will face less traffic in the future. This is an external effect and, again, its value is difficult to calculate.

Another externality is even more difficult to translate into money terms. New roads are safer than old ones, so one benefit of roadbuilding is that lives are saved and fewer people are injured. What value should we put on a life? One solution is to calculate the value of the output the individual would produce if he or she had lived. This is obviously unsatisfactory, but it is the procedure often adopted. Consequently, there are large differences in estimates from different people. In 1989 the Public Accounts Committee of the House of Commons

calculated the true cost of a fatal accident at £500,000. This was far higher than the £238,000 which was used by the government in its investigations. If the higher figure was accepted, cost-benefit analysis would cause the government to invest far more in road building that is designed to reduce accidents.

Cost-benefit analysis of education

Investment in education involves both costs and benefits. If we take the example of a government considering whether or not to expand higher education, some costs will be direct (lecturers' salaries and other wage costs, spending on books and other materials, costs of premises etc.) and others will be indirect (the opportunity cost of the goods and services which would have been produced by students if they had not been studying).

The main economic benefit to society is that education makes people more productive. Cost-benefit analysis of education usually assumes that this extra productivity can be measured by the higher salaries received by educated people; that employers pay educated people more because they are more productive. Because these extra earnings arise in the future, they must be discounted. In addition, there are external benefits arising from education, such as a more civilised society.

However, many of these costs and benefits are difficult to measure. How do you measure the benefits of a more civilised society? And do educated people earn more because they are more productive, or because employers use education as a 'screening' device and tend to promote people with higher qualifications whether or not they produce more?

Table 10.2: *The percentage returns to education by level and region*

Region	Secondary education	Higher education
Developing	16	13
Intermediate	14	10
Advanced	10	9

Source: Psacharapolous, G. *Returns to Education*, Elsevier, 1973.

Table 10.2 summarises a large number of cost-benefit analyses of education. It shows that returns to education tend to be higher in less-developed countries, partly because in developed countries there are proportionately more graduates and this higher supply tends to bring down their wages. One limitation of these results is that they exclude the external benefits, which are difficult to quantify. Despite this, they do tend to support government investment in education. Figure 10.1 shows the approach which is used to calculate the results obtained in Table 10.2. The numbers used in the Figure illustrate the position in the UK.

Having examined the methods used to calculate a cost-benefit analysis, we can now examine the debate concerning the use of the technique.

Figure 10.1: *Should society invest in higher education?*

COSTS	
(£ per student)	
Direct, e.g. salaries	£6,000
Loss of production (measured by salary forgone)	£6,000
Total costs each year	£12,000
Total costs for 3 years	£36,000

BENEFITS	
(£ per student)	
Extra production (measured by higher salary forgone)	£2,000 rising to £7,000
Externalities	£x
Total benefits over perhaps 40 years	£200,000? but must be discounted

Rate of return

Key ideas

1. **Cost-benefit analysis involves a comparison of all the costs and benefits of a proposed investment.**
2. **Costs and benefits arising in the future need to be discounted.**
3. **Cost-benefit analyses can be undertaken by calculating the net present value of costs and benefits or else by finding the internal rate of return.**
4. **Many external costs and benefits are difficult to translate into monetary values.**

The case for cost-benefit analysis

Essentially the case for using cost-benefit analysis is that, although it has problems, it is better than any of the alternatives. Since governments have to use some criteria in order to decide whether to proceed with a project, it is better to use this technique rather than to leave it to personal prejudice on the part of civil servants or politicians or to even less satisfactory methods of evaluation, such as guesswork.

The great advantage of cost-benefit analysis is that it forces people to take account of all the costs, including those not easily translated into money terms. This forces decision makers to face up to the value judgements that arise in many proposals. For example, one argument in favour of building new roads is that it removes traffic from town centres. It is, however, impossible to put an agreed value on quietness. What is possible in cost-benefit analysis is to undertake **sensitivity analysis.** This can be done by first putting a low value on quietness, then running the calculation again with a high value. If this makes little difference to the rate of return, the value put on quietness does not matter. If there is a large difference in the two rates of return, the decision makers are forced to discuss and debate the value of quietness. The problem cannot be evaded. Instead people are forced to discuss the issue. They cannot ignore it, as would happen without such a rigorous investigation.

Many supporters of the technique would claim another advantage. They suggest that even when projects with high returns are passed over in favour

of others with lower returns, the technique can still have been useful. This can happen when political considerations are important. For example, it may be better to locate a new project in Northern Ireland than in the South-East of England because not only would it help to reduce unemployment in the province, but it would also strengthen the unity of a disaffected part of the UK. This may be the best decision even if the Northern Ireland project has a lower rate of return. Cost-benefit analysis would force decision makers to realise the extra costs they were incurring in order to obtain the political benefit.

Key ideas - summary of the case for cost-benefit analysis

1. **It takes a structured approach to the evaluation of proposed developments.**
2. **It takes into account all the costs and benefits, including those cases where social costs and benefits differ from private ones.**
3. **Sensitivity analysis can show the importance or otherwise of value judgements.**

Arguments against the use of cost-benefit analysis

A major criticism of the technique is that it is inaccurate and yet gives a spurious impression of accuracy. The computer takes in all the figures and gives out a precise rate of return. Yet many of the figures which go into the computer are extremely imprecise, rendering the results almost worthless.

Moreover, it is so difficult to quantify many of the variables that the figures entered into the computer frequently represent the prejudices of the investigators rather than any objective reality. Hence the results obtained are those which the investigator wants; they merely confirm the original intention. A specific example will illustrate the point. Cost-benefit analysis is often used to investigate the desirability of governments investing in education, yet many of the benefits are not quantifiable. Education plays a part in the creation and maintenance of civilised society; this is a factor which cannot be represented in money terms and so is either ignored, or an entirely arbitrary figure is entered as a benefit. If the government wants the project to go ahead, a high figure can be entered for such a benefit. If the government is opposed to the project, such a benefit can be ignored or its value cut. Thus one benefit of building new roads is that they reduce accidents and deaths. Because these are difficult to measure, a government wishing to build more roads can give a high figure for the benefits arising from fewer accidents and deaths. A government opposing extensive road building would insert a low figure.

Conclusion

Cost-benefit analysis is a method of investigating proposed developments which takes into account all the costs and benefits. If the present value of the benefits exceeds the present value of the costs then the development should go ahead. Alternatively, if the internal rate of return method is used, developments should proceed if the internal rate of return exceeds the chosen discount rate. Supporters of the technique argue that it is a rational way to evaluate proposals. Critics say that it is inaccurate and reflects the value judgements of the researcher.

Key ideas - summary of the case against cost-benefit analysis

1. The results are inaccurate, yet give the impression of accuracy.
2. If you put garbage into a computer, garbage comes out. And many of the figures that go into cost-benefit calculations are garbage.
3. Many of the costs and benefits are impossible to quantify.
4. There is no agreed way to choose a discount rate, yet this can be the crucial factor in deciding whether an investment should proceed.

Data questions

BR's SLOW TRAIN TO PARIS

With the agreement of £5 billion worth of bank loans only one major obstacle now remains in the way of Eurotunnel's £750 million flotation this October. Before the prospectus can be released, the French and Belgian governments must agree a formula to link the public and private finance for the new lines to carry the 186mph TGV trains from Calais to Paris and Brussels. A third of the French investment of £1.8 billion is for a fleet of 64 TGVs (out of a total fleet of 100) to link London, Paris, Brussels and Cologne. Both governments want the whole TGV project to be financed privately.

However, while the projected rate of return on the project is only around 10 per cent, some guarantees will be necessary - and the revenue forecasts in the prospectus assume that 16 million rail passengers will use the tunnel in its first operational year - 1993.

The major problem for the French part of the operation is BR's reticence in upgrading British lines to increase speed or capacity. BR is committed to a 'leave alone' policy, since the ever increasing cost of a new Dover-London route was largely responsible for the cancellation of the last tunnel project in 1975. The French, however, cannot understand the logic when Nicholas Ridley (then Transport Secretary) claims the M20 extension from Maidstone to Ashford is environmentally acceptable, while an upgraded railway line is environmentally damaging. The French are worried that any attempt to force BR to increase the basic £400 million investment could kill the project. Moreover, Mrs. Thatcher is worried that if BR did increase this investment she could be accused of pouring more public money into the project via the back door.

BR Chairman, Sir Robert Reid, does not, however, believe the new line can be justified financially. Half of the £400 million is for new rolling stock and only £20 million is for improved track and signalling on the main Eurotunnel route. Thus TGV's will only average 60 mph on the British Section compared to 100 mph on the newly electrified East Coast main line. If the East Coast is electrified why not theSouth Coast?

A very basic improvement package should at least be possible, for example, upgrading the straight Tonbridge-Tunnel section to 140 mph (though this would require overhead power) would increase speed, while upgrading the Orpington-Tunnel section from two track to four track would significantly increase line capacity. BR is currently evaluating the financial case for this based on higher traffic estimates.

Source: Adapted from *The Guardian*, August 28, 1987.

Question 1

1. Outline the potential:
  (i)   private costs and benefits and
  (ii) external costs and benefits
of the proposed investment in Eurotunnel.

2. Using examples from the Eurotunnel investment, explain how supporters and critics of cost-benefit analysis would justify their claims.

How is the economy doing? National income accounting attempts to answer this question. It does so by measuring the performance of the economy in various ways, for example, by calculating the output produced in the country during a year. There is some disagreement about the accuracy and usefulness of the figures which are produced:

- Some economists think that, although not perfect, they are a reliable indicator of what is happening in the economy.
  - Others feel that the figures are extremely inaccurate.

The debate is important because national income statistics are used in many areas of economics, for example, in measuring living standards and in examining economic trends.

Constructing the accounts

Before considering the uses and limitations of national income statistics, we must first examine how the figures are obtained and evaluate their accuracy.

National income can be defined as the total money value of all the goods and services produced by a country during a year. Hence the rate of growth of national income is probably the most important indicator of a country's economic performance. Governments of all political parties boast of the rise when it is high and find excuses when the growth rate is low.

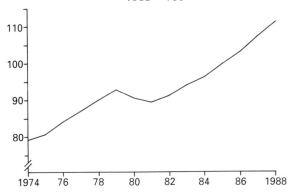

Figure 11.1: GDP at factor cost, 1985 prices
1985 = 100

Source: Adapted from *Economic Trends*, HMSO, 1989.

Figure 11.1 shows the growth rate of the UK economy in real terms (that is corrected to eliminate the effects of inflation) between 1974 and 1988.

Over this period the economy has grown at an average rate of just over 2.3% a year. However, there have been large variations in this rate and in some years national income has actually fallen.

Three ways to measure national income

National income can be measured in three ways. By definition these must be equal because they are different ways of measuring the same thing - the growth in output of the economy. The three different methods are shown in Figure 11.2. This is a simplified explanation and is developed further in Chapter 12.

One way to measure national income is to calculate the value of all goods and services produced by the people of a particular country. This is called Gross Domestic Product (GDP) by the output method. Unless people from outer space come to earth and steal some of these goods, GDP calculated by the **output method** must equal the amount of goods and services which is either bought, or not purchased and put into store. When GDP is calculated in this way it is called the **expenditure method.**

When something is produced it gives rise to incomes. These can accrue to several people - the workers who make it, the people who sell it, or as profits to the owners. The income generated must equal the amount spent on the product; if a table is sold for £100, then this £100 must go to one or more people as income. Hence GDP calculated by this **income method** equals that calculated by the expenditure method.

We will now consider each of these methods in turn.

Figure 11.2: *The national income accounts - three ways of measuring economic activity (1987)*

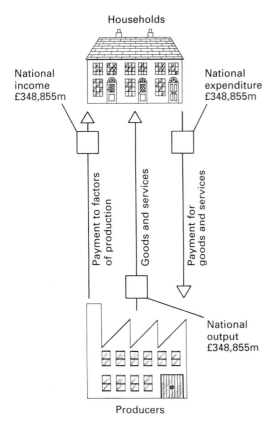

The output method

This involves adding together the final output of all the producers in the economy. **Final** output is stressed in order to avoid double counting. Assume that the chair on which you are sitting was bought for £20; that is the value of the chair. However, this output came from several industries. The forestry industry contributed the wood, the furniture industry manufactured the chair and the distribution industry sold it. In order to avoid double counting we need to add together the **value added** by each of these industries. An over-simplified example will show the procedure:

Forestry: value of inputs £0, value of output £5, value added £5.

Furniture: inputs from forestry £5, value of output £15, value added £10.

Distribution: inputs from furniture industry £15, value of output £20, valued added £5.

Hence in constructing the national output table the contribution of each industry can be shown by its value added, in this case £5 + £10 + £5 = £20. The sum of values added by all the firms in the economy becomes the nation's national output.

Figure 11.3: *Share of national output*

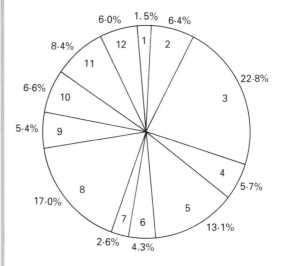

1. Agriculture, forestry, fisheries
2. Energy & water supply
3. Manufacturing
4. Construction
5. Distribution, hotels, catering
6. Transport
7. Communication
8. Banking, finance, insurance
9. Ownership of dwellings
10. Public administration, defence, compulsory social security
11. Education, health
12. Other services

Source: *Annual Abstract of Statistics*, HMSO, 1988.

Figure 11.3 shows the relative importance of the various industries in the UK economy. As can be seen, manufacturing contributes less than a quarter of the nation's output - far short of what services provide. Table 11.1 contains similar information, but in the form of a table. In this Table a figure for financial services is deducted. This is to prevent double counting, since the services of banks and other financial institutions contribute to the output of individual industries and are therefore also included separately. Hence a deduction is made here.

Table 11.1: *National income statistics, UK, 1987 - Output method*

	£ million
Agriculture, fishing and forestry	5,901
Energy and water supply	24,184
Manufacturing	85,552
Construction	21,524
Distribution, hotels and catering	48,963
Transport	16,227
Communication	9,688
Banking, finance and insurance	63,903
Ownership of dwellings	20,180
Public admin., defence, social security	24,895
Education and health services	31,681
Other services	22,366
Total	375,064
Adjustment for financial services	- 20,545
Statistical discrepancy	- 5,664
Gross domestic product at factor cost	348,855
Net property income from abroad	5,523
Gross national product	354,378
(Less) Capital consumption	- 48,238
National income	306,140

Source: *Annual Abstract of Statistics*, HMSO, 1988.

The expenditure method

As Table 11.2 shows, by far the largest item of expenditure is that undertaken by consumers on durable consumer goods, such as video recorders or washing machines, on non-durable goods, such as bread or gas and on services, such as hairdressing or bank charges. The difference between durable and non-durable goods is taken, rather arbitrarily, to be whether or not they last longer than one year.

Government expenditure is another major item. Note that this excludes transfer payments, such as student grants or pensions, because these are transfers from one part of the population to another and do not represent final consumption. Investment (called 'gross domestic fixed capital formation' in the Table) is another important item. This tends to be difficult to forecast in advance because it fluctuates quite considerably. This means that the share of investment in national income also

fluctuates. Finally, to get a full measure of expenditure we need to add exports (which are bought by foreigners) and subtract imports (because the money spent on these goes abroad).

Table 11.2: *National income statistics, UK, 1987 - Expenditure method*

	£ million
Consumers' expenditure	258,431
Central government	51,689
Local authorities	34,083
Gross domestic fixed capital formation	70,767
Value of physical increase in stocks and work in progress	627
Exports	107,506
(Less) Imports	- 112,030
Gross domestic product at market prices	411,073
(Less) Taxes on expenditure	- 67,980
Subsidies	5,762
Gross domestic product at factor cost	348,855
Net property income from abroad	5,523
Gross national product	354,378
(Less) Capital consumption	- 48,238
National income	306,140

Source: *Economic Trends*, Annual Supplement, HMSO, 1989.

We can represent the economy's total expenditure on goods and services by the equation:

Expenditure = C+I+G+X-M

where C = consumption, I = investment, G = government spending, X = exports and M = imports. We will meet this equation again when we discuss aggregate demand in Chapter 12 and it is worth remembering.

The income method

The data required to complete the figures for 'incomes' in the national income statistics are obtained by the Inland Revenue. These figures are shown in Table 11.3. As you can see, by far the largest item is income from employment, which accounts for about two-thirds of total incomes. The share of profits varies from year to year, rising when the economy is expanding, but falling in years of depression. Transfer incomes, such as student grants and pensions, are not included. This is because the figures only measure incomes arising from the production of goods and services (and students are assumed not to produce anything!).

During the year, some people will have become 'richer' because they own stocks of goods which have become more valuable. Since GDP is concerned with items which are produced during a

Table 11.3: National income statistics, UK, 1987 - Income method

	£ million
Income from employment	226,343
Gross trading profits of companies	65,596
Gross trading profits of public corporations	6,623
Gross trading surplus of general government enterprises	- 177
Other income, e.g. rent, self-employment	60,992
(Less) Stock appreciation	- 4,858
Residual error	- 5,664
Gross domestic product at factor cost	348,855
Net property income from abroad	5,523
Gross national product	354,378
(Less) Capital consumption	- 48,238
National income	306,140

Source: *Economic Trends*, Annual Supplement, HMSO, 1989.

given year, changes in the value of existing stocks should not count, so a figure for stock appreciation is deducted when the income method is calculated.

Some complications

Measuring the output of an entire economy is clearly a complex process and a number of complications arise which need to be discussed:

● Market prices or factor cost? The value of a product, so far as consumers are concerned, is the price paid for it in the shop - the market price. This often includes tax, so if the retail price was used to calculate national output, it would lead to the ridiculous result that the nation's output would rise if the Chancellor put up VAT. Similarly, a government subsidy to an industry would lead to a fall in national income. Hence the figures are sometimes shown at market prices, but more often at factor cost. This means that the

market price has been adjusted to remove the effect of any tax on the goods and also any subsidy. Taxes are removed and subsidies are added to GDP at market prices in order to change the figure to one at factor cost.

● Transfers. If I sell you a book I have read, no current production is involved. Consequently such transfers are excluded from the accounts. However, the same book bought from a second-hand bookshop would involve a payment for the seller's service and would be included in the accounts.

● Non-marketed goods. The national accounts only include goods which are bought. Hence DIY activities are not counted. Neither are the activities of 'housewives'. Cooking a meal in a cafe where it is bought adds to GNP; cooking at home does not. This omission is criticised by some people, and is discussed later in this chapter.

● The public sector. What is the value of the output of your school or college? Something is being produced - at least occasionally - but how can it be measured? In the private sector the value of a product is what the purchaser is willing to pay, but this method cannot be used in state schools or for defence, the services of the police or the health service. The unsatisfactory solution used in the national accounts is to use the cost of the service as a measure of its output. Hence we can have the position where if there is an increase in efficiency, so that a service is produced at less cost, this then shows as a fall in output.

● Residual error. The three approaches to measuring the national income must come to the same total. However, the complexities of collecting the statistics are such that in practice they do not agree. To solve this dilemma a figure for residual error is added to make the figures agree. Note that this figure for residual error is not an accurate measure of the actual error, since this is not known. It is merely a statistical device to make the three totals agree. This leads to questions about the validity of using the figures in economic analysis.

Which measure of national income?

So far we have been discussing Gross **Domestic** Product (GDP). However, if you happen to own an oil well in Alaska, or a tea estate in Malawi, you will realise that some people receive incomes from property they own in other countries. Similarly, some foreigners own property in this country. When these flows of money into and out of the country are taken into account, we obtain a figure for Gross **National** Product (GNP). For the UK this has always been a positive item because British people own more overseas assets than foreigners own assets in this country. Hence GNP is greater than GDP in the UK.

The relationship is shown by the equation:

GDP ± net property income from abroad = GNP

Capital consumption

Another complication takes account of the fact that, during any one year, machines and buildings deteriorate. In the official statistics this is called capital consumption or depreciation and is shown by a move from **Gross** National Product to **Net** National Product (NNP).

An increase in NNP is the best measure we have of the real change in living standards and NNP is the official measure of national income (though the term is often used more vaguely to include other measures such as GDP or GNP). One problem which arises is that any precise measure of depreciation is impossible; imagine the difficulty in trying to list all the cars in the country and then estimating the fall in their value during the year. Hence it is estimated by using a series of accounting conventions and does not vary much from year to year.

The relationship between GNP and NNP is shown by the equation:

GNP - capital consumption = NNP

Figure 11.4

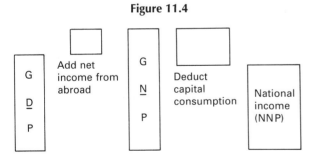

Figure 11.4 illustrates the above two formulae in the form of a diagram.

Key ideas

1. National income is the money value of all the goods and services produced in a country during a year.

2. It can be measured in three ways: by counting output, expenditure and income. In theory, all three should give the same result.
3. The figures can be expressed at market prices or at factor cost. The statistics exclude transfers and non-marketed goods. The output of government services, such as education, is measured at the cost of producing the service.
4. GDP measures what is produced in the domestic economy. GNP adds to this property income from abroad. When capital consumption is deducted from GNP, the result is national income.

Uses of the national income statistics

The previous sections dealt with the problems of obtaining an accurate figure for the national income of a country. Despite the difficulties, most economists would argue that the national income statistics have important uses for economists both inside and outside the government.

The prime purpose of the national income statistics is to facilitate government planning. If the Chancellor is considering cutting the rate of income tax, the statistics make it possible to forecast the effect that this would have on such things as economic growth and the balance of payments. This can be done by feeding the figures into a computer model of the economy.

National income statistics are the usual way to measure the rate of economic growth. They are also used to compare the current rate of economic growth with the rate in the past and with the rate of growth and standard of living in other countries. That is because most countries use similar methods to construct the national income statistics, so comparisons are possible.

Economists in industry make considerable use of the statistics to analyse economic developments and their effect on individual firms. For example, they can make predictions about the future growth of the economy and how this will affect particular industries. Similarly, academic economists use the accounts to comment on matters as diverse as the share of wages in the national income or to compare the relative importance of manufacturing in one country with another.

"... Whereas with investment Plan B..."

Key ideas - uses of national income statistics

1. **National income statistics are essential for governments when planning their budgets.**
2. **The figures are used to make comparisons with the past and with other countries.**
3. **Economists use the statistics to analyse particular sectors of the economy.**

Criticisms of the national income accounts

Economists generally agree that the national income accounts have their uses, but there is substantial argument about these uses in any particular situation. This is because the accounts have considerable limitations and are sometimes used for inappropriate purposes.

Limitations of the figures

● They are not accurate. This is inevitable because measuring the economic activity of an entire country can never be done precisely. People sometimes fail to fill in forms or they complete them inaccurately.

● The 'black economy' distorts the figures. This is the name given to work that is not reported to the authorities. Teachers giving private lessons have been known to 'forget' to inform the tax authorities about the income they have received. The black economy is probably most prevalent in the area of domestic repairs, where discounts are often given for cash payment. This means that the statistics for this and similar areas of the economy are inaccurate. However, they do not distort the comparisons between total GNP in one year and the next because the size of the black economy does not vary much over one year, so that the error is similar in both years. Comparisons over a longer period will be affected by changes in the size of the black economy.

● A rise in national income may not mean a rise in living standards. This is because the rise may occur as a result of increased spending on items such as defence, which do not improve living standards. Similarly, an increase in national income may be accompanied by a rise in undesirable externalities, such as pollution, or a fall in the quality of goods.

● The accounts only measure **paid** activities. They

therefore exclude DIY activities and the work of housewives. If over a period of years there is a rise in DIY activities, then this will not be shown in the official figures and comparisons over several years will be inaccurate.

These omissions are a severe problem in some countries where many economic activities are unpaid. In large parts of Afro-Asia, women collect water and wood, people build their own houses and live off food that they have grown. If these unpaid activities are not counted, then the figures will greatly under-estimate the level of GNP in these countries. If some attempt is made to estimate their value in order to give a truer picture, then insoluble problems of valuation arise. Imagine trying to estimate the value of all the water collected by all the women in India over a year!

- National income often rises in time of war, or the threat of war, because money is spent on weapons. This will push up GNP, but the people may be acutely short of goods to buy.
- When making comparisons with the past, adjustments have to be made to allow for inflation. If prices have risen by 5% and GNP has also risen by 5%, then the country is no better off. Hence it is important when looking at the figures to see whether they are in **nominal** terms, i.e. the actual figures not adjusted to remove the effects of inflation. If GNP rises by a nominal 5%, but inflation is 3%, then the real rise is 2%.

  The extent of inflation can be calculated fairly accurately over a short period, such as one year, but it is much more difficult to do so over a long period. One reason is that new products appear and existing ones become obsolete, so it is impossible to measure price rises accurately.
- Another adjustment that has to be made when making comparisons with the past is that the figures have to be adjusted to allow for population changes. If national income has risen by 10%, but population has also risen by 10%, the average person is no better off.
- Many factors affect the quality of life but are excluded from GNP. Over the last few decades, people have come to enjoy more leisure, largely because they work fewer days. The national accounts take no note of this. Similarly, the quality of many products has improved - a modern TV is far superior to one made many

UK (£m)
GDP 1980 199,915
GDP 1988 352,237

Pollution kills trees
Ozone layer weakened by CTCs
Stress of high pressure work kills executives

Does a rise in GDP mean a rise in living standards?

years ago. On the other hand, economic growth may be accompanied by increased pollution, overcrowded cities and a frenetic lifestyle - factors ignored by statisticians. The national income accounts measure some of the **quantitative** factors affecting life, but they ignore many features of the **quality** of life.
- The figures say nothing about the **distribution** of income within a country. In some countries a small elite has a large share of the economic cake; in such countries figures showing a high average income per head may give the wrong impression of typical living standards.

International comparisons

Comparisons between countries may be misleading for other reasons:
- National income figures are compiled in national currencies. In order to make comparisons, these have then to be converted to a common currency, usually US dollars. However, exchange rates vary daily and changes in exchange rates can give a misleading impression of changes in living standards.
- People's needs are not the same in all countries. In warm countries less needs to be spent on heating and clothing, so that even if two countries have identical national incomes, they may have different living standards.
- Countries are not always consistent in the way they prepare the statistics. For example, some countries may exclude or conceal spending on items such as defence.

Key ideas - criticisms of national income statistics

1. **The national income accounts are inaccurate, for example, they exclude the 'black economy' and ignore unpaid activity such as DIY.**
2. **They also ignore many factors affecting the quality of life, such as the existence of pollution.**
3. **Comparisons with the past are difficult because the composition and the quality of goods change over time.**
4. **Comparing living standards between countries is particularly inaccurate because the statistics are compiled in different currencies and because people in different countries have different needs.**

Conclusion

The national income accounts are essential for the modern economist. They provide a wealth of detail about the economy and, considering the problems involved in compiling them, they can provide a reasonably accurate picture provided they are used sensibly. However, they can be put to uses for which they are inappropriate or used to support precise conclusions when they can give only approximate indications, such as when they are used to compare living standards in different countries.

Data questions

UK national income (£ million)

	1977	1978	1979	1980	1981	1982	1983	1984	1985	1986	1987
Factor incomes											
Income from employment	86 572	98 843	115 866	137 639	149 584	158 621	169 580	180 096	194 573	209 542	226 343
Income from self-employment	12 129	13 723	15 802	17 485	19 405	22 066	24 523	27 149	28 302	30 485	32 959
Gross trading profits of companies	19 864	22 484	29 429	27 951	27 940	31 883	39 810	45 085	53 500	51 358	65 596
Gross trading surplus of public corporations	5 095	5 393	5 594	6 162	7 821	9 410	9 918	8 267	7 020	8 016	6 623
Gross trading surplus of general government enterprises	183	216	180	180	236	216	50	-92	256	105	-177
Rent	8 715	10 036	11 951	14 244	16 366	17 697	18 775	19 849	21 619	23 261	24 798
Imputed charge for consumption of non-trading capital	1 287	1 449	1 711	2 107	2 338	2 408	2 473	2 594	2 808	3 067	3 235
Total domestic income	133 845	152 144	180 533	205 768	223 690	242 301	265 129	282 948	308 078	325 834	359 377
less Stock appreciation	-5 095	-4 228	-8 837	-6 391	-5 974	-4 276	-4 204	-4 206	-2 816	-2 005	-4 858
Gross domestic product (income-based)	128 750	147 916	171 696	199 377	217 716	238 025	260 925	278 742	305 262	323 829	354 519
Statistical discrepancy (income adjustment)	188	919	692	539	93	-728	-1 168	311	-527	-1 608	-2 282
Gross domestic product (average estimate) at factor cost	128 938	148 835	172 388	199 915	217 809	237 297	259 757	270 053	304 735	322 221	352 237
Net property income from abroad	265	806	1 205	-196	1 210	1 446	2 847	4 433	2 800	5 079	5 523
Gross national product (average estimate)	129 203	149 641	173 593	199 719	219 019	238 743	262 604	283 486	307 535	327 300	357 760
less Capital consumption	-16 501	-19 378	-22 827	-27 952	-31 641	-33 653	-36 150	-38 686	-41 899	-45 165	-48 238
Net national product at factor cost (average estimate): "National income"	112 702	130 263	150 766	171 767	187 378	205 090	226 454	244 800	265 636	282 135	309 522

Note: The figures for national income (1987) in the table differ slightly from those figures in Table 11.3 because the above table is an average whereas Table 11.3 is corrected so that it agrees with the estimates in Tables 11.1 and 11.2.

Source: *Economic Trends,* Annual supplement, HMSO, 1989.

Question 1

1. Explain what is meant by:
   (i)   capital consumption
   (ii) factor cost
   (iii) property income from abroad.

2. Which categories of incomes have increased most rapidly over the period illustrated? What reasons can be put forward for their increase?

3. To what extent do the figures show that the standard of living was rising rapidly over the period illustrated?

The black economy

The 'black economy' is basically illegal, but it flourishes. Teachers offering private lessons, builders doing roof repairs and market traders often 'forget' to declare all their earnings. This affects the national income statistics. For example, if shops do not invoice purchases, then actual consumption of goods will be higher than that shown by the official statistics. Fringe benefits also affect the figures, since many benefits received by workers are not counted as income. To give just one example, office workers often make use of company telephones and stationery.

Economists' explanations of the black economy usually focus on the costs and benefits of such activities. Rational individuals will calculate the costs and the benefits of participating in the black economy compared to either not working at all or to getting a 'proper' job.

Question 2

1. (i) How does the black economy affect the national income statistics? Which sectors of the economy do you think are particularly affected?
(ii) What problems are involved in assessing the size of the black economy?

2. Elaborate the costs and benefits involved in participating in the black economy.
3. Do you think the black economy is a good thing? Justify your answer.

12 Determinants of National Income

This chapter and the next could well be regarded as one because they each emphasise a particular approach to macro-economics - the study of the economy as a whole. In that sense they are crucial because many of the chapters that follow elaborate and develop the ideas found here:

● This chapter is largely, though not entirely, concerned to elaborate the Keynesian approach to the problem of analysing the factors that determine the level of national income. It will set up a theoretical model of the economy as a whole, and then look in some detail at two of the most important variables - consumption and investment.

● The next chapter will give more emphasis to the supply side approach to macro-economics.

The circular flow of income model

There are a number of ways in which the basic Keynesian model can be developed, but a relatively easy way is to build up a model of the circular flow of income in the economy. A simplified version of this model was presented in the last chapter in Figure 11.2.

Figure 12.1: The circular flow of income

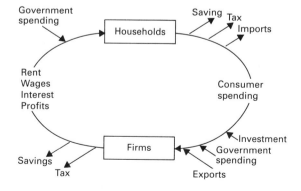

As Figure 12.1 shows, income flows from households to firms in the form of consumption spending by households on goods and services produced by firms. Similarly, income flows from

firms to households in the form of wages, rent, interest and profits (remember the income approach to measuring national income in the last chapter?). These flows are disturbed by various **injections** into the system and by **withdrawals** from the system. Injections and withdrawals change the level of the flow, just as the level of water in a bath varies according to the amount of water coming in from the tap and the quantity escaping from the plug hole.

Withdrawals

Withdrawals, which remove income from the circular flow, come in three ways. Both firms and individuals save money in the sense that they do not pass it on. Later in this chapter we will explore in some detail the determinants of an individual's saving and consumption. For the present, it is enough to note that an increase in savings will lead to a fall in the level of the circular flow of income. Another withdrawal from the flow comes in the form of spending on imports; in this case the money is leaked to firms in other countries. The final withdrawal arises when the government takes money from firms and families in tax. Note that the prime determinant of all these withdrawals is the level of income. People with high incomes will tend to save more, buy more imported goods and pay more in tax.

Injections

There are also three injections into the system. These raise the level of incomes in the circular flow. Some firms receive money from other firms when they sell investment goods such as factories or machines. A firm such as ICI receives most of its income not from selling consumer goods to families, but by selling chemicals to other firms. A second injection arises when firms export goods to other countries. In this case they receive money from foreign families and firms.

The final injection comes from government spending. This takes many forms. For example, households obtain money from the government when they work in the public sector whether they are typists, teachers or tank drivers. Some households also receive income from the government, for example, when they receive transfer payments such as pensions or student grants. Similarly, firms obtain money from the government when they receive grants or sell goods as varied as chalk or aeroplanes to the public sector. All these injections into the system increase the circular flow of income.

To summarise:

Injections	**Withdrawals**
Investment	Saving
Exports	Imports
Government spending	Tax

Figure 12.2

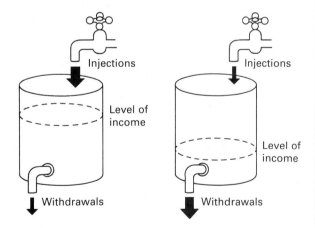

The size of withdrawals is largely determined by the level of incomes; the level of injections is determined by other factors and is discussed in later chapters. Injections are said to be 'autonomous' of income.

Policy implications

An increase in injections will raise the circular flow of income, while a fall will lower the level of incomes. On the other hand, a rise in withdrawals will lead to a fall in the circular flow, while a fall in withdrawals will lead to a rise in incomes. Although this circular flow model of the economy is rather simplistic, it can be a powerful tool of analysis and it does suggest policies. For example, if the government wishes to stimulate the economy (in order to increase the rate of growth or create more jobs) then it should either increase injections by spending more, or reduce withdrawals by cutting taxes.

Real life is more complex than this and in the next few chapters we will explore the implications and limitations of this model in some detail. In the meantime we need to give a more formal exposition.

Equilibrium

'Equilibrium national income' means that the level of national income shows no tendency to change.

National income will be in equilibrium when injections equal withdrawals. We can deduce this because, as the last chapter made clear, national income calculated by the income method equals national expenditure.

Now:

National Income (Y) = Consumption (C) + Tax (T) + Savings (S) + Imports (M)

that is, income is either spent, taxed, saved or spent on imports.

Similarly:

National expenditure = Consumption (C) + Government spending (G) + Investment (I) + Exports (X)

that is, national expenditure on economic activity arises from consumption, government spending, investment spending and exports.

Since National income = National expenditure then:

$$C + T + S + M = C + G + I + X$$

Subtracting C from both sides gives:

$$T + S + M = G + I + X$$
or Withdrawals = Injections.

Since withdrawals equal injections, we need to discover how this comes about. How does the

Figure 12.3: Equilibrium level of national income

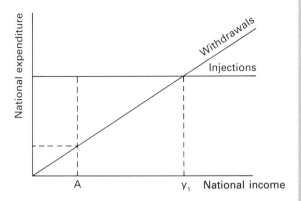

Figure 12.5 shows the effect of a fall in withdrawals. The slope of the withdrawals line measures the rate at which withdrawals rise as incomes rise (the top part of the Figure shows that as incomes rise by 10 withdrawals rise by 6). If there is a fall in withdrawals, caused, for example, by a cut in income tax, then the rate of withdrawals would fall, in this case to 4 in 10. The effect would be a rise in national income from y_1 to y_2.

Figure 12.5: A fall in withdrawals

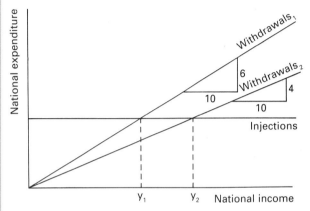

economy operate to maintain this equality? In Figure 12.3 the vertical axis measures national expenditure; the horizontal axis measures national income. In this model the level of injections is taken as given - or at least injections do not vary with the level of income, whereas withdrawals do rise as incomes increase. The equilibrium level of national income occurs where injections equal withdrawals at y_1. At any other position the economy would not be in equilibrium and changes would take place which would move the economy towards equilibrium. For example, if the economy was at point A, injections would be higher than withdrawals. This would lead to a rise in the circular flow of income - shown on this diagram by a movement to the right - until injections equal withdrawals at y_1.

The effect of changes

Figure 12.4 shows the effect of changes. A rise in government spending leads injections to rise from z_1 to z_2. This leads to an increase in national income, which rises until injections equal withdrawals at y_2. A fall in injections, for example from z_2 to z_1, has the opposite effect.

Figure 12.4: A rise in injections

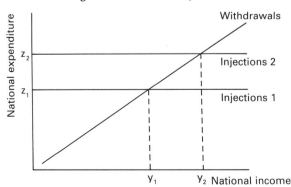

The paradox of thrift

The paradox of thrift arises because the result of people wishing to save more may lead to a fall in the level of savings. This may occur in the following way.

If people desire to save more, this will lead to a rise in the level of savings in the short run. However, in the longer run, this rise in savings means an increase in withdrawals and so a fall in incomes. Now the prime determinant of how much is saved is the level of income. A fall in incomes will cause people to save less. Hence the paradox; a desire to save more may lead to a fall in savings.

The multiplier

Look back at Figure 12.4 and compare the extent of the original rise in injections with the resulting rise in national income. It is clear that the rise in income is larger than the rise in injections. Why?

Let us begin with a simple explanation. If I were to win a million pounds on the pools and invest it by building a diamond mine in Birmingham, there would be a rise in injections of a million pounds. That is stage one.

The people who received this money - landowners, workers etc., would then spend some of the money on extra goods, such as cars, leading to a rise in national income, its size depending on the extent to which the withdrawals took money out of circulation. That is stage two.

In turn, people in the car industry would spend more money, say on furniture. Again there would be a rise in national income. The process would continue, with each successive rise in income becoming smaller because at each stage some money would be withdrawn.

This relationship between a change in injections and a resulting change in income is called the multiplier. It is defined as the amount by which a change in injections will lead to a multiplied change in income. We can show the effect numerically. If we assume that £6 in every £10 is consumed, then £4 will be withdrawn (because income must be either consumed or withdrawn - see the circular flow diagram to confirm this).

Original injection £1,000,000
Extra income stage 2 £600,000 (60% of 1000,000)
Extra income stage 3 £360,000 (60% of 600,000)
Extra income stage 4 £216,000 (60% of 360,000)
etc.

A quicker way to calculate the full effect is to use the multiplier formula:

The multiplier $(k) = \dfrac{1}{\text{MPW}}$

where MPW is the marginal propensity to withdraw. This is the proportion of any increase in income which is withdrawn. In the example above this was 0.4, so that the multiplier was 2.5. Hence the total effect of an increase in injections of £1,000,000 would be to raise national income by £2,500,000. If more is withdrawn, then the multiplier will be smaller. If the marginal propensity to withdraw is 0.5, then the multiplier would be 2.

The extent of any change in income can be found by using the formula:

$$\Delta \text{ Income} = k \times \Delta \text{ Injections}$$

In the formulation of the multiplier given here, the determinant of the size of the multiplier is the marginal propensity to withdraw. In some formulations this is split up into its components of savings, taxes and imports, so that the multiplier is shown as:

$$k = \dfrac{1}{\text{MPS} + \text{MPT} + \text{MPM}}$$

where MPS = marginal propensity to save, MPT = marginal propensity to pay tax and MPM = marginal propensity to import.

An alternative approach

So far we have analysed the determination of national income by using an approach using injections and withdrawals. An alternative way to look at this problem is to use an approach focusing on income and expenditure.

In the last chapter, we saw that national income calculated by the output and income methods equalled that calculated by the expenditure method, and that national expenditure was composed of C + I + G + X - M (consumption + investment + government spending + exports - imports). The approach to the determination of national income discussed in this section builds on this relationship and is illustrated in Figure 12.6.

The equilibrium level of national income occurs where aggregate planned expenditure equals total output. In the Figure this is shown by a line drawn at 45°. At every point along this line planned expenditure equals total income. E_1 shows planned expenditure. This line slopes upwards because the largest item in national expenditure - consumption - rises as income rises.

Original equilibrium is at A where planned expenditure equals national income y_1. If there is then a planned rise in some part of national expenditure, such as investment or government spending, the result is a new equilibrium at B, with national income rising to y_2. A cut in planned expenditure would have the opposite effect, leading to a fall in national income.

Figure 12.6: *The income-expenditure approach*

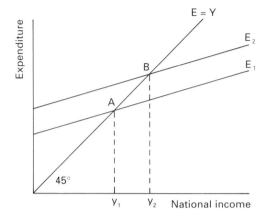

Inflationary and deflationary gaps

This model suggests that the economy can be in equilibrium at less than the full employment level of output. This has clear policy implications since it suggests that the government should intervene to change the equilibrium.

Keynes developed the model in order to reduce the level of unemployment. His ideas are developed in detail in the chapter on unemployment, but in brief he argued that the level of employment depended on the level of aggregate demand. If demand for furniture rises, then employment in this industry will also rise. If demand for cars increases, then the number of jobs in car manufacturing will also rise. By increasing aggregate demand - that is, demand for all goods and services - the government can increase the number of jobs. If the government goes too far so that the demand for goods outstrips the economy's capacity to supply them, the result will be a rise in prices. These two possibilities are usually called deflationary and inflationary gaps (though other terms such as expansionary and output gaps are also used).

The deflationary gap is the amount by which desired aggregate expenditure is less than the level of national income needed to ensure full employment. If it is estimated that at full employment the country could produce goods to the value of £400,000 million, but the economy is only producing goods worth £350,000 million, then there is a deflationary gap of £500 million. In order to secure full employment, national expenditure would

have to be increased by this amount. The position is shown in Figure 12.7 (i).

In this Figure, E shows total expenditure and yf is the full employment level of national income. However, the actual level of national income is y_1 which is less than yf; hence there is a deflationary gap which is shown as AB. This is the amount by which expenditure needs to rise in order to reach the full employment level of output. Note that the economy is in equilibrium, but not at a full employment level. The rise in expenditure needed to bring equilibrium at the full employment level can be brought about in a number of ways; for Keynesians, the most usual policy prescription would be for the government to increase its spending.

Figure 12.7: *(i) Deflationary gap*

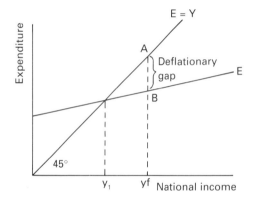

(ii) Inflationary gap

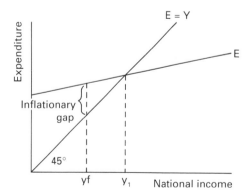

An inflationary gap exists when the equilibrium level of national income is greater than the level of output which can be produced at full employment. Since the demand for goods is greater than the supply, prices will rise. This is shown in

Figure 12.8

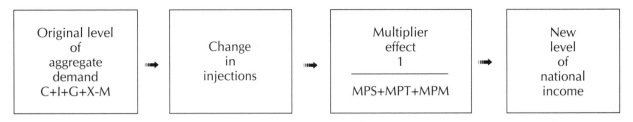

Figure 12.7 (ii) where the economy is in equilibrium at y_1. However, the economy can only produce yf goods and services. Since this is less than y_1 there is an inflationary gap, AB. This is the amount by which aggregate expenditure would have to fall if there was to be equilibrium at the full employment level of output. This situation is sometimes called **demand pull inflation** because it illustrates the position when prices rise due to excess demand. This is discussed in more detail in Chapter 17.

Supply side critique of this model

This account of the determinants of national income is essentially that presented by Keynes. Supply side economists do not accept all the features of this model. In particular they reject the conclusion that the government can increase national income and employment by spending more. They suggest this would merely lead to a rise in inflation. The reasons which lay behind this conclusion are presented in detail in the next chapter.

Key ideas

1. One approach to the determination of national income is to use a model focusing on planned expenditure and income.

2. The equilibrium level of national income occurs when planned expenditure equals total output. A change in planned expenditure will lead to a change in national income.

3. A deflationary gap is one where desired aggregate expenditure is less than the full employment level of output. An inflationary gap exists when the equilibrium level of national income exceeds the full employment level of output.

The components of aggregate demand - consumption

So far in this chapter we have set up a model of how the economy as a whole operates. Now we need to flesh out the model by looking at some of the components of aggregate demand. In later chapters we will look at government spending and tax, and at imports and exports. Here we will focus on consumption and investment. Consumption is the largest item in aggregate expenditure. Therefore in order to predict future levels of expenditure we need to be able to understand what factors affect the level of consumption.

One obvious influence is the level of income. This can be deduced from the circular flow diagram which shows that income affects the level of saving. Indeed after taxes have been deducted, consumers have the choice of saving or spending their money, so we can write:

Disposable income = Consumption + Saving

This makes it clear that in this approach 'saving' can be defined as 'not spending'.

Determinants of consumption

It is quite easy to draw up a list of the factors which influence families to consume:

- Level of income. We would expect people with higher incomes to spend more than those with low incomes.
- Level of wealth. Millionaires spend more than paupers. More generally, changes in the level of wealth will cause people to adjust their spending patterns. Thus a rise in house prices may make people feel richer and induce them to spend more.
- Rate of interest. High rates of interest may encourage some people to save more and spend

less. It may also discourage people from borrowing to buy durable goods. Moreover, if people are paying high interest rates on their mortgages, they will have less to spend on other goods.

- Credit terms. If it is easy to obtain credit and repayment terms are attractive, then people may borrow more to buy goods. On the other hand, if they have to make large deposits and pay back the money quickly, then less will be borrowed and spent.
- Expectations. If people expect prices to rise in the future, they may decide to buy now. Similarly, if they expect their incomes or wealth to rise in the future, they may spend more now. If you are the only relative of a 90 year old millionaire there may seem little point in saving.

The consumption function

The phrase 'consumption function' describes the relationship between what households plan to spend on consumption and all the other factors which influence this amount. In order to develop a theory, we will adopt a typical economist's practice and assume all the variables except one are constant and then see what happens when that one variable is changed. In this case the variable to be considered is income.

Figure 12.9: The consumption function

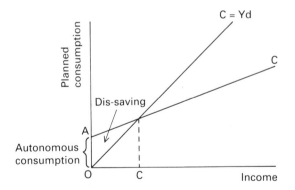

Figure 12.9 illustrates the relationship between planned consumption and disposable income. The 45° line shows the points at which consumption equals income - that is, where people spend all their income. At low levels of income people's spending is higher than their income - they 'dis-save'. Even when their income is zero, people will still spend something on consumption. In the diagram this is labelled OA and is called 'autonomous

consumption'. At point C all income is spent. At higher income levels than this people save - their income is higher than their spending.

Propensities to consume

Two terms need to be understood. The **average propensity to consume** (apc) is the total spending on consumption, C, divided by total income, Y:

$$APC = \frac{C}{Y}$$

The marginal propensity to consume (mpc) is the change in consumption divided by the change in income:

$$MPC = \frac{\Delta C}{\Delta Y}$$

(The Greek letter Δ in this equation stands for 'change in'. For example, if income rose by £10 and consumption rose by £8, the mpc would be 0.8.)

Look back at Figure 12.9. The slope of that line shows the mpc. A steep slope would show a high mpc - consumption rising quickly with rises in income. A gentle slope shows a low mpc - a large rise in income leads to only a small rise in consumption.

Saving and consumption

Saving and consumption are tightly linked. If we ignore taxes and foreign trade, then income must be either spent on domestic goods or saved. Hence saving can be defined as 'not spending'. Consequently any rise in income must lead to a rise in either consumption or saving or in both these variables. Similarly, where mpc is the marginal propensity to consume and mps is the marginal propensity to save we can write:

$$MPC + MPS = 1$$

The Keynesian theory of the consumption function

Keynes developed a theory of the consumption function in his book *The General Theory of Employment, Interest and Money* (1936). He wrote:

'The fundamental psychological law, upon which we are entitled to depend with great confidence . . .

is that men are disposed, as a rule and on the average, to increase their consumption as their income increases, but not by as much as their increase in income.'

Figure 12.10: *The Keynesian consumption function*

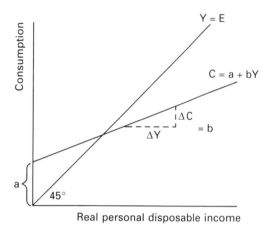

This line of argument leads to the Keynesian consumption function which is usually expressed as:

$$C = a + bY$$

where a is the autonomous consumption shown in Figure 12.10, and b is the marginal propensity to consume.

The Keynesian view is that when income rises, so does consumption, but by a smaller amount. In other words the mpc is less than one. Keynes also argued that the rich would spend more than the poor, but their consumption would be a smaller proportion of their income than that of poorer people. For example, students often spend all of their income, whilst millionaires spend much more in total, but this large total represents only a small part of their total income. Put formally, this means that the average propensity to consume falls as income rises. There is some evidence to support this argument. If data on real personal disposable income and consumption for the last thirty years are plotted on a graph the result is that shown in Figure 12.11.

As the diagram shows, autonomous expenditure is about £14 billion (at 1980 prices) and the mpc is about 0.8. This result is obtained by using time series data - that is data generated over a long period of time. However, more detailed analysis suggested that if cross section data is used, i.e. data for different groups of people at one particular point in time, then a much flatter consumption function

results. Moreover, subsequent investigation showed that Keynes' formula did not always allow accurate predictions to be made of future levels of consumption. Thus if economists entered actual data into the Keynesian consumption function, and then attempted to predict future levels of consumption, the results were not entirely satisfactory.

Figure 12.11: *Empirical evidence for the Keynesian consumption function*

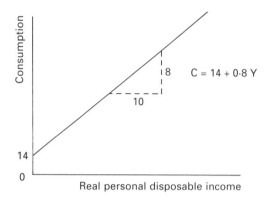

Key ideas - summary of the Keynesian consumption function

1. **Consumption depends on current disposable income.**
2. **The marginal propensity to consume is positive but less than one.**
3. **Average propensity to consume falls as income rises.**

Friedman's Permanent Income Hypothesis (PIH)

Since Keynes put forward his theory a number of refinements have been suggested and a number of alternative theories expounded. One, put forward by Milton Friedman, is called the Permanent Income Hypothesis (PIH). As its name implies, the essence of this theory is that people's spending depends less on their current income than on the basis of their long-term expectations. Current spending is determined by 'permanent income', which is what an individual expects to receive over a lifetime. Hence students may be poor, but have expectations of higher income in the future and so be willing to spend virtually all their income. In contrast, middle-aged people will expect their incomes to fall on retirement and therefore save a relatively large part of their income. In general, this theory suggests that people's level of consumption will be fairly constant over time, since temporary fluctuations in income, such as an unexpected bonus, will not have much influence on the individual's expectations of permanent income. The theory also implies that periods of boom will have little effect on spending plans unless they last long enough to change expectations about permanent income. Friedman also suggested that the proportion of future income that is spent would depend on a number of other factors, such as the interest rate, education, age and tastes.

Its supporters claim that the PIH can explain much of the data about consumption, but one difficulty in testing the theory is that it is difficult to measure people's expectations about the future and consequently to match these with spending patterns.

Key ideas - the PIH

1. **Current spending is determined by permanent income.**
2. **Permanent income is determined by expectations about the future.**
3. **Temporary fluctuations in income have little effect on current spending.**

The components of aggregate demand - investment

The importance of investment

Understanding investment is important to economists for two reasons. In the first place, investment is an important part of aggregate demand, so that if we are to understand and predict aggregate demand we need to be able to predict future investment. This is difficult because the level of investment tends to fluctuate quite considerably. Secondly, the amount of investment will affect future standards of living. More investment today will tend to mean higher standards of living in the future, though the relationship is not automatic.

What is investment?

Investment can be defined as expenditure on productive physical assets, such as factories,

machines and raw materials. It can be defined in gross terms, which is the total amount of money spent, or net of depreciation of assets which have become obsolete or worn out. Investment can also be divided into various categories. 'Fixed capital formation' is concerned with expenditure on fixed assets (which includes vehicles!) whereas the other prime component of investment is inventories or stocks of goods. Whatever the category, investment usually involves giving up present consumption in order to produce more in the future.

Investment is undertaken by different groups of people as Table 12.1 shows. The relative importance of each sector varies over time. One reason for this is political; the number of public corporations has fallen in recent years because of privatisation and consequently the level of investment undertaken in this sector has also fallen.

Alternative explanations

Because investment is so diverse, both in its type and in its origins, it is not surprising that no one theory gives a fully satisfactory explanation. In this section we will consider what determines the level of fixed capital formation.

The accelerator

This suggests that the **level** of investment depends on the **rate of change** in the level of GDP. In other words, an increase in GDP from £100 to £105 billion will lead to a rise in investment, but if GDP stays at this high level no new investment will be undertaken.

A simplified example will clarify the idea. Assume consumers usually buy 20,000 radios a year. These radios are produced on ten machines, each of which produces 2,000 radios a year. Each machine lasts ten years so that the producers replace one machine each year. In this case gross investment is one machine, net investment is zero.

What will happen if GDP rises by 10% and spending on radios also rises by 10%? Consumers will wish to buy 22,000 radios. In order to produce this quantity, producers will need to buy two new machines; one to replace the worn out machine and one to satisfy the extra demand. In this hypothetical example, a 10% rise in GDP has led to a 100% rise in investment in machines. However, if GDP, - and demand for radios - remains constant at the new higher level, then only one new machine is needed in the next year to replace the machine which will have worn out. This means a fall in investment from two to one machine, despite the fact that GDP

Table 12.1: *Gross domestic fixed capital formation*

	Private sector	General government	Public corporations	(£ million, 1987 prices) Total
1980	38,557	6,290	8,491	53,416
1981	35,990	4,632	7,775	48,298
1982	38,892	4,313	7,906	50,915
1983	39,085	5,901	8,490	53,476
1984	43,845	6,605	7,625	58,075
1985	48,043	6,584	5,656	60,283
1986	48,947	6,952	5,394	61,293
1987	55,190	6,792	4,391	66,373
1988	64,023	5,975	4,221	74,219

Note: Due to rounding, totals do not always add up to the sum of the parts.
Source: *Economic Trends*, HMSO, March, 1989.

remains at a high level.

The accelerator principle can be expressed as:

$$\text{Net } I_t = v (Y_{t2} - Y_{t1})$$

where I_t is investment in year t, $Y_{t2} - Y_{t1}$ is the change in income or GDP between one year and the next and v in the equation is the accelerator coefficient, or 'capital-output ratio'. This is the relationship between the amount of capital in the economy and the quantity of goods that this produces. If £6 of capital was needed to produce £1 of goods, then the capital-output ratio would be 6. This means that if GDP rises by £10 million, then £60 million of new investment will be needed to satisfy this rise.

Complications and criticisms

The outline of the accelerator principle so far given would account for large fluctuations in the level of investment, but it is too simplistic. In the first place there may be excess capacity in the economy so that firms can produce extra output without buying any more machines. Secondly, the capital-output ratio will vary over time. One reason for this is that **expectations** vary. Sometimes entrepreneurs will be confident and buy new machines even though they have some spare capacity. At other times they will be cautious and not invest, even though demand for their product is rising.

Finally, firms may be unable to invest even if they want to, because companies making capital goods may be unable to increase output as they are already working at full capacity.

One complication which this account has so far ignored is that there are time lags in the process; firms do not adjust their investment plans immediately. This makes the theory difficult to test

because different lags may give different results. Research does give some support to the theory and the accelerator principle is used to predict the level of investment in many economic models, but it cannot give a full explanation of changes in the level of investment.

The rate of interest

It seems plausible to suggest that the rate of interest will affect the level of investment. If a firm expects an investment to give a return of 10%, but it has to borrow the money at 11%, it will not go ahead. If it could borrow the money at 5% the firm would undertake the investment. Figure 12.12 shows the demand for investment as a typical demand schedule, sloping down to show an increase in the demand for investment as the price (in this case the rate of interest) falls.

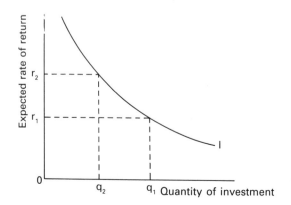

Figure 12.12: *An investment demand schedule*

Unfortunately the common sense implicit in this line of argument is not given much support by the evidence. Almost every investigation shows there is little relationship between the rate of interest and the level of investment. One reason is that the other factors discussed here are more important. Another is that small changes in the rate of interest will not have much effect if the firm believes the investment will be very profitable or that it will pay off very quickly. Hence the evidence suggests that the demand for investment schedule shown in Figure 12.12 is very inelastic.

Profitability

Firms invest in order to make profits. Hence we should expect the level of investment to be linked to the level of profits. Moreover, when profits rise entrepreneurs may become more optimistic and so be more inclined to increase investment. Another reason is that firms making high levels of profit can use some of their profit to finance investment and they also find it easier to borrow money. Research evidence does suggest a link between profits and investment. For example, profitability and the level of investment have both been lower in the UK than in competing nations. However, this link does not take us much further in the job of constructing a full theory of investment, because if we adopt this approach we then need to construct a theory of profits. There is no generally accepted theory of profits, but one influence is the level of incomes; as incomes rise so do profits.

Other influences on investment

New discoveries affect investment. Historically, the invention of the railway and the car led to a huge amount of investment. More recently, the discovery of oil in the North Sea caused some firms to spend large sums of money on new investment. The availability of finance may also affect the decision to invest. If firms find it easy to obtain money from financial institutions they will be more likely to invest. Small businesses often complain that it is difficult to obtain long-term finance, but this is disputed by the banks and by some independent commentators. In any case the availability of finance does not vary much from year to year, yet the level of investment does fluctuate. Hence it appears that while this may influence the total amount of investment it does not explain the fluctuations.

Government policy also affects investment in a number of ways. If entrepreneurs approve government actions they will become more optimistic and invest more. Governments can also influence some of the variables, for example, by making finance available to small firms, or by bringing down the rate of interest. Finally, much investment is undertaken either directly by government - roads are a good example - or indirectly by public corporations, such as the Post Office. In this case commercial considerations, such as profitability, will influence the decision to invest, but government intervention can force nationalised industries to invest more than they would wish. Similarly, government can constrain investment in these public sector industries. Finally, an entrepreneur's decision to invest will depend on the methods used to analyse possible projects. These are discussed in Chapter 12.

Key ideas - the factors influencing investment

1. The accelerator principle suggests that investment is largely determined by changes in the level of national income.
2. High rates of interest may deter investment; low rates encourage it.
3. Expectations, for example about future profitability, will also have an effect.
4. Other factors, such as the availability of finance and government policy, influence the level of investment.
5. There is no completely satisfactory theory of investment.

Conclusion

This chapter began by attempting to explain the Keynesian theory of the determinants of national income. This was approached in several ways. The circular flow of income with various injections and withdrawals provided a simplified way. This was then developed more formally.

Two of the variables were then analysed in more detail - consumption and investment. In both cases a number of explanations were analysed, none of which could give a complete explanation of such complex phenomena.

The Keynesian theory of national income focuses on aggregate demand. As the introduction pointed out, supply siders criticise this approach and instead emphasise aggregate supply, the subject of the next chapter.

Data questions

Treasury model

In the Treasury model, for example, a one per cent increase in manufacturing output results in a 2 per cent increase in investment five quarters later; for private non-manufacturing, the figure is 4.5 per cent. Another important determinant of investment is the cost of capital relative to the return on capital. This depends on the relationship between the price of capital goods and the price of industrial equities, together with the rate of interest and the cost of labour compared with that of capital. In this analysis, we concentrate on the effect of output on investment.

This link could be termed a decelerator as much as an accelerator, since the falls in both investment and output, particularly in manufacturing, have been bigger than the rises, notably between 1979 and 1982. The changes in investment have averaged about 2.5 times the changes in output in manufacturing since 1970, measuring between peaks and troughs in the business cycle. Between 1972 and 1979, the usual time lag was six months. In the case of the two-year decline in manufacturing output from the middle of 1979, the fall in investment began at about the same time, but lasted for four years, until the first quarter of 1983.

Source: *Lloyds Bank Review,* January, 1984.

Question 1

1. (i) Describe how changes in output affect investment.

(ii) Why are there time lags in the process?

2. What factors other than output influence the level of investment?

3. What effect will these changes in the level of investment have on national income?

Year	Real personal disposable income £million	Real consumers' expenditure £million
1966	159 072	143 617
1967	161 455	147 162
1968	164 266	151 271
1969	165 769	152 112
1970	172 246	156 336
1971	174 463	161 208
1972	189 069	171 052
1973	201 034	179 852
1974	199 421	177 233
1975	200 353	176 273
1976	200 029	176 853
1977	195 606	176 016
1978	209 894	185 950
1979	221 673	193 794
1980	224 885	193 806
1981	222 254	193 832
1982	221 709	193 561
1983	227 931	204 318
1984	232 426	207 927
1985	237 802	215 267
1986	244 797	226 839
1987	252 185	238 460

Note: Real personal disposable income revalued by the implied consumers' expenditure deflator (1985 prices).

Source: *Economic Trends,* Annual Supplement, HMSO, 1989.

Question 2

1. Comment on the relationship between disposable income and consumer spending.

2. What factors other than income might explain the level of consumer spending?

3. Critically discuss any of the theories of the consumption function. Use the figures to illustrate your argument.

13 Aggregate Demand and Aggregate Supply

- Until recently Keynesian economists have focused largely on the demand side of the economy. Hence a typical Keynesian policy for unemployment would be to increase aggregate demand for goods in the belief that this would encourage employers to produce more and take on more workers.
- Supply siders argue that this is a mistaken belief. They emphasise supply and they argue that governments should take measures such as cutting taxes in order to give individuals incentives produce more. Thus they take what is essentially a micro-economic approach to macro-economics. The argument between these two lines of thought is fundamental to macro-economic policy.

Aggregate demand and aggregate supply

In micro-economics, prices and the level of output of firms are determined by the interaction of the forces of demand and supply. In macro-economics, the interaction of aggregate demand and aggregate supply determines the level of prices in the economy as a whole and also the level of real national output.

The aggregate demand and supply model (AD/AS for short) presented here has the same basic framework as the large computer models of the economy which are used to predict future economic variables and hence to influence economic policy decisions. The AS/AD model focuses on the short and medium term and assumes a given amount of capital equipment and technical knowledge. Hence it is particularly useful for analysing problems such as inflation, unemployment and the balance of payments, all of which require short and medium-term management of the economy. It is less useful in analysing longer-term problems, such as economic growth.

Aggregate demand

Aggregate demand is the amount of money which people wish to spend in the **domestic** economy. This may not be the same as they actually spend. If aggregate demand exceeds actual national expenditure, then some people will be unsatisfied; they cannot buy the goods they want. If the opposite position applies so that aggregate demand is less than national expenditure, then some firms end up with unsold goods. This unintended rise in stocks counts as part of national expenditure so far as the national income accounts are concerned.

Because aggregate demand is concerned with domestic expenditure, it includes exports but excludes imports. Aggregate demand can be subdivided into various components: consumption, investment, government expenditure and exports minus imports. That is:

$$AD = C+I+G+X-M$$

Since aggregate demand is the sum of all the individual demand curves in the economy, it slopes down to the right, just like the demand curves used in micro-economics, that is because prices would have to fall to encourage people to consume more.

Aggregate supply

The last chapter was largely concerned with the analysis of aggregate demand, and so here we will focus more on the supply side of the economy. The aggregate supply schedule shows the quantity of output which firms wish to supply at each price level. Since the aggregate supply curve is the sum of all the individual supply curves in the economy, it is

Figure 13.1: *A perfectly elastic aggregate supply curve*

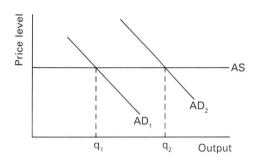

often drawn rising up to the right, just as individual supply curves are conventionally drawn. However, the actual shape of the aggregate supply curve is a matter of considerable disagreement.

The aggregate supply schedule will be perfectly horizontal as shown in Figure 13.1 if the average costs of firms are constant as output expands. If firms increase output by 10% and total costs rise by 10%, so that unit costs remain the same, then this is the shape of the AS curve. This could occur when firms have excess capacity. In this case, an increase in aggregate demand will lead to an increase in output, not prices. Figure 13.2 shows the opposite extreme. Here total output cannot be increased because the physical capacity to produce more does not exist. Whatever price is offered, firms will not produce more goods. This may be the case when the economy is at full employment. An increase in aggregate demand in this case will only lead to a rise in price and not output.

The actual shape of the curve will depend on two factors:

● The nature of the production function. This is the technical relationship between output and the factors of production. The production function will determine the productivity of labour in the short run. This is because the quantity of capital and state of technology are fixed in this period.

● The behaviour of wages as output changes in the short run. If to produce 5% more output, firms are forced to pay 20% more in wages, then the supply curve will slope steeply upwards because firms will only be willing to increase output if they can put up prices to cover their higher costs. On the other hand, if firms can increase output without any rise in average costs, then they may be willing to increase output without putting up prices. In this case, the AS curve will be horizontal. Hence the behaviour of the labour

market is a crucial determinant of the shape of the AS curve.

Figure 13.2: *A perfectly inelastic aggregate supply curve*

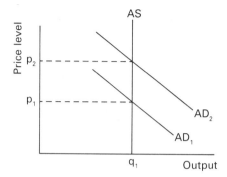

Shifts in the AS curve

If input prices can change in the time period being analysed, then a rise in the price of wages or other inputs will lead to a fall in aggregate supply. This will cause the AS curve to shift to the left, showing that less will be supplied at any given level of prices or that higher prices would be charged at a given level of output. The same result would occur if workers chose more leisure instead of work. According to some economists this would occur if there was a rise in taxes since this would encourage workers to believe that it was no longer worth while to work, or else it would encourage them to work shorter hours.

When these changes are substantial they are called **supply side shocks.** The best example of this is the rise in oil prices in 1973/74 when the price of oil doubled and then doubled again. The result is shown in Figure 13.3. The AS curve moved to the left so that at every level of AD prices were higher and output lower. The reason the curve moved was that firms' costs had risen, so that it was no longer profitable to produce goods at the prevailing price; that is, the supply curves of many firms moved to the left.

The aggregate supply curve sometimes moves to the right, for example, if it becomes more acceptable for women to work or there is a rise in the population of working age. A rise in the stock of capital has the same effect. In both cases the AS curve moves to the right causing output to rise and prices to fall. Unfortunately changes such as these tend to be long-term and not easy for the government to influence directly, though supply siders believe that lower taxes will encourage more people to choose work and also encourage entrepreneurs to invest. The aggregate supply curve also moved to the right as a result of the fall in raw material prices in the early 1980s.

Figure 13.3: A supply side shock

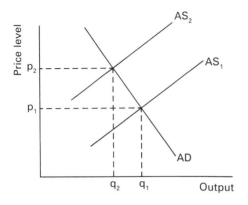

Key ideas

1. **The aggregate demand curve shows the amount of money which people wish to spend in the domestic economy. It is usually expressed in the formula:**

$$AD = C+I+G+X-M$$

2. **The aggregate supply curve shows the quantity of goods which firms wish to supply at each price level.**
3. **The shape of the aggregate supply curve depends on the production function and on the behaviour of wages as output changes.**
4. **The aggregate supply curve will shift to the right when the supply of labour increases or there is a cut in raw material prices. It will move to the left if input prices rise.**

The Keynesian approach

There are two Keynesian approaches to the shape of the AS curve. The first is shown in Figure 13.4. This was developed by followers of Keynes in order to illustrate his ideas. When the AS curve is this shape, the AD curve is the major determinant of economic events. The government can increase aggregate demand and the result will be a rise in output without any rise in prices until the full employment level of output is reached at yf. Then any increase in aggregate demand will lead to a rise in prices as shown by AD_3.

Figure 13.4: The Keynesian long-run aggregate supply curve (version 1)

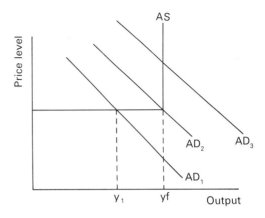

Two assumptions need to be satisfied for the AS curve to be this shape. The first is that the level of money wages must not rise as output rises. This is unlikely to be true; in some cases firms will have to pay overtime rates in order to produce more goods. The second assumption is that firms' marginal product of labour is constant until the full employment level of output is reached. The law of diminishing returns would suggest that this assumption is also untrue since, if more labour is employed, its marginal product will fall if the quantity of capital is held constant as it is in the short run. Arguments such as these led Keynesian economists to return to the AS curve which is closer to the original Keynesian formulation. This is shown in Figure 13.5.

This version accepts that the marginal product of labour falls as the level of employment rises and that the demand for labour by firms will fall as real wages rise. However, Keynes argued that although workers would be unwilling to work for a lower **money** wage, they would be willing to work for a lower real wage than that which currently exists. Thus if money wages do not change when prices rise, some unemployed people will be willing to take jobs and firms will be able to take on more workers at existing wage rates. The same argument applies if money wages rise, but prices rise faster so that the real wage falls - firms will be able to recruit more workers.

This line of argument is shown in Figure 13.5. If the government increases its spending so that aggregate demand rises from AD_1 to AD_2 real output will rise from y_1 to y_2, but there is also a small rise in prices. If there is a further rise in aggregate demand

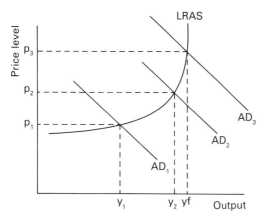

Figure 13.5: The Keynesian long-run aggregate supply curve (version 2)

to AD_3, the rise in output is less and the rise in prices is greater. Any attempt to increase aggregate demand beyond the full employment lefel yf will just lead to a rise in prices with no increase in output.

The fundamental belief behind this argument is that some firms can increase output without putting up wages and hence prices; that there are unemployed people who are willing to work at existing or lower wage rates. If this belief is true, then the government can increase its spending in order to push up aggregate demand and this will lead to rises in output and employment. Note, however, that as the economy approaches full employment any given rise in output is accompanied by a proportionally larger rise in prices. In other words, there is a trade-off between output and employment, and the terms of this trade-off worsen as full employment is reached. When full employment is reached, any increase in aggregate demand will lead to a rise in prices without any compensating increase in output.

Behind this discussion lies a key idea. Keynesians argue that markets do not necessarily clear to give full employment. In particular they believe that labour markets are imperfect, so that workers do not rush into and out of the labour market every time there is a change in real wages. Moreover, they argue that in areas of high unemployment, employers can take on more workers at existing wages and so increase output without putting up prices. Therefore there is still room for government to increase aggregate demand in order to achieve full employment.

Keynesian policies

These are discussed extensively in the chapter on unemployment and need only be outlined here. In essence Keynesian economists suggest that markets do not always solve the problem of allocating resources in a satisfactory way, and that this is particularly true of the labour market. Hence when there is unemployment, the government should intervene to increase national output and employment by increasing aggregate demand. The most convenient way to do this for the government to increase its own spending.

The supply side approach

At the heart of the supply side approach is the belief that individuals and firms respond to incentives. Lower taxes will stimulate people to work longer and harder, and to be more innovative. Similarly, higher real wages will cause more people to want to work - but it will also cause firms to reduce demand for labour. Because of these incentives, the demand for labour will equal the supply, and the labour market will clear.

Supply siders dismiss the Keynesian arguments and argue that the AS curve is unstable because workers will not accept a cut in their real wages when prices rise. If they cannot push up real wages they will choose to leave the labour market. They claim that the Keynesian arguments only apply in the short run because markets clear very quickly, and that the short run is so short it can be disregarded.

Figure 13.6

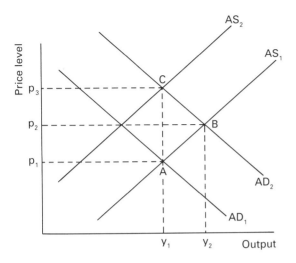

Figure 13.7: *Long-run aggregate supply curve*

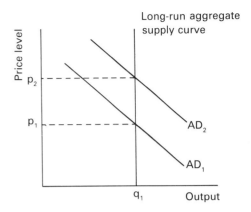

The supply side approach is shown in Figure 13.6. This assumes that the supply of labour is positively related to the level of real wages. If prices rise workers will force up money wages until the original level of real wages is restored. Since there is no change in the level of real wages, there will be no change in the demand or the supply of labour. Original equilibrium is at A where AD_1 meets AS_1, the price level is p_1 and output y_1. If the government then increases aggregate demand to AD_2, the short run effect will be a move along the AS_1 curve to B giving a rise in prices to p_2 and a rise in output to y_2.

However, supply siders believe this is only temporary. The rise in prices means that real wages have fallen. Workers do not accept this cut in real wages and force up money wages to their equilibrium level. This rise in real wages cuts firms' demand for labour so that the AS curve shifts to the left leading to a final equilibrium at C, where output is at the original level y_1, but prices are higher at p_3. The government's attempt to stimulate the economy has only resulted in higher prices; output is unchanged in the long run.

(Note that in the Figure the vertical distance between AS_1 and AS_2 is the rise in the money wage rate. This equals the rise in prices $p_3 - p_1$ showing that the real wage rate is unchanged.)

If this supply side argument is correct it means that the long-run aggregate supply curve is vertical - AC in the Figure 13.6. Figure 13.7 reproduces this vertical long-run AS curve and shows that the implication of this shape is that demand management policies have no part to play in the management of the economy. Any attempt to increase aggregate demand only results in a rise in price; output is unchanged. This is because output will always be at the full employment level, if labour markets are allowed to clear. In this view the level of real national output depends not on aggregate demand, but on supply side factors such as changes in technology, the size of the capital stock and the supply and productivity of labour.

A key point in this approach is 'How long is the long run?'. If it is several years, for example, because wages are slow to respond to changing circumstances or because workers do not respond quickly to changes in real wages, then the move from A to B in Figure 13.6 may lead to a real rise in output which continues for some time. However, if adjustment is swift then this rise may be over before people realise that it has even happened. Supply siders tend to believe that the adjustment is quick because of 'rational expectations'.

Rational expectations

The emphasis on rational explanations in economics rests on two assumptions:
- People are well informed and use all available information so they are as knowledgeable as the government. This means the government cannot fool the people; workers realise that when prices rise their real wage falls and so modify their behaviour, for example, by demanding higher wages or by leaving the labour market.
- That the labour market is very flexible so that demand and supply are in equilibrium in all markets. This means markets clear at all times.

If these assumptions are true, then workers will anticipate the effects of government policy and the labour market will adjust so quickly that any attempt to increase aggregate demand will lead to an almost immediate rise in wages and spending. There will be a move directly up the long-run supply curve without any temporary increase in output. However, these underlying assumptions have been criticised. Many people have little knowledge of economic facts and relationships so they are unable to predict the results of government action.

The second assumption is also criticised on the grounds that the labour market is slow to react. Once people are in a job they often find it difficult to move to another and are reluctant to leave the labour market even if their wages fall behind the rise in prices. Moreover, shortages of particular skills continue for long periods. For several decades people have said that there is a shortage of physicists in general and of physics teachers in particular, yet the shortage persists. If the labour market adjusted quickly, then wages for physicists would rise quickly, thousands would train to be physicists, and the shortage would disappear. Hence it is argued that the labour market is very slow to adjust. If these criticisms are accepted, then the AS curve is not vertical and there is a place for demand management in running the economy.

Key ideas - summary of the supply side approach

1. **Markets are generally the best way to allocate resources and government intervention should be undertaken only in special circumstances.**
2. **The market is the best way to allocate resources in the labour market. Demand and supply of labour adjust quickly to allocate resources. One reason for this is that people have rational expectations.**
3. **The long-run AS curve is vertical and, because the labour market clears rapidly, the short-run AS curve hardly exists.**
4. **Attempts to increase output and employment by raising aggregate demand will only lead to rises in price; output will be unchanged since the labour market will be at full employment if markets are left to clear.**

Supply side policies

According to this group of economists, real national output will only be increased when the AS curve moves to the right. Hence policies should be adopted which will encourage such shifts. These policies include tax cuts which will encourage people to enter the labour market. Tax cuts will also provide an incentive for entrepreneurs to innovate and invest in new machinery. Supply siders also favour measures to weaken trade union power, since unions distort the labour market and push up wages. Cuts in some social security benefits will also help to keep down wages, since they can receive similar sums for social security.

Other measures favoured by this group of economists are those which would reduce the extent of government intervention in the economy, such as the privatisation of publicly-owned industries. They also advocate measures in industgry and education which would encourage a spirit of enterprise and an increase in investment.

Conclusion

Economists' approach to macro-economics often reflects their personal value systems rather than the application of accepted 'proofs'. One reason for this is that the economy is not a laboratory in which one variable can be examined whilst all others are held constant. Hence it is extremely difficult to judge the claims of competing theories. Moreover, an entire economy is too complex for any theory to explain in full and evidence can always be found to support or to criticise a theory.

In essence, Keynesian economists believe there is a greater place for government intervention than do supply siders. They believe that, left to itself, the economy will often be in equilibrium at less than full employment. Government intervention, for example by increasing aggregate demand, can raise the equilibrium level of output and employment, though this may lead to a rise in prices.

This approach is criticised by neo-classical supply siders who argue that the labour market adjusts quickly. If this is so, any attempt by the government to increase aggregate demand will merely lead to a rise in prices with no effect on output. Instead the government should focus its efforts on improving the supply side of the economy.

This chapter has so far given the impression that these two schools of thought are completely opposed. There is some truth in this impression, but in recent years some Keynesian economists, while maintaining their belief in aggregate demand as a policy variable, have given increasing support to measures which would improve the supply side of the economy. For example, they advocate an extension of education and training to make workers more efficient.

The end of government?

I start my call to rebellion from the observed tendency for government to dispose of a growing slice of the community's resources. Precise figuring to several decimal places is hardly necessary. In broad orders of magnitude the total governmental sector has grown in most Western democracies since the war from around 25-35 per cent to nearer 45-55 per cent of national income, and commonly employs between a quarter and a third of the labour force. (These measures do not include the ever-increasing 'compliance costs' which government regulation throws on private individuals, families, companies and trade associations.)

The obverse is seen in the contraction of the market sector which provides the goods and services consumers are prepared to pay for and so feeds, clothes and shelters the quarter or third of non-producing consumers in what I would prefer to call the 'parasitic' rather than the 'public' sector. (A shrewd wit has said the private sector is the part of the economy controlled by government and the public sector is the part controlled by nobody!)

Source: Harris, R. *The End of Government?* Institute of Economic Affairs, 1980.

Question 1

1. Outline the economic theory which lies behind the 'call to rebellion'.

2. What criticisms would Keynesian economists make of this argument?

14 Taxation and Public Spending

Governments - and therefore government spending and taxes - are inevitable. However, there is considerable argument between economists about the most desirable level of taxation and government spending:

● Supply siders believe that the role of government should be reduced. They also argue that high levels of taxation discourage work and initiative.

● The opposite point of view is often Keynesian. These economists argue that government spending is needed to correct market failure, that high levels of taxation usually do not discourage effort, and that government spending and taxation should be used to redistribute resources from rich to poor.

Fiscal policy is the use of taxation and government spending to influence the level and composition of output, and we will consider each of these in turn before examining how the above perspectives view fiscal policy.

Taxation

What is a good tax?

One approach to the study of taxation is to consider the characteristics of a good tax. A cynical approach would be to suggest that a good tax is one paid by someone else; this is why total abstainers favour huge taxes on alcohol, non-smokers press for higher taxes on tobacco and the poor shed no tears about taxes on the rich. However, there are certain characteristics to be found in a 'good' tax and many of these were listed by Adam Smith who suggested four **canons** of taxation:

● The amount of tax should be linked to people's ability to pay.
● The payment of taxes should be clear and certain, both to the taxpayer and the tax collector (so that everyone knows how much is due).
● The way in which taxes are collected should be convenient to the taxpayer.
● The cost of collecting a tax should be small in relation to the amount of money collected.

These canons still apply today. A tax on beards would be a poor tax; it would not be linked to ability to pay and it would be difficult to calculate how much was due. If the beard grew would more tax be payable? And would someone who had forgotten to shave be liable for tax?

However, these original canons need to be augmented by others which are applicable to a modern society:

● The tax collector should be able to assess fairly accurately how much money will be received from the tax.
● Taxes should promote economic efficiency, or at least not significantly worsen the efficient allocation of resources. Thus a tax on pollution may improve the allocation of resources because it would reduce the production of goods with negative externalities (that is those goods that adversely affect people not directly involved in their production or consumption).
● Taxes should increase equity (fairness); though of course it is possible to argue about precisely what is meant by 'equity'.
● Taxes should promote desirable economic goals such as full employment.

Unfortunately no tax has yet been discovered that fulfils all these criteria. Consequently the tax authorities have to consider the **relative** advantages and disadvantages of particular taxes.

Direct or indirect taxes?

A traditional way to classify taxes depends on whether they are paid directly, such as income tax or corporation tax, or indirectly like VAT. Supply siders, who dislike income tax, argue that direct taxes such as this are less desirable than indirect taxes and that the government should shift the burden of taxation away from direct towards indirect taxes. They claim that these have fewer disincentive effects and that to some extent individuals can largely avoid paying such taxes if they choose not to buy highly taxed goods. It was this kind of argument which led the 1979 Conservative government to cut income tax and to raise VAT from 8% to 15% instead. Economists who would like a more equal society tend to see greater merit in direct taxes because they usually take more from the rich than the poor. These arguments are part of the debate about the progressiveness of a tax system.

Progressive, proportional or regressive taxes?

An alternative way of considering taxes is to focus exclusively on their equity aspects - how they affect rich and poor.

There are three possible relationships between taxes and income. Taxes are progressive if they take a larger share of income as incomes rise, proportional if the share of taxes remains constant as incomes rise, and regressive if they take a larger share from those with a low income.

Figure 14.1: Taxes and income

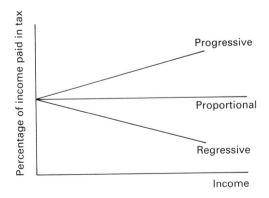

An example will clarify the difference. If A has an income of £10,000 a year and pays £2,000 tax (=20%), whilst B with an income of £5,000 pays £1,500 tax (=30%), the tax is regressive since the tax is taking a larger share of the poor person's income than it does of the rich person's income. If B paid only £1,000 (=20%), the tax would be proportional. If B paid only £500 (=10%), the tax would be progressive. The best example of a progressive tax is income tax because those with low incomes pay little or no tax and those with high incomes pay at a higher rate. Indirect taxes are often - but not always - regressive. Thus taxes on cigarettes take up a larger share of the income of poor people than they do of the better off.

Poll tax/community charge

The community charge illustrates many of the points made above. It also shows how the choice of words can be used to influence the debate. The government prefers to call this tax a 'community charge' because this phrase implies that people are paying for local services. Opponents refer to it as a 'poll tax' because this is the traditional term for such a tax; also it implies that people are being taxed for voting. The essence of the tax is that everybody in an area pays the same amount of money. Hence the tax is very regressive, though this is mitigated to some extent because those on social security pay a smaller amount. Another disadvantage is that it is expensive to collect because it involves listing all the adults in an area, a time consuming and difficult task. Supporters of the tax claim it will make people realise the costs of local services, so that public opinion will force local councils to cut costs.

Taxes and equity

Two principles can be considered when discussing equity and taxation. The first is **horizontal** equity - that people in similar circumstances should be treated similarly. This sounds fair; but if two people are in an aeroplane about to crash and there is only one parachute, what is the equitable solution? Horizontal equity may suggest that neither should have the parachute. This is clearly stupid. So far as taxation is concerned, horizontal equity breaks down when people can reduce their tax burden, either by obtaining specialist advice or by not notifying the tax authorities. **Vertical** equity exists when people in different circumstances are treated unequally. Most people would suggest that those on higher incomes should pay more tax, but there would be considerable disagreement about how much extra tax they should pay.

Tax incidence

Sometimes people can shift the burden of a tax on to others. 'Tax incidence' refers to the eventual distribution of the burden of taxation. Thus the tax on tobacco is paid to the tax authorities by the trader who draws the tobacco from a bonded warehouse. However, the trader will try to pass the burden of the tax on to the customer by putting up the price of cigarettes. Thus the **formal** incidence of the tax falls on those who have the legal liability to pay, but the **effective** liability falls on those who are less well-off as a result of the tax. Traders who say that they have to charge VAT are talking nonsense; they have to pay VAT, but in charging the customer they are seeking to shift the burden.

The effect of the imposition of a tax on price and quantity was discussed in Chapter 3. This showed that a tax on a good raised the price of the good and cut the quantity. The extent of the changes depended on the price elasticity of demand. When demand is inelastic, the price paid by consumers will rise to cover most of the tax, so that producers escape relatively lightly.

Governments usually impose taxes on goods where demand is inelastic. If they put taxes on goods with elastic demand, not only would firms have to bear the brunt of the tax, but the price rise would cause a relatively large fall in the quantity of goods bought, and the result would often be bankruptcy.

Poverty and unemployment traps

A poverty trap exists when a low paid worker gains little or nothing from an increase in earnings because this causes benefits to be lost and tax to be paid. The unemployment trap is similar. It exists when jobless people obtain work and find themselves no better off than when they are unemployed because they may loose benefits, have to pay income tax and National Insurance, and have job-related expenses such as travel to work.

In both traps the argument is that the tax and social security system combine to provide substantial disincentive effects. In some cases people are, in effect, paying marginal tax rates of up to and over 100%. In many other cases the rate is less than this, but still very high. One solution is to cut tax rates for the low paid, but this is difficult because the government loses large amounts of revenue whilst the effect on any one individual is small. A cut of 1p in the pound in the rate of income tax costs the government over £1,000 million, but would provide little incentive for people to change their way of life. An alternative approach is to cut welfare benefits, but this is opposed on welfare grounds.

Key ideas

1. 'Good' taxes have certain qualities; for example, they are cheap to collect.
2. Taxes can be classed as progressive, proportional or regressive; direct or indirect.
3. Suppliers can sometimes change the incidence of taxation by passing the burden on to other people.
4. The tax system sometimes interacts with the social security system to produce poverty and unemployment traps.

Government spending

Everyone benefits from government spending, but some benefit more than others. As Table 14.1 shows, by far the largest item of public expenditure in the UK is social security, followed by defence and health and personal social services. The relative importance of these items changes over time. For example, when unemployment rises so will spending on social security. An ageing population will have the same effect whilst a rise in the birth rate will be followed several years later by more spending on education.

Table 14.1: *Public money 1988-90*

Pence in every £1[1]

Receipts		Expenditure	
Income tax	23	DHSS: social security	27
National Insurance contributions	17	DHSS: health and personal social services	11
Value added tax	14	Defence	11
Local authority rates	10	Education and science	10
Road fuel, alcohol and tobacco duties	10	Scotland, Wales and Northern Ireland	9
Corporation tax[2]	9	Other departments	18
Capital taxes	3	Interest payments	10
Interest, dividends	3	Other	5
North Sea taxation	2		
Other	9		
Total	100		100

[1] Rounded to the nearest penny.
[2] Excluding North Sea.

Source: *The Budget in Britain,* HMSO, 1988.

Despite changes in the relative importance of particular items, it is clear that the long-term trend is for public expenditure to rise over time. There are various explanations for this. Economists interested in micro-economics explain the growth by referring to government action to reduce market failure and so provide goods, such as defence, which become more expensive over the years because the technology grows more sophisticated. Moreover, many public services have a high income elasticity of demand, so that as incomes rise over time people want better educational and health services. Structural factors, such as a rise in the number of old people, also lead to more spending.

At the macro level, Keynesian explanations are also used to explain the growth in public spending because this theory suggests that the government should not attempt to balance the budget, but vary its spending and taxation levels according to the state of the economy. And once government spending has been increased it is difficult to bring it down to its former level. Thus the Conservative government elected in 1979 on a promise to cut public spending found itself unable to do this.

Economists interested in the economics of public choice also suggest that politicians obtain popularity by increased spending and that civil service bureaucrats aim to enlarge the size of their individual department. The result is increased government spending. Supply siders in particular would support this line of argument.

The interaction of government spending and taxation

So far this chapter has considered taxation and public spending separately, but their interaction has a number of important effects.

Effect on the level of national income

Keynesian economists suggest that cuts in taxation and increases in public spending lead to rises in national income and falls in unemployment, assuming there are sufficient unemployed people to make this possible. As was seen in the last two chapters, this line of argument was criticised by supply side economists.

Government spending and taxation can act as **automatic stabilisers** in the economy. Thus when the economy starts to decline government receipts from taxation fall (since fewer people will be paying income tax and government income from VAT may also decline) whilst public spending on unemployment and social security rises. These increases in injections and cuts in withdrawals will both help boost the economy. On the other hand, when the economy is booming, public spending on

unemployment falls and government tax receipts rise, thus dampening down the expansion.

Effect on the National Debt

The National Debt is mis-named; in reality it is the **government's** debt. Most of the debt is owed by the government to British citizens who own National Savings Certificates, government bonds and so on. Only a tiny proportion is owed to foreigners. The National Debt increases whenever the government spends more than it receives in taxes, which has been the position in most years. In any one year the difference between what the government spends and what it receives is called the Public Sector Borrowing Requirement (PSBR). When the government receives more in taxes than it spends, this is called the Public Sector Debt Repayment (PSDR).

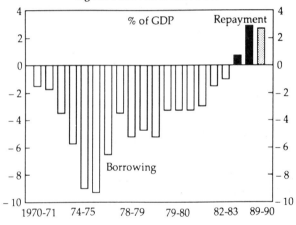

Figure 14.2: *PSBR and PSDR*

Source: *The Budget in Brief*, The Treasury, HMSO, March 14, 1989.

The National Debt currently amounts to over £130,000 million - a huge sum. Is this a problem? One effect is that the interest on this money forces up taxes. As Table 14.1 shows, 10% of government spending is in the form of interest payments and the government has to raise the money to pay this interest. If instead of increasing taxes the government increases the quantity of money, this may push up inflation. Thus the National Debt may have some undesirable consequences, but it does not mean that the country is in hock to foreigners, nor that future generations will be impoverished - their standard of living will depend on the quantity of goods and services which the country then produces.

An increase in the National Debt does have one undesirable effect. The government has to borrow large sums of money, and this pushes up the rate of interest causing difficulties to borrowers. However, there are many other factors which influence interest rates and increases in the National Debt probably have only a small effect.

Effect on Equity

Government spending and taxation interact to redistribute money from some people to others, as Table 14.2 shows. This shows how the people who are a fifth from the bottom and the top of the income

Table 14.2: Redistribution of income through taxes and benefits, all households, 1986

United Kingdom

	Quintile groups of households ranked by original income	
	Bottom fifth	Top fifth
Average per household (£ per year)		
Total original income	130	24,790
+ Benefits in cash		
Contributory	1,750	270
Non-contributory	1,620	410
Gross income	3,500	25,470
- Income tax and NIC	-10	5,650
Disposable income	3,510	19,820
- Indirect taxes	880	4,250
+ Benefits in kind		
Education	370	850
National Health Service	910	720
Travel subsidies	50	100
Housing subsidy	130	20
Welfare foods	50	20
Final income	4,130	17,260
Average per household (numbers)		
Adults	1.4	2.6
Children	0.4	0.7
Economically active people	-	2.2
Retired people	0.8	0.1

Source: *Social Trends*, HMSO, 1989.

range are affected. Both groups benefit from cash payments, such as child benefit, but the poorer group gain much more from social security. They also lose less because of income taxes and National Insurance payments and from indirect taxes, such as VAT. The poor also gain from 'benefits in kind', such as education and health care, but the difference is very small. Indeed, for some benefits

such as education, the better-off gain more than the poor. This is because the children of the better-off are more likely to stay on at school beyond the age of 16 and then go on into higher education. As these are the most expensive parts of the education system they receive most benefit.

Key ideas

1. Government spending has tended to rise over time, partly because many government services have a high income elasticity of demand. Also politicians may favour increased spending in order to gain popularity.
2. Taxes and public spending act as stabilisers in the economy.
3. The National Debt is really the government's debt. It may have some undesirable consequences, but it does not impoverish future generations.

The supply side perspective

The argument about fiscal policy is often just a special case of the general disagreement among economists about the role of markets. Supply side economists tend to suggest that markets are the most efficient way to allocate resources and therefore the role of government should be limited. They argue that government activity impedes the working of the market and so reduces choice and efficiency. For example, if the state provides goods that would not be provided by the market, this means fewer resources are available to produce those goods that people would actually choose to buy. Supply siders argue that the state should provide public goods, such as defence, but that its activities in other areas should be severely restricted. One reason for this is the 'crowding out' argument. This asserts that the private sector is the source of wealth creation and that public sector activities crowd out these wealth-creating activities by employing resources in relatively unproductive activities.

Government failure

A variation on the above line of argument is concerned with government failure. Even if markets fail to achieve the most efficient allocation of resources, there is no guarantee that government action would improve matters. One reason why government activities are inefficient is that these are so broad that the government simply does not have the knowledge needed to achieve smooth co-ordination. Hence one branch of government does not know what the other is doing. Moreover, to achieve efficient government intervention, the government needs detailed information on the social costs and benefits of its activities and this is often unavailable. For example, if the government were to extend the health service, what precisely would be the costs and benefits to society? And if a local authority builds a sports centre, does this represent an efficient allocation of resources?

Bureaucratic self-interest is another reason for government failure. In the absence of markets there is no reason to suppose that the interests of the providers - in this case civil servants - will accurately represent the wishes of those they are supposed to serve. This may result in X-inefficiency. In a market system the entrepreneur benefits from increased profits if the business is run efficiently; but no such incentive operates in the public sector. Instead, bureaucratic self-interest may lead to the growth of the bureaucracy rather than the service of the citizen. One reason for this is that status and pay may depend on the size of the department that they manage. Thus it is claimed that whilst self-interest in the market leads to greater efficiency, in the public sector it can lead to a lower level of allocative efficiency.

A final reason for government failure is that decisions are often made as a result of political bargaining between pressure groups so the final decision represents the strength of the group rather than the merits of the argument. Hence people buying houses can claim tax relief on the interest they pay on their mortgage. It is widely agreed among economists that this leads to a mis-allocation of resources and also subsidises a better off section of the community - those who can afford to buy their own house. Yet the political strength of this group is such that no government can abolish this privilege.

Taxation and incentives

The supply side argument suggests that high tax rates discourage initiative and cause people to work less. Hence the Conservative government elected in 1979 cut the top rate of income tax to 40%. The argument suggests that some people will have a choice between working and not working, or between working more or less hours; in other words they will have a choice between work and leisure. If the marginal rate of income tax is raised, then it is argued that some people will say 'It's no longer worthwhile working', and choose leisure instead. A cut in tax rates will have the opposite effect and encourage people to work harder. Note that this effect depends on the **marginal** rate of tax - the proportion of extra income that goes in tax. Supply siders assert that governments should therefore make great efforts to cut marginal tax rates.

Other economists dispute this and assert that in addition to this substitution effect there is an income effect that is more important. They suggest that a rise in tax rates will leave some people worse off and these may actually work harder in order to maintain the real value of their income.

In other words, they need a certain income to maintain their standard of living and if taxes are increased they will be forced to work harder in order to pay the bills. Moreover, many people have little choice; whatever the tax rate their employers will dictate the hours of work. Empirical evidence seems to support this line of argument, though it is a very difficult area to investigate. The classic British survey is by C.V. Brown (1983) who concludes:

'There are no studies of labour supply that are not open to serious objection on at least one serious ground. Therefore the most intellectually defensible position . . . is that we can say very little about labour supply elasticity.'

Brown goes on to suggest that for men changes in tax rates have little or no effect, though the effect may be stronger for women.

The Laffer curve

A similar analysis has been developed by an American economist, Professor A. Laffer. He asserts that cuts in the **rate** of taxation lead to an increase in government **receipts** from taxation. This is shown in Figure 14.3. At very low rates of tax, government receipts will be very low. This will also be true at high rates; at a tax rate of 100% people cease to work and tax receipts will be zero. Below this level, high rates will stimulate tax evasion and discourage work so reducing government income from tax. Tax receipts will be maximised at A, which Laffer suggests is much lower than most current tax rates. Hence cuts in rates will lead to a rise in receipts. Many economists dispute this, though there is some agreement that extremely high rates (for example, over 90%) will be counter-productive.

Figure 14.3: *The Laffer curve*

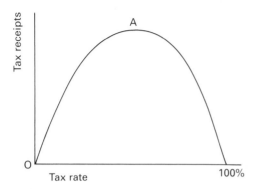

Control of the money supply

'Supply siders' is a term which covers a wide group of economists and some of these, known as monetarists, pay particular attention to controlling the money supply in order to control inflation. This is considered in more detail in Chapters 15 and 17, but one aspect of this line of thought is that high levels of government spending will lead to a high Public Sector Borrowing Requirement. In turn this causes the government to issue more securities, such as Treasury Bills (which are a kind of short-term government IOU) and which will be used by the banking system to expand the money supply, thus causing inflation.

Key ideas - summary of the supply side argument

1. Markets are the best way to allocate resources; government spending and high taxes limit the work of markets and are therefore to be deplored.
2. Governments fail in their attempts to improve markets because bureaucrats follow their own self-interest rather than that of the citizen. Also there are no automatic incentives in a government-run system as there are in markets.
3. Cuts in government spending and taxes give people incentives to work harder and lower tax rates increase government receipts from tax.

4. High levels of government spending tend to cause increases in the money supply and the rate of inflation. They also crowd out resources which could be used by the private sector.

Supply side policies

Supply side policies seek to reduce the size of government. One way to do this is to privatise publicly-owned industries. This reduces the size of government, increases the private sector and also raises government income so that taxes can be reduced. Supply siders also suggest privatising activities such as the cleaning of hospitals and government offices. Similarly, they suggest that social security spending often leads to a 'dependency culture' whereby people lose initiative and become over-dependent on the state. Hence social security spending should be cut, or at least targeted more closely at the really poor. This may also reduce unemployment (as explained in Chapter 16) by encouraging those who have been living on public benefits to go out to work.

Incentives need to be increased, hence tax rates should be cut, especially for those with high incomes because these are the people with initiative whose efforts will invigorate the entire economy.

The case for government intervention

Essentially the case for government intervention derives from the failure of markets to allocate resources in a satisfactory manner. This was discussed in some detail in Chapter 2. Markets are not very good at providing public goods, such as defence, nor allowing for externalities, such as pollution, where the social cost to the society as a whole may be different from the private cost to the producer. Hence government needs to intervene to correct these failures. Keynesian economists also argue that the labour market can be in equilibrium at a high level of unemployment and that governments should make active use of fiscal policy to reduce the level of unemployment. They suggest that government spending should be increased, and possibly taxes cut, in order to obtain a desirable level of aggregate demand and employment. In order to do this the government may have to borrow money. This may have some undesirable

Table 14.3: *Tax burdens as percentage of GDP, 1986*

	Total*	Personal*	Corporate*	Goods and Services	Other
France	44.2	10.9	14.4	13.0	5.9
UK	39.0	14.1	7.6	12.1	5.2
Germany	37.5	16.7	9.4	9.5	1.9
Italy	36.2	11.7	12.1	8.9	3.5
USA	28.9	13.5	7.0	5.1	3.3
Japan	28.8	10.3	10.4	3.8	4.3

*Including income and capital gains taxes and social security contributions.
Source: *OECD Revenue Statistics*, HMSO, 1965-87, tables 3, 10, 12, 16, 18.

consequences, such as pushing up interest rates, but these are outweighed by the benefits. This is a fundamental difference between Keynesian and supply side economists and is discussed in detail in Chapters 12, 13 and 16. Moreover, the interventionists would attack the assumption behind the supply side approach that taxes are too high in the UK. They point out that UK tax rates are typical of those in advanced industrial countries as Table 14.3 shows. Therefore the sometimes unsatisfactory performance of the economy cannot be blamed on high tax rates.

Merit goods

Merit goods are those which society believes are intrinsically desirable. When this is the case markets would provide too few of these goods because the benefits to society are greater than those accruing to the individual who might buy such goods on the open market. Hence if the provision of swimming pools were left to the market, entry would be very expensive and there would be far fewer pools. Society, through the actions of local councils, has decided that swimming is a desirable activity and, consequently, provides pools even though they usually run at a loss. Sports centres and playing fields are other examples. Left to market forces they would be comparatively rare.

Education and housing are other examples of merit goods. People sometimes talk about the right to education and health care. Whilst many economists would be cautious about using terms such as 'right', a statement such as this does represent a consensus among many people in society that access to education and health should not be dependent on the ability to pay the market price of such services. Hence the state must provide, or at least finance, such services and provide a greater quantity than would market forces.

Individualism

The supply side/market forces argument rests on the assumption that individuals know what is best for themselves and are competent to make utility maximising choices. Interventionists accept that in many cases, perhaps most, this assumption is valid; but they believe that in some cases it is not. Left to themselves, some people would not insure their health, or provide for their old age. So society steps in and forces people in work to contribute so that old age pensions are provided to all and that social security benefits are available to those in need. A strict individualistic approach would suggest this reduces the freedom of the individual to choose whether to insure against these possibilities. Hence some supply siders would abolish state provision in these areas, leaving it to the market. Interventionists believe that state intervention is needed to prevent or reduce poverty. Therefore spending on social security should be a major part of the state's economic responsibility.

Equity

Values influence the way people approach economic policies. Economists who believe in greater equality contend that without state intervention, market forces would lead to a society with great differences between rich and poor. Those who start life with substantial assets will find it relatively easy to increase them. Similarly, people with scarce skills that are valued in the labour market will also grow rich. On the other hand those with few such assets, or who have poor health, suffer accidents, or have to care for children or the old, will find that the market gives few rewards and that the result is poverty. Hence they suggest that state intervention is necessary, not only to help the poor, but also to reduce the gap between rich and poor because they believe that a society without great differences of wealth and income is desirable.

Key ideas - summary of the interventionist approach

1. Markets fail so government spending is needed to correct these failures.
2. The level of government spending and taxes should be adjusted so that the level of aggregate demand is sufficient to reduce the level of unemployment.
3. Merit goods, such as education, health and recreational facilities, would only be provided in small quantities by the market; government spending is needed to provide a desirable supply of these services.
4. Government spending is needed to alleviate poverty. Fiscal policy should be used to reduce inequalities in society.

Interventionist policies

At the heart of the interventionist approach is the belief that positive government action is needed to prevent or mitigate the undesirable consequences of unregulated market forces. The work of Keynes has had a profound effect on many economists and suggests that government spending and taxation should be varied in order to maintain an appropriate level of aggregate demand. ('Appropriate' in this context means a level which would reduce unemployment without generating much inflation.)

Moreover, government should spend money on social services in order to improve the lives of the citizens. One problem is that although this is generally agreed, it is open to argument exactly how much should be spent on these services and how to provide the money in ways which would be most efficient.

Similarly, there is agreement among this group of economists that the fiscal system should be used to create a more equal society. This means that government spending should focus on the needs of the poor and that the taxation system should be progressive. However, there is some disagreement about how progressive the system should be. Some economists favour a wealth tax which exists in many other countries and which compels rich people (for example, those with assets over £250,000) to pay a special tax on their assets. Not all this group of economists would agree with this suggestion, but most would agree that the better off should pay proportionately more tax than the poor. This suggestion, like so many in economics, derives from a value system which dislikes extremes of poverty and wealth in a society and seeks to use the fiscal system to reduce these differences.

Conclusion

Over the years government spending has grown and, though tax receipts have also risen, in most years the government has had to borrow to make up the difference. These trends have led supply siders to argue that government spending and taxes should be reduced whenever possible in order to stimulate the economy. Interventionists respond by saying that markets often fail and that government spending is needed to correct these failures and to promote a more equal and caring society.

Data questions

- Lower public spending, tax cuts, removal of rigidities in the labour market and elimination of administrative and legislative disincentives to business growth represent the only viable policy for medium and long-term economic growth and job-creation.
- Increased public spending would weaken business confidence at home and confidence in financial markets abroad; it is the primary cause of employment levels lower than the economy would otherwise generate.
- Capital spending on roads or infrastructure renewal, although desirable, is among the least effective means of increasing the number of permanent jobs.
- Wages Councils should be abolished because they stifle job prospects for many young and part-time workers.
- Employment protection laws deter some businesses from taking on staff. Their impact should be reduced, especially for smaller firms. Qualifying periods for unfair dismissal compensation should be lengthened to reduce disincentives to taking on extra workers.

Source: Adapted from *Institute of Directors*, 1984.

Question 1

1. What view of market forces is taken by the Institute of Directors?
2. Which groups in society would lose and which would benefit if these suggestions were implemented?

3. What criticisms would you make of these proposals?

Faith in the city

The idea of partnership in promoting urban regeneration is welcome, and needs to be developed to promote greater consultation of, and participation by, local people at neighbourhood level.

Inner city policy has seen a shift in emphasis from tackling social problems, to physical problems, to economic problems. All three are important. But a major emphasis is needed on economic regeneration: for thriving local economies to be developed which can offer employment. This will require three things:

— the public sector must provide more employment opportunities and increased income support to those who are unemployed;

— all those living in the UPAs (Urban Priority Areas) should be given the best possible opportunities in education and skill-training;

— the physical environment of the UPAs must be improved.

The heart of the problem is the national decline in manual jobs, and the concentration of manual workers in UPAs. By 1981, there were nearly 2.5 million fewer manual jobs in the UK than a decade earlier.

Policy should be as concerned with the distribution of wealth as with its creation. What seems to be lacking at present is an adequate appreciation of the importance of the distributive consequences - for cities, regions and groups of people - of national economic policies. Modern technology means that wealth creation tends not to result in job creation. And arguments that wealth will 'trickle down' are not borne out by the facts.

A more open debate is needed about economic policies and about the type of society present economic policies are shaping. Their main assumption is that prosperity can be restored if individuals are set free to pursue their own economic salvation. But pursuit of self-reliance must not damage our collective obligation to those who have no choice, or only forced choices. At present too much emphasis is being given to individualism, and not enough to collective obligation. The costs of present policies are unacceptable in their effect on whole communities and generations. The greatest burdens of economic changes are being carried by those least able to bear them.

Source: *Faith in the City*, Christian Action, 1986, St. Peter's House, Kennington Lane, London SE11 5HY.

Question 2

1. What view does the article take of the workings of the market?
2. What would be the consequences for fiscal policy of these ideas?

3. What economic ideas could be put forward to:
   (i)   support and
   (ii) oppose
   the arguments in the article?

15 Money

● One of the central propositions of monetarist economics is that the control of inflation is the major goal of economic policy. Its supporters believe that the way to achieve this end is to control the money supply. Economists such as Milton Friedman argue that if the government keeps control of the money supply, prices in general cannot rise and money will be able to fulfil its necessary functions in the economy.

● Keynesian economists do not deny the importance of money - indeed the title of Keynes' major work was the *General Theory of Employment, Interest and Money* (1936). However, they argue that the supply of money in a modern economy is largely determined by the economy's need for money to undertake transactions, and that attempting to control the money supply leads to higher levels of unemployment and lower rates of economic growth. The interaction of the demand and supply of money can have a significant effect on the economy, and we need to examine what factors affect the demand and supply for money before considering the above perspectives.

The supply of money

Money and its functions

Money is often defined as anything which is generally acceptable for the purchase of goods and services or repayment of debt. This is a broad definition and in the past a wide range of objects have been acceptable as money. Gold and silver coins were the usual forms of money in many countries, but tobacco, cowrie shells and even dog's teeth have served as money. What is important is not the precise form which money takes, but whether it is generally accepted. In a modern economy only a small part of the total money supply is in notes and coins. Most money is created by the banking system and moved around electronically. Cheques and credit cards are accepted as a means of payment, yet no notes or coins are involved when purchases are made using these methods. Whatever the precise form taken by 'money', it must fulfil four functions:

● It must act as a medium of exchange; that is it permits people to exchange goods and services of different value. Without money an economy has to rely on barter and this has the same disadvantage as sex - it requires not only that someone has what you want, but also that the same person wants what you have! To use the jargon, barter requires the double coincidence of wants.

● It must act as a unit of account; that is, it is a standard of value that allows people to compare the relative worth of various goods and services.

● It must act as a standard of deferred payment. This is a way in which spending can be postponed, for example, when someone signs a contract or buys goods on credit.

● It must act as a store of value - a way in which today's wealth can be kept for use in the future.

If money does not fulfil all these functions, then the economy will suffer. For example, when there is inflation money ceases to be a good store of value. Some commodities fulfil some of the functions of money, but not all. Credit cards act as a medium of exchange and a way of making deferred payments, but do not fulfil the other functions of money.

Some forms of money - notes and coins - are supplied by the Bank of England. These are not 'backed' by any security, such as gold, but are in general printed in sufficient quantities to ensure the economy is not short of cash. The Bank of England can do this without there being severe consequences because most money in a modern economy is created by the commercial banks such as Barclays and National Westminster in a process usually called 'credit creation'.

How do banks create credit?

When a bank receives a deposit from a customer, it keeps only part of the money in case the customer wants it back and lends out the rest. Since borrowers pay interest, the bank wishes to lend as much as possible, but is constrained by the need to maintain adequate assets. If we assume for simplicity that the bank keeps 10% as security, it can lend out 90% of each deposit received. Since most of the money lent will sooner or later be deposited in a bank, it follows that the bank receiving this deposit can then lend more money. The process is illustrated in Table 15.1.

If Mr A deposits £1,000 in a bank, the bank's assets will be £1,000 (the cash it holds) and its liabilities also £1,000 (the money it owes Mr A). The bank keeps 10% as security and lends out £900 to Ms B who wishes to buy some furniture. The bank's assets are now £100 cash and £900 owed to it by Ms B. Ms B (or the furniture company) then deposits the £900 in the bank. Hence the bank's assets are now £1,000 cash (the £100 it kept as security on Mr A's deposit plus the £900 received from Ms B or the furniture shop) plus the £900 owed it by Ms B. Its liabilities are also £1,900 (£900 deposited by the furniture shop plus the original £1,000 deposited by Mr A).

The next step is a repetition of the first, but with a smaller amount. Since the furniture shop has deposited £900, the bank will keep 10% of this, i.e. £90 and lend out the remaining 90%, i.e. £810 to Mr C, perhaps to buy hi-fi equipment. In turn this will be deposited at the bank which will keep 10% and lend out 90% to Mr D. The process will be repeated with ever decreasing amounts. Eventually the original £1,000 will have been turned into £10,000 by the banking system. If the banks keep 10% of liabilities in reserve, then they can create 10 times their original deposit. This is known as the **credit multiplier.** If the bank keeps 25% in reserve, it can only create 4 times the original amount deposited.

This account is simplified, but it does illustrate the way in which the banking system can create money. One simplification is that we have talked about 'the' bank when in reality there is a whole system. This complicates the process, but it does not invalidate the description. The account also assumes that money lent by the system is always returned to the bank as a deposit; in practice some will remain outside the banking system. Another simplification is the assumption that the banks keep 10% as security. The real world is more complex than this.

However, banks do have to keep some deposits for their own security and in order to comply with

Table 15.1: *The creation of credit*

	BANK	
	Assets	**Liabilities**
Mr A deposits £1000	£1000 cash	deposit £1000
But the bank knows that he will withdraw only £100 so the rest may be lent to Ms B	£100 cash £900 loan	deposit £1000
Now Ms B deposits her new £900 with the bank	£1000 cash £900 loan	deposits £1900
But the bank realises that Ms B will withdraw only £90 of her deposit so the rest is lent to Mr C	£190 cash £1710 loans	deposits £1900
Now Mr C deposits his new £810 with the bank	£1000 cash £1710 loans	deposits £2710
But the bank realises that Mr C will withdraw only £81 of his deposit so the rest is lent to Mr D	£271 cash £2439 loans	deposits £2710
Mr D deposits his new £729 with the bank	£1000 cash £2439 loans	deposits £3439

and so on . . .
Eventually the original £1000 will be held by the bank as the one-tenth it needs to cover withdrawals by its customers. If £1000 represents one-tenth, then total deposits must total £10,000, as follows:

	£1000 cash £9000 loans	deposits £10,000

Capital Adequacy Rules imposed by the Bank of England. These rules were agreed in 1987 and are similar in the UK and USA. From 1990 banks will have to keep a minimum capital ratio of 7.25%. This 'capital ratio' is the bank's capital expressed as a percentage of its assets weighted in terms of risk.

What measure of money?

There is no single, universal definition of money. This is because, as we have seen, money fulfils a number of functions and some kinds of money fulfil certain functions better than others. This means that there is no single way to measure the money supply. So far we have been talking implicitly about a definition of money which includes cash in circulation, plus sight deposits in the banks ('sight deposits' is the phrase used to denote deposits in banks which can be withdrawn immediately as opposed to 'time deposits' which require some notice to be given before withdrawals can be made). This definition of money is called M1, but, as can be

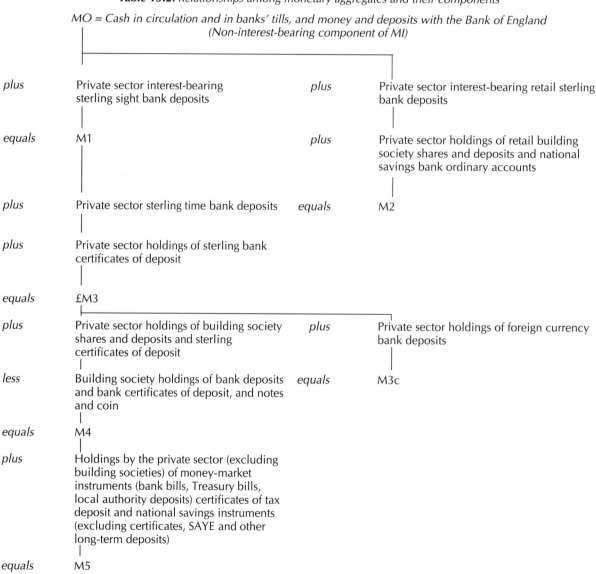

Table 15.2: *Relationships among monetary aggregates and their components*

MO = Cash in circulation and in banks' tills, and money and deposits with the Bank of England
(Non-interest-bearing component of MI)

plus	Private sector interest-bearing sterling sight bank deposits	plus	Private sector interest-bearing retail sterling bank deposits
equals	M1	plus	Private sector holdings of retail building society shares and deposits and national savings bank ordinary accounts
plus	Private sector sterling time bank deposits	equals	M2
plus	Private sector holdings of sterling bank certificates of deposit		
equals	£M3		
plus	Private sector holdings of building society shares and deposits and sterling certificates of deposit	plus	Private sector holdings of foreign currency bank deposits
less	Building society holdings of bank deposits and bank certificates of deposit, and notes and coin	equals	M3c
equals	M4		
plus	Holdings by the private sector (excluding building societies) of money-market instruments (bank bills, Treasury bills, local authority deposits) certificates of tax deposit and national savings instruments (excluding certificates, SAYE and other long-term deposits)		
equals	M5		

Source: *Bank of England Quarterly Bulletin*, 1987.

seen from Table 15.2, other definitions are possible. MO includes only cash in circulation, banks' till money, and their deposits in the Bank of England. This gives a relatively small total for the money supply. At the other extreme a definition such as M5 is much larger because it includes such things as deposits in building societies, Treasury Bills and some national savings.

Controlling the money supply

Because there are several definitions of money, there is no one way in which the government can control the money supply. Indeed, because one type of 'money' can easily be converted into another, the authorities find that when they try to control one type people switch to another that is unregulated.

If 'money' is narrowly defined in terms of notes and coins, then the problem of how to control the supply is relatively simple - just control the print run.

However, if broader definitions of money are used, the problem of control is more complex. The change in a broad money supply such as £M3 depends on:
● the public sector borrowing requirement,
● - the change in private sector lending to the public sector,
● + the change in bank lending to the private sector,
● + external flows,
● - the increase in banks' non-deposit liabilities.

Each of these will be discussed in turn.

The Public Sector Borrowing Requirement

The PSBR was discussed in the last chapter. Other things being equal, a rise in the PSBR, followed by increased borrowing from the banking sector through the sale of Treasury bills, will give the banks greater assets allowing them to create credit. This will lead to a rise in the money supply. Hence economists who believe that it is important to have firm controls on the money supply tend to argue that government spending should be kept as low as possible. This is difficult to accomplish. There are often strong political pressures to increase spending and in any case, public expenditure next year is largely determined by spending this year. It is not possible suddenly to close a hospital, or make a battalion of soldiers redundant. Moreover, it is quite difficult to predict how much the government will have to borrow in any one year. Hence some

economists argue that controlling the PSBR is not a good method to use to control the money supply.

Private sector lending to the public sector

A rise in public sector borrowing from the non-bank private sector will reduce the money supply. This is because when the public buy National Savings certificates, gilt edged securities or other government securities, they sign cheques payable to the government. (Gilt edged securities or bonds are a kind of IOU. To simplify, they say something like 'The government will pay the bearer the sum of £1,000 in January 2005 and £100 interest annually until that date'.) When these cheques are cashed by the Bank of England, money is withdrawn from the banks so their deposits fall. When their deposits fall the banks can create less money (this is the reverse side of the credit creation process described earlier). Hence a major way for the authorities to reduce the money supply is to sell more gilt edged securities. (You can see lists of these in the financial pages of some newspapers and they can be bought through banks or the Post Office.) This method of controlling the money supply is called 'open market operations' or funding the Public Sector Borrowing Requirement. One problem with this method is that an increase in government borrowing may push up interest rates which may be undesirable.

Bank lending to the private sector

A rise in bank lending to the private sector will tend to push up the money supply. There are a number of ways in which the authorities can attempt to reduce bank lending. One way is to push up interest rates so that some people are unwilling to borrow money. Unfortunately this also puts up costs to businesses. Moreover, it often requires large rises in interest rates before there is much effect on the willingness of people to borrow. An alternative approach is to require the commercial banks to make Special Deposits at the Bank of England. This means that the banks will then have less money to lend to the private sector.

External flows

External flows also affect the quantity of money. For example, when the balance of payments is positive (i.e. when UK exports exceed UK imports) money will flow into the country. It is possible for the authorities to intervene in the foreign exchange market in order to influence the flow of money, but this will have undesirable effects on the whole balance of payments.

Banks' non-deposit reserves

Increases in banks' non-deposit reserves will also affect the money supply. If the banks choose to increase their capital base by retaining profits they will be transferring banks' liabilities into banks' assets. Such a transfer will reduce the monetary aggregate £M3 since assets are not included in measures of the money stock.

An alternative way to control the money supply

The methods described above do not offer a trouble-free way to control the supply of money when this is broadly defined. An alternative way would be to control the monetary base. The idea is that the banks tend to keep a fairly stable ratio between their deposits and their reserves. They may do this because the law says that they must, or because they are prudent. If the law lays down requirements, then one way to influence the money supply is to change the requirements. If the banks are forced to keep bigger reserves, then their ability to create money will be reduced. In the credit creation example given earlier, a reserve of 10% was used as an example. If this was increased to say 12.5%, then much less money would have resulted from any increase in deposits (£8,000 instead of £10,000). However, this method of attempting to control the supply of money is criticised on a number of grounds. For example, if the reserve ratio is not fixed by law, then the banks may vary their reserves and so make it difficult to calculate the effect of any government sale or purchase of bonds. Even if a minimum reserve ratio is fixed by law, the effects of any intervention may be difficult to predict because prudential banks may keep more reserves than the law requires. Critics also claim that this method of monetary control would lead to very unstable interest rates, which are undesirable, particularly for firms wishing to borrow money to finance expansion.

The methods used to control the supply of money are complex. The detailed methods used by governments vary over time because no method is perfect, so as time passes governments look for improved techniques, but all have some disadvantages.

Key ideas

1. Money is anything that is generally accepted as payment for goods and services.

2. Because money has to carry out a number of functions, there are a number of different ways of measuring it.
3. Banks create most money by the process of credit creation.
4. There are several different ways to control the money supply. These include high interest rates, open market operations and controlling the banks' monetary base.

The demand for money

The phrase 'demand for money' has a curious ring to it; in commonsense terms we demand as much money as we can get. However, 'demand' has the same meaning here as it has in the context of the demand for goods. It is therefore important to find out what factors influence whether people wish to hold their assets as money or in some other form. One consideration is **liquidity.** Money is a perfectly liquid asset because it can be used immediately to buy goods or services. At the other extreme, a building may be very valuable but it is not very liquid - ownership of a house is no use if you want to buy an ice cream. Buildings are illiquid; it takes time to change them into a form which can be used to buy things and selling in a hurry may result in a capital loss.

The level of income

One factor which affects the demand for money is the level of incomes. This is because people need money to finance transactions (hence this is called the **transactions** motive for holding money). When incomes are high people buy more goods and services and hence need more money to finance these transactions than do people with low incomes.

There is also a precautionary reason for holding money. Because firms and individuals are not absolutely sure that future receipts and payments will occur as expected, they will wish to keep some money in reserve in case they need to make some payment quickly. The amount of money kept as a precaution will depend largely on the level of income. A rich person may wish to keep large sums of money available as a precaution; a poor person could not.

Money

The rate of interest

Whilst the level of incomes is the chief determinant of the amount of money held for precautionary and transactions motives, the rate of interest may also play a part. That is because there is an opportunity cost of holding money. Particularly when interest rates are high, some people or firms may decide that it would be better to transfer their money into some other form of asset which would earn high interest. Hence high rates of interest may reduce the demand for money balances.

There is also a **speculative** motive for holding money. We have seen that there is an opportunity cost of holding money, and that this will encourage people to choose to hold other assets, such as bonds, instead. However, the price of bonds is not constant; speculators can gain or lose money if they buy bonds at the right (or wrong) time.

The price of bonds tends to vary inversely with the interest rate. When interest rates are expected to fall, the price of bonds will rise and vice versa. The reason is that bonds have a face value and pay a fixed interest. Hence a bond with a face value of £100 which pays £5 a year interest will be worth £100 when the current rate of interest in the economy is 5%. However, when interest rates generally are 10% no one would be willing to pay £100 for such a bond because they would only receive £5 interest on it compared to £10 on other assets. Hence the value of the bond would fall to £50; this would mean that someone with £100 could buy two bonds and receive £10 interest on their investment. Conversely if interest rates

generally fell to 2.5% the bond would be worth more than £100 because it would give much better interest than other assets. Its price would increase to £200 and the holder would receive £5, i.e. 2.5% interest on the investment.

This account of the speculative motive for holding money is largely Keynesian. It suggests a negative relationship between the rate of interest and the demand for money. When interest rates are high and expected to fall, speculators will exchange money for bonds because the value of bonds will rise. When interest rates are low and expected to rise they will tend to sell bonds and hold money instead.

Figure 15.1 summarises the Keynesian demand for money function. It shows that there are two principal determinants of the demand for money: the level of national income and the rate of interest. A change in either of these will cause a change in the demand for money.

The monetarist approach to the demand for money

The modern monetarist approach to the demand for money differs from the Keynesian in that it considers assets other than money and bonds. Monetarists argue that money is only one of a whole range of assets and that if the supply of money exceeds the demand, then individuals and firms will not just buy bonds, but also other assets, such as buildings, shares, jewellery and consumer durable goods. If this view is accepted, then the level of incomes will still have a major effect on the demand for money.

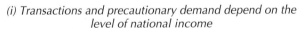

Figure 15.1: The demand for money

(i) Transactions and precautionary demand depend on the level of national income

(ii) Speculative demand varies inversely with the rate of interest

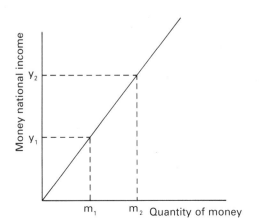

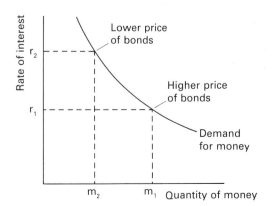

The rate of interest will also have an effect because when interest rates are high, the opportunity cost of holding money will also be high. However, monetarists argue that changes in interest rates have relatively little effect on the demand for money, and that the demand curve for money is inelastic.

The big difference between this view and that of Keynes is that the monetarist approach suggests that the demand for money is stable. Friedman claimed:

'A wide range of empirical evidence suggests that the ratio which people desire to maintain between their cash balances and their income is relatively stable over fairly long periods of time aside from the effect of two major variables.'

(These two variables are the level of real incomes and the cost of holding money - the opportunity cost in terms of interest foregone.) As we will see, this conclusion that the demand for money is stable has important implications for monetary policy.

Empirical evidence on the demand for money

In principle these differences could be resolved by research. Is the demand for money stable as monetarists argue, or does it fluctuate as Keynesians believe? After reviewing the evidence Gowland (1979) concluded:

'There seems to be a stable demand for money function.'

A few years later Howells and Bain (1985) concluded:

'The evidence seems now to favour the presumption that in Britain in the 1970s the demand for money function was decidedly unstable.'

The safest conclusion seems to be that the evidence is ambiguous!

Equilibrium in the money market

In the market for goods and services equilibrium was brought about by changes in the price level. Similarly, in the money market equilibrium between the demand for money and the supply of money is brought about by changes in the rate of interest as shown in Figure 15.2.

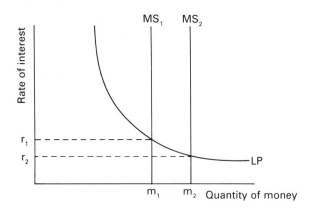

Figure 15.2: Monetary equilibrium and the rate of interest

In this Figure the money supply is drawn as a vertical straight line because it is assumed to be controlled by the authorities and does not vary with the rate of interest. The demand for money curve is labelled LP because it measures the liquidity preference of the population; at high rates of interest people will have a low liquidity preference - that is they will desire bonds instead of money. The market will be in equilibrium when the interest rate is r_1. If the interest rate was higher than this, the supply of money would be greater than the demand for money. Since people held more money than they wished, they would use this excess money to buy bonds and so cause the price of bonds to rise and the interest rate to fall until equilibrium was reached. When the demand for money is greater than the supply, people will sell their bonds to obtain money and this will push up the rate of interest.

A change in either the demand for money or its supply will affect the rate of interest, just as a change in the demand or supply of goods affects the price. An increase in the supply of money will move the MS curve to the right and lower the interest rate, while a cut in the money supply will have the opposite effect. If there is an increase in the demand for money, caused, for example, by a rise in incomes, then the LP curve will move to the right, pushing up the interest rate. A fall in the demand for money will lead to a fall in interest rates.

The influence of government

So far this chapter has developed what is sometimes called the **liquidity preference theory of interest rate determination.** It is given this name because it focuses on people's desire to hold money or other assets. However, the theory as explained ignores an important influence - that of the government. In a modern economy governments are not content to leave important variables, such as the interest rate, to market forces and they often intervene to move the rate up or down. One reason for this is to influence the rate of exchange - the rate at which the pound is exchanged for other currencies. This is explained in detail in Chapter 20; for the present we will consider competing perspectives on monetary policy as it affects the domestic economy.

Key ideas

1. By 'demand for money' we mean the demand to hold money rather than other assets.
2. The Keynesian approach stresses three motives for holding money: transactions, precautions, and speculative. The variables which affect these motives are the level of income and the rate of interest.
3. Monetarists consider money as one of a broad range of assets. This means that the demand for money is stable.

The monetarist approach

The quantity theory

The theory underlying the monetarist view is called the **quantity theory of money.** This theory is derived from an equation which is accepted by all economists:

$$MV = PT$$

In this equation:
M = the quantity of money
V = the velocity of circulation
(this is the number of times a year that money changes hands in order to purchase goods and services)
P = the average level of prices
T = the number of transactions, a measure of the quantity of goods produced by the economy in a year.
Thus the equation says that the quantity of money multiplied by its circulation will equal the number of goods produced multiplied by their price.

If this seems complicated, a simplistic example may clarify the point. Imagine a desert island where the quantity of money is 100 coins each worth £1. During the year each coin changes hands five times. Hence MV equals £500. If the economy produces £50 units of goods, then the average price of these goods must be £10, i.e.:

$$M \times V = P \times T$$
$$100 \times 5 = 10 \times 50$$

This equation is accepted by all economists because it is true by definition. In words it says that the total amount spent in the economy (MV) must equal the total amount received by producers (PT). The argument between economists arises not over the equation itself, but about how this equality comes about and whether this causal mechanism should be the basis for economic policy.

The essence of the monetarist argument is that if the government controls the money supply (M), then the result will be to prevent prices (P) from rising. This is because monetarists argue that the velocity of circulation (V) is fairly constant, since it is determined partly by social and institutional factors which do not change much in the short run (for example, if people are paid monthly instead of weekly, then they will tend to pay their bills monthly instead of weekly and this will reduce the velocity of circulation, but only very slowly and over a long period). Similarly, monetarists believe that real national income (T) is fairly constant because it depends on slowly moving variables such as productivity. Over a period of years it could be expected to rise by (say) 3% a year. Hence if we look at the equation again we see:

M	x	V	=	P	x	T
controlled by government		constant		determined by M		rises slowly

From this analysis it follows that if the government keeps tight control over the money supply, then prices cannot rise. If a powerful union succeeds in obtaining a large wage increase this will not lead to inflation, unless the government allows the money supply to rise to fund the increase. Instead the wage rise will mean that there is less for others. This may be very undesirable, but it does not cause inflation. Hence in this view, **inflation is always a monetary phenomenon,** caused by the government allowing the money supply to rise too rapidly.

In support of this line of argument, the monetarists have undertaken a good deal of research into the relationship between the money supply and the rate of inflation. According to Friedman (1966):

'There is perhaps no empirical regularity among economic phenomena that is based on so much evidence for so wide a range of circumstances as the connection between substantial changes in the stock of money and in the level of prices. To the best of my knowledge there is no instance in which a substantial change in the stock of money per unit of output has occurred without a substantial change in the level of prices in the same direction . . . instances in which prices and the stock of money have moved together are recorded for many centuries of history, for countries in every part of the globe, and for a wide diversity of monetary arrangements.'

Friedman himself has undertaken a good deal of this research and concluded that a change in the supply of money will lead to a change in the rate of inflation, but with a time lag. For example, if a government cut the rate of increase of the money supply from (say) 10% to 5%, the effect in the short run would be on T, the real level of national income. Firms and individuals would be short of money, interest rates would rise, and there would be a fall in the quantity of goods produced and a rise in the level of unemployment. But this would be temporary. Depending on the flexibility of the economy, in a year and a half or two years the period of readjustment would come to an end and the rate of inflation would start to fall.

One factor which could affect this relationship is the amount of money which the public desires to hold relative to its income. If the demand for money is unstable, then the velocity of circulation of money may also vary. This means that changes in the quantity of money would have little or no effect on the level of prices. However, if the demand for money is relatively stable, then changes in the stock of money will have a significant effect on the level of prices and monetary policy should concentrate on controlling the supply of money.

The transmission mechanism

By the phrase 'transmission mechanism' we mean the way in which changes in the money supply affect the economy. The monetarist view of the consequences of a rise in money supply is shown in Figure 15.3.

As can be seen, the increase in money supply means that the supply of money exceeds the demand for it. Since people have more money than they want, they use some of the money to buy financial assets such as bonds. This raises the price of bonds and brings down the rate of interest. They also use some of the excess money to buy more goods. However, since supply siders assume that the labour market is in equilibrium, there are no additional workers available to produce more goods. Hence the result is that prices rise, without any increase in output.

> **Key ideas - summary of the monetarist argument**
>
> **1. Inflation is an economic phenomenon which must be eradicated.**
> **2. The way to control inflation is to control the money supply. This is because the velocity of circulation of money is fairly stable and national income tends to rise in the long run. Hence if M is controlled, P cannot rise.**
> **3. In the short run, controlling the money supply will reduce the national income and increase unemployment, but this effect is only temporary.**

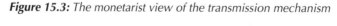

Figure 15.3: *The monetarist view of the transmission mechanism*

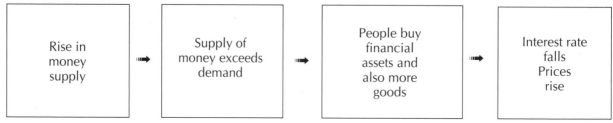

Monetarist policies

The short summary of monetarist policy would be 'The government should control the money supply'. As we have seen earlier in this chapter, there are various ways in which this can be done, and there is also some dispute among monetarists about the extent of the control. Should the money supply be brought down quickly, or should its rate of growth be brought down gradually?

For most monetarists, the foundation of their ideas is the belief in the tendency of a free market economy to achieve economic efficiency. Hence monetary policy should be carried on in a way which will not disturb the real economy. This suggests that the money supply should be allowed to grow at a rate equal to the rate of growth of the productive capacity of the economy. If factors such as productivity and the labour supply suggest that the economy could grow at 3% a year, then the money supply should also grow at this rate. The precise rate is less important than the principle that the growth should be steady, with governments given no discretion because they are likely to react to difficult circumstances by expanding the money supply.

The government should control the money supply by controlling the banks' ability to create credit, and this can be done by:

- Defining clearly which assets the banks can use as reserve assets.
- Controlling the issue of these assets.
- Having a minimum ratio of reserve assets to total assets.
- Keeping a close watch on banking practice.

Other policies can help achieve control over the money supply. Because there is a link between government borrowing and the supply of money, control will be easier if the government controls its own spending. And of course, the government should take whatever measures are needed to increase the efficiency with which market forces can operate in the economy.

The Keynesian approach

Keynesian critique of the monetarist approach

Keynesian economists make a number of criticisms of the monetarist approach.

Control

Is it possible for the government to control the money supply? A policy which takes this as its central feature will not be successful if banks and firms can find ways to increase the money supply. As we have seen, 'money' can be defined in several different ways. Many Keynesians claim only money narrowly defined as notes and coins can easily be controlled by the government. In other cases, firms can borrow from abroad, make greater use of credit, or use 'near money' in order to avoid monetary

Table 15.3: £M3 targets and out-turns

Target Period	Target Range	Out-turn	Overshoot from Target Mid-Point
4.75- 4.77	9-13%	17.7%	+ 6.7%
4.77- 4.78	9-13%	16.0%	+ 5.0%
4.78- 4.79	8-12%	10.9%	+ 0.9%
10.78-10.79	8-12%	13.3%	+ 3.3%
6.79- 4.80	7-11%	10.3%	+ 1.3%
6.79-10.80	7-11%	17.8%	+ 8.8%
2.80- 4.81	7-11%	18.5%	+ 9.5%
2.81- 4.82	6-10%	14.5%	+ 6.5%
2.82- 4.83	8-12%	11.0%	+ 1.0%
2.83- 4.84	7-11%	9.7%	+ 0.7%
2.84- 4.85	6-10%	12.2%	+ 4.2%
2.85- 4.86	5- 9%	16.6%	+ 9.6%
2.86- 4.87	11-15%	19.0%	+ 6.0%

Source: 'Financial Statement and Budget Reports'; *Bank of England Quarterly Bulletin.*

controls. Keynesians go on to argue that the statistical links which monetarists have found between the money supply and the price level are only found in periods when the authorities have not tried to control the money supply. 'Goodhart's Law' says that:

'any observed statistical regularity will tend to collapse once pressure is placed on it for control purposes'.

This is because businesses find it relatively easy to switch into some other medium of exchange not under government control.

Table 15.3 illustrates the point. Even the Conservative government elected in 1979, which made control of the money supply a central feature of its economic policy, failed to achieve its target.

Velocity of circulation

Even if the government has some success in controlling the money supply, this will have little effect unless the velocity of circulation is reasonably constant. Keynesians claim that the velocity of circulation of money is unstable. A committee chaired by Lord Radcliffe as long ago as 1959 made the point:

'. . . during the last few years the volume of spending has greatly increased while the supply of money has hardly changed . . . we cannot find any reason for supposing, or any experience in monetary history indicating, that there is any limit to the velocity of circulation; it is a statistical concept that tells us nothing directly . . .'

The reason for rejecting the monetarist view is simple; that if money is scarce, people will make greater use of the existing money supply. For example, if money is short then firms will cease to give a month's credit and insist on prompt payment. As a result the velocity of circulation will increase.

Every economist accepts that $MV=PT$, but there is disagreement about how this comes about. Whilst monetarists argue that controlling M will lead to changes in P, Keynesians argue that the line of causation is reversed - from P to M. In other words, they say the quantity of money responds to changes in the real economy; if individuals and firms need more money to finance their activities, then the sophisticated financial system will create more money, and this is why governments find it so difficult to control the money supply.

Effects

Finally, Keynesians disagree about the effects of attempting to control the money supply. Monetarists suggest that when the money supply is brought under control there will be a temporary effect on the 'real economy'. Keynesians believe that this will be permanent and that such a policy will lead to a fall in national income and employment. Hence the economic consequences of attempting to control the money supply will be worse than the original problem.

The Keynesian view of the transmission mechanism

The Keynesian approach agrees that money is important. The disagreement with the monetarists is in part about the time which the economy takes to react to changes. Monetarists tend to assume that markets adapt quickly and accuse Keynesians of only concentrating on the short run. To this Keynes retorted, 'In the long run we are all dead'. In other words, markets are often slow to react and changes that are predicted for the long run may never come about because new developments will have occurred and changed the entire position.

Keynesians focus on the link between the supply of money and aggregate expenditure; this is called the monetary transmission mechanism.

The first link is between the supply of money and the interest rate. As we have seen in Figure 15.2, an increase in the supply of money will lead to a fall in the rate of interest, just as an increase in the supply of a good would be expected to lead to a fall in its price.

The second link is between the interest rate and the level of spending on investment and consumer goods. Chapter 12 discussed the determinants of the level of investment and consumption; all we need to do here is summarise the main points. So far as consumption is concerned, a fall in interest rates will make borrowing cheaper and so encourage people to borrow money to finance the purchase of consumer durables. Similarly, lower interest rates will encourage firms to invest more. The links between money supply, interest rates and investment are shown in Figure 15.4. Original equilibrium is at interest rate r_1 and desired investment is i_1. When the money supply is increased from M_1 to M_2, the rate of interest falls to r_2 and desired investment rises to i_2.

The third link in the Keynesian explanation of the monetary transmission mechanism is that a rise in the level of investment will lead to a multiplied rise in aggregate demand as shown in Chapter 12.

Putting the three links together, we see that a rise in the supply of money will lead to a rise in aggregate demand and national income, the extent depending on such factors as the elasticity of the demand for money, the size of the multiplier and the interest elasticity of investment; that is the extent to which a fall in the rate of interest stimulates investment. A fall in the demand for money will have the same effect as shown in Figure 15.5.

However, there are limits to the expansion which can be achieved by this means. As the economy approaches full employment an increase in the supply of money will lead to a rise in prices because the T in the equation $MV=PT$ will no longer rise (since the economy cannot produce more goods in the short run because there is full employment). Hence an increase in M will lead to a rise in P.

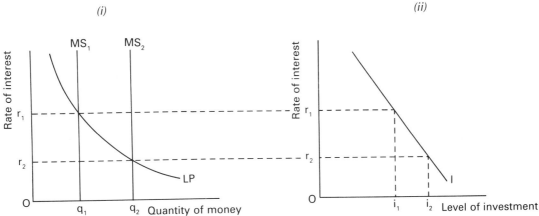

Figure 15.4: *The supply of money and the level of investment*

Key ideas - summary of the Keynesian approach

1. Keynesian economists tend to concentrate on the short run.

2. The demand for money will be determined by the level of national income and expected changes in the rate of interest. When the rate of interest is expected to fall, there will be a fall in the demand for money because people will buy bonds.

3. Changes in the supply of money will affect the interest rate; a higher money supply will lower the interest rate and encourage investment.

Keynesian policies

Keynesian policies tend to concentrate on the rate of interest rather than the money supply as such. This is because Keynesians tend to believe the money supply is difficult to control and that the attempt to

control it will lead to a rise in unemployment. This does not mean that the money supply is unimportant. It must not be allowed to grow at an excessive rate and particular care must be taken as the economy nears the full employment level. In general, Keynesian economists believe the supply of money should be allowed to grow fairly freely so that it does not impose limits on the economy's rate of expansion. Moreover, the government should attempt to keep down the rate of interest so that firms are encouraged to invest more. However, this may be difficult.

As we will see when we discuss foreign trade and the rate of exchange, the rate of interest influences the value of the pound compared to other currencies (rich people and companies will switch their money to countries where interest rates are high and so force up the value of those currencies). Hence foreign trade and exchange rate considerations will sometimes determine policy on interest rates. Because these are interrelated, some Keynesian economists would adjust monetary policy so that it helped to achieve balance of payments and exchange rate goals.

Figure 15.5: *The Keynesian view of the transmission mechanism*

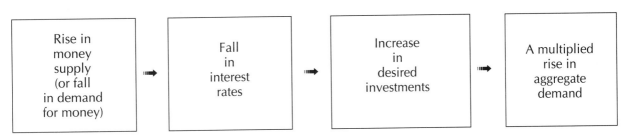

Another policy associated with Keynesian economists is that they emphasise controlling **credit** rather than money supply. This is because there is a close link between the cost and availability of credit and the amount which consumers spend. Since Keynesians emphasise the importance of aggregate demand, it is not surprising that they advocate policies to control credit.

Conclusion

All economists agree that money matters; but there is not much agreement about other aspects of money - not even about how it should be measured. In essence, the difference between the two approaches depends in part on how they view markets. Keynesians believe that markets only adjust slowly; monetarists that the process is very quick. Monetarists believe that money affects prices because changes in money will affect asset switching behaviour which then affects all prices, including the price of goods. The real economy - the quantity of goods and services produced - is not affected by money in the long run because it is determined by supply side forces, such as changes in the working population and in productivity.

On the other hand, Keynesians tend to give less emphasis to monetary policy. Some Keynesians believe that the supply of money adjusts to the demand for it, and that attempts to control money supply lead to undesirable side-effects on output and employment. Some would argue that changes in the money supply affect the rate of interest and hence the real economy through changes in the level of investment. In turn this will affect the level of national income and employment. There will be little effect on prices, except when the economy approaches full employment. Keynesians also argue that it is often more important to control credit than the money supply since this has a strong effect on the level of consumer spending.

Data questions

The velocity of circulation

The basic contention of monetarists is that there is a stable function of money in relation to income (which comes to the same as saying that there is a stable velocity of circulation, invariant to changes in the quantity of money in circulation). This assertion, first put forward by the early followers of the quantity theory of money in the eighteenth and nineteenth centuries, was denied by Keynes and reasserted by Friedman on the basis of statistical evidence which shows a high correlation between changes in the amount of money in circulation and changes in the money value of the national income. Friedman admitted, however, that there was nothing in his findings which logically excluded an interpretation diametrically opposite to his own, i.e. that the change in the money supply may be the consequence, not the cause, of the change in money incomes (and prices), and that the mere existence of time-lag - that changes in the money supply precede changes in money incomes - is not in itself sufficient to settle the question of causality; one cannot rule out the possibility of an event A which occurred subsequent to B being, nevertheless, the cause of B (the simplest analogy is the rumblings of a volcano which frequently precede an eruption). Apart from that it is notoriously difficult to establish the existence of a lead of one factor over another, when both move in the same direction in time and the whole question of the existence of a 'lag' is by no means established.

Source: Kaldor, N. *The Scourge of Monetarism*, Oxford University Press, 1985.

Question 1

1. Explain what is meant by the 'velocity of circulation'.

2. How will changes in the velocity of circulation affect the economy?

3. To what extent are Keynesians justified in arguing that the velocity of circulation is not stable?

The central propositions of monetarism

1. There is a consistent though not precise relationship between the rate of growth of the quantity of money and the rate of growth of nominal income.

2. It takes (a variable amount of) time for changes in monetary growth to affect income.

3. A change in the rate of monetary growth produces a change in the rate of growth of nominal income about six to nine months later.

4. A change in the rate of growth of nominal income typically shows up first in output and hardly at all in prices.

5. The effect on prices comes about six months after the effect on income and output, so the total delay between a change in monetary growth and a change in the rate of inflation averages around twelve to eighteen months.

6. Even after allowance for the delay in the rate of monetary growth, the relation is far from perfect.

7. In the short run, which may be as much as five or ten years, monetary changes mainly affect output. Over decades, monetary changes affect only prices; while output remains unaffected since, in the long run, output depends only upon such real factors as enterprise, ingenuity and thrift.

8. Inflation is always and everywhere a monetary phenomenon.

9. Government spending may or may not be inflationary. It will be inflationary if it is financed by creating money, i.e. by printing currency or creating bank deposits.

10. An increased rate of monetary growth raises the amount of cash which people and businesses have in relation to other assets. With the attempt to reduce cash balances, the effect spreads from one asset to another. This tends to raise asset prices and to reduce interest rates, which encourages expenditure on the production of new assets. It also encourages spending on current services rather than upon existing assets. Thus the initial impact on balance-sheets is translated into an effect upon income and spending.

11. Monetary expansion initially lowers interest rates but, as spending and price inflation increases, it also produces a rise in the demand for loans which will tend eventually to raise interest rates. This two-edged relation between money and interest rates explains why monetarists insist that interest rates are a highly misleading guide to monetary policy. Moreover, rising (or falling), prices introduce a discrepancy between real and nominal interest rates which disturbs real sectors of the economy.

Source: Steele, G. 'Monetarism' in Atkinson, G.B.J. (ed). *Developments in Economics* Vol. III, Causeway Press, 1987.

Question 2

1. Select three of the above propositions and develop arguments in favour of and against them.

16 Unemployment

Everybody knows what unemployment is, yet it is surprisingly difficult to define and measure, so that there are disagreements about the extent to which the published figures actually measure the level of unemployment. This chapter analyses the above problem and also the costs of unemployment - why unemployment matters to the individual and to society. It then discusses various types of unemployment and the theoretical approaches of supply siders, Keynesians and Marxists:
- ● Supply siders urge more emphasis on market forces.
- ● Keynesians believe government intervention in order to increase aggregate demand is needed.
- ● Marxists argue that more radical changes are the only solution.

However, before we examine the topic in depth, we must first understand exactly what is meant by unemployment.

Defining and measuring unemployment

Defining unemployment

In everyday speech there is usually no need to make precise statements. If we say someone is unemployed, people will understand what we mean. In economics, however, we need to make precise statements and so precise definitions are needed. A useful simple definition of unemployment is someone who is willing and able to work, but cannot find a job. This approach is taken and developed by the International Labour Organisation, whose definition focuses on 'people without a job and seeking work for pay or profit'. However, this does not solve the problem of measuring unemployment because it is not always obvious if people are really seeking work. One reason for this difficulty is that people do not want any job; they want a job in a convenient place that pays reasonable wages. An unpleasant job in London, at a wage of £25 a week, would not appeal to many unemployed workers in Newcastle.

Measuring unemployment

There are two approaches to measuring unemployment. The first is to carry out a survey of the labour force in which a sample of members of the public are asked details of their work, or lack of it. This method is used in a number of countries, including the USA, Japan and Sweden. It gives a fairly accurate picture of the unemployment position on a national scale, but because the size of the sample in any one area is usually small, it does not give a clear picture of the position in particular parts of the country.

An alternative way of collecting unemployment statistics is to count people registering for work (or benefit) at state unemployment offices. This is the method used in the UK, where people are counted as unemployed if they register, are eligible for benefit and are actively seeking work. This gives a good picture of what is happening in small areas. The great weakness of the method is that if administrative arrangements change, then the statistics will show variations in the number registering as unemployed, even though there has been no change in the numbers actually unemployed. For example, in November 1982 the Department of Employment changed the system. Before that date the unemployment figures included all those seeking work, even if they were not entitled to benefit. Since November 1982 the basis of the figure has been the number of people entitled to benefit. The new system reduced the number of 'unemployed' by 100,000. In the decade following 1979 there were 24 changes in the way the unemployment statistics were compiled. According to the Unemployment Unit, an independent organisation which monitors the changing position, these changes reduced the number of unemployed by over 750,000.

Do the statistics over or underestimate unemployment?

The measurement of unemployment is a political issue and people's views influence the way the unemployment figures are interpreted. Those who wish to emphasise other aspects of government policy, such as the need to reduce inflation, tend to argue that the official figures overestimate the size of the problem, whilst others (often on the political left) believe there are far more people out of work than the figures show.

The first group claims that there are many people who are registered as unemployed who are not really seeking work, or who are not in financial difficulties as a result of being out of work. For example, someone who is between jobs might be quite happy to be unemployed for a week or two whilst receiving benefit. Indeed, unemployed people sometimes take on work and 'forget' to declare the income so they continue to receive benefit. Some people do not really want work and there are some people who are so physically or mentally handicapped that however much they want a job, they have little or no chance of finding one. If all

these were deducted from the unemployment figures, the number of unemployed - those who are really searching for work - would be much smaller and less effort need be devoted to solving the problem.

However, there are powerful arguments to suggest that the official figures underestimate the number of people seeking work. There are many people who are 'without a job and seeking work for pay or profit' but who are not counted as unemployed because they are not claiming benefit. Many married women are in this position, because if they have left paid employment to care for children they may be ineligible for benefit. Survey data suggests this group may number over half a million people. Other groups who are not counted as unemployed are those 'temporarily stopped' (that is those suspended by their employer but expecting to resume work) and workers on short time. Some people would also add those on special government schemes for the unemployed because they do not have a 'real' job. If this line of argument is accepted, then unemployment is much more serious than the official figures show and more effort ought to be devoted to solving the problem.

Stocks and flows

When unemployment is discussed, it is usually in the context of the number of people unemployed at

Table 16.1: *Jobless - the great divide*

Official total: 2,000,000

Left-wing critics ADD:		Right-wing critics SUBTRACT:	
Unemployed excluded by statistical changes	700,000	School leavers	150,000
Effect of special employment measures	400,000	Claimants who are not really looking for jobs	500,000
Unregistered unemployed	500,000	Severely disabled	20,000
		'Unemployables' - mentally or physically incapable	130,000
		'Job changers' - out of work for four weeks or less	350,000
		'Black economy' workers, illegally claiming benefit	250,000
Total additions	**1,600,000**	**Total subtractions**	**1,400,000**
TOTAL UNEMPLOYED	**3,600,000**	**TOTAL UNEMPLOYED**	**600,000**

Note: Approximate totals for 1988.

Source: Adapted from *The Daily Telegraph*.

a particular time. This can be misleading because it emphasises unemployment as a stock - a figure at a particular time. A more realistic approach is to view it as a flow, because each month many thousands of people become unemployed and thousands of others obtain work.

Figure 16.1: *Number of 16 year olds available to enter the labour market*

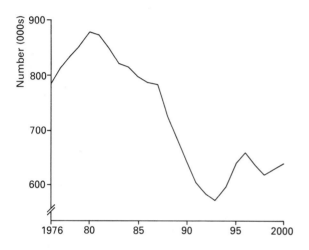

Note: The figures have been obtained by extrapolating the birth rate 16 years earlier. They therefore ignore migration and death.

Source: Adapted from OPCS.

One explanation of the rise in unemployment at the end of the 1970s focuses on the rise in the number of 16 year olds at this time as shown in Figure 16.1. Whilst some of these young people continued in full-time education, a large proportion sought employment. As the number of jobs on offer did not rise at the same rate, the result was a rise in unemployment. There is not much that can be done about the age structure of the population, but governments can take measures to reduce its effect on the labour market. Thus youth training schemes take some people off the unemployment register and at the same time increase the level of skills in the labour force. Figure 16.2 shows the extent of such measures. At the other end of the age range, early retirement can reduce the number of people counted as unemployed.

Key ideas

1. **People can be regarded as unemployed if they have no job and are actively seeking work.**
2. **Unemployment is often viewed as a stock. A better approach is to consider the flow of people into and out of employment.**
3. **There are two ways to measure unemployment: the first is to survey the labour force; the second to count those registering as unemployed or seeking benefit. The UK uses the latter method.**
4. **Some people believe the official unemployment figures exaggerate the problem because certain people who register as unemployed do not want work, or could get a job if they were less 'fussy'. Moreover, some unemployed people are not in financial hardship.**
5. **Others believe that the real unemployment total is higher than the figures suggest because many people wanting jobs are not counted as unemployed because they are not eligible for benefit.**

Figure 16.2: *Special employment measures, 1989*

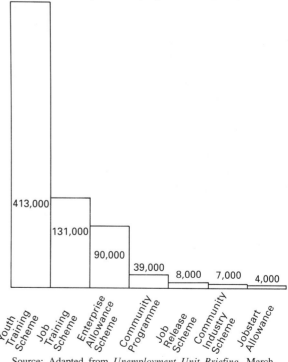

Source: Adapted from *Unemployment Unit Briefing*, March, 1989.

Does unemployment matter?

Everyone agrees that unemployment can be an unpleasant experience that imposes costs on the individual and on society, but there is disagreement about the size of these costs.

Unemployment and the individual

The obvious cost to the individual who is unemployed is relative poverty. Most unemployed people are poorer than those who are in work. It is true that for a few people social security benefits may mean they are better off unemployed than working, but they are exceptional. The extent to which people are poorer will depend on their particular circumstances, so that there are large variations from the average. However, a study by White (1983) into the long-term unemployed found that 59% of men were receiving benefits which amounted to less than half of the amount they had earned in their last job, and that a further 25% were receiving between 50% and 75% of their last net wage. Only 7% were better off unemployed than working. Women's incomes followed a similar pattern.

A fall in a family's income affects its whole lifestyle; parents cannot afford to 'treat' their children as they would wish and Christmas may become a time of stress, when youngsters compare their meagre presents with those of their more fortunate friends. Social life is restricted and it is difficult to buy essentials, such as clothes. Unemployment leads to stresses in the family. In most surveys, about one fifth of the unemployed report a deterioration in their mental health after becoming unemployed, and the longer they have been unemployed the more likely they are to report a deterioration. The unemployed tend to be more anxious, depressed, unhappy, suffer loss of self-esteem and sleep less than those with jobs. There is also evidence to suggest that the unemployed are more likely to have poorer physical health than the employed; they also have higher death rates. This type of evidence has its critics. It is difficult to prove cause and effect, and in some cases people may become unemployed because they have poor health rather than the other way round. Moreover, it is claimed that many unemployed people do not suffer very much from unemployment. In some cases, their out of work income is not much lower than they would earn in work, particularly if additional costs of working, such as travel, are counted. In

addition, the unemployed have more leisure time. And, the argument continues, if they really wanted work, they could find it if they were willing to be adaptable and accept low wages. This is examined in more detail later in this chapter.

Costs to the community

Communities also suffer when unemployment rates are high. Young people may move away, leaving behind an ageing community that needs to spend increasing amounts of money on social services. Throughout the country high levels of unemployment may lead to rises in the crime rate as people steal to increase their incomes, or break the law in search of excitement to break the monotony often associated with unemployment. This link between unemployment and crime is disputed; for example, in the mid-1980s, reported crime rose whilst unemployment fell.

Costs to the government

Unemployment increases government spending and cuts government revenue. Government spending increases because more public money is spent on unemployment benefit and on other social security payments, such as free school meals. It is hard to calculate the precise amount of increased spending

Table 16.2: *Approximate cost to the government of a million people unemployed*

	£ million (1981)	£ million (1989)
Increased expenditure:		
National Insurance benefits	700	700
Other social security	1,400	1,500
Housing benefit	100	100
Administration	300	300
	2,500	2,600
Lost revenue:		
Income tax	1,100	1,100
National Insurance contributions	950	1,000
Indirect taxes	950	1,000
	3,000	3,100
TOTAL	5,500	5,700

Source: Adapted from Dilnot, A.W. and Morris, C.N. 'The Exchequer Costs of Unemployment', Fiscal Studies, vol. 2 no. 3, 1981, and updated to give an indication of costs in 1989.

that results from unemployment because it depends on the family characteristics of the people who become unemployed. A rough estimate, such as that illustrated in Table 16.2, suggests that in the UK, for each million people who are unemployed, government spending will rise by £2,600 million. Unemployment also means that the government receives less money because jobless people pay less income tax.

Since their incomes are lower, they also buy fewer goods and services, so that the government takes less in VAT and in excise duties on goods such as petrol. A rough estimate of this cost would be £3,100 million. Note that these figures are estimates and the actual figures will vary as changes are made in benefit levels and tax rates. As Table 16.2 shows, the overall cost to the UK government is roughly £5,700 million for each million people unemployed.

Costs to society

The country as a whole is poorer as a result of unemployment. If the unemployed had been working, they would have produced goods and services which would have raised the standard of living of the country. This foregone output is the opportunity cost of unemployment. The Manpower Services Commission (now the Training Agency) calculated that each extra million people unemployed cost nearly £6,000 million of output foregone in 1981.

However, some short-term unemployment is inevitable and can bring some benefit to society in the form of increased efficiency. When workers lose their jobs, they become available for employment elsewhere and this increase in labour mobility helps growing firms to expand.

Key ideas

1. **Unemployment imposes costs on the unemployed, their families, the community, the government and society as a whole.**
2. **Individuals and their families suffer from lower incomes, poorer health and a lower status in society.**
3. **Communities with high levels of unemployment may deteriorate.**
3. **The government loses tax revenue and has to spend more on benefits.**
4. **National output falls as a result of unemployment.**

Types of unemployment

One approach to the study of unemployment is to analyse the different types of unemployment. Over a period of time the relative importance of each type will change. There is some disagreement about the relative importance of each type.

Seasonal unemployment

More people are unemployed in January than in July. This is because some industries are affected by the weather. In agriculture, tourism and construction, employers tend to take on more workers as the summer approaches and to reduce employment in winter. Consequently unemployment in these industries rises in the winter months.

This has implications for measuring unemployment. In a particular winter, the actual number of unemployed people may rise, but this may be due entirely to seasonal factors; the long-term trend may be falling. The opposite may apply in summer. Hence the employment figures are sometimes presented as 'seasonally adjusted'. This means that the actual figures have been adjusted to eliminate seasonal influences.

Whilst seasonal unemployment can be painful for the individuals concerned, it is not a major problem. This is just as well, because there are no easy cures for it. One approach is to attract new industries to tourist areas, or to extend the tourist season.

Frictional and search unemployment

Everyone agrees that the labour market has special characteristics which make it different from other markets. In the market for consumer goods, for example, buyers and sellers can usually exchange information quickly and purchases be made immediately. However, in the labour market both firms and workers need to search for information. Firms need information about the supply of labour and prevailing wage rates, whilst workers also incur costs when looking for work. Time is spent looking for appropriate posts and there may be travel and postage costs too. Sometimes workers have to decide between accepting a job now or waiting in the hope that a better one will become available in the future. The unemployment which occurs as a result of these search costs is called search unemployment. A key to understanding this type of unemployment is that people are ignorant about job opportunities. Some supply side economists believe it is a primary cause of the length of time that certain people are unemployed.

A closely related type of unemployment is frictional unemployment. Like search unemployment, this is present even when the economy is booming. In the twenty years after the Second World War, UK unemployment averaged less than 2%; most of it was frictional. As its name implies, this type of unemployment is caused because people do not move smoothly from one job to the next. It is not a serious problem because workers who are frictionally unemployed obtain jobs fairly quickly.

Structural unemployment

There is a good deal of agreement between economists about the existence of structural unemployment, but disputes about the causes and measures appropriate to deal with it. As its name implies, structural unemployment is caused by changes in the structure of the economy. In other words, there is dis-equilibrium in individual labour and product markets. Changes take place and the labour market is slow to adjust, causing unemployment. Thus changes in technology can cause unemployment. To give just one example of technological unemployment, for centuries dockers loaded individual items on to ships. When containers were introduced, items for transit were put into containers at the factory and far fewer people were needed on the docks because standard sized containers could be easily loaded on to specially designed ships.

Foreign competition can also cause structural unemployment. Britain used to have a substantial industry which manufactured motor cycles, but this was destroyed by competition from Japan. Changes in demand can have the same effect. At one time, almost every adult used to wear a hat or cap. This is now very rare, so employment in the hat making industry has declined substantially.

In all these examples, the labour market was affected by changes and unemployment was the result. The most spectacular examples arise from the decline of manufacturing industry in the UK, so that industries such as steel and car manufacturing have experienced huge falls in employment. Thus the British Steel Corporation (later British Steel) employed 254,000 people in 1968/69; twenty years later the number had fallen to less than 50,000. Since declining industries are highly concentrated in

particular areas, the effects can be very severe. This was the heart of the discussion of the regional problem in Chapter 8.

Policies for structural unemployment

Disagreements arise when policies are being suggested. Supply siders suggest policies which would emphasise market forces. Thus they believe that removing rent controls would lead to more houses becoming available for rent, so making it easier for people to move from areas where jobs have been lost to those where they are relatively plentiful.

Critics of this view argue that even if more houses did become available, the rents would be so high that those seeking jobs would be unable to afford them. These critics believe that market forces need to be curtailed by government action if much progress is to be made in reducing structural unemployment. Both groups would agree that one approach to reducing structural unemployment is that workers should retrain. However, supply siders would put the responsibility for this on individuals and firms. Keynesian economists would place more emphasis on government initiatives. This debate was discussed in more detail in Chapter 8.

Cyclical unemployment

Over a period of years, the level of unemployment rises and falls. This is sometimes called 'cyclical unemployment', though the term is not precise, because 'cyclical' implies a regular pattern and changes in unemployment are not regular. The rest of this chapter is largely concerned with explaining these changes in the level of unemployment. In order to do that, we need to develop theories about causation. Such theories are important, because policies develop from theories. Supply siders explain changes in unemployment by looking at changes in the demand and supply of labour, paying special attention to supply side factors. Keynesian economists argue that fluctuations in the level of unemployment are largely caused by changes in aggregate demand. Marxist economists argue that they are caused by conflicts which are inevitable in a capitalist society.

The supply side approach

Although this section is headed 'supply side approach', it could equally well have been called the 'market forces approach' or even the 'monetarist approach' because all these phrases identify particular aspects of a fairly common approach to unemployment. It represents a return to pre-Keynesian economics and is also known as neo-classical economics'. One of the popularisers of supply side economics, an American called Arthur Laffer (1983), has explained the position:

'Supply side economics provides a framework of analysis which relies on personal and private incentives. When incentives change, people's behaviour changes in response . . . The role of government in such a framework is carried out by the ability of government to alter incentives and thereby affect society's behaviour.'

The starting point of this approach is the labour market. As in any other market, the forces of demand and supply determine the quantity of the good or service bought and sold. The factors which determine the demand and supply of labour were discussed in Chapter 9. All we need to do here is repeat the central supply side argument; that the demand and supply of labour are primarily determined by the price of labour and that a fall in the real wage rate will cause firms to take on more workers. It will also lead to a decline in the number of people wanting work so that there will be fewer people wanting jobs who could not find them.

The natural rate of unemployment

This is one of the most important concepts in the supply side analysis of unemployment.

The natural rate of unemployment is the rate of unemployment which exists when the labour market is in equilibrium. Alternatively, it can be defined as the amount of unemployment which still exists when the labour market has cleared, that is when the demand for labour equals the supply because real wages are at a level which will bring about equilibrium. This implies that at the natural rate of unemployment the rate of inflation will be constant. Hence it is sometimes given the clumsy title of NAIRU - the Non-Accelerating Inflation Rate of Unemployment. (Some economists would distinguish between the natural rate of unemployment and NAIRU, but for practical purposes it is a distinction without much difference.)

The implication of this approach is that involuntary unemployment does not exist. If some people are unemployed it is because they choose not to take up employment at the going wage rate. They prefer unemployment to work at existing wages. The argument is illustrated in Figure 16.3. In this Figure, Ld shows the demand for labour. Lf is the size of the labour force and Ww the number of workers willing to take jobs at any level of real wages. The difference between Lf and Ww is that some workers are between jobs and some are unwilling to take jobs at the existing wage rate, perhaps because they are hoping for better offers. The labour market is in equilibrium at E, and ED is measure of natural unemployment.

If this supply side argument is accepted, then it is necessary to find out what factors determine the natural rate and then take appropriate measures to reduce it. According to Milton Friedman (1966) the natural rate is determined by:

'the actual structural characteristics of the labour and commodity markets, including labour imperfections . . . variability in demands and supplies, the costs of gathering information about job vacancies and labour availabilities, the costs of mobility and so on'.

Consequently the crucial factors on which this group of economists focus are the composition of the labour force, mobility of labour, costs of employing workers and imperfections in the labour market caused by government 'interference' and trade unions. According to one of the leading supply siders in the UK, Patrick Minford (1985), the natural rate was low until 1965 when there was a 'sharp rise in union power, in benefits and in taxation' and then the rate rose until it reached a maximum of 13.5% (about 3.25 million people) in 1980.

The natural rate of unemployment approach is criticised by some economists. In the first place, the word 'natural' seems to imply that it is 'God given' and that nothing can be done about it. In addition, they point out that the amount of natural unemployment is impossible to measure precisely. However, the main criticism they make is that the natural rate approach assumes the labour market is in equilibrium at the full employment level of output, and therefore any attempt by government to

Figure 16.3: *The natural rate of unemployment*

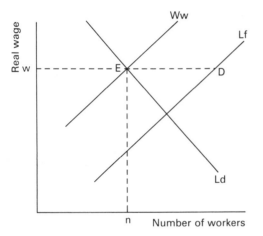

cut unemployment by stimulating the economy is doomed to fail. This assumption is criticised by Keynesian economists who argue that the economy can be in equilibrium at less than full employment. Hence governments should intervene to stimulate the economy.

Unemployment benefits

Supply siders argue that government intervention reduces the effectiveness of market forces by keeping the real wage above the point where the demand and supply of labour are in equilibrium. This prevents the labour market from clearing. According to Minford (1985):

'The first and fundamental cause of unemployment is the operation of the unemployment benefit system.' Anyone who is unemployed will receive benefits and *'Such a man will very naturally expect to be re-employed at a wage after tax and work*

Figure 16.4: *Effect of social security on employment*

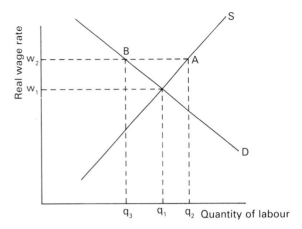

expenses which is at least as high as this benefit, and probably somewhat higher because he may not wish to "work for nothing" . . . Hence wages cannot effectively fall below this level for even the most unskilled worker. This level then acts as a floor under the whole wage structure . . . It follows that shifts in economic conditions which would warrant a fall in real wage costs, will have only a limited effect on them and unemployment will result instead.'

The argument is illustrated in Figure 16.4. Without any social security the market will clear at wage w_1 and q_1 units of labour will be employed. If a social security system is then put into operation so people can receive an income of w_2 when on the dole, then no one will work if wages are less than this. Hence the supply of labour is zero for wages below w_2 and the new supply of labour curve is w_2 BAS. At this level of wages the supply of labour exceeds the demand by AB. The social security system has created unemployment.

The replacement ratio

The amount of social security an unemployed person receives depends on family circumstances, so that a married person with a large family receives much more than a single person. The relationship between income when not in work and that received when working is called the replacement ratio. When this is 1.0 a person would receive the same income whether at work or unemployed. The rational person would therefore choose to be unemployed - why work when you can obtain the same income from being unemployed? Very high replacement ratios of 0.8 or 0.9 are found in cases where people only receive low incomes when at work and whose family circumstances would mean they receive high levels of social security. At the opposite end of the spectrum some single people earning high wages will have low replacement ratios. The social security system will not have much effect on their decision to work or not.

If this line of argument is correct, then the relationship between benefit levels and earnings will have a large impact on the level of unemployment. Minford (1985), for example, believes that replacement ratios are very high in the UK, exceeding 0.90 for over one in five single people and one in ten married people. Inserting this data into his model of the UK economy leads him to the conclusion that a 10% cut in benefits would lead to a fall in real wages of 2.1% and cause unemployment to fall by 500,000 and output to rise by 2.5%.

Very different results have been obtained by other researchers making different assumptions about family circumstances and behaviour (for example, Minford assumes that married women do not go out to work and also that people claim all the benefits to which they are entitled). Nickell and Andrews (1983) developed a computer model and concluded that for the long-term unemployed the replacement ratio was quite low - only 0.56. They concluded that they were unable to find any strong replacement ratio effects and that the level of employment benefit had only a marginal impact on unemployment.

One reason for these differences is that the calculation of replacement ratios can be complex because detailed analysis is needed to discover precisely what social security benefits an individual would be entitled to in different circumstances. For example, the birth of a child or an increase in rents may lead to an increase in benefits. The argument is about the extent to which the existence of unemployment benefits raises unemployment. Everyone agrees that for some people the possibility of receiving benefits will encourage them to go on the dole. The consensus seems to be that the effects are smaller than strong supply siders, such as Minford, would suggest. The policy implications of his approach are that radical reforms are needed to the social security system because:

'the current system of unemployment support is dangerously inefficient because it does not limit replacement ratios as work incomes fall'.

He therefore proposes that individual social security benefits should be limited so that, in all cases, net income whilst out of work would be substantially below net income whilst in work.

Tax rates

Supply siders also claim that high tax rates increase unemployment. This is because high rates discourage initiative. On the other hand, when income tax is low entrepreneurs will have more incentive to invest because they will be able to keep more of the profits. In this way, low tax rates help to develop an enterprise economy which leads to higher growth in the economy and so more people will be employed.

Trade unions

Supply siders dislike trade unions. Hayek (1984), a Nobel Prize winning economist, claims that the:

'powers of the unions have become the biggest obstacle to raising the living standards of the working class . . . They are the prime source of unemployment. They are the main reason for the decline of the British economy . . .'.

The main reason for this dislike is the belief that unions distort the working of market forces. If labour is mobile, wages will rise in expanding industries and in profitable firms and fall when industries decline and firms make losses. Trade unions attempt to prevent such wage cuts. They also attempt to maintain high levels of employment in declining industries. Such activities introduce rigidities into the labour market and increase the natural rate of unemployment. Even where the economy is expanding and level of employment is rising, supply siders claim that unions cause unemployment by pushing up the level of wages for their members. This cuts employers' demand for labour, causing unemployment. If unions do manage to maintain jobs for their members, then it is argued that the burden of unemployment falls on those not in unions.

The effect on the labour market of unions succeeding in an attempt to raise real wages is shown in Figure 16.5. Original equilibrium is at wage w_1, when q_1 units of labour will be employed. If real wages rise then the quantity of labour employed falls to q_2. Note that this analysis assumes that unions can push up real wages and not just nominal wages. If firms raise prices in line with wages there will be no rise in real wages. Moreover, even if there was a fall in employment in the unionised sector of the economy, some of those displaced would drift to the non-union sector. This increase in supply would force down wages and increase employment in that sector so that the overall result may be no change in the employment level.

Figure 16.5: *A shift in supply due to union action*

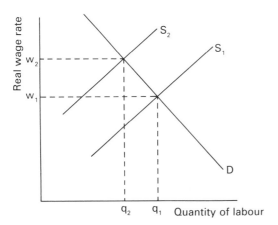

A number of estimates have been made of the effects of union power on employment, though all such studies lack precision, if only because it is difficult to quantify 'union power'. One measure often used is the number of people in unions, though this is not entirely suitable because the statistics of union membership are not very accurate and because numbers may not necessarily measure power or militancy.

Minford's model of the economy makes use of the unionisation rate and suggests that, other things being equal, a fall in the unionisation rate would lead to a fall in real wages of 0.8%, a fall in unemployment of 170,000 and a rise in output of 1%.

Other economists obtain very different results, even where they agree that unions do push up unemployment. Nickell and Andrews (1983) calculated that since the Second World War unions have pushed up unemployment by about 400,000. However, they also believe that it would be wrong to attempt to weaken the power of unions because they help the less privileged sections of society. Another estimate, this time by Layard and Nickell (1985) suggests that only 8% of the rise in unemployment after 1979 could be explained by union activity. They also calculate that in the post-war period the direct impact of unions on employment has been about 2 percentage points. One reason for the difference between this result and that of Minford is that Layard and Nickell use different measures of union militancy.

Key ideas - summary of the supply side approach

1. The labour market responds to market forces. If real wages are cut then employers will take on more workers.
2. The level of unemployment cannot be reduced below its natural rate.
3. Unemployment is largely voluntary; people could obtain work if they were willing to accept lower wages.
4. People need incentives to work. Social security payments and high tax rates reduce the incentive to work.
5. Trade unions distort the working of the labour market and cut employment.

Supply side policies

Policy proposals in this area follow from the basic belief that the labour market should be free of all restraints on competition and that any action which causes workers to join unions to fix the terms of their employment is a restraint of competition. Therefore it follows that laws should be passed which weaken the unions, for example, by making them liable for damages to employers who suffer losses as a result of strike action. Such legislation is opposed by those who believe that union power is necessary because otherwise individual workers would be powerless against the huge financial resources available to employers. According to the supply side argument, governments intervene in the labour market in a number of ways, causing unemployment to rise. They believe that high rates of income tax act as a disincentive to effort, so that some people will choose not to work. This is because rational people will consider the net effects of any action. High tax rates will shift the relative advantages against work causing people to choose leisure. National Insurance contributions paid by employees will also have the same effect.

But National Insurance contributions are also paid by companies on each employee. It is therefore argued that they act as a tax on jobs - the more people employed, the more tax which has to be paid. (This line of reasoning is also accepted by economists from other schools of thought.) The difficulty is that National Insurance contributions bring in large sums of money to the government which would find it difficult to raise the revenue in other ways. According to one estimate, the rise in

employers' National Insurance costs since the 1960s has increased unemployment by about 2%.

Governments also impose several non-wage labour costs on employers. Employment protection legislation may help workers to avoid unfair dismissal, but it also makes it more expensive to dismiss workers so employers are more reluctant to take on workers in the first place. Redundancy payments have the same effect. If the government imposes costs which make it more expensive to take on new workers, then employers will tend to encourage overtime among existing employees instead of increasing the number of jobs. However, empirical investigation suggests that whilst government legislation may be annoying to firms, it has relatively little effect on employment. In any case, these non-wage labour costs are usually lower in the UK than in other comparable countries.

Other policies favoured by supply side economists include measures to reduce the replacement ratio, for example, by cutting social security payments. They also favour cuts in income tax and other measures to improve industrial efficiency.

The Keynesian approach

The 1930s, like the 1980s, was a decade when unemployment was high and when economists disagreed strongly. The supply side analysis was the orthodox approach, but to the younger economists this failed to explain the high levels of unemployment. Their leader, John Maynard Keynes, believed that it was possible for the economy to be in equilibrium at less than the full employment level of output because markets fail to ensure that all those who want work can obtain it. He claimed:

'The system is not self-adjusting and, without purposive direction, it is incapable of translating our actual poverty into our potential plenty.'

His basic idea can be put simply. The number of people employed by a firm will depend on the demand for its products. If demand for shoes rises, more people will be employed in shoe factories and in shoe shops. If people buy more books then employment in publishing will rise. For the economy as a whole, the level of employment will depend on the level of aggregate demand. As was seen in Chapter 12, this is made up of consumer spending, investment, government spending and exports. Variables such as investment and exports are not easily manipulated by the government. Consequently governments attempting to increase aggregate demand either cut taxes, so that consumers spend more, or preferably (because consumers will save some of their extra take home pay or spend it on imports) increase its own spending. If the government spends more on schools, hospitals or housing, then employment in these industries will rise and unemployment will fall.

There are many theoretical and practical difficulties which this brief outline has ignored, but the basic idea is clear. The government should intervene in the market to ensure a satisfactory level of aggregate demand.

Modern Keynesians

Contemporary Keynesian economists have adapted and developed his original analysis to take account of modern conditions. For this group of economists the basic cause of mass unemployment remains too low a level of aggregate demand. Thus Layard and Nickell (1985) found that about a quarter of the increase in unemployment between 1966 and 1977 was caused by falls in aggregate demand, whereas almost three-quarters of the rise since then was caused by inadequate aggregate demand. Similar results were obtained by Junankar and Price (1983) who estimated that in the period between 1979 and 1981, when unemployment rose very rapidly, 67% of the increase in unemployment was caused by falls in aggregate demand. However, even if this theoretical analysis is accepted, there may be complications when attempts are made to implement the theory.

Complication 1: Inflation

One complication is the danger of inflation. Keynesian economists accept that as the economy nears the full employment level of output some prices will rise. If demand rises some firms will be able to increase output without putting up prices because they will be able to take advantage of economies of scale.

Other firms will be in a very different position. To increase output they will have to pay overtime rates of pay or increase wage rates in order to attract new staff. This will push up prices and cause inflation, particularly when there are only a relatively small number of unemployed workers. This effect will be greatest in those regions of the country where unemployment rates are low. The position is shown in Figure 16.6. This shows the aggregate demand and aggregate supply curves for the economy. At the original equilibrium position the average level of prices in the economy will be p_1 and the quantity of labour employed q_1. The government then expands aggregate demand to AD_2 and the result is an increase in the quantity of goods and services produced and hence in employment. However, prices also rise to p_2. If the government continues to increase aggregate demand to AD_3 the result is a much greater rise in prices and a relatively small increase in output and employment.

The Keynesian approach to this dilemma is to attempt to shift the aggregate supply curve to the right. This can be done in part by adopting some of the supply side measures discussed in the last section. Thus Layard (1986) titles one of his chapters

Figure 16.6: Increasing aggregate demand

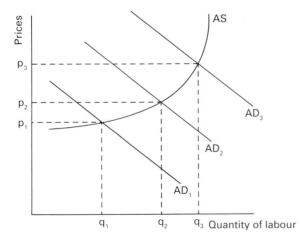

Figure 16.7: Supply side approach to an increase in aggregate demand

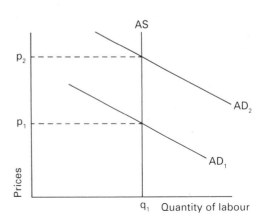

'Cutting Unemployment with Both Blades of the Scissors: More Demand and Improved Supply'. If these policies are successful they will encourage firms to produce more goods without putting up prices. This example illustrates that economists do sometimes agree!

A more typically Keynesian response is to adopt an incomes policy. This can take many forms, but all seek to control increases in wages. If these policies are successful then firms will be able to attract more workers without putting up wages and so increase output and employment without putting up prices.

This line of argument is rejected by supply siders. Strict supply siders believe that the long-run aggregate supply curve is vertical as shown in Figure 16.7. The reasons for this conclusion were discussed in Chapter 13. If the aggregate supply curve is this shape, any attempt to reduce unemployment by increasing aggregate demand will fail. The only result will be a rise in prices.

Complication 2: The balance of payments

A second problem which may occur when attempting to implement a Keynesian policy towards unemployment is that the economy will run into a balance of payments problem. As the circular flow of income diagram in Chapter 12 shows, the prime determinant of the level of imports is the level of incomes in the economy. If incomes rise, many people respond by taking a foreign holiday or buying foreign-made goods, such as compact disc players or video recorders. Thus the result of an increase in aggregate demand may be a fall in unemployment, but the rise in incomes which accompanies this will suck in imports and lead to a balance of payments deficit. There are a number of ways in which such a deficit can be tackled, and these are discussed in Chapter 19. However, none are particularly effective except the imposition of a deflationary policy which requires the imposition of higher taxes and cuts in government spending - precisely the measures which will cause unemployment to rise.

In recent years the balance of payments problem in the British economy has been eased by the flow of North Sea oil, but as the economy expanded in the 1980s the problem returned. Keynesian economists accept that there is no easy solution to this problem. One approach is to cut the value of the pound compared to other currencies. For the reasons given in Chapter 20, this will mean there is a fall in the price of British goods in overseas

markets which will encourage exporters and increase employment in exporting industries. A fall in the value of the pound will also mean that imports are more expensive. This will help domestic manufacturers fight off foreign competition.

Key ideas - summary of Keynesian ideas

1. **The level of income and employment is largely determined by the level of aggregate demand.**

2. **The government should vary its spending and taxation policies in order to obtain the full employment level of aggregate demand.**

3. **Two problems which may arise are the likelihood of inflation or a deficit on the balance of payments. Appropriate measures to solve these problems include an incomes policy and a fall in the value of the pound.**

Keynesian policies

Keynesians accept that there is no easy solution to the problem of unemployment. Their policies derive from the theoretical analysis which suggests that aggregate demand is the prime determinant of the level of employment. Since some components of aggregate demand are not under government control, Keynesians focus their policy measures on government spending and taxation. Cutting taxes may help, but some of the extra income received by consumers will be saved or spent on exports. Therefore a better measure is to increase government spending which should be targeted on sectors of the economy which require few imports - health, education and construction are examples. Expenditure on training is another example; this would also make industry more competitive. Government spending should also be targeted on those regions where unemployment is highest. If these measures lead to inflation, an incomes policy will mitigate this. Similarly, a fall in the value of the pound will help keep British exporters competitive.

The Marxist approach

The Marxist approach is very different. Both supply siders and Keynesians are attempting to make the existing system work better. Underlying the Marxist approach, however, is the belief that conflict and crises are inevitable in any capitalist system and

that, in the long run, problems such as unemployment will only be overcome by a change in the nature of the system itself.

From this it follows that, for Marxists, the Keynesian analysis is inadequate. They accept that stimulating aggregate demand would relieve unemployment, but believe the improvement would not solve the basic problem which is inherent in the system itself. For example, they criticise the Keynesian view of the way the state is supposed to operate. For most Keynesians, the state - the government, civil service, police etc. - is politically neutral. For Marxists the position is very different. They argue that the state and its institutions are the instruments of the ruling class and the aim of the state is the continuance of the system. Thus when unemployment rises, as it did after 1979, they are not surprised to see this accompanied by large increases in spending on the police and the armed forces which will then be in a position to crush any trouble arising from increased unemployment.

So far as Keynesian economic policies are concerned, some of these would be supported by Marxists, some would not. If the effect of a Keynesian reflation was a fall in unemployment, this would strengthen the power of the workers relative to that of the employers. This power shift would be opposed by the capitalists and since in the Marxist view these control the state, the state apparatus would ensure that such reforms did not succeed; for example, many capitalists would move their money overseas thus causing a sterling crisis. Hence any improvement in unemployment resulting from Keynesian policies would only be temporary because it would be followed by a new crisis. Some other Marxist-orientated economists are rather more sympathetic to certain elements of Keynesianism so long as it is coupled with structural reforms, for example, the nationalisation of key industries which would weaken the power of the capitalists and could be used by a socialist government to increase investment and employment.

Marxist analysis of crisis

In a capitalist society the aim of the owners of capital is to increase profits rather than production. Decisions will be made using the criterion of profitability. This will lead to conflict. There will be conflicts with other firms as they all compete for markets and there will be conflicts with workers, as employers try to keep down wages and workers try to raise them. Because these conflicts are integral to the system, they inevitably produce crises from time to time.

Falling profits

These crises can originate in a number of ways. Marx believed there was a long-run tendency for the rate of profit to fall. That is because the search for profits forces business people to accumulate more and more capital goods, such as machinery. The process of accumulation will lead to a relative increase in the amount of capital power compared to labour power. However, in the Marxist view profits arise because the value of the output produced by the workers is higher than the wage received by the workers. This is called 'surplus value' and, since it is produced by workers, the rate of profit will decline over time because the ratio of workers to capital will decline.

Consequently Marxist economists frequently produce evidence of the falling rate of profit. This decline is a long-run phenomenon, countered in the short run by other factors, such as increased productivity or wage cuts. However, from time to time the rate of profit will fall and for some firms this will mean losses and bankruptcies which will lead to a rise in unemployment. This creates a 'reserve army of labour' which is beneficial to employers. This reserve army provides an easily-available supply of workers which can be used when the economy starts to expand again. It also helps to keep down wages and makes those in work less militant because they know there are others who would like their jobs. As Marx put it, the reserve army of labour:

'creates, for the changing needs of the self expansion of capital, a mass of human material always ready for exploitation'.

In this way unemployment is beneficial to capitalists and it is not surprising to Marxists that it is a characteristic feature of such economies.

Contradictions in the system

The desire to keep down wages leads to a basic contradiction within capitalism. On the one hand, workers are buyers of goods and services and the money they spend is necessary if profits are to be maintained. On the other hand, higher profits also require low wages in order to keep down costs. If employers succeed in keeping down wages the result will be a crisis of overproduction (under-consumption). This is very similar to the Keynesian notion of unemployment caused by insufficient aggregate demand. For Marxists, the crisis is one of **realisation;** the capitalist cannot sell sufficient goods to realise the full surplus value. Profits fall and so will investment, causing problems in firms which

produce investment goods. For Marx this was a crucial cause of unemployment:

'The last cause of all real crisis always remains the poverty and restricted consumption of the masses compared to the tendency of capitalist production to develop the productive forces in such a way that only the absolute power of consumption of the entire society would be their limit.'

Translated into intelligible English, Marx is saying that the system forces firms to compete by investing in more and more machinery, but workers' incomes will not grow fast enough to enable them to consume all the goods that could be produced!

Secondary causes

So much for the basic cause of unemployment. In any particular case the basic causes will be exacerbated by secondary factors, such as the structural weakness of the UK economy caused by low investment. Another cause is the international monetary and trade system which has meant that Britain has faced competition from less developed countries and other countries in the European Community. Moreover, the international monetary system has caused some countries to threaten to default on their international debts thus causing repercussions in other countries. For example, when the world price of oil rises, many of the poorer countries of the world are forced to cut back on imports of other goods, thus causing unemployment to rise in other countries. They also respond to the higher price by borrowing money from abroad, but in the longer run this causes further problems when the debt has to be repaid.

Criticisms of the Marxist approach

These Marxist ideas are criticised on a number of grounds. Both supply side economists and Keynesians reject the basic Marxist belief that unemployment is inevitable in a capitalist system. They argue that appropriate policies can solve the problem - though, of course, they disagree about the policies. In other words they want to improve the working of the present system, not change the entire system. Moreover, both groups would be likely to reject the amount of state intervention which the Marxists would like (though some radical Keynesians would advocate an increase in public ownership). They tend to argue that state intervention is inefficient, leading to a waste of resources because large numbers of bureaucrats would be needed to run the system. The notion of a

falling rate of profit is also criticised. Empirical evidence is inconclusive because it is possible to measure profit in several ways and the data is not always accurate. Critics of the Marxist position argue that the rate of profit will rise and fall over time, rising when the economy expands and falling in periods of depression.

> ### Key ideas - summary of the Marxist approach
>
> 1. **Economic crisis is inevitable in a capitalist society. If wages are too high, owners will suffer from low profits. If wages are too low, sales will fall and so will profits.**
> 2. **In the long run, unemployment can only be wiped out by a revolutionary change to a socialist society.**
> 3. **The basic causes of unemployment are exacerbated by structural factors, such as low investment and the international monetary system, both of which lead some countries to build up huge debts.**

Marxist policies

There is some disagreement between Marxists about the precise policies which should be adopted in the short run because they believe that unemployment is caused by the nature of the system itself and can only be overcome by changing it. For these Marxists, what is needed is that production should be organised for need, not profit. This implies that about 200 of the largest firms should be nationalised in order that the state can control output and employment. Other Marxists suggest less radical measures, many of which are along Keynesian lines of increased public expenditure. Marxists would reinforce this by including some nationalisation, for example, of part of the banking sector in order to ensure cheap loans for industry.

'To ensure that financial resources are fully used for the programme of industrial regeneration, key sectors of banking and finance would become part of a publicly owned system'

argues the Marxist economist Aaronovitch (1981).

Many Marxists also favour some measure of import controls so that the economy can expand without running into a balance of payments problem. Some radical Keynesians also advocate such measures. Marxists also argue that unemployment can also be reduced by measures which reduce the supply of labour, for example, a reduction in overtime so that existing work could be shared out more evenly.

Behind all these proposals is a belief that radical state intervention is required to reduce unemployment. Planning output and employment is needed to bring stability into the system.

Conclusion

The three approaches to unemployment discussed here have been presented as three separate and distinct theories. Whilst this is largely true, it should be remembered that it is something of an oversimplification. There is disagreement within each group and some overlap of views. Thus some Keynesians accept the need to improve the supply side of the economy whilst some would agree with Marxist views about the need for an increase in public ownership.

Nevertheless, it is possible to identify three distinct strands of thinking, each with its own policy proposals. The economists who are here called supply siders focus on the market and on incentives. Their strategy leads to less government intervention and cuts in taxation and public spending, particularly on social security benefits. Keynesians believe government intervention is necessary, particularly to ensure an adequate level of aggregate demand and help hard hit regions. Marxists would like a much greater degree of government intervention in the economy and a substantial increase in the public sector. These three views are not compatible; it is not possible to select the 'best' of each approach and advocate this package because the policies are often contradictory. For example, supply siders argue that cuts in real wages will increase employment, whilst many Keynesians would oppose such cuts because they believe that they lead to a fall in aggregate demand and hence employment.

Data questions

Charter for jobs

1. We believe that the present level of unemployment is economically wasteful and socially corrosive. The Government can and must stimulate the creation of more jobs.

2. There is useful work crying out to be done. With extra spending we could renovate our cities and improve the health of our people, while lower taxes on jobs would raise private spending power and make us more competitive. To make this possible there has to be some increase in Government borrowing. Government borrowing should normally rise in a depression. When there is useful work to be done, it is as sensible for the Government to borrow money as for firms or families to do so.

3. The Government has a special responsibility for the million and a quarter people who have been unemployed for over a year.

These people should be guaranteed the offer of a job on socially useful projects, such as the Community Programme supports.

We can cut unemployment.

Source: Charter for Jobs, London.

Question 1

Examine the 'Charter for Jobs'.
1. Explain why unemployment can be 'economically useful and socially corrosive'.
2. Which economic theory lies behind these public proposals?
3. What problems could result from such a policy proposal?

Proposals for reducing unemployment

1. Cutting the tax on jobs
2. Easing the unemployment trap
3. Reforming the unions
4. Community work for all who want it
5. Fostering new work patterns
6. Encouraging profit sharing
7. Reducing the replacement ratio

Source: Adapted from the *Daily Telegraph*, January 29 and 30, 1985.

Question 2

1. Explain the proposals, stating exactly how they would help to reduce unemployment.

2. What criticisms would Keynesian economists make of the suggestions? What alternative policies would they advocate?

17 Inflation

When prices are more or less steady there is little interest in inflation; but when they do rise it becomes the prime focus of economic attention. Everyone recognises that when inflation gets out of control it can have severe consequences:

● Monetarists believe that inflation is the supreme economic evil and that the government should give top priority to eradicating it. The background to their methods was discussed in Chapter 15. For these economists, the only way to conquer inflation is to control the money supply.

● Keynesian economists argue that the undesirable effects of inflation are often exaggerated, though they do recognise that high inflation rates cause problems. They put forward two possible causes of inflation. In the first place they suggest that excess aggregate demand can lead to rising prices. Secondly, they point to supply factors, such as wage increases or rises in the price of raw materials like oil, as the causative factors. A variation of this approach comes from sociologists who suggest that inflation derives from social conflict. As this increases, disadvantaged groups seek to improve their position by forcing up their incomes, and this leads to inflation.

How accurate are the measures of inflation?

Inflation can be defined as a **persistent** increase in the general level of prices. Hence a rise in the price of one or two goods is not called inflation; nor is a once and for all increase in the general price level.

There is no perfect way to measure inflation. In practice, the first step is to find out what goods and services people actually buy. This is done through a survey of about 7,000 households. The items purchased are given 'weights' according to their importance. This is because it does not matter much to most people if there is a rise in the price of drawing pins or shoe laces, but rent or food price increases will have a significant effect. Table 17.1 shows the weights used for a group of items. Their precise importance varies over time. Over the last few years we have spent **relatively** less on food and more on transport and housing. From this survey, the authorities derive a notional 'basket' of goods which represents the spending pattern of a typical household. However, since few households are typical, these average figures will not be an accurate measure of the inflation rate for particular households. This is because some families spend much more on, say, cars so a rise in the cost of motoring would have a much bigger effect on them than on others who rely on public transport. The second stage is to find out the prices of these goods and services. For some items, such as electricity, this is done nationally, but the prices of most goods are found by officials visiting a range of shops. The information is then used to calculate the cost of a notional basket of goods. This is repeated each month, making it possible to compare the change in prices over time.

The Retail Price Index

In order to make comparisons easier, the actual price of the basket is translated into an index number. Essentially this involves comparing the cost of the basket of goods in one year with that in a base year which is given the value of 100. That is:

$$\text{Price index} = \frac{\text{Cost of basket today}}{\text{Cost of basket in base year}} \times 100$$

Hence if the cost of the basket of goods rose by 50% over a period of time, then the price index would rise from 100 to 150. Percentage changes in the Retail Price Index (RPI) for the UK in recent years are shown in Figure 17.1.

Table 17.1 *Weights used in compiling the Retail Price Index*

	At January 1988 prices	At January 1989 prices	
	1988 weights	1988 weights	1989 weights
Food	163	158	154
Catering	50	50	49
Alcoholic drink	78	77	83
Tobacco	36	35	36
Housing	160	179	175
Fuel and light	55	55	54
Household goods	74	72	71
Household services	41	40	41
Clothing and footwear	72	71	73
Personal goods and services	37	36	37
Motoring expenditure	132	128	128
Fares and other travel costs	23	23	23
Leisure goods	50	47	47
Leisure services	29	29	29
All items	**1,000**	**1,000**	**1,000**

Source: *Employment Gazette*, HMSO, April, 1989.

Figure 17.1: *The Retail Price Index: increases over previous year*

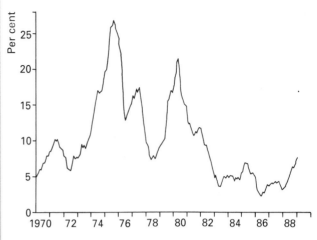

Source: *Employment Gazette*, HMSO, April, 1989.

The Retail Price Index is only one way in which the level of inflation can be measured. A separate index is calculated for pensioners, since this group has different spending patterns to the population as a whole. Another index takes into account changes in tax and National Insurance and is called the Tax and Price Index. This attempts to measure the changes in income before tax which the average person would need to maintain their purchasing power.

Two more indexes can be mentioned. The Producer Price Index measures changes in the cost of primary products and is, therefore, a useful predictor of future changes in the Retail Price Index. Finally, the GDP deflator takes account of changes in the cost of non-marketed goods, such as health and education. It is used when economists want to eliminate the effects of inflation when comparing changes in national income over time.

All price indexes have limitations. We have already mentioned that the RPI only measures the goods bought by the average family, and few people are average. Moreover, it is difficult to take proper account of the effect of new goods that appear on the market, since these will not appear for some years in the 'basket' of goods used to construct the index. During this time their price may fall. This is what has happened to the prices of items such as calculators and computers.

Another limitation arises because the RPI is concerned with changes in prices. If the quality of goods improves or deteriorates this will not be reflected in the index. If the price of cars rises by 5% but their quality improves by 10%, consumers will be better off, but this will not be reflected in the index. Finally, problems arise when making international comparisons. In the UK mortgage repayments are included in the 'basket', so when interest rates rise so will the measured rate of inflation. In most other countries these payments are not included.

Key ideas

1. **Inflation is a persistent increase in the general level of prices.**
2. **In the UK, the Retail Price Index measures the changes in the price of a basket of goods bought by the average family. Other measures include the producer price index and the GDP deflator.**

Does inflation matter?

What are the effects of inflation on the economic life of the community? In everyday life, people tend to assume that inflation is undesirable, but it is necessary for economists to be more precise and analyse the exact effects. This is easier to say than to do. One reason is that the effects depend to a large extent on whether the inflation is anticipated. If people expect inflation to be 10% and it is 10%, then they can change their behaviour to take account of this. However, if they expect a zero or low rate of inflation and the actuality is a high rate, then the effects are much more serious.

Perfectly anticipated inflation

If we assume that people can anticipate inflation perfectly, then the main costs will tend to be relatively minor because people can change their behaviour to minimise the undesirable effects.

Shoe leather costs

This takes two forms. Since not all prices rise at the same rate, people spend time shopping around for the lowest price. Secondly, money loses its value in inflationary times, so the rational individual holds little money and consequently has to make frequent trips to the bank to withdraw money.

Menu costs

Firms have to spend time and money changing price tags, altering vending machines and so on.

Psychological costs

Even though people anticipate rises, they can still be annoyed when they find that prices have actually gone up. This cost is much greater when the inflation is unexpected. For example, some people will find they have not enough money to pay the bill when they reach the supermarket till.

Unanticipated inflation

If people do not anticipate the rate of inflation perfectly, then the effects are more severe.

Redistributional costs

These take several forms. In the first place, people tend to pay more in tax. This is because many incomes rise with inflation so that some people will move into higher tax brackets (unless tax allowances are increased at the rate of inflation). Also, as prices rise, the government will obtain more money from a standard rate of VAT.

Secondly, inflation reduces the real value of the National Debt. Hence the government benefits, but people who have lent money to the government lose out. This is a specific example of a general point; inflation benefits borrowers while lenders lose. That is because the money paid back by borrowers is worth less than the money which they borrowed. One consequence of this is that in recent years people who have borrowed money to buy houses have benefited greatly. Another group of losers are those on fixed incomes. People receiving state pensions do not lose because these are increased to take account of inflation, but some people receive incomes which do not rise with inflation and risk sinking into poverty.

These redistribution effects are undesirable because they are arbitrary. Whether they are **serious** is open to debate. The extent of the gains and losses is unclear. In some cases the redistribution may be from rich to poor (which some people may think is desirable), though some will be from the less well-off to those with greater resources.

Balance of payments

When prices rise in a country it tends to become more difficult for that country to export because its goods are less competitive. Moreover, the high prices which can be charged will encourage foreigners to send more goods to that country. Hence it can be argued that inflation will worsen the balance of payments. However, this assumes that the rate of exchange remains the same. If prices in country A rise by 10% more than those in the rest of the world, but the value of A's currency falls by 10%, then this balance of payments effect will disappear.

Investment

Monetarists tend to argue that inflation will lead to a decline in investment because it makes entrepreneurs less certain about the future. However, it may encourage investment if firms see their profits rising (even though they may be constant in real terms). In addition, since firms often borrow money to invest, they will benefit as borrowers and so be encouraged to invest. The overall effect is uncertain. In most cases it may be that the effect of inflation is small compared to the other influences on investment.

Unemployment

According to supply side economists, such as Milton Friedman, inflation is likely to increase the level of unemployment. That is partly because he believes it will reduce investment as mentioned above. An indirect reason is that he believes inflation leads to a fall in efficiency, since firms and workers find it difficult to judge if price rises result from inflation or from an increase in demand. In other words, inflation prevents the price system from working as well as it should. Misleading messages replace the clear signals of the price system. Efficiency falls, with the result that unemployment rises. Friedman also argues that inflation can lead to stronger trade unions and to governments introducing inappropriate policies, such as prices and incomes policies. Both these developments weaken the market and cause a less efficient allocation of resources and possibly higher unemployment.

These claims by Friedman are not universally accepted by economists. The relationship between inflation and unemployment is discussed in the next section in more detail.

Hyper-inflation

Some economists believe that inflation can lead to political and social disintegration. In part this depends on the rate of inflation. In the First World War, several countries suffered from very high inflation and this led Keynes to write:

'There is no subtler, no surer means of overturning the existing basis of society than to debauch the currency.'

This is an opinion of Keynes with which Friedman heartily agrees. There is little evidence to suggest that 'ordinary' rates of inflation lead to the overthrow of society. Countries as diverse as Brazil and Israel have experienced inflation rates of over 100% per annum and show no signs of disintegration. However, hyper-inflation can accelerate and destroy a currency's usefulness as a means of exchange. The best known example of this was the depreciation of the German mark in the period 1921-1923 as shown in Table 17.2. A change such as this means that people can find their life savings become worthless, and as a result they turn to political extremists.

Key ideas

1. **The effects of inflation differ according to whether or not it is anticipated.**
2. **Even when inflation is anticipated, there are shoe leather, menu and psychological costs.**
3. **Unanticipated inflation can affect income distribution, the balance of payments, investment and employment.**

Inflation and unemployment

In the 1950s, A.W. Phillips compared the rate of change of money wages in the UK with the rate of unemployment over 100 years. Since there is a close statistical link between the rate of change of money wages and the rate of inflation, money wages are sometimes used as a proxy for inflation and used to analyse the relationship between inflation and unemployment. The link between these variables found by Phillips is called the Phillips curve and is shown in Figure 17.2.

The curve suggested a trade-off between these two variables. This meant the government had a choice between a position such as A where unemployment is low, but wage rates (and hence inflation) are rising quickly, and B where unemployment is high but wage rates (and inflation) are rising very slowly. Note that the terms of the trade-off vary over the length of the curve. To the right of B, for example, unemployment has to increase substantially in order to achieve only a small fall in the rate of inflation. To the left of B a much bigger fall in inflation is achieved for a relatively small rise in unemployment.

Table 17.2: *The depreciation of the German mark, 1921-23*

Date	Price index	Currency in circulation (billion marks)
1921 July	1	123
1922 July	7	1,295
1923 January	195	
1923 July	5,230	
1923 August	66,017	
1923 September	1,674,755	
1923 October	496,209,790	2,500,000
1923 November 15	54,448,000,000	92,000,000

Source: Jefferson, M. *Inflation*, Calder, 1977.

Figure 17.2: *The Phillips curve*

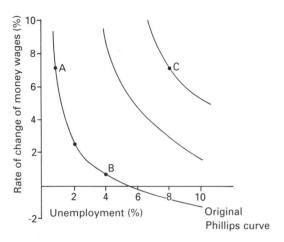

A number of explanations were put forward to explain this relationship. At a position such as A, unemployment is very low, so many people have money to spend, aggregate demand is high and this pulls up prices. Moreover, at A there will also be a shortage of labour in some areas and this will push up wages (and prices).

Phillips' analysis of the relationship between inflation and unemployment was published in 1958 and the relationship seemed to hold true for a decade after that. Then it broke down; the economy suffered high rates of inflation and unemployment at the same time. The Phillips curve had moved to the right to a position such as C, with relatively high levels of both inflation and unemployment. These reasons are discussed in detail later in this chapter, but briefly the monetarists suggested that people had come to expect higher rates of inflation and so claimed higher wages, and that the government financed the inflation by allowing the money supply to rise. Keynesian economists on the other hand stressed

changes in costs, such as the rise in oil prices and the strength of trade unions. These pushed up prices, irrespective of the unemployment level.

In 1985, Lewis attempted to identify the main sources of inflation and considered five categories as shown in Table 17.3. He found that increases in wages accounted for over a third of the rise in prices, but that the relative importance of each factor varied over time. Hence in 1973/74 import prices (particularly oil) were the most important source of inflation.

An analysis such as this identifies possible sources of inflation, but it does not offer a coherent theory of why inflation occurs and why the rate of inflation varies over time. It will come as no surprise to discover that economists have competing theories about these matters.

Key ideas

1. The Phillips curve suggested a statistical relationship between the rate of change of money wages (which was used as a proxy for inflation) and unemployment.
2. Many economists interpreted this relationship to imply a trade-off between the two variables.
3. Subsequently the curve shifted to the right, showing high levels of inflation and unemployment.

The monetarist approach

The monetarist approach to the control of inflation has three elements: the quantity theory of money, expectations and the Phillips curve, and the system of exchange rates.

Table 17.3: *Components of inflation in the UK, 1970/71-1982/83*

Components of inflation rate	1970/1	1971/2	1972/3	1973/4	1974/5	1975/6	1976/7	1977/8	1978/9	1979/80	1980/1	1981/2	1982/3
Labour costs	2.5	4.1	2.7	7.2	11.2	3.5	3.2	3.9	5.6	7.6	3.8	1.5	1.2
Capital costs	3.2	3.9	2.6	0.8	4.3	5.0	7.4	3.4	2.6	3.0	2.5	2.8	2.7
Imported goods	0.8	0.6	5.0	9.0	3.0	4.7	3.0	0.6	1.6	2.0	1.1	1.6	1.7
Indirect taxes	0.2	0.4	-0.1	-0.3	3.8	3.1	4.4	1.6	4.7	3.8	3.1	1.8	0.2
Residual	1.7	-2.4	-1.6	0.6	1.3	-0.6	-2.8	-0.7	-1.7	0.1	0.4	0.8	-0.4
Inflation rate	8.4	6.6	8.6	17.3	23.6	15.7	15.2	8.8	12.8	16.5	10.9	8.5	5.4

Source: Lewis, M. 'Money and the control of inflation in the UK', *Midland Bank Review*, Summer, 1985.

The quantity theory of money

This has been extensively discussed in Chapter 15. Here we can examine it in a slightly different way. If we assume that the supply of money is unaffected by the demand for it (an assumption which non-monetarists would not accept), then for the monetary sector to be in equilibrium the demand for money must equal the supply and we can write:

$$\Delta Md = \Delta Ms$$
$$\text{and}$$
$$\Delta Md = a\Delta Y - b\Delta R + \Delta P$$

where Δ = change in. This equation says that the change in the demand for money (ΔMd) has three parts. In the first place, it depends on changes in the level of national income ($a\Delta Y$), a rise in which will lead to a rise in the demand for money for transactions purposes. The a in the equation measures the income elasticity of the demand for money, that is the extent to which a rise in incomes will lead to a rise in the demand for money.

The second element in the equation says that the demand for money will depend on the rate of interest ($b\Delta R$). A rise in the rate of interest will increase the opportunity cost of holding money and so lead to a decline in demand for it. The b in the equation measures the interest elasticity of the demand for money, that is the extent to which a rise in the rate of interest will lead to a fall in the demand for money. The final element says that a rise in the rate of inflation (ΔP) will lead to a rise in the demand for money - as prices rise people will want more money to finance their transactions. The monetarist argument is that any increase in the supply of money will lead to a rise in the demand for money in order to maintain equilibrium. In the short run, the effect will be on Y and on R, but in the longer term, Y - the level of national income - is determined by 'real' factors, such as productivity and the size of the labour force. Monetarists also argue that b (the size of changes in the demand for money resulting from changes in the rate of interest) is very low. Hence it follows that, in the long run, changes in the supply of money will affect the price level.

Expectations and the Phillips curve

As we saw earlier, the original Phillips curve suggested an inverse relationship between the rate of inflation and the level of unemployment, but that in the 1970s the relationship broke down and the economy was faced with high rates of inflation and

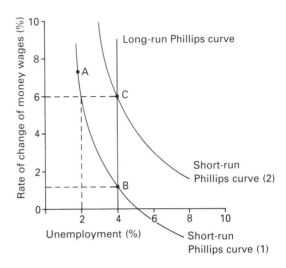

Figure 17.3: *Expectations-augmented Phillips curve*

unemployment. Monetarist critics, such as Friedman, claimed that the reason why this relationship broke down was because there was no trade-off in the long run. His argument was that workers were interested in **real** wages. If they expected prices to rise by 5%, they would demand wages which increased by at least this amount.

The effect of including expectations is to shift the curve to the right. If at a position such as B in Figure 17.3 workers expect inflation to be 5%, they will demand an extra 5% in wages; this will push up prices by an extra 5%, and the result will be a point on a new Phillips curve (at C). In fact, this is a point on a **vertical** Phillips curve. For this group of economists, there is no trade-off and the long-run curve is vertical.

Their reasoning is this. If at a point such as B the economy is in equilibrium, but the government tries to stimulate the economy, the immediate result will be an increase in the money supply which will increase aggregate demand. This causes an increase in the demand for labour to produce the extra goods. However, since this group of economists believes that the labour market is in equilibrium, the only way for firms to attract more workers is to put up wages. But this then pushes up prices by an equivalent amount. This means the real wage falls so the extra workers drop out of the labour market leaving production at its original position. The only effect of the attempt to stimulate the economy has been a rise in prices and wages; with output and unemployment unchanged. The Phillips curve will be vertical at the natural rate of unemployment.

The exchange rate

This is discussed more extensively in Chapter 20. Here it is sufficient to note that in a system of fixed exchange rates (that is one where the value of a currency is fixed against other currencies so that the pound always equals, say, $1.70) a balance of payments surplus or deficit will affect the supply of money. For example, a surplus will mean that money will flow into the country and so increase the money supply. However, if the exchange rate is floating - so that the value of the currency varies each day - the authorities have more control over the money supply because they can allow the value of the currency to vary if there is a surplus or deficit in the balance of payments. This means that if money is flowing into the country as a result of a balance of payments surplus, they can allow the value of the currency to rise, so making exports more expensive and reducing the surplus.

Non-causes of inflation

In *Free To Choose* (1980), Milton and Rose Friedman list factors which non-monetarists sometimes suggest as causes of inflation, and which

they claim are not causal factors:
- Unions may provide useful services for their members. They may also do a great deal of harm by limiting employment opportunities for others, but they do not produce inflation. Wage increases in excess of increases in productivity are a result of inflation, rather than a cause.
- Similarly, businessmen do not cause inflation. The rise in the prices they charge is a result or reflection of other forces. Businessmen are surely no more greedy in countries that have experienced much inflation than in countries that have experienced little.
- Neither is inflation imported from abroad. If it were, how could the rates of inflation be so very different in different countries?

They conclude:

*'We return to our basic proposition. Inflation is primarily a **monetary phenomenon,** produced by a more rapid increase in the quantity of money than in output . . . Many phenomena can produce temporary fluctuations in the rate of inflation, but they can have lasting effects only insofar as they affect the rate of monetary growth.'*

Monetarist policies

The essential feature of a monetarist policy towards controlling inflation will come as no surprise - the government must keep the supply of money under control. The quantity of money should only be allowed to increase at a steady rate linked to the rise in the output of the economy. If output is expected to increase by 2% a year in the long run, then the money supply should also be increased by 2% a year. However, there are pressures on government to increase the money supply. Three causes in particular lead government to do this. In the first place governments can 'import' inflation if they attempt to maintain fixed exchange rates. An expansion in the role of government and its spending, and government's attempt to increase the level of employment by expanding aggregate demand will also encourage weak governments to increase the money supply.

It follows that governmental attempts to control the money supply will be made easier if flexible exchange rates are adopted, government spending is cut and supply side measures are used to improve employment prospects.

Some monetarists, such as Friedman, also suggest that it can be made politically more feasible to end inflation if measures are taken to reduce the side-effects which result from **unanticipated** inflation and can be reduced by 'escalator clauses'. These are devices to increase wages, pensions and benefits in line with the rise in prices. This is already done in some cases, for example, state old age pensions are

raised each year as prices rise. Friedman would like tax allowances to rise with inflation (this is also done in some cases), and he would also like these type of arrangements to become more common in the private sector. For example, financial transactions involving borrowing and lending should contain clauses linking the interest to the rate of inflation. Friedman believes that measures such as these would reduce the ill-effects of inflation and make it easier for the government to take the essential measures needed to end inflation. Some monetarists disagree with him on this and argue that escalator clauses make inflation easier to live with, thereby reducing the government's incentives to control the money supply.

The Keynesian approach

All economists accept that large increases in the quantity of money will lead to rises in prices. If £10 notes showered down from the skies like rain at an Old Trafford test match, then some of this money would increase demand for goods and push up

Figure 17.4: *Demand pull inflation*

(i) An increase in aggregate demand leads to a rise in price

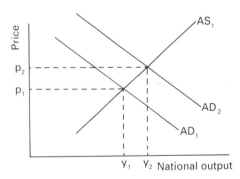

(ii) The rise in price leads to a fall in aggregate supply and a further price rise

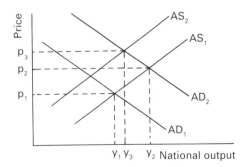

189

Figure 17.5: The wage-price spiral

prices. However, no government is likely to increase the money supply in this way. The argument is about what factors cause inflation in the real world and what policies should be adopted to reduce the likelihood of it happening. As was seen in Chapter 15, non-monetarists believe that attempts to control the money supply will fail since the supply of money responds to the demand for it. Moreover, attempts to control the money supply may have undesirable side-effects, such as higher unemployment. Instead they stress two causes: inflation caused by excess aggregate demand and inflation resulting from increased costs of production.

Demand pull inflation

This explanation of inflation begins with an increase in aggregate demand. This can occur in any of the components of aggregate demand. Consumers may spend more on goods or services, firms invest more, government increases its spending, or exports increase. If this is accompanied by a rise in the money supply, then the result will be an increase in prices as shown in Figure 17.4.

However, this does not explain inflation, which implies a continuing rise in prices. In order to explain this we need to describe a process. In this case, the rise in prices makes workers less well off; they respond by demanding higher wages. This rise in real wages will put up costs and cause the aggregate supply curve to shift to the left (just as in micro-economics a rise in costs causes the supply curve to move to the left). This will push up prices, lead to a new demand for higher wages and so on. This wage-price spiral is shown in Figure 17.5.

Cost push inflation

This is the second Keynesian explanation of inflation and is also the reason they put forward to explain the movement of the Phillips curve to the right. The explanation starts with an increase in costs. One

Figure 17.6: A supply side shock

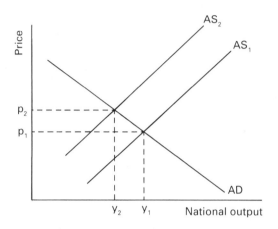

reason this can occur is because of a push by trade unions for higher wages. Several economists have attempted to test this theory by linking rises in wages to the strength of unions, but monetarist critics say that union strength does not vary enough to explain the considerable variations in the rate of inflation over time. An alternative source of the increase in costs can occur because of a rise in the price of raw materials, such as the huge rise in oil costs in 1973/74 and again in 1979. This is sometimes called a supply side shock. Alternatively, the rise in prices can occur because of a push for higher profits by business people. The effect of an increase in costs on prices is shown in Figure 17.6. This original rise in prices then leads to a wage-price spiral. The rise in prices leads to a demand for higher wages, a further rise in prices and so on. Note that this argument suggests that there is still a trade-off between inflation and unemployment.

A sociological approach

This can be considered as a quite separate perspective, or as a variation of the Keynesian emphasis on the costs of production approach as it

is here. Some sociologists, such as Rowthorn (1977), see inflation as the outcome of conflict between workers and capitalists over the share of wages in the economy. According to Rowthorn:

'The working class can shift distribution in its favour by fighting more vigorously for higher wages, although the cost of such militancy is a faster rate of inflation, as capitalists try, with only partial success, to protect themselves by raising prices.'

This view rests on an increase in social conflict. This may occur because the old social order has been replaced by one in which workers feel less socially inferior, recognise their power and are prepared to use it. This power rests on the ability of workers to cause disruption due to the increased interdependence of a modern economy.

Behind this approach is a view that wages are not set by the forces of demand and supply because the labour market never reaches equilibrium. Instead they are set by collective bargaining and hence by sociological and political pressures. It follows that changes in political factors (such as a change in government or in a dominant ideology) can lead to a rise or a fall in wages and hence in prices.

Key ideas - summary of the Keynesian approach

1. The supply of money tends to respond to changes in the demand for money. The velocity of circulation varies and will nullify control measures. Hence attempts to control the money supply will probably fail. Moreover, such attempts will have severe effects on the economy.

2. One cause of inflation is a rise in aggregate demand (consumer spending, investment, government spending or exports). This pulls up prices.

3. In addition, inflation can be caused by increases in costs (for example, wages and raw materials). This pushes up prices.

4. Many Keynesian economists argue that the labour market does not clear. Hence wages are not determined by demand and supply, but by collective bargaining. This means that changes in wages are caused by political and social factors.

Keynesian policies

Since Keynesian economists identify two main causes, their policies focus on two areas.

One set of policies seeks to reduce aggregate demand. One way to do this is to cut government spending or increase taxes. This would mean that consumers would have less money to spend. Both measures would shift the aggregate demand curve to the left. A disadvantage of this is that it would probably increase unemployment.

A variation on this approach would be to control consumer credit, for example, by putting up interest rates. However, this seems to have little effect and has undesirable effects on industry, perhaps reducing investment. Alternatively, the government can try to pass laws which restrict the ease with which people can obtain credit, or which makes them pay back loans more quickly. This has become more difficult in recent years because of the expansion of credit cards and the diversification of building societies into institutions which provide personal loans for the purchase of consumer goods.

The other approach seeks to cut costs, or at least to slow down the rate at which they rise. One way in which this can be done is through an incomes policy. This attempts to reduce public sector incomes in the hope that these will then set levels which the private sector follows. Teachers feel that they have often been used in this way. Such measures reduce morale in the public sector and then lead to strikes and other action designed to ensure parity with the private sector. In the past, governments have adopted formal prices and incomes policies. These have sometimes been voluntary, for example, by making agreements with the TUC, or imposed by law, for example, outlawing any wage increase over a certain amount. Such policies have been criticised on the grounds that they distort the allocation of resources, for example, by making it difficult for growing firms to attract more workers by putting up wages. More-over, it is claimed that these policies have only a temporary effect, so that after a while the policy breaks down and wages catch up to where they would have been without a policy.

These criticisms have led to new ideas. James Meade (1984) has suggested a compulsory system of 'pendulum' arbitration. This means that the arbitrators would not be able to split the difference between claim and offer, but have to choose one or the other. This would prevent unions making excessive claims. Moreover, the arbitrators would have to make their decision bearing in mind the effects on the level of employment.

Another new idea is associated with Richard Layard (1986). This is a tax-based system, whereby companies paying excessive wage increases to their workers would have to pay higher taxes. The rationale is that this would force companies to resist high wage increases and the workers would also realise that sales and employment might fall if companies' costs were increased not only by large wage increases, but also by higher taxes. They would therefore reduce their wage demands.

Conclusion

For monetarists, inflation is a major economic disaster. Hence strong measures have to be taken in order to bring it under control. Since they believe that the basic cause of all inflation is that the money supply is rising faster than national output, it follows that the essential policy is that the money supply should be brought under control. In addition, measures should be taken to reduce pressures on the government to increase the money supply; hence the government should cut its spending.

Keynesians take a very different view. They also believe that inflation is undesirable, but perhaps not so bad as monetarists claim. They see two causes of inflation. The first is too much aggregate demand; hence this must be cut, for example, by putting up taxes or cutting government spending. Another cause is that costs rise and so push up prices. The usual response to this is some form of prices and incomes policy.

In principle it ought to be possible to test these two approaches, but in practice this is very difficult. In the real world it is not possible to undertake economic experiments to see what happens. Hence much economic investigation takes the form of statistical investigation. In the USA, Friedman and Schwartz provided a comprehensive statistical case in favour of monetarism. However, Hendry and Ericsson (1983) reviewed Friedman's evidence and concluded that the evidence did not support his claims. Instead they suggested that the velocity of circulation of money was very variable, so that a policy of controlling the money supply would have little effect. One reason why investigations such as these can come to different conclusions is that some of the variables are difficult to quantify. For example, which measure of money supply should be used? Or how should investigators measure union strength? Moreover, different time lags give different results. If the money supply and prices are both rising, it is not easy to test whether the money supply is causing prices to rise, or if rising prices lead to increases in the money supply.

Data questions

Year	M3 (£ million)	Retail Price Index 1985 = 100
1978	49,273	53.0
1979	55,340	59.7
1980	65,536	70.7
1981	82,537	79.1
1982	89,878	85.8
1983	99,851	89.8
1984	109,904	94.1
1985	124,918	100.0
1986	150,607	103.3
1987	184,698	107.6
1988	223,026	113.1

Source: *Economic Trends*, HMSO, 1989.

Question 1

1. What is meant by:
   (i) M3 and
   (ii) the Retail Price Index?
2. (i) From the data, calculate the rate of change of M3 and the Retail Price Index.
   (ii) Is there any relationship between the two variables?
3. If time lags were taken into consideration, how would this affect your answer to 2(ii)?
4. What economic theory could be used to explain the figures? Use examples from the table to support your answers.

Conclusions

Five simple truths embody most of what we know about inflation:

1.   Inflation is a monetary phenomenon arising from a more rapid increase in the quantity of money than in output (though, of course, the reasons for the increase in money may be various).

2.   In today's world government determines - or can determine - the quantity of money.

3.   There is only one cure for inflation: a slower rate of increase in the quantity of money.

4.   It takes time - measured in years, not months - for inflation to develop; it takes time for inflation to be cured.

5.   Unpleasant side effects of the cure are unavoidable.

The United States has embarked on rising monetary growth four times during the past twenty years. Each time the higher monetary growth has been followed first by economic expansion, later by inflation. Each time the authorities have slowed monetary growth in order to stem inflation. Lower monetary growth has been followed by an inflationary recession. Later still, inflation has declined and the economy has improved. So far the sequence is identical with Japan's experience from 1971 to 1975. Unfortunately, the crucial difference is that we have not displayed the patience Japan did by continuing monetary restraint long enough. Instead, we have overreacted to the recession by accelerating monetary growth, setting off on another round of inflation, and condemning ourselves to higher inflation plus higher unemployment.

We have been misled by a false dichotomy: inflation or unemployment. That option is an illusion. The real option is only whether we have higher unemployment as a result of higher inflation or as a temporary side effect of curing inflation.

Source: Friedman, M. and R. *Free to Choose*, Penguin, 1980.

Question 2

1. Discuss the arguments for and against the views expressed in the article.

2. What policies would follow from this analysis?

18 International Trade

Debates about international trade focus on the extent to which completely free trade - trade without any barriers - is desirable:

● One group of economists, those who favour market forces and dislike government 'interference', tend to argue that trade between countries should be free from all, or almost all, restrictions. They argue this will give consumers a greater choice of goods at lower prices and that they will gain from the benefits of specialisation.

● Critics of free trade suggest it can have substantial disadvantages. They argue that barriers to trade can help new and also declining industries. They can protect industries from dumping by foreigners, and barriers may be needed to help essential defence industries. Finally, some economists believe that trade restrictions may be needed if a country suffers from a deficit on the balance of payments.

The case for free trade

Three hundred years ago, the prevalent theory of foreign trade was mercantilism. This suggested that a country should do all it could to increase exports, but should restrict imports and so build up 'treasure'. This view was criticised by Adam Smith in *The Wealth of Nations* (1776). He argued that restrictions on foreign trade limited the benefits which could be obtained from market forces. In essence, the case for free trade is the case for markets on a larger scale. If complete free trade were introduced the market would consist of the whole world and consumers benefit from a huge choice of goods. Moreover, international competition would force domestic firms to keep down prices. Innovations in production techniques and product design would spread more rapidly, so benefiting consumers.

Absolute advantage

Smith argued that trade should be based on absolute advantage. This phrase describes the position when one country is absolutely more efficient at producing good A, whilst another country is absolutely 'better' at producing good B. Both countries would benefit if they specialised in producing the good at which they have the advantage and then exchanged their products. Thus Britain has an absolute advantage compared to Jamaica in the production of cars whilst Jamaica has

an absolute advantage in the production of tropical fruits. It will benefit both countries if they specialise and trade. Absolute advantage is a specific example of the advantages of specialisation and the division of labour. In Smith's words:

'It is the maxim of every prudent master of a family, never to attempt to make at home what it will cost him more to make than to buy. The tailor does not attempt to make his own shoes, but buys them off the shoemaker. The shoemaker does not attempt to make his own clothes, but employs a tailor . . . What is prudence in the conduct of a private family can scarce be folly in that of a great kingdom . . . If a foreign country can supply us with a commodity cheaper than we ourselves can make it, better buy it off them with some part of the produce of our own industry . . .'

Comparative advantage

Smith's argument about absolute advantage was developed by David Ricardo in 1817 in his book *On the Principles of Political Economy and Taxation*. Ricardo was concerned about the position where a country was able to produce every commodity at an absolutely lower real cost than another country. He suggested that in this case each country should specialise in the production of those goods where its comparative advantage was greatest. This can be explained by using the division of labour as an example; if A is ten times more efficient than B as a surgeon and twice as efficient as a road sweeper, then A should devote all his efforts to surgery (particularly if I am the patient!) and leave all the road sweeping to B.

Table 18.1: *Comparative advantage*

Country	Amount of labour (man hours) required to produce 1 unit	
	wine	cloth
Portugal	80	90
England	120	100

Ricardo developed his theory by comparing two countries, England and Portugal, and two commodities, wine and cloth. Table 18.1 shows that Portugal was more efficient in the production of both goods, but Ricardo argued that both countries could benefit if they specialised where their advantage was comparatively greater and then traded. Portugal's labour costs were lower than England's in both cloth and wine, but the comparative advantage was greater in wine. The cost ratios were 9:10 for cloth and 8:12 for wine. Thus it cost England roughly 1.1 times as much labour to produce cloth as it did Portugal, but 1.5 times as much to produce wine.

Ricardo showed that both countries would benefit if England specialised in cloth and Portugal in wine and they then exchanged a unit of wine for a unit of cloth. England would gain 20 hours since it costs her 100 hours to produce cloth but 120 to produce wine. Portugal would also benefit because she would trade a unit of wine which took 80 hours to produce and receive a unit of cloth which would have taken her 90 hours to produce. Hence Portugal gains 10 hours. In Ricardo's words (referring to Portugal):

'It would be . . . advantageous for her to export wine in exchange for cloth . . . she would obtain more cloth from England than she could produce by diverting a portion of her capital from the cultivation of vines to the manufacture of cloth.'

Ricardo's model is a simple one. It ignores factors such as transport costs and assumes that goods are homogeneous. It also ignores intra-firm trade, such as that between subsidiaries of a multi-national firm. Nevertheless, its conclusion is clear. Countries should specialise where their advantage is comparatively greatest (or comparative disadvantage is least) and then trade. The principle has been restated in various ways, for example, by including all costs and not just labour costs. Another approach uses the terminology of opportunity costs to reach

the same conclusion. In the example above, the opportunity cost to Portugal (what is given up) is minimised if Portugal concentrates on producing wine.

Factor endowments

In order to improve Ricardo's theory, two Swedish economists, Heckscher and Ohlin (Heckscher, 1919 and Ohlin 1933), developed a theory which stressed factor endowment as the basis for international trade. They suggested that countries such as India, with a huge supply of relatively cheap labour, would specialise in labour-intensive products and countries such as the USA, with abundant capital, would specialise in the production of capital-intensive products. However, an investigation by Leontief (1954) found a paradox. His research showed that the USA actually exports labour and land-intensive products rather than capital-intensive goods. Despite this paradox, more sophisticated versions of Heckscher and Ohlin's ideas still provide the most widely accepted theories of international trade.

The terms of trade

The extent to which countries benefit from trade depends on the price at which the goods are exchanged. Ricardo's example simply assumed that one unit of cloth was exchanged for one unit of wine; in the real world both would be sold for a price.

Because world trade involves many goods and many prices, the terms of trade is compiled as an index. This index is itself compiled by making use of two other index numbers, one for the price of exports and one for the price of imports:

$$\text{Terms of trade} = \frac{\text{Index of the price of exports}}{\text{Index of the price of imports}}$$

In the base year the terms of trade will be $\frac{100}{100} = 1$.

Thus if the index of export prices changes from 100 to 150 and the index of import prices changes from 100 to 50, then the terms of trade will be $\frac{150}{50} = 3$.

The terms of trade are said to have become favourable when the index rises; that is when the price of exports rises relative to the price of imports. This means more imports can be bought for a given quantity of exports. However, 'favourable' can be misleading because a rise in the price of exports may make them more difficult to sell abroad. The precise effect will depend on the price elasticity of demand for exports.

Gains from large-scale production

The extent to which a firm can specialise depends on the size of the market. When this is large, firms can employ specialised machines and labour and obtain the benefits of other economies of scale. Free trade extends the potential market and so permits extensive specialisation. This benefit is greater for small countries such as Ireland or Switzerland than for larger countries like the USA, where the market is already large. Moreover, the potential benefits will differ between industries; in cases such as personal services there are no advantages to be gained from free trade. In others, however, there are substantial benefits from being big, as was shown in Chapter 5.

Key ideas - summary of the case for free trade

1. Free trade extends the market and so brings consumers the benefits of competition, such as lower prices and greater choice.

2. When two countries each have an absolute advantage in producing products, it will pay both to specialise and then to exchange. Britain could grow oranges, but it would be a waste of resources; hence Britain should specialise in other products and then exchange these for goods it cannot produce efficiently.

3. Ricardo's theory of comparative advantage shows that even where a country is better at producing several goods than another country, both will benefit when they specialise in products where their advantage is comparatively greater (or their disadvantage is comparatively least). The extent to which each benefits will depend on the prices at which the goods are exchanged.

4. Ricardo's theory has been developed by later economists such as Heckscher and Ohlin.

5. Free trade makes possible greater economies of scale.

Free trade policies

Free traders wish to see the removal of all, or nearly all, barriers to trade. For them, life is a constant struggle against special interest groups which seek to protect their industry against foreign competition by introducing new restrictions on imports. Hence at one level their policy involves a defence of the present position.

To extend free trade is difficult. The growth of the European Community extends free trade within its area, but puts up substantial barriers to those outside the Community, especially in agricultural products.

On a world arena, much of the struggle takes place at meetings of GATT (the General Agreement on Tariffs and Trade). This is a body which, since the Second World War, has negotiated substantial reductions in customs duties and helped to remove other barriers to international trade. Economists who support freer trade would like this to be given more emphasis.

The case for protection

Criticisms of the case for free trade

Some economists criticise the case for free trade on a number of grounds. According to Joan Robinson in her book *Reflections on the Theory of International Trade* (1974):

'. . . the models imply trade between countries of equal weight and at the same level of development. This rules out imperialism and the use of power to foster economic advantage. In Ricardo's example Portugal was to gain as much from exporting wine as England from exporting cloth, but in real life Portugal was dependent on British naval support, and it was for this reason that she was obliged to accept conditions of trade which wiped out her production of textiles and inhibited industrial development . . .'

Moreover:

'Investment in expanding manufactures leads to technical advance, learning by doing, specialisation of industries and accelerating accumulation (of **profits** and **capital**), while investment in wine runs up a blind alley into stagnation. In a similar way the British cotton industry grew up under protection from superior Indian exports. When it was developed, free trade was imposed on India and the Indian textile industry decimated.'

Infant industries

Joan Robinson's views underlie one of the arguments put forward in favour of protection; that many less developed countries have the conditions necessary to compete successfully, but lack experience and expertise which take time to acquire. The infant industry argument suggests that new industries should be given protection for a time in order to allow them to build up this experience. This argument applies where the industry is small and young, and where costs are high but fall as the industry grows. Critics of this line of argument claim that most infant industries never grow up; that they continue to demand protection so their customers continue to pay high prices. Once protection is given to such industries, it is very difficult, politically, to remove it.

Protection to improve the terms of trade

Countries can improve their position when they are the sole (or dominant) buyer of a world commodity. This is rare, but if British importers of tea agreed with each other to restrict imports, then the world price would fall. Of course this would lower the incomes received by the producers of tea and so might be thought undesirable as they are mostly poor countries.

Protection against low-cost imports

This line of argument takes a number of forms. One suggests that declining industries need a period of protection in order to allow the decline to take place gradually, so that workers can retrain and new industries develop. This would apply to industries in the UK such as cotton, coal mining and shipbuilding.

A variation on this approach says that industries in high-wage countries should have protection against goods made by low-paid labour. This, of course, denies the advantages of comparative advantage which derive from lower costs. Instead the argument is that if foreign firms pay low wages, this is a form of unfair competition and domestic firms should be protected. This would safeguard the position of British workers. Critics argue that this would, in fact, reduce the wages of workers in poor countries and would make British consumers pay higher prices.

Protection against unfair foreign competition

'Unfair' competition can take various forms. Sometimes foreign governments can subsidise their export industries. This means that domestic industries cannot compete fairly. Similarly, foreign firms may 'dump' their products overseas, either because they cannot be sold on their domestic market, or in order to destroy competitors. They could then increase their prices and make large profits.

In some cases what is seen as dumping is no such thing. Firms can sometimes sell abroad at low prices because their domestic sales cover high fixed costs and allow prices abroad to reflect the low marginal cost of production.

Macro-economic arguments for protection

So far we have considered economic arguments which have suggested protectionist measures to help particular industries. However, some economists have suggested protection on a much wider scale. One of the problems of the British economy is that, as the economy expands, the level of imports rises leading to a deficit on the current account. This can then force the government to deflate the economy by putting up taxes and cutting government spending. As an alternative to this it is suggested that the government should take measures to restrict the overall level of imports. This would then allow the economy to be expanded without the constraint of a balance of payments problem. A variation on this approach is to target the protection against a particular country which has a huge surplus on its trade with the country concerned. In recent years this has usually been Japan. There is no doubt that in the past Japan employed many protective devices to build up its industry and that a few of these still exist. What is also clear is that Japan is so successful as an exporter because it is efficient.

Critics of this argument for protection say that it would contravene many international agreements. They also argue that protectionist measures would lead to retaliation from other countries, so the ultimate effect would be to reduce the level of world trade and increase unemployment in many countries. That is what happened in the 1930s when world trade plummeted as a result of the growth of restrictions on imports.

Non-economic arguments for protection

The economic arguments used to support free trade usually assume that it is desirable to maximise national income. However, other objectives may also be desirable. For example, the people of a country may wish to preserve a way of life that is desirable, such as a certain way of farming or traditional crafts. If these are theatened by foreign competition it may be desirable to protect them. Similarly, politicians may suggest that defence requirements necessitate the protection of an industry; for example, that Britain needs a shipbuilding industry. Such arguments depend on political grounds and not on economic considerations.

Key ideas - summary of the protectionist argument

1. The case for free trade using comparative advantage arguments is oversimplified. In particular it rests on the assumption that power is spread equally so the strong do not impose on the weak. In the past, countries such as Britain and the USA have used their power to force poor countries to concentrate on producing raw materials and to exchange these for manufactured goods.
2. Countries should be able to use protection to acquire comparative advantage, for example, by helping infant industries.
3. Protection can help countries improve the terms of trade, particularly where they import a large part of the world's output of a commodity.
4. Declining industries should be helped to decline in an organised way so that new industries can be developed to replace them.
5. The level of imports should be controlled in order to prevent balance of payments problems developing. This would allow countries to expand their economies more rapidly.
6. There are also non-economic arguments, such as the protection of a way of life, or to safeguard essential defence industries.

Protectionist policies

There are a number of ways in which protectionist policies can be introduced.

Tariffs

Tariffs are a traditional way to help particular industries and also to reduce the level of imports as a whole. They are a tax on imports and can be

Figure 18.1: *Effect of a tariff*

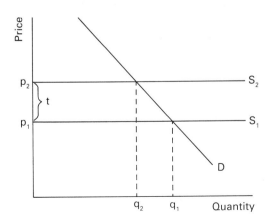

specific, that is so much per item, or **ad valorem,** that is a percentage of the value of the good. Another advantage of tariffs is that they raise money for the government.

Figure 18.1 illustrates their effect. The tariff shifts the supply curve upwards because it puts up the costs of the foreign producer. In the Figure the new supply curve S_2 is above the original curve by t - the amount of the tariff. Imports fall from q_1 to q_2 and the price rises from p_1 to p_2.

Quotas

Quotas can also be used to restrict imports. A quota is a limit on the number of goods that are allowed to enter the country; thus a country may say that only 10,000 video recorders will be allowed to come into the country during the year. The effect is shown in Figure 18.2. The original equilibrium is at price p_1 and quantity q_1. The quota shifts the supply curve so that it becomes vertical, and the new equilibrium is at price p_2 and quantity q_2.

Both these methods will reduce imports. Comparing the two we see that in both cases there is a rise in price. A tariff benefits the Treasury, whilst a quota may benefit foreign suppliers because they can charge a higher price for their product.

199

Figure 18.2: *Effect of a quota*

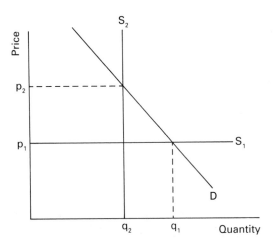

Non-tariff barriers

Imposing tariffs and quotas will certainly reduce imports, but they are illegal under many international agreements. Hence in recent years they have become less important as barriers to trade. However, there has probably been an increase in non-tariff barriers. There are a number of such devices. Some are uncontroversial, such as the imposition of strict quality controls in the form of regulations to reduce the likelihood of food poisoning in imported foodstuffs.

Sometimes governments insist that importers need a special licence before they are allowed to import goods. Another variation occurs when two or more governments come to an agreement that imports should be limited. This is usually referred to as voluntary export restraint. Two examples are the Multi-Fibre Agreement, which restricts the importation of textiles from less developed countries, and the agreement restricting the number of Japanese cars which are allowed to enter the UK. Their advocates say that barriers such as these can be used to reduce unfair competition. Such barriers do work in the sense that the level of imports is reduced. Their opponents say that they restrict trade in ways which make it very difficult for foreign companies to overcome, and so reduce consumer choice.

Devaluation

Devaluation means cutting the value of a currency. This will probably also work, but as we have seen, it will increase the price of imports and so push up the rate of inflation. Also it may make matters worse in the short run because people will often continue to

buy imports even though their price has risen. Hence this is a long term measure.

Interest rates

An alternative way to reduce the demand for imports is to increase interest rates. This will make borrowing more expensive and so discourage those consumers who borrow to buy goods. It will also mean that those people buying houses with mortgages will have less money to spend on goods, many of which would have been imported. However, higher interest rates make domestic industry less competitive because they push up costs. The CBI estimates that a 1% increase in interest rates puts up industry's costs by £250 million; hardly the way to encourage exports.

Higher interest rates will also tend to push up the rate of exchange. This is because people with money to invest will tend to move it to those countries with high interest rates, and this will push up the value of those currencies. A high exchange rate will have the opposite effect to a devaluation.

Deflation

The certain way to improve the balance of payments is to deflate the economy. Since the prime determinant of the level of imports is the level of income, then a cut in incomes will reduce imports. Hence governments with balance of payments difficulties often cut government spending and increase taxes. These measures succeed in their purpose, but the side-effects are extremely undesirable. National income falls (or rises more slowly) and the level of unemployment rises.

There are therefore a large range of policies which can be used to restrict imports. The precise measures advocated to restrict imports will depend on the circumstances. If the aim is to help a particular industry, measures to restrict the importation of specific goods should be adopted. If the aim is to rectify a balance of payments deficit, more general measures are needed.

Conclusion

Economists who support freer trade claim that world trade brings consumers the benefits of the market; lower prices and greater choice. They are supported by research from organisations such as The Organisation for Economic Co-operation and Development (OECD), which surveyed research in this area in a book called *Costs and Benefits of Protection* (1985) and concluded:

- The spread of protection has yielded few benefits, but imposed substantial costs.
- Protection has not proved to be an efficient means of sustaining employment. Jobs saved in the industries protected are often offset by viable jobs foregone elsewhere in the economy.

However, this research would be criticised by those who favour an element of protection. Some would suggest that free trade favours the powerful and that industries in less developed countries are not able to compete on fair terms. Even in developed countries they suggest that some protection should be given to declining industries to allow adjustments to take place in an orderly way. On the macro level, they suggest that imports should not be allowed to rise when the economy expands because this leads to a balance of payments crisis. This may force the government to impose deflationary measures, which would have the effect of reducing imports, but in an uncontrolled way.

Data questions

The costs and benefits of protection

The 1979 recession drastically lowered demand for cars, particularly in the United States, where it coincided with the launch of many fuel-efficient models and the necessity of servicing the debt incurred to re-equip production lines and redesign cars.

The severity of the recession was such as to seriously impede the return to profitability.

A division between winners and losers in adapting to new competitive conditions became increasingly apparent. The major winners - the Japanese industry - found their continued access to export markets increasingly impeded. The United States negotiated a Voluntary Export Restraint agreement with Japan, initially effective within the limit of three years from March 1981. Already subject to strong restraints in France and Italy, and to 'prudent marketing' in the United Kingdom, Japan entered into a bilateral arrangement for 'forecasting' Japanese car exports to Canada and undertook unilaterally to exercise discretion on the German and Belgian markets. These developments were partly a result of the 'demonstration effect' of the US agreement. As agreements expire, they have been renewed, lengthening the 'breathing space' provided to the automobile industry of the major importing countries. The recent decision by the US Government to allow its VER (Voluntary Export Restraint) with Japan to lapse is a major reversal of this trend.

Source: OECD, *Cost and Benefits of Protection*, 1985.

Question 1

1. Explain what is meant by 'a bilateral arrangement'.
2. Who benefits from such restrictions on free trade?
3. Summarise the economic theory which could be used to oppose such arguments.

19 The Balance of Payments

The balance of payments is a statement of a country's transactions with the rest of the world. The most useful way to approach this topic is to consider the flow of funds into and out of a country. For example, when someone in the UK buys a foreign car, money flows out of the UK. When someone from abroad comes to the UK for a holiday, money comes into the country. Over a period of several years, these flows into and out of the country should at least balance. If the flow of money out of the country is greater than the flow into it, a balance of payments crisis may result and force the government to take unpleasant measures to remedy the position. Since none of the measures is guaranteed to work, and the most successful have undesirable side-effects, there are considerable arguments between economists about which policies to adopt:

● Some economists believe that no government intervention is necessary because market forces will solve the problem by cutting the value of the currency.

● Others argue that government intervention, for example to deflate the economy, is needed to solve a deficit.

Components of the balance of payments

There are two main areas of the balance of payments: the current account, and transactions in assets and liabilities.

The balance of payments of any one country must always balance. The central bank will hold assets in the form of foreign currencies and gold, and these reserves increase or decrease according to changes in the current or asset accounts. For example, if there is a surplus on the current account, the foreign exchange reserves will rise by the amount of the surplus. In this sense the balance of payments must always balance, because the change in the reserves always equals the change in other items.

When the accounts do not balance, then a **balancing item** is introduced in order to make them balance. This is another name for 'errors and omissions' as Nigel Lawson, the Chancellor of the Exchequer, put it.

Language can be confusing in this context because economists sometimes talk about 'a deficit on the balance of payments'. When they use this phrase they usually mean a deficit on the current account of the balance of payments, but the phrase 'current account' is often omitted. A deficit on the current account can be serious if it is prolonged because it will lead to a fall in the reserves; foreigners will demand payment in foreign currency and the government may be forced to adopt new policies to remedy the position. A deficit on capital items such as investment abroad may be less serious, because it can be seen as building up a nation's assets abroad. If this is the position, foreigners may be happy to accept payment in domestic currency.

Table 19.1: *UK balance of payments, 1988*

		£ million
CURRENT ACCOUNT		
Visible balance		-20,500
Invisibles:		
Services balance	3,500	
Interest, profit & dividends	6,000	
Transfers	-3,600	
Invisible balance		5,900
CURRENT BALANCE		-14,600
TRANSACTIONS IN EXTERNAL ASSETS AND LIABILITIES		
UK external assets	51,000	
UK external liabilities	-50,500	
NET TRANSACTIONS		-500
BALANCING ITEM		15,100

Source: *Economic Trends*, HMSO, 1989.

Table 19.1 shows the UK balance of payments. The precise figures vary each year, but the overall picture does not change rapidly.

The current account

This includes all international payments which are deemed to be related to income. It covers money received from the sale of goods and services to other countries, and also money in the form of receipts and payments from property and gifts. Overall the current account in the UK amounts to about 50% of GDP (goods 25% of GDP, services 7%, property incomes 16%, transfers 1%). The UK tends to run a surplus on the current account when the economy is doing badly. This is because, when unemployment is high, we spend less on imports. However, as the economy expands we tend to go on foreign holidays and buy imported consumer goods, such as electronic equipment and, as a result, the current account goes into a deficit. The current account in the UK can be sub-divided into various components.

Trade in goods

This is sometimes called 'visible trade' because it refers to goods passing through customs barriers. It includes such things as the import and export of manufactured goods such as cars, chemicals and computers. The UK used to have a surplus of these items, but now runs a deficit on manufactures. Raw materials, such as iron ore and food, are also 'visibles', and the UK always runs a deficit on this item. Finally, trade in oil appears in this section. The UK always used to run a deficit in the trade in oil, but North Sea oil has changed this into a surplus. Overall, the UK runs a deficit on trade in goods.

Invisible trade

The other components of the current account are often called 'invisibles', because they (usually) cannot be seen:

- Services. The UK earns money from the activities of its insurance companies in other countries. Shipping, banking, air travel and tourism are other examples of trade in services. The UK runs a surplus on its trade in services.

- Interest, profits and dividends. Some individuals and firms in Britain own property abroad and this gives rise to incomes which then come into this country. Similarly, foreigners own assets in this country and send the income they receive abroad. Some of the profits Nissan receive from their factory in the UK will be sent back to Japan and will therefore appear as a deficit on the UK current account and as a surplus on the Japanese current account.

- Transfers. These include international gifts from governments or individuals and also payments to bodies such as the European Community.

Table 19.2: UK trade balances, 1977-87

Year	Non-oil Primary Products		Oil		Manufactures		Total Goods	
	£b	%GNP	£b	%GNP	£b	%GNP	£b	%GNP
1977	-5.7	-4.4	-2.8	-2.2	6.2	4.8	-2.3	-1.8
1978	-4.9	-3.3	-2.1	-1.4	5.5	3.7	-1.6	-1.1
1979	-5.3	-3.1	-1.1	-0.6	3.0	1.7	-3.4	-2.0
1980	-4.3	-2.2	-0.1	-0.1	5.8	2.9	1.4	0.7
1981	-4.4	-2.0	2.7	1.2	5.0	2.3	3.3	1.5
1982	-4.6	-1.9	4.1	1.7	2.7	1.2	2.2	0.9
1983	-5.5	-2.1	6.3	2.4	-1.9	-0.7	-1.1	-0.4
1984	-6.4	-2.2	5.4	1.9	-3.6	-1.3	-4.6	-1.6
1985	-6.2	-2.0	6.6	2.1	-2.7	-0.9	-2.3	-0.8
1986	-6.2	-1.9	2.7	0.9	-5.2	-1.6	-8.7	-2.7
1987	-6.5	-1.8	2.9	0.8	-6.6	-1.8	-10.2	-2.8
Mean 1977-79		-3.6		-1.4		3.4		-1.6
Mean 1985-87		-1.9		1.3		-1.4		-2.1

Note: Non-oil primary products = food, drink and tobacco and basic materials. Oil = Oil + other mineral fuels and lubricants. Manufactures = manufactures, semi-manufactures and unclassified.

Source: *United Kingdom National Accounts*, HMSO, 1988, and *United Kingdom Balance of Payments*, HMSO, 1988.

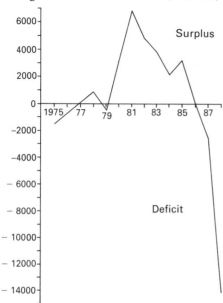

Figure 19.1: *Current account (£ million)*

Source: Adapted from *Economic Trends*, HMSO.

Transactions in assets and liabilities

This is the second main component of the balance of payments. It includes payments which are made, not from income, but from capital. It covers such things as money spent and received on the sale of shares in foreign companies (as when Nestle bought Rowntrees in 1988). This is known as portfolio investment. This account is also affected when domestic firms build factories overseas, or when foreign firms build here (as when Nissan built a factory in the North East of England. In this case some of the money to pay for the construction came from Japan). Short-term lending by banks is also included. The published figures for this part of the balance of payments are often inaccurate because the people concerned do not always notify the authorities.

Some people believe that a deficit in capital transactions is not a bad thing because it builds up the country's assets abroad. The total value of the UK's overseas assets is about £700 billion, whilst external liabilities are about £100 billion less.

Foreign exchange reserves

Part of the assets of a country are in the form of foreign exchange reserves. These can be regarded as the nation's savings. In principle, foreign exchange reserves can be used to pay for imports in a crisis, but their total is small compared to the amount spent on imports so they could not really fulfil this

function. Instead their real use is to enable the government to intervene in the foreign exchange market. Put another way, the reserves mean that the government can buy and sell currencies in order to obtain a desirable value for the pound. The reasons they should do this are discussed in the next chapter.

How accurate are the figures?

In some cases, there is a widespread feeling that the authorities adjust the basis of the statistics in order to obtain better results. Unemployment figures are the best example of this. In other cases the figures are known to be inaccurate, not because of government alterations, but because of genuine difficulties in obtaining accurate figures. One reason for this is that almost all governments are concerned about the possibility of a substantial deficit on their current accounts and so pay particular attention to imports - which also often bring in tax revenue from tariffs. One consequence of such action is that world imports exceed world exports. This should not take place in theory as the combined balance of payments deficits of all countries should be equal to the combined surpluses that exist in other countries. Since it is unlikely that creatures from outer space are trading with the earth, it follows that the figures are inaccurate. One reason is that the people responsible for making the transactions are more concerned with the success of their business than with sending accurate figures to the authorities.

This means that it is difficult to test the accuracy of predictions made about future movements in the balance of payments and therefore it is hard for the government to decide if corrective measures need to be taken to prevent future deficits. In any case, predictions in this area are extremely difficult. This is not surprising because any deficit (or surplus) is the difference between a huge sum for imports and a huge sum for exports. A small percentage error in either of these will lead to a large error in forecasting the difference between them.

Key ideas

1. The balance of payments statistics have two main areas: the current account and transactions in assets and liabilities.
2. The UK now runs a deficit on trade in manufactures, but has a surplus on invisibles.
3. The UK has substantial assets abroad.
4. Balance of payments statistics are very inaccurate and are also difficult to forecast.

What factors determine imports and exports?

A short-term deficit on the current account is not significant; there are large swings from month to month in the figures and a deficit in one month may well be corrected in the next without any action from the authorities. A deficit can be pleasurable; a country in deficit is receiving more goods than it is sending abroad. However, a large deficit which seems likely to continue over a period of years can lead to serious problems. Foreigners will demand payment in a 'hard' currency - one which is acceptable anywhere in the world. A persistent deficit will cause reserves of such currencies to fall and the authorities will be forced to take action to correct the position. In order to discuss possible government action we first need to discuss the determinants of the level of imports and exports.

The rate of exchange

A fall in the value of the pound will make exports cheaper and make it easier for firms to sell their products abroad. A firm exporting cars, such as Jaguar, may want (say) £10,000 for each car it sells (ignoring taxes and retailers' costs etc.). If the pound is worth three dollars, then the price of the car in the USA will be $30,000. If the pound fell in value so that was worth only one dollar, then the same car could sell for only $10,000. In each case the firm would receive £10,000 for each car sold, but the lower price would make it much easier to sell cars abroad. Hence a fall in the value of the pound encourages exports. It also makes imports more expensive. The extent to which this benefits the balance of payments depends on the price elasticity of demand of imports and exports. If this is high, then a relatively small fall in the exchange rate will have a substantial effect. However, if demand for imports and exports is inelastic, a fall in the exchange rate will make matters worse. The reason for this is that the country will not sell many more goods abroad and these will be at a lower price. Moreover, it will continue to import nearly as many goods, and at a higher price.

Inflation rate

If a country has a higher rate of inflation than its competitors, then this will attract imports and at the same time its products may be too expensive to sell abroad. However, a fall in the exchange rate can compensate for this. For example, if the inflation rate in country A is 5% greater than in other countries, a fall in the value of its currency of 5% will maintain the original price in real terms and eliminate the effect of inflation on imports and exports.

Competitiveness

This refers not only to price, but also to such factors as reliability, design, reputation and ability to deliver on time. These are not variables which the government can control and are difficult for individual firms to change in the short run.

Barriers to trade

These include a variety of measures, such as tariffs, quotas and various administrative barriers which were discussed in the last chapter.

Levels of income

This is perhaps the most important factor. Figure 19.2, a simplified version of the circular flow of income model, shows that the main determinant of

Figure 19.2: Imports, exports and the circular flow of income

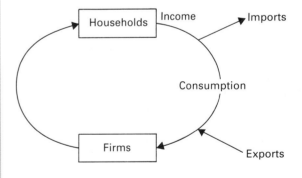

imports is the level of incomes. As incomes rise, people are more likely to go on foreign holidays and to buy goods such as electronic equipment which are made abroad. The relationship between the level of incomes and the balance of payments on the current account is shown in Figure 19.3. As domestic incomes rise, imports also rise, but exports are largely unaffected by the level of domestic incomes. Instead the quantity of exports depends largely on the level of foreign incomes.

Figure 19.3: *Income and the current account*

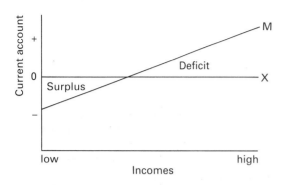

Policies to reduce a deficit

There is no easy solution to a severe balance of payments problem. This is not surprising because the factors affecting exports and imports also affect the economy as a whole so that policies to improve the current account will also affect many other things, such as the level of unemployment.

Because it is so complex, a wide range of policies is possible.

Market forces approach

One approach to a deficit on the current account is to leave any adjustment to market forces. If there is no government intervention, then any country whose imports exceed its exports will find that the value of its currency falls. This is because people in the country will be exchanging their own currency for foreign money in order to buy foreign goods. Since more people are selling the currency than are buying it, its price will fall. This will make exports

cheaper, so that the country will export more. The fall in the value of its currency will also make its imports more expensive, so less will be imported. This argument assumes that imports and exports are sensitive to price changes - that demand is price elastic.

This argument is explored in detail in the next chapter; here it is enough to say that many economists believe that adjustments do not take place so easily and that the government needs to intervene to solve the problem. Hence most of the argument is about the precise form any intervention should take.

However, if the market forces approach is adopted, its supporters claim that not only will a fall in the exchange rate end any deficit on the balance of payments, but the country will benefit because market forces will encourage it to specialise in those industries where it has comparative advantage. In the UK, for example, the deficit in manufacturing would continue because the UK cannot compete successfully with other countries. Instead resources would be concentrated on services, such as insurance and banking, where the UK has comparative advantage. This would enable resources to be used more efficiently.

Interventionist approach

Several of the protectionist measures discussed in the last chapter are relevant here. Some, like tariffs and quotas would probably succeed, but are impossible to implement because this would break international agreements such as GATT. They would also break the rules of the European Community.

The effects of a devaluation would be similar to the consequences following from a decision to leave adjustment to market forces. The difference is that devaluation implies that the fall in the value of the currency is determined by the government.

Supporters of devaluation suggest that this gives a more controlled fall and prevents the uncertainties which result from a policy of leaving everything to the market. The consequences of a devaluation are discussed in the next chapter.

One undesirable consequence of a fall in the value of the currency is that the price of imports rises and makes any inflation worse. In order to avoid this, the British government in the second half of the 1980s adopted a policy of high interest rates. They argued that this would reduce domestic demand for goods since borrowing would be more expensive, and people buying houses on mortgage would have less money to spend on consumer goods because they would be paying more on their mortgage.

A less painful way would be for the government to encourage exports. However, this is not easy. British embassies abroad provide potential exporters with information, and the Export Credit Guarantee Department provides insurance cover for exports. New ways in which the government can increase exports are not easy to find.

In the past the UK government imposed controls on the movement of money out of the country. For example, tourists were limited in the amount of money they could take abroad. This reduced invisible imports. People have also argued that firms should be prevented or discouraged from investing abroad since this helps other countries. Instead they should be forced, or encouraged, to invest their money at home. Supporters of market forces dislike such restrictions on the capital market and argue that entrepreneurs should be allowed to invest where they wish. Moreover, in recent years the electronic transfer of funds has made it much easier to transfer money, and government controls would be bureaucratic and relatively easy to avoid. An alternative suggestion is to give tax advantages to firms which keep money in the UK.

Another approach involves deflating the economy. Since incomes are the prime determinant of imports, deflating the economy would reduce incomes and hence imports. Moreover, if domestic markets declined, some firms would be encouraged to make bigger efforts overseas. Deflation does work, but at a price. Since incomes fall, people are poorer, output falls, and employment rises.

Key ideas - summary of the interventionist approach

1. Government should plan the value of a currency and devalue when needed to correct a balance of payments deficit.
2. In certain circumstances, restrictions should be made on people's ability to transfer currency out of the country.
3. Deflating the economy may be necessary to correct a deficit, but it has undesirable side-effects such as an increase in unemployment.

Conclusion

The balance of payments has been a persistent problem for the British economy. When the economy expands, imports are sucked in causing a deficit on the current account. To remedy this problem, the government deflates the economy leading to a fall in living standards and a rise in unemployment. Eventually the current account moves into surplus and the economy expands, leading to another balance of payments crisis. This sequence was called 'stop-go' and was only interrupted by the advent of North Sea oil which greatly reduced imports. The crisis re-appeared in the late 1980s after several years of economic expansion. The root cause of the problem is probably that the UK economy is often not as competitive as it should be.

Supporters of free markets would argue that the problem will only be resolved when government intervention is reduced. Interventionists would retort that government measures such as devaluation and deflation are needed to correct a persistent deficit.

Data questions

Lawson's law

Correction is being undertaken solely through the rate of interest, which is maintained at a high enough level not only to finance the deficit but also to reduce domestic demand. The great inconsistency is that high rates of interest involve high rates of exchange and the classic text book remedy for correcting a balance payments deficit on current account is to depreciate the exchange rate so as to make exports more attractive to overseas buyers and imports dearer to domestic buyers. 1989 and 1990 will see whether the Chancellor can inaugurate a new economic theory - correcting a balance of payments deficit by keeping the exchange rate high (Lawson's Law?).

Source: *Financial Review*, HMSO, 1989.

Question 1

1. Explain how:
   (i) depreciating the exchange rate and
   (ii) a high rate of interest
   might be used to correct a deficit on the current account.
2. What disadvantages might arise from using these methods?
3. Discuss the benefits and problems of alternative solutions to balance of payments deficits.

Manufacturing

The seriousness of the problem may be illustrated by some key facts about manufactured products, related to exports and our share of world trade; to imports; to manufacturing output in Britain; and to productivity and competitiveness.

Britain's share of world trade in manufactured goods has declined steadily throughout this century, with some short pickups. The actual volume of exports of manufactured goods has risen substantially in the last twelve years (with some decline in 1975 and 1980 to 83), and in 1985 reached a record level. Our share of world trade had, however, fallen to 7.6 per cent by 1984 - from 14.2 per cent in 1964 and 20.5 per cent in 1954. Happily, in 1985, our share recovered a little to about 8 per cent, but exports of manufactured goods in the first twelve months of 1986 were lower than in the first five months of 1985.

Imports of manufactured goods into Britain have risen in the last twenty years by much more than our exports. Our exports as a percentage of imports had fallen from 220 per cent in 1963 to under 100 per cent in 1983, and have moved lower since. There was a very sharp rise in the volume of imports in 1986 compared with the early part of 1985.

Hence the balance of trade in manufactured goods has changed from a surplus of between £1.5 billion and £6 billion in each year from 1963 to 1982, to a deficit in 1983, which widened to nearly £4 billion in 1984, with only a small improvement in 1985, small despite a splendid export achievement. Reasons for anxiety are not confined to the global figures. It is clear that trade in more 'modern' products (such as electronics) is in deficit as well as in the 'traditional' even 'declining' groups. And the deficit is mainly attributable to the very large imports of capital and consumer manufactured goods. Lack of competitiveness has led to a sizeable reduction in Britain's manufacturing base; and the consequent reduction in capacity has made it easier for importers.

Between 1960 and 1983 in our manufacturing industry

output rose by	26 per cent
exports rose by	130 per cent
imports rose by	500 per cent

Source: *The Royal Bank of Scotland Review*.

Exports

Prospects for services exports are not particularly good, even though the UK relies more heavily on services for its export revenue than do other industrial countries. The UK's share of world services trade fell slightly faster than its share of world manufacturing trade between 1968 and 1983, from 11.9 to 7.3 as opposed to from 9.6 to 6.2 per cent. The volume of services exports rose by only 0.5 per cent a year in the decade to 1984, while that of goods other than oil rose by about 2 per cent. Apart from oil, civil aviation and some of the other services show the best coverage of imports by exports, while food, raw materials and sea transport have the worst. Financial services, although they have a high export margin, yield no more than 3 per cent of total export revenue. Semi-manufactures are in balance; it is finished manufactures which have an unfavourable ratio of only 89 per cent coverage of exports by imports.

Source: Lloyds Bank, *Economic Bulletin*, January, 1986.

Question 2

1. Describe and give reasons to explain the above data.
2. What action should the government take to deal with these problems?

20 The Exchange Rate

Just as potatoes are sold in a supermarket, so are currencies such as the pound sterling bought and sold in the foreign exchange market. However, arguments arise about the extent to which the foreign exchange market should be allowed to operate without government intervention:

● Some economists argue that the foreign exchange market should be allowed to operate like any other; that the forces of demand and supply will operate efficiently to bring about equilibrium, and that this equilibrium will reflect the underlying strength of the currency. Consequently the value of the currency will alter to bring about equilibrium in the current account of the balance of payments.

● Critics of this approach suggest that, left to itself, the market will produce great fluctuations in the value of a currency. Hence the value of a currency should be fixed, either by government intervention or by establishing an international system of fixed exchange rates. This will provide stability for international traders.

● A variation on these approaches is provided by those who advocate that Britain should join the European Monetary System (EMS) which provides a stable relationship between the values of most of the currencies within the European Community. If Britain joined this system, the value of the pound would be fixed against other European currencies, such as the French franc. However, the European currencies as a whole would continue to fluctuate against the currencies outside the EMS.

Before considering these approaches, we need first to explain what factors determine the rate of exchange.

Determinants of the rate of exchange

Defining and measuring the exchange rate

Every time someone from the UK planning a foreign holiday goes to a bank and asks for (say) some Spanish pesetas, that person is selling pounds and buying pesetas. If many people do this, the bank will sell pounds in order to buy pesetas required by customers, but on a much bigger scale. Such transactions take place every day and determine the value of currencies such as the pound. If more people are selling pounds than are buying them, the value of the pound will tend to fall.

The price which the pound sterling is worth in terms of foreign currency is called the exchange rate for sterling.

Because the American dollar is the most important world currency, the exchange rates of most currencies are usually expressed in terms of the dollar. If we read that £1 = $1.50, we know the price in dollars of one pound sterling - that it costs $1.50 to buy £1. The same information can also be expressed in reverse - that it costs £0.667 to buy $1. When the pound falls in value so that it costs more pounds to buy a dollar (or fewer dollars to buy a pound), we say that the pound has depreciated. When the pound rises in value against other currencies, we say it has appreciated.

A currency such as the pound sterling is exchanged for many other currencies. Some of these exchanges are on a huge scale; others with small countries, such as Burma or Burundi, are of relatively little importance. Hence when calculating the value of sterling compared to all other currencies, these other currencies are weighted according to their importance. The **trade weighted** exchange rate is an average of the exchange rate between the pound sterling and the UK's main trading partners. Figure 20.1 shows the changes in the value of the pound as measured by this index.

Figure 20.1: *The value of sterling (1975 = 100)*

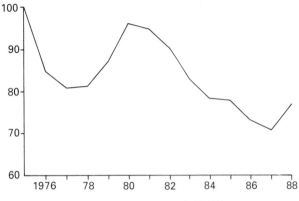

Source: Adapted from *Economic Trends*, HMSO.

Demand and supply

The value of a currency will be determined by the forces of demand and supply. The demand and supply curves for currency are the same shape as those for goods. Other things being equal, a fall (depreciation) in the price of one currency against another will cause more of that currency to be demanded, but less to be supplied. Other factors can also affect the quantity demanded and supplied. These will cause a shift in the curves.

The demand for sterling will be determined in part by the desire of foreigners to buy British goods. If they buy more British cars or whisky, or come to the UK as tourists, then they will want sterling. They will also want sterling if they wish to invest in the UK. This increased demand will cause an appreciation in the value of the pound.

Similarly, the supply of sterling will depend in part on the amount of foreign goods and services which UK residents wish to buy. Hence imports and exports of goods and services, and the movement of capital into and out of the country will influence the exchange rate.

There are two other important influences. In recent years there has been a large growth in currency speculation. Individuals and institutions try to buy a currency cheap and sell it for a higher price. If they think the pound is going to rise in price, they will buy pounds. If they believe that the pound will fall compared to the dollar, they will sell pounds and buy dollars. Tourists sometimes do this

on a much smaller scale, when they decide to exchange pounds for a foreign currency prior to departure in the hope that more foreign currency will be obtained that way. This speculation tends to increase the extent of the fluctuations in the value of a currency.

The government also affects the value of a currency. If the government wants the pound to rise in value (say because it wishes to cut the price of imports) then it can use its reserves of foreign exchange to buy pounds, so restricting their supply and forcing up the exchange rate as shown in Figure 20.2(i). On the other hand if the government sells pounds, then the value of the currency will fall as shown in Figure 20.2(ii).

Figure 20.2: *The market for sterling*
(i)

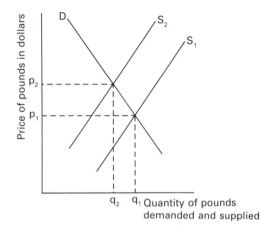

(ii)

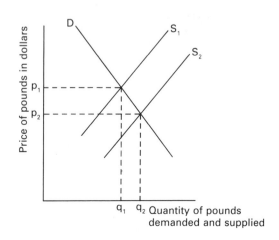

The government can also influence the value of the pound by changing the rate of interest in the country. A high rate of interest in the UK will cause some people to buy sterling, thus raising the rate of exchange. For example, if a firm has some money to invest for a short period and the interest rate is 10% in the UK and only 5% in the USA, its managers may move the money to the UK - unless they believe that the pound will fall in value. Hence expectations also play a part in determining the value of a currency.

Purchasing Power Parity (PPP)

The factors discussed above will often affect the value of a currency in the short run. But what factors will be important in the long run?

One approach to this is called Purchasing Power Parity (PPP). This suggests that the long-term value of the exchange rate will vary according to the cost of buying a representative basket of traded goods in competing countries. If prices in the UK rise by x% more than in its competitors, then the theory predicts that the value of the pound will fall by x% compared to the value of the currencies of competing countries.

Table 20.1: *Hamburger prices in several countries*

	Price in local currency	Implied purchasing power points of the dollar (1)	Actual exchange rate	Percentage over and under-valued
Britain	£1.10	0.69	0.67	-3
France	FF16.4	10.30	6.65	-35
Ireland	IR £1.18	0.74	0.74	0
USA	$1.60	—	—	—
W. Germany	DM4.25	2.66	2.02	-24
Australia	A$1.75	1.09	1.65	+50

Note: (1) Foreign price divided by dollar price.
Source: Adapted from *The Economist*, September 6-12, 1988.

The essence of this theory is that changes in relative price levels change the PPP rate. If the actual exchange rate between two countries mirrors the PPP rate, then neither will have a commercial advantage over the other. This is because each country's goods would have the same prices as the other's. This would cause each country to export the goods it can produce at home at a relatively low price and to import those goods that it would otherwise produce at a relatively high price. There is some evidence to support the theory that the long-run exchange rate will reflect changes in PPP. However, there are many variations from this rate. One reason is that international competitiveness is not determined solely by price, but by factors such as design and reputation.

A simple way to test if exchange rates reflect PPP is to compare the price of a particular product in several countries. If the exchange rate reflects PPP, such a product will have an identical price in each country. In 1986, *The Economist* did this for a Big Mac. Their results are shown in Table 20.1. They found that in several countries, such as the UK and Ireland, the cost of a hamburger reflected PPPs very accurately, but in others, such as Germany and Australia, there were large variations. This analysis suggests that, so far as hamburgers are concerned, the US dollar was undervalued against the German mark, but overvalued against the Australian dollar.

Key ideas

1. The price which a particular currency is worth in foreign currency is called its exchange rate.
2. In a free market, the exchange rate of a currency will be determined by demand and supply.
3. The demand for a currency will depend in part on demand by foreigners for goods produced in the country.
4. The supply of a currency will depend in part on the amount of foreign goods which the people in the country wish to buy.
5. Speculation, interest rates and government intervention will also affect the value of a currency.
6. In the long run, the main determinant may be Purchasing Power Parity.

What are the effects of changes in the rate of exchange?

Effect on the balance of payments

The rate of exchange affects the prices of imports and exports. A fall in the value of a currency will make imports more expensive and exports cheaper. Hence we should expect a sterling depreciation to lead to a fall in the quantity of goods imported and to a rise in the quantity of goods exported. The extent of the change will depend on the price elasticity of these goods. If (say) the demand for imports is inelastic (so that people are not deterred from buying imports even though the price has risen), then a country will continue to import nearly as many goods and to pay a higher price for them. The result will be a worsening of the balance of payments. If demand is elastic, then a fall in the value of the currency will lead to an improvement in the balance of payments because the rise in import prices will lead to a sharp fall in the quantity of imports.

The same analysis also applies to exports. If the demand for exports is elastic, then a fall in the exchange rate will lead to a large increase in the quantity of goods exported. This analysis has been formulated as the 'Marshall-Lerner condition'. This states that a fall in the exchange rate will improve a trade deficit if the sum of the price elasticities of demand for imports and exports is greater than one. There will be a time lag before these changes take effect and, in the short run, a fall in the value of a

currency may make things worse as shown in Figure 20.3. The reason for this is that, for a while, people will continue to buy the goods they have always bought and domestic manufacturers will take some time to replace imported goods; imports may therefore remain high and will also cost more. For example, when the price of oil rose in the period 1973/74, it took some time before car manufacturers could develop models which used less petrol per mile. Until this occurred, the quantity of oil imports fell very little after the price rose. After a while, a depreciation in the value of the currency should lead to an improvement in the current account. The length of the lag will vary according to the circumstances, but for an economy such as the UK, it will probably be well over a year before a currency depreciation leads to a significant improvement in the current account, and the full effect may not be felt for two years.

Effect on inflation

A rise in the value of a currency will cut the price of imports. Does this suggest a good way for the government to reduce inflation?

The extent of the fall in the Retail Price Index will depend on a number of factors. For example, will producers use the fall in import prices as a way to increase their profit margins and not pass the price cut on to consumers? Secondly, the effect may be very small in a country which imports relatively little, and the effect may be only temporary unless the fall in prices leads to a slowdown in the rate at which wages rise. Even if all these factors are favourable, it must be remembered that a rise in the exchange rate will probably lead to a worsening in the current account of the balance of payments. Hence this method can only be used to bring down inflation by those countries which have a strong surplus in their foreign trade.

Effect on unemployment

Another reason for not using the exchange rate to fight inflation is that a high rate of exchange for sterling will make exports more expensive and therefore cut output and employment in industries which export a large proportion of their production. It will also encourage imports and therefore lead to job losses in firms which face competition from abroad.

As can be seen from Figure 20.1 above, the pound rose rapidly in value around 1980 and this was followed by a collapse of output and employment in manufacturing industry. This suggests that there may be a trade-off between

Figure 20.3: *Effect of a currency depreciation over time*

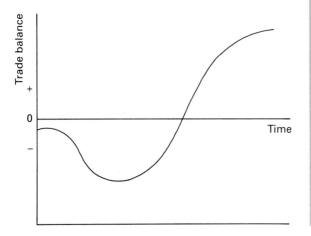

Table 20.2: Effects of a change in the value of a currency

Direction of change in value of the currency	Effect		
	On current account of the balance of payments	On inflation	On output and employment
Rise	Fall in exports and rise in imports Improvement if demand and supply are inelastic Deterioration if demand and supply are elastic	Lowers prices	Fall in output and rise in unemployment
Fall	Rise in exports and fall in imports Improvements if demand and supply are elastic · Deterioration if demand and supply are inelastic	Raises prices	Rise in output and fall in unemployment

objectives. A high exchange rate will help bring down the rate of inflation, but it will also lead to a worsening of the balance of payments and a fall in output and employment. A low rate will have the reverse effects. Hence car manufacturing firms such as Rover Group and Jaguar do very well when the pound is falling, but consumers may be faced with higher prices for imported goods. Table 20.2 summarises the overall position.

Key ideas

1. A fall in the value of a currency will make imports dearer and exports cheaper. This should increase the quantity of exports and reduce imports, the extent depending on how consumers react to price rises. A rise in the value of a currency will have the opposite effect.

2. Since a fall in the exchange rate makes imports more expensive, it will make inflation worse.

3. A fall in the value of a currency will cut export prices and so help exporters. It may lead to an increase in employment in these industries.

The market approach - floating exchange rates

A system of floating exchange rates treats a currency as a commodity which is bought and sold in the market place and its supporters tend to be those economists, such as Milton Friedman, who are enthusiastic about markets in general.

For most of the nineteenth century most international transactions took place under the gold standard system. The price of each major currency was fixed in terms of gold and therefore was also fixed in terms of other currencies. The system tended to be self adjusting. Countries which had a surplus on their foreign trade received payment in gold. This increased their money supply and incomes, which in turn led to a rise in imports and eliminated the surplus. A deficit led to an outflow of gold, a fall in incomes and hence in imports. Again the deficit was eliminated. In other words the system - output and employment - adjusted to the balance of payments. This system broke down about the time of the First World War which had an enormous disruptive effect on world trade. After that, countries were not willing to allow their economies to be dominated by foreign trade considerations.

Since about 1970, most world trade has taken place under a system of floating exchange rates in

Figure 20.4: *Self-equilibriating function of free exchange rates*

| UK BOP Deficit with Japan IMP > EXP | ⮕ | Sell £ for Yen Value £ ↓ Value Yen ↑ | ⮕ | UK Exports become cheaper in Yen UK Imports become more expensive in £ | ⮕ | EXP ↑ IMP ↓ | ⮕ | UK trade deficit with Japan eliminated IMP = EXP |

which the value of a currency is determined by the forces of demand and supply. However, this has not been a period of pure floating exchange rates because governments intervene to increase or decrease the value of their currencies; this is known as 'dirty floating'.

Benefits of floating rates

Under a system of floating exchange rates, the forces of demand and supply determine the value of a currency. Supporters of markets argue that these forces give a truer valuation of a currency than could a government. The rate of exchange will vary quickly to bring demand and supply into equilibrium. Put another way, the system is self-regulating. If the UK has a deficit in its trade with Japan, then the pound will fall in value because UK importers will sell pounds in order to obtain yen to buy Japanese goods. This fall in the value of the pound will cause British exports to Japan to become cheaper and imports from Japan will become more expensive. The fall in the value of the pound will only cease when trade between the two countries comes into equilibrium.

Another advantage claimed for floating exchange rates is that there is no need for government to hold large quantities of gold or foreign currency reserves. More important, since the balance of payments ceases to be a problem requiring government action, the government can concentrate its efforts on other problems. For example, a system of floating exchange rates makes monetary policy more effective. This is because a cut in the money supply will increase interest rates which will attract money from abroad and push up the exchange rate. In turn this will cut import prices and deflate the economy. Flexible exchange rates combined with a tight monetary policy therefore offer a good combination of policies for economists who favour a tough monetary policy. Some economists have argued that floating exchange rates will tend to be stable because they will not deviate much from the PPP level. Since this can be forecast fairly accurately, speculators will only do so within narrow margins.

However, experience does suggest that without any government intervention there will be fluctuations in the value of a currency; hence no government allows its currency to float unhindered. Instead they practice 'dirty' or 'managed' floating whereby the government buys and sells currency and varies interest rates in order to iron out fluctuations and obtain a desirable level for the currency. Managed floating therefore attempts to get the best of both worlds by letting the exchange rate float in order to obtain a payments balance, while maintaining some stability in the value of a currency.

Key ideas - summary of the case for floating rates

1. **Markets can judge the worth of a currency better than governments. Demand and supply will quickly bring the foreign exchange markets into equilibrium.**
2. **Freely floating exchange rates will automatically bring about a balance between imports and exports, so eliminating the possibility of a balance of payments crisis.**
3. **Floating exchange rates make monetary policy more effective and so help eliminate inflation.**
4. **Some economists in this group prefer perfectly free floating. Others want managed floating to reduce fluctuations in the value of the currency.**

Policies associated with floating exchange rates

These can be described very briefly; the government should not try to influence the value of the currency. Instead it should allow the forces of demand and supply to determine the value of the currency. Other economists would modify this generalisation to suggest that the government should intervene discreetly in the market to reduce the extent of fluctuations. The government can do this by buying and selling currency on the foreign exchange market.

The interventionist approach - fixed exchange rates

Critique of the case for floating rates

Supporters of the case for fixed rates of exchange point to experience in the last few years to suggest that, even with managed floating, exchange rates fluctuate considerably. Figure 20.1 showed the annual variations in the rate of exchange of sterling over the last few years - a period when the government was 'managing' the float. This conceals the extent of the variations in the value of the pound because within any one year the currency fluctuates considerably.

Do these fluctuations matter? Critics suggest that they do. International trade flourishes best in conditions of certainty. If currency fluctuations mean entrepreneurs do not know how much they will receive for their products, trade will suffer. This is because an export order may become more or less profitable between signing the contract and the final payment. Individual consumers are also affected when firms pass unexpected costs on to the customer. A good example of this is the surcharges which travel firms pass on to travellers when variations in the exchange rate put up their overseas costs. For these reasons it is argued that floating exchange rates are destabilising and so harm international trade.

Another criticism is that floating rates pass their destabilising effects on to other countries. If the balance of payments of country A is brought into equilibrium by cutting the level of imports from country B, there will be a rise in unemployment in B. The home country will have exported its unemployment. Similarly, if the exchange rate falls the price of imports will rise causing inflation.

Benefits of fixed rates

So far the case for fixing rates has been put in terms of the disadvantages of floating; but there are positive advantages claimed for fixing exchange rates.

The International Monetary Fund System (IMF)

was set up after the Second World War. Currencies were fixed against each other, but could be adjusted ('devalued' or 'revalued') when a country had a deficit or surplus on its balance of payments, causing market forces to put pressure on the existing value of the currency. International liquidity was increased by the provision of a pool of money to which all countries contributed and from which they could draw when in trouble. The IMF system of fixed exchange rates worked well for many years and contributed to a large rise in world trade, but this system broke down at the end of the 1960s, partly as a result of rising inflation. Despite this, supporters of fixed rates claim that this period was one in which the world economy expanded faster than ever before, and that this was made possible by the IMF system which gave the stability needed by international traders.

Supporters of fixed rates claim that they help to prevent speculation. Since the rate of exchange is fixed, there is no point in buying currencies in order to speculate. However, critics point out that this advantage disappears when it becomes obvious that a currency is over or under-valued, because then the government will be forced to change the value of the currency - to devalue or revalue. Speculators can forecast such developments and benefit from them. Proponents of fixed rates also claim that one cause of economic depression in the 1930s was that countries pushed down the value of their currency in order to obtain lower prices for their exports. This caused other countries to retaliate and caused confusion on the foreign exchange markets. Fixed exchange rates would prevent such policies. Critics of fixed rates deny these advantages. Firms can guard against future losses by buying currencies in advance. And even under a system of fixed rates of exchange, some countries do devalue their currencies in order to obtain competitive advantage.

Key ideas - summary of the case for fixed rates

1. **Part of the case for fixing exchange rates rests on the disadvantages of floating rates. These include destabilisation caused by large variations in the value of a currency and speculation.**
2. **Positive advantages include the encouragement of international trade arising from stable rates, a reduction in speculation and less likelihood of competitive devaluations.**

Policies associated with fixed rates

The essence of the policies associated with this point of view is that the rate of exchange should be kept stable at a desirable level. What is meant by 'desirable' will depend on the circumstances. Some would argue that the value of a currency ought to correspond more or less with its PPP. Others would argue for a value which reduced the cost of imports and hence brought down inflation. Perhaps the largest group would favour a level which was low enough to stimulate exports and hence employment.

Whatever the actual value chosen for the rate of exchange, the government would buy and sell currency in the foreign exchange markets in order to maintain the value. Hence if the pound was falling below its desired level, the government would intervene to buy pounds and so push up the price. Often this intervention would be done in conjunction with foreign governments who would sell their currency and buy pounds. If the value of the pound was thought to be too high, then the government would sell pounds and buy foreign currency. One difficulty which might be faced is that the government's ability to buy pounds depends on the amount of foreign exchange reserves. If these are too low compared to the level required to buy pounds, then the government will be unable to buy enough pounds to keep up the value, and will be forced to devalue. This will destroy the stability which is the prime reason for the policy.

Governments may be forced to devalue if the long-term trading position of the country deteriorates compared to that of its competitors. This can happen if competitors are more efficient, or if their inflation rate is lower. In both cases the country would be unable to compete and would have to make unpleasant decisions, such as devaluing the currency or deflating the economy in order to reduce demand for imports. A more pleasant solution would be to increase efficiency, but it is difficult to improve the efficiency of a country's industries.

A kind of a compromise - EMS

Both fixed and floating exchange rates appear to have benefits and problems. Historical evidence suggests that neither system is totally beneficial. An alternative approach, which attempts to obtain the benefits of both systems, is the European Monetary System (EMS). However, this system is closer to the interventionist approach, because it requires government intervention.

In the EMS, governments fix their exchange rates against each other. This means that currencies such as the French franc, German mark and Italian lire are only allowed to fluctuate by a tiny amount against each other. This gives the system stability which firms like and stimulates trade. However, against currencies outside the system, these currencies float together. Hence they all rise or fall together against the US dollar. Its supporters claim that this captures some of the advantages of a floating system.

Opponents of the system say that it reduces the freedom of individual countries to determine policy, and means that countries lose their independence. They also claim that it does not gain the advantages of either system. For example, supporters of markets would argue that it does not allow markets to allocate resources, and that this leads to a misallocation of resources. In addition, since some European economies are stronger than others, periodic devaluations and revaluations are needed, so that the stability claimed for the system is only temporary.

In addition to its purely exchange rate functions, the EMS has two other elements. It makes use of a unit of account called an ECU (European Currency Unit). The ECU is used as a unit of account in many Community transactions and the central banks use it to buy each others' currencies and to settle debts. The third element in the EMS is the European Monetary Co-operation Fund which lends money in ECUs to members in difficulties and which could eventually become a central bank for Europe. Indeed, some supporters of the EMS favour it because they see it as a step towards the creation of a single European currency.

Key ideas

**1. The EMS makes use of a common unit of account, the ECU. It also has a monetary co-operation fund.
2. Participants in the EMS exchange rate mechanism have fixed exchange rates against each other, but the currencies as a whole float against non-member currencies.
3. Supporters of the exchange rate mechanism say that it helps European business. Critics argue that it reduces the freedom of individual countries to determine economic policy.**

Conclusion

The basic question to be faced when discussing the foreign exchange market is the extent to which governments should intervene in the market. One group of economists suggest that the market will work best without any action from government. The market will determine the value of the currency and will bring about a balance between imports and exports. It will also increase the effectiveness of monetary policy. Critics of markets suggest that government intervention will prevent excessive fluctuations in exchange rates and will encourage international trade.

The EMS can be seen as an attempt to get the best of both systems, but the real goal of many of its supporters is European monetary union. Consequently EMS is opposed by those who dislike greater Community influence in the domestic economy.

Data questions

The exchange rate

The Committee received much evidence of the difficulties caused to manufacturing by the exchange rate. There were two principal complaints, first that the level of sterling *vis-à-vis* other currencies has been too high and secondly that the rate has been too unstable. Many witnesses stressed the adverse effect on manufacturing output of the rises in sterling between 1977 and 1981 and its continued high level in 1981-82. The high level which sterling attained against the United States dollar and major European currencies made British goods less competitive in home and foreign markets. Exports fell, import penetration rose, and for those exporters who held on to their markets, profit margins were squeezed severely. The witnesses who complained of this were drawn from all sectors and included the TUC, the CBI, the Bank of England, the motor, textile, electrical, chemical, engineering, paper and furniture industries. Many also complained bitterly of the instability of the exchange rate rather than the problem of coping with any particular rate. The problem here is that long-term contracts have to be undertaken for purchase and supply and imports may have to be purchased in a currency which is rising relative to the pound while exports compete against currencies which have changed far less. This can lead manufacturers to source components in the countries to which they are selling so as to reduce currency losses. Whilst it is possible, at a cost, to hedge against some changes in exchange rates to cover future orders or deliveries, this cannot protect the domestic supplier to the home market against exchange rates which give the foreign importer price advantages that cannot be matched - hence the rapid growth of import penetration and the demise of many United Kingdom industrial concerns.

Source: House of Lords Select Committee on Overseas Trade, 1984-85.

Question 1

1. Outline the disadvantages to British firms of:
   (i) a high and
   (ii) a fluctuating
   level of the pound.

2. What reasons would the government give for allowing the value of the pound to float?

Sterling: the cost of over-valuation

It does seem that, after a long period of belly-aching, it is now understood that an artificially strong pound damages the export prospects of industry.

It also seems that more people realise that the inability to export manufactured goods - and that the propensity to import more - is a bad thing, bound to end in tears. What still does not seem to be understood, however, is the nature of the long-term damage that may be done, and why this occurs.

It may take five or more years of persistence to sell to a customer. It may mean arranging contingency stocks on his doorstep, or altering your product to meet his projected need. Moreover, once in position, you take him for granted at your peril. As a rule of thumb, if it takes you five years to sell to him in the first place, you should consider at least another five as your period of probation. Nor will your competition be quiet and passive during this period. They will play every trick in the book, and many you have never heard of, to get you out.

Real damage

This is where the real damage to industry of overvalued currencies occurs. The pressure for performance placed on the average company by institutions and the stock market necessitates courage and determination to hold on to a market position when you lose money on every item you sell. Yet you know the investment you have made and you know that re-entry, once you have pulled out, is even more difficult.

This is why, despite the revival of strength and pride of our manufacturing capability, we have yet to replace the 30 per cent which closed down losing their markets for ever. This is why a prolonged period of overvaluation of a currency, caused, for instance, by the internal necessity of high rates to dampen demand, has a much greater effect than just the loss of exports in the short term. It was this point that many of us have been trying to emphasise and it is this point, as far as I can see, that fails to be adequately understood. The market does rule, but in its own time.

Source: Sir John Harvey-Jones, 'Sterling: the cost of over-valuation', *The Observer,* August 14, 1988.

Question 2

1. Explain what is meant by 'a strong pound' and 'the propensity to import'.

2. Put forward economic arguments:
(i) to support and
(ii) to oppose
the views in the article.

21 Economic Development

There are a number of controversies in the field of development economics; indeed this is such a broad area that it is only possible here to outline some of these arguments. Many of them focus on the efficiency of market forces:

● Some economists suggest that the incentives provided by an unhindered system of markets will stimulate economic development. Low wages in poor countries will attract capital and new technology, and development will result.

● Others suggest that most poor countries need intervention from domestic governments and from the international community in the form of aid, cheap finance and trade advantages if they are to develop at an acceptable pace.

● Many Marxists argue that the real cause of poverty in less developed countries is the direct result of the wealth found in richer countries; that rich countries exploit poorer ones, and that revolutionary change is needed.

What is development?

It is both true and an over-simplification to say that the world is divided into rich and poor countries. It is true because some countries, such as Haiti or Burma, are poor by any standards, whilst others, such as Sweden or Swizerland, are clearly rich. The statement is also an over-simplification because some people in poor countries are quite rich whilst there are poor people in rich countries. Moreover, between the two extremes there are many countries which have some characteristics usually found in rich countries but also some features common to poor countries. For example, some countries have low incomes per head but relatively high levels of education. In other countries the position is reversed. Hence we need to begin by exploring the problem of defining and measuring economic development. Terminology is important because it colours the way we think about problems. For example, to call countries 'backward' implies that they are uncivilised. In this chapter we will use the expression 'less developed countries' (LDCs) when we refer to those countries with low levels of income per head.

Classifying development

There are a number of ways to classify development. One method is to construct some measure of welfare. This could include measures of life expectancy, infant mortality and levels of education, and also take into account the distribution as well as the average level of income. This is a valid approach to the study of development, but it does raise questions about which measures should be included. There are other problems; for example, it is not possible to add an infant mortality rate to a low literacy rate to obtain a single measure of development. Hence in this chapter we will use the conventional measure of national income per head. As you may recall from Chapter 11, this is far from a satisfactory measure for a number of reasons. The figures are often inaccurate, they say nothing about the distribution of income and unpaid activities are excluded. Moreover, international comparisons are particularly difficult because this requires data on national income for different countries to be converted into a common currency, usually US dollars. Since exchange rates vary daily, this would imply daily changes in living standards, which is nonsense. Moreover, prices are usually lower in LDCs. The figures suggest that a country such as Chad has a per capita income of only $80 per annum. In a country such as Britain, people would starve to death on an income as low as this. Clearly comparisons between countries with very low incomes and those with high ones can be misleading.

Diversity among LDCs

There is enormous variation between countries conventionally described as 'less developed'. Some, such as China, cover a huge geographical area, whilst others are tiny. Some have large populations, others small. Some are densely populated, in others the population is sparse. Similarly, some have low levels of education and health whilst some have high standards. Certain countries rely on markets to allocate resources whilst others have extensive planning mechanisms. Despite this massive diversity, the division of the world into rich and poor countries is real. As Table 21.1 shows, the 75% of the world's population who live in poor countries such as China, India, Pakistan and sub-Saharan Africa produce only 21% of the world's output.

Table 21.1: Share of world output

	Developed countries	Less developed countries
Share of world population	25%	75%
Share of world production	79%	21%

Source: *World Development Report*, 1984, World Bank.

Table 21.2: Growth of Gross Domestic Product, by region, 1965-86

Group	1980 GDP (US$ billions)	1980 population (millions)	1980 GDP per capita (US$)	Average annual percentage change in GDP					
				1965-73	1973-80	1980-83	1984	1985	1986[a]
All developing countries	2,115	3,123	680	6.5	5.4	2.5	5.1	4.8	4.2
Regional group									
Sub-Saharan Africa[b]	187	331	560	6.4	3.2	-0.8	-1.7	2.2	0.5
East Asia	604	1,300	470	7.9	6.6	6.2	10.1	7.3	6.8
South Asia	211	921	230	3.8	4.5	5.5	4.0	6.3	4.7
Europe, Middle East and North Africa[c]	329	198	1,670	6.6	5.9	2.8	3.0	2.8	2.9
Latin America and the Caribbean	706	344	2,050	6.6	5.4	-0.9	3.2	3.7	3.0
Income group									
Low-income countries	564	2,118	270	5.5	4.6	6.0	8.9	9.1	6.5
Large low-income	449	1,667	270	6.1	4.9	6.8	10.4	10.3	6.9
Small low-income	115	451	260	3.4	3.3	2.8	2.4	3.6	4.7
Middle-income countries	1,552	1,005	1,540	7.0	5.7	1.2	3.6	2.8	3.2
Miscellaneous group									
Exporters of manufactures[d]	958	1,886	510	7.4	6.0	4.1	7.8	7.8	7.0
Oil exporters[e]	522	405	1,290	6.9	6.0	0.8	2.3	2.2	-1.1
Highly indebted countries[f]	890	492	1,810	6.9	5.4	-0.9	2.0	3.1	2.5
Industrial countries	7,570	716	10,570	4.7	2.8	1.0	4.6	2.8	2.5
High-income oil exporters	216	16	13,500	8.3	7.9	-1.9	1.2	-3.8	9.4

NOTE: Developing countries refers to the ninety-country group used for analytical purposes in the *World Development Report* and other Bank documents.
a. Preliminary
b. Excluding South Africa
c. Does not include Hungary, Poland and Romania
d. Includes Brazil, China, Hong Kong, India, Israel, Republic of Korea, Portugal, Singapore and Yugoslavia.
e. Includes Algeria, Cameroon, Congo, Ecuador, Egypt, Gabon, Indonesia, Mexico, Nigeria, Syria, Trinidad and Tobago and Venezuela.
f. Includes Argentina, Bolivia, Brazil, Chile, Colombia, Costa Rica, Côte d'Ivoire, Ecuador, Jamaica, Mexico, Morocco, Nigeria, Peru, Philippines, Uruguay, Venezuela and Yugoslavia.

Source: The World Bank.

The development record

Table 21.2 summarises recent world economic development. Over the period as a whole living standards have been rising, but there are substantial differences between areas. African economies have done relatively badly and this is likely to continue. The reason for this is that they tend to have high rates of population growth, weak domestic policies and poor export performance. Oil exporting countries did relatively poorly in the 1980s because of the low price of oil. On the other hand the major exporters of manufactured goods (countries such as Brazil, Korea, Singapore and the Philippines) have developed rapidly.

Factors affecting economic development

Economists do not possess a generally accepted theory of economic development. If such a theory existed it would be possible to predict growth and, indeed, to adopt policies which would ensure growth. In the meantime it is possible to note some of the factors which seem to be associated with rapid development.

Natural resources

Britain's development at the time of the industrial revolution was helped by the possession of coal and iron ore. Similarly, oil has helped the development of countries such as Saudi Arabia and Kuwait. However, countries such as Japan have had rapid economic growth despite the lack of natural resources.

Political stability

Countries in political turmoil, such as Lebanon do not develop, if only because investors have little confidence in the future. However, stability on its own is not enough. Salazar ruled Portugal for nearly forty years from the 1920s, but this stable government was used to oppose change and the country stagnated.

Investment

Investment today leads to future growth. A resource consumed today cannot also be used to increase future consumption. Put another way, the opportunity cost of an investment such as a dam may be houses that are urgently needed to accommodate the homeless. Hence investment requires saving, but this is difficult in countries where incomes are low.

Skilled labour force

The quality of the labour force is a crucial factor in economic development. The human capital approach to development approaches the problem by analysing people as they would an ordinary capital investment and asking 'Would this be a good investment?'.

In general this line of approach suggests that investment in education is worthwhile for developing countries. An educated labour force tends to be more productive than one which is ignorant. Good health also helps increase productivity, and in turn this is improved by education as well as by factors such as suitable diet and pure water.

Attitudes towards change

For centuries China seemed to have all the requisites necessary for development, but remained desperately poor. It had long periods of stable government, a tradition of scientific investigation, mineral resources and a hard working people. The reason that it remained poor was that the whole ethos of the society opposed change. Business people had a low status in society and the government did little to encourage growth.

Some societies, such as Japan, do not question the need for constant change and are rewarded by rapid growth; others are less willing to adapt and consequently develop at a slower rate.

Appropriate government policies

Countries grow quickly if the government adopts appropriate policies. Of course, economists being economists, there is room for considerable argument about which policies are correct! (President Roosevelt of the USA once asked his advisers to find him some one-handed economists. When asked to clarify his request he said 'I'm tired of economists saying "on the one hand this, but on the other hand that".') This debate is expanded later in the chapter when policy alternatives are analysed.

Key ideas

1. **Economic development is conventionally measured by using national income statistics, though these have considerable limitations.**
2. **LDCs vary considerably in size, economic characteristics and rates of growth.**
3. **Factors influencing development include the extent of natural resources, political stability, the level of investment, the quality of the labour force, attitudes towards change and appropriate government policies.**

Some controversies in development economics

Development economics is a large subject and it is not possible to cover all the controversies here. However, it is possible to focus on some particular issues.

Costs and benefits of development

Change can be painful. People have to adapt to new working methods, existing skills become obsolete and traditional products may disappear, being replaced by mass produced goods which lack individuality. Some people may have to move in order to obtain work, so breaking up families. This can cause a fall in the welfare of old people who in LDCs are cared for at home by their children, but who in advanced countries often have to go into 'homes'.

There are other costs associated with development. As industries grow the problems of pollution increase and there is more congestion on the roads. Moreover, when people move into cities they suffer from overcrowding as huge slums develop, and there is often a rise in crime.

Despite all these costs, the potential benefits of economic development are enormous. Rising levels of national income do not only mean more goods, they also permit higher standards of education and health. Rising incomes also give people greater choice, not only in goods, but in the whole way of life. For example, in richer countries people have a much greater choice of jobs than they do in poor countries.

Population

At the birth of Jesus, the population of the world was about 300 million people. It took 1,500 years to double. It then grew rapidly and by 1900 it had reached 1.7 billion. The rate of growth continued to increase and in the thirty years after 1950 the world's population doubled again. Estimates now suggest that it has reached about 5 billion.

Attitudes towards population are strongly affected by religious beliefs and by nationalistic feelings. Some people argue that it is wrong to limit the number of births. In some countries, leaders advocate more births because they believe that this increases the importance of the country. In addition some economists would argue that the size of population is not a constraint on growth; more people means more workers and more demand for goods and services. However, most economists would probably support the argument that a rapidly rising population hinders growth. In many LDCs half the population is aged under 20, and this means that they cannot afford to provide adequate education. Consequently the labour force remains poorly qualified. In addition, an increasing population means that there are fewer capital resources per head of the population, and simple arithmetic shows that if GNP increases at 3% a year and the population also rises by 3%, then the average person is no better off.

Agriculture and industry

For many LDCs industrialisation is a prime objective. They see the path of development as one in which their countries move from a position where agriculture is the dominant sector to one where industry predominates. One reason is that this was the path by which more developed countries increased their national income. They also argue that industrialisation will raise output per head and help their balance of payments by reducing the need for imported manufactured goods. In order to develop their industries many countries have used scarce funds to build up large-scale, capital-intensive factories and have protected their industries with high tariff barriers. Critics of this approach argue that it is wasteful to build industries which cannot compete and that the money should be used instead on less glamorous small-scale developments in agriculture. Since most people live in rural areas, the prime objective should be to improve living standards of small farmers. Thus in many LDCs, the quality of life would be improved if peasants could afford to keep a few chickens. The provision of pure water would have a similar result. Rising rural living standards would also stem the rush to the towns which has created huge slums in many countries.

Key ideas

1. Economic development can have undesirable side-effects, but it increases living standards.
2. World population is growing rapidly. Some people welcome this, but it causes problems such as a large number of young people who have to be educated.
3. Many LDCs have emphasised industrial development, but some critics say that agriculture should have greater priority.

The case for intervention

The conventional view of most development economists is that positive action by both domestic and foreign governments is needed if development is to be stimulated. And official international organisations, such as the World Bank and the Food and Agriculture Organisation, must also play a part. The reason for such policies being advocated is that these economists believe market forces are inadequate to the task of fostering development.

Criticisms of market forces have already been discussed in detail, particularly in Chapter 2, but there are special reasons why intervention is advocated in the case of LDCs. When we say that a country is poor we mean primarily that its inhabitants have a low standard of living. But we also mean much more than this. One assumption behind the market forces approach is that people are knowledgeable and so are able to make informed decisions. In most LDCs, however, the standard of education is low and people do not have the sources of information - for example, about new crop possibilities - which would allow them to make reasoned judgements about new initiatives. Consequently the incentives which provide the stimulus for change in market economies may not work in LDCs. Moreover, since many people live in a subsistence economy, growing their own food and building their own houses, the price system may only operate to a very limited extent. Hence it is argued that the necessary conditions needed to make markets work efficiently are not met in these countries.

Investment

Poor countries need to spend a huge part of their income on the basics which are necessary for life. There is little left over to finance extensive investment, whether in infrastructure such as roads, education or health, or in new factories or farms. Hence government and even international help is needed. This is largely given in the form of aid, sometimes through bilateral (that is state to state) help, sometimes through international agencies and sometimes through the efforts of the voluntary sector. The rationale behind long-term aid is that funds made available in this way will provide investment which poor countries could not afford and enable them to break out of a circle of poverty. This exists when poor countries cannot afford to invest; consequently they cannot compete with other countries, so that incomes and investment remain low.

Balance of payments

Most LDCs face chronic balance of payments problems and owe huge sums of money. As Figure 21.1 shows, LDCs as a whole have huge debts and consequently pay large sums in interest. Hence in the world as a whole there is a transfer of funds from poor countries to rich.

One reason for this debt is that in the 1970s the price of oil increased enormously and there was little they could do in the short run to reduce the level of oil imports. Then in the 1980s world interest rates rose and debts which had been manageable could no longer be financed.

Figure 21.1: *The third world financial haemorrhage*

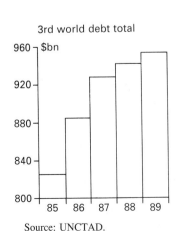

3rd world debt total

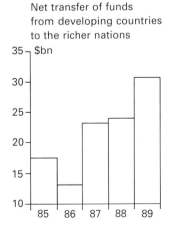

Net transfer of funds from developing countries to the richer nations

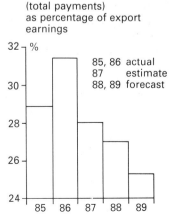

Debt service (total payments) as percentage of export earnings

85, 86 actual
87 estimate
88, 89 forecast

Source: UNCTAD.

There is another reason why many LDCs face persistent balance of payments problems - that is because they tend to export agricultural products. One characteristic of most of these products is that demand for them does not rise much with income, i.e. income elasticity of demand is inelastic. When we become richer we do not increase our consumption of tea, nor eat more bananas or sugar. Because many LDCs have attempted to solve their problems by increasing the output of cash crops such as these, world production has increased substantially whilst consumption has remained fairly static. This has caused the price to fall as shown in Figure 21.2. Hence the value of exports from LDCs has fallen compared to the price they have to pay for imports - that is the terms of trade have become more unfavourable.

Figure 21.2:

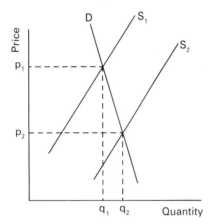

Trade in Manufactures

One way out of this dilemma is for LDCs to produce manufactured goods to sell in the richer countries. Over the last two or three decades LDCs have developed their manufacturing industries, so that exports of manufactures now amount to nearly a quarter of their total exports. For some countries, such as South Korea or Singapore, the proportion is much higher than this. However, it is easier to suggest that countries should increase their exports of manufactured goods than it is to achieve this goal. In the first place there is only a limited market in rich countries for products such as textiles or other manufactured goods that do not require highly skilled labour or expensive machinery and so can be easily made in LDCs. Moreover, countries that are already industrialised often take measures to prevent competition from LDCs - look in almost any shop

selling textiles and very few will come from poorer countries. Hence it is suggested that governments should remove these barriers to trade. (This argument is also supported by economists who advocate the use of market forces to allocate resources.)

The reason why markets in richer countries are barred to many products from the LDCs is that vested interests keep up these barriers. An additional reason is that many poor countries do not have the ability to produce goods of the quality that is required to sell in advanced countries. Hence some economists suggest that aid in the form of experts or machines is needed in order to help raise standards.

Population control

Without government intervention many LDCs would be faced by rapid growth in population. The problems this can cause have already been mentioned, and these have caused many economists to urge government intervention to reduce the rate at which population grows. This can take many forms. In some countries governments run publicity campaigns urging people to have fewer children. Some provide cheap contraceptives. In others, such as China, individuals with large families have faced official disproval and lose social benefits.

> **Key ideas - summary of the case for intervention**
>
> **1. As in developed countries, market forces sometimes fail to achieve satisfactory ends.**
> **2. However, these inadequacies are exacerbated in LDCs; for example, low educational standards mean that people lack knowledge of the opportunities which may be present.**
> **3. LDCs face particular problems in accumulating capital and in balancing their external payments. This needs government intervention and international aid.**

Interventionist policies

A long list of policies could be produced; those that follow are largely taken from *Common Crisis* (1983), the report of an international commission chaired by Willie Brandt, formerly the Chancellor of the German Federal Republic:

- Finance. The International Monetary Fund should make more credit available to LDCs which face balance of payments problems. Similarly, more resources should be made available to the World Bank so that it can lend more to poor countries. In addition, individual developed countries should increase their aid so that it amounts to 0.7% of GNP.
- Trade. Developed countries should resist protectionist pressures and encourage imports from LDCs.
- Agriculture. There should be increased food aid and more research into agriculture, especially in an African context.
- Energy. A new international agency should be established in order to increase self-reliance in developing countries. This could provide advice and expertise, not only on how to produce more energy, but also on energy saving methods.

The case for non-intervention

The case against government intervention is essentially an extension of the case favouring market forces as the way to allocate resources. Economists such as Bauer and Yamey in their book *The*

Economics of Underdeveloped Countries (1957) argue that decision making should be decentralised in order to extend choice:

'The role of the state is seen primarily as that of making it possible for individuals to have access to a wider range of alternatives and to more adequate knowledge of them.'

They believe that this can only be achieved by using the forces of demand and supply to allocate resources through the market.

One reason for this approach is that they believe politicians and civil servants are not competent to take decisions in the interests of the country as a whole and so make decisions which are in their own interest. This often includes expanding the public sector because it extends the power and patronage of politicians. Bauer (1982) also claims that:

'Third World rulers use economic controls primarily to promote their own political and financial purposes, including the undermining or destroying of opponents and rewarding of supporters'.

In this view the functions of government should be limited to activities such as maintaining law and order, providing public goods such as defence, helping in catastrophes, providing an institutional framework which encourages individual initiative, and breaking down monopoly power.

In support of their approach, economists such as Bauer would argue that the rapid economic growth of countries such as Singapore and South Korea has occurred because their economies have been driven by entrepreneurs and not politicians.

Aid

Foreign aid plays little or no part in this approach. According to Bauer:

'If the conditions for development other than capital are present, the capital required will either be generated locally or be available commercially from business . . . If the required conditions are not present, then aid will be ineffective and wasted.'

Note that this line of argument assumes that capital is not a constraint on development because it is mobile and will switch from rich to poor countries if economic opportunities arise. This assumption is not accepted by advocates of aid. There are other arguments against aid. Bauer argues that aid is often wasted on unproductive projects because it is not expected to yield a commercial return. Moreover, aid goes to governments which are inefficient. It increase the politicisation of life, the power of politicians and encourages the development of the state sector. Thus many LDCs spend large sums of money on armaments which contribute nothing to development.

International debt

Table 21.3: *Heavily indebted countries (1984)*

1 = Debt, US$bn.
2 = Debt, %GNP.
3 = GNP/Capita US$

	1.	2.	3.
Argentina	38.1	46.8	2230
Brazil	87.2	44.0	1720
Chile	17.2	100.2	1700
Mexico	87.5	54.2	2040
Morocco	10.6	79.9	670
Nigeria	12.7	17.0	730
Peru	11.3	68.2	1000
Philippines	14.1	43.9	660
Venezuela	23.7	52.7	3410
Yugoslavia	17.0	42.2	2120

Source: *North South Issue paper*, Trocaire, Dublin, 1987.

As Table 21.3 shows, many LDCs have extensive debts to richer countries. This is sometimes used as an argument to support an increase in aid or cancellation of debts. However, the debts arose because of the transfer of real resources and any failure to repay is clear evidence that the capital was wasted by the governments that received the resources. Cancelling such debts therefore favours the incompetent and the dishonest. Critics of this would claim that debts have built up because of factors outside the control of LDCs, such as the rise in oil prices, and because rich countries have put up interest rates after loans have been agreed.

Key ideas - summary of the case against intervention

1. **Markets are the best way to allocate resources. Interference with market forces will delay economic growth.**
2. **Governments should limit their activities and instead stimulate the local private sector by providing incentives for innovation.**
3. **Foreign aid is not needed because private sector capital will flow automatically to economically desirable projects whilst aid will encourage the growth of the inefficient public sector.**

Policies advocated by economists opposed to intervention

The group of economists who dislike intervention favour measures which will limit the role of government to relatively few activities, such as defence, law and order, and the provision of incentives which will stimulate private sector entrepreneurial activity. Hence government should cut both taxes and public spending. They should also encourage the private ownership of land because private owners will be more efficient than co-operatives or other forms of ownership. This group also favours the elimination of barriers to international trade. Indeed, the best way in which the richer countries can help the poor is by removing the barriers which restrict the opportunity of poor countries to export their goods.

The Marxist approach

A third alternative is put forward by Marxist economists. They suggest that a 'Marxist' economic system should be established in order to promote development. Evidence in support of this approach can be found in countries such as Cuba, where there has been a huge fall in the infant mortality and a large expansion in education since Marxist methods were adopted. In addition, some countries such as Tanzania have adopted Marxist ideas and used a 'socialist' approach, for example, encouraging peasants to move into co-operative villages where facilities such as health centres can be provided.

For Marxists, the process of development is dialectical. This means that development produces disequilibrium as well as equilibrium; conflict as well as harmony. In the long run, conflict will lead to the break up of existing capitalist states and their replacement with socialist ones, where the people own the capital. It follows from this that the process of development cannot be one of smooth progress; instead it is characterised by conflict and frequent crises.

Most Marxists would accept that the capitalist accumulation process produces both poverty and wealth, and that the wealth found in the richer countries was largely the result of the destruction of living standards in poorer, exploited countries. This will continue until the system itself is changed. In Marx's words:

'. . . only then will human progress cease to resemble that hideous pagan idol, who would not drink the nectar but from the skulls of the slain.'

An example will illustrate the point. Until the Industrial Revolution in Britain - when power passed to the capitalist class - India had a large textile industry. As a British colony, India was forced to accept textiles made in British factories and this decimated the Indian industry, causing enormous poverty, whilst the profits led to rising standards in Britain. Consequently the wealth of the West rests on the poverty of the world's poor.

Other examples of this exploitation can be given. Marxists claim that economies such as Mexico are organised in the interests of the USA, supplying cheap labour and providing a market for the products of American industry. The products produced in Mexico tend to be those requiring low wages or those which cannot be easily produced in the USA. Similarly, international capitalists move production of products such as electronic goods to a few LDCs where wages are low and governments keep down business taxes and discourage trade unions. South Korea is an example. Production in countries such as these maintains profits and stimulates growth in one or two countries, but this cannot be spread to others - there is only a limited number of video recorders which are needed by the developed world. Hence capitalist investment in the less developed world does little to raise living standards there because it is organised in the interests of the capitalists who live in the richer countries. The profits are expropriated by foreign capitalists or squandered on luxury consumption by domestic elites who form an alliance with foreign capitalists and, in return, reap some of the benefits.

The prevalent Marxist view of the 1960s and 1970s argued that LDCs experienced under-development (or dependent development) because they were part of the international capitalist system. This made them vulnerable to fluctuations in the price of primary products which they produced, to penetration and exploitation by trans-national companies, to dependence on international capital markets, and to a subservient military position.

More recently, some Marxists have suggested that capitalism can spread to LDCs and that it can be a progressive force. By this they mean that it can replace more backward economic systems as it did in Europe in the nineteenth century. This group of Marxists argues that LDCs are able to absorb imported technology and that they can negotiate on strong terms with transnational companies. In this view there are good possibilities for sustained development.

Key ideas - summary of the Marxist approach

1. The general Marxist position since the War has been that the poverty of LDCs is a direct result of the wealth found in richer countries.
2. In this view the wealth found in rich countries is caused by the exploitation of poorer countries whose economies are geared to supplying the needs of the rich countries, such as raw materials and markets.
3. A different Marxist approach suggests that LDCs can take the capitalist path and become wealthier, at least in the short term.
4. Both groups believe that economic crises are inevitable in development and will continue until the whole system is changed.

Marxist policies

In the long run Marxists believe that revolutionary change is needed; this can be peaceful in certain circumstances. In the shorter run they advocate the strengthening of workers' organisations, such as trade unions, and the growth of public ownership. Since resources are particularly scarce in poor countries, government intervention is needed to prevent them being wasted on the pleasures of the rich. Instead, more money should be spent on education, providing basic health facilities and on building up the economic infrastructure such as roads, electricity and pure water. Government farms and factories can also be set up to force the pace of development.

Conclusion

Economists agree that there are large differences in living standards between rich and poor countries. Arguments arise when the causes and significance of these differences are considered and when policies are suggested. The debate centres around the role of government. Those who admire the efficiency of market forces seek to limit the role of government to a relatively few essential activities. Interventionists argue that market forces cannot cope with the circumstances found in many LDCs and that intervention is needed from domestic governments and from the international community if development is to be stimulated. Finally, Marxists believe that strong government action is needed to prevent exploitation.

Data questions

The South

Industrial economies transmit their troubles to developing countries by a number of routes. Uncoordinated policies in the North to eliminate payments deficits due to oil price increases or to reduce inflation have increased the adjustment burden on oil-importing developing countries. For the poorer countries this burden has been particularly severe because the recession has dramatically reduced their commodity export earnings, and they cannot borrow to finance deficits. But for other countries too debt service payments have risen steeply as a result of high interest rates, and increased borrowing is becoming difficult to sustain. Even the better-off developing countries are now reducing imports, which further aggravates the recession. In fact the developing countries today are, with few exceptions, in a desperate plight. With the prices of commodities - the main exports of many countries - at their lowest level for over thirty years, recession and protectionism affecting their exports of manufactures, a slowing up in the flow of commercial capital and aid, their balance of payments problems have reached intolerable proportions.

Cutting back on growth is the order of the day - for those countries which have been growing. For numerous countries - especially in Sub-Saharan Africa, where there has been no growth in recent years - lack of capacity to import translates directly into increased hardship, even threatened starvation, for tens of millions of the most vulnerable people.

Source: The Brandt Commission, *Common Crisis,* Pan, 1983.

Question 1

1. Explain what is meant by:
(i) 'payments deficits' and
(ii) protectionism.
2. Critically analyse the way in which 'industrial economies' transmit their troubles to developing countries.

3. What action should industrial countries take to help LDCs?

Role of the state in development

We prefer a society in which policy is directed towards widening the effective range of alternatives open to members of that society. It follows that we think it should be the function of the state to widen the range of opportunities and facilitate access to them, but that it is for the members of society to choose among the alternative opportunities open to them and develop them with the aid of their personal endowments and the property they own. We believe that the widening of the range of effective choice is the most valuable single objective of economic development as well as the best single criterion of its attainment. We shall show that our approach does not confine the state to a passive and negligible role, but that on the contrary it envisages state action on a wide scale, on a scale, indeed, which is sufficient to tax the political and administrative resources of most governments in under-developed countries. Our political position influences the direction in which we prefer official policy to go; it does not postulate state inaction.

Source Bauer, P.T. & Yamey, B.S. *The Economics of Under Developed Countries*, C.U.P., 1957.

Question 2

1. What functions for the state do you think Bauer and Yamey would advocate?

2. What additional functions to these advocated by Bauer and Yamey (if any) would you advocate, and why?

22 Conclusion - Economic Models and Theories

Facts don't speak for themselves. They have to be interpreted. If two cars collide, the interpretation of the facts offered by the drivers will often vary considerably. Their perspectives will alter the way they perceive the events and their perspectives will probably be determined by their self-interest.

In economics the position is much more complicated. The number of possible facts surrounding any economic problem is so large that no individual - and no computer - can comprehend them all. Therefore the economist has not only to interpret the facts, but also to decide which facts are important. In order to do this economists build models.

Economic models

An economic model is a simplification of reality which abstracts from the complexities of the real world in order to explain economic phenomena and to make predictions. In everyday life we build and make use of models all the time. Most people have a simplistic model of how a television works. If they press a certain button, the result will be a particular programme. This model has simplified reality by ignoring everything inside the set. If something goes wrong, people have to call a repairer who has a much more sophisticated model which allows them to make predictions about the causes of television failure.

Models can be expressed in various ways. The most obvious is to use words; most of the models in this book are verbal models. They can also be expressed diagrammatically. The circular flow of income model is a good example. In this model reality is simplified so that just six variables are considered; but this is sufficient to allow predictions to be made. Professional economists would extend the model, bring in more variables, and probably specify their relationships mathematically. The Treasury model of the British economy has some 600 equations which make it possible to forecast the consequences if some variable, such as the money supply, is altered. Despite its complexity, even this model is a considerable simplification of reality.

Figure 22.1: Theorising in economics

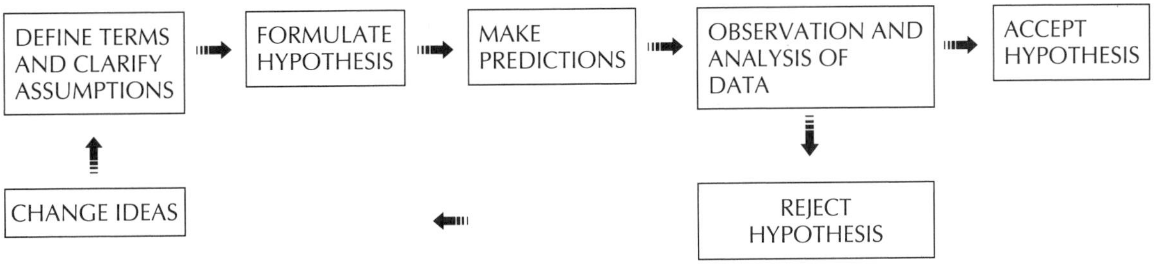

Testing models

In order to use models we usually have to be able to **quantify** the variables involved. In principle this may seem an easy task. In practice it is quite difficult. Statistics are often not available or are inaccurate. If we are investigating income, for example, most data comes from the Inland Revenue and people have been known to give inaccurate information to the tax authorities! If we knocked at doors asking people their income we would be more likely to get a black eye than accurate information. Take another instance; there is no perfect way to measure 'housing conditions', so we have to use **proxies,** such as overcrowding or lack of facilities.

Economic method

According to Keynes:

'The theory of economics does not furnish a body of settled conclusions immediately applicable to policy. It is a method rather than a doctrine, an apparatus of the mind, a technique of thinking which helps its possessor to draw correct conclusions.'

This economic 'way of thinking' has been used throughout this book and is closely related to the methods used by other scientists, particularly other social scientists. However, there are special difficulties which occur when scientific method is applied to people.

One difficulty is that most economic analysis assumes people behave rationally and this manifests itself in an attempt to improve their utility. However, people can be capricious, behaving differently in the same circumstances, perhaps just because they feel like a change. This makes it difficult to predict how individuals may behave.

The position is different when we consider large groups of people because of the 'law of large numbers'. This suggests that while particular individuals may behave in odd ways, this will be offset by the behaviour of others. Hence it may be impossible to predict whether a particular individual will buy an ice cream on a particular day, but it is predictable that more ice cream will be bought when the weather is hot than when it is cold. Similarly, a 'Scrooge' may spend only tiny amounts of money whatever his income, but it is safe to suggest that on average people will spend more when their income rises.

Evaluating theories

Theories can never be proved correct because it is not possible to check a theory against every possible observation. A statement such as 'Every person will eventually die' cannot be **proved** correct until every person is dead - and then there would be no one to confirm the accuracy of the prediction. Consequently instead of trying to prove theories true, social scientists seek evidence to refute them. Again, this can never be done with complete certainty, if only because people are not perfect and are liable to make mistakes. However, if data is accumulated which suggests that a theory does not accord with the evidence, it is discarded or amended. To test a theory, economists ask questions such as 'Does it account for all the evidence?' and 'Does it predict the consequences of a change more accurately than the alternative theory?'

From this viewpoint, a good theory is one that makes wide ranging claims which can be tested, while leaving itself open to falsification. Newton's theory of gravity is such a theory. It allowed scientists to make predictions about the orbits of planets as well as about the way objects would fall to the ground. Scientists could therefore make many predictions and test them. The theory therefore gave rise to many opportunities for falsifying it. The more it resisted attempts to falsify it, the more likely it was to be true. However, because of the special difficulties facing social scientists it may never be possible to achieve this amount of certainty in economics.

Values

Some economics textbooks begin by distinguishing between **positive** and **normative** economics. Positive economics deals with what is; with **objective explanations** of the working of the economy. Normative economics is about what ought to be; it puts forward views based on **personal value judgements.** Thus positive economics deals with questions which, in principle at least, are testable. 'Students taking A level economics are better looking than those taking physics' is a testable statement, though there might be a problem in deciding how to measure 'good looking'.' Students taking 'A' level economics ought to be grateful to their teachers' is a normative statement concerned with values. Similarly, 'A tax on a good will raise its price' and 'Business people will invest more when interest rates are low' are positive statements about economics. Normative statements would include

'Britain ought to give more aid to poor countries', and 'Unemployment is a more serious problem than inflation'.

In practice the distinction between positive and normative may not be so clear. People's values can have a substantial effect on their economics. The issues examined by economists - poverty, money, unemployment - are ones where people have strong views. These views influence the areas which economists choose to investigate; for example, someone who believes in greater equality may investigate the causes of poverty. This belief will affect the way the researcher perceives the problem, the way it is investigated and the way the results are interpreted and reported. Similarly, in investigating world poverty Marxist economists would focus on explanations which emphasised exploitation, while supply siders would emphasise evidence which supported their views that inappropriate government intervention retarded development. The **facts** are the same, but the facts which are seen as significant differ between perspectives. The explanations given by economists reveal their values and affect the way they perceive the facts.

The assumptions underlying research are often not made clear. Marxist economists would make very different assumptions about the nature of economics in a capitalist economy than someone who believed in the virtues of the private ownership of the means of production. These differing assumptions would influence their methodology and their findings.

Differing values and assumptions are one reason why economists disagree and give rise to the old jibe that 'if all the economists in the world were laid end to end they would not reach a conclusion'. Readers of all economics texts should be aware that however much the authors may try to present a value free science, they cannot do so.

The problem of relativism

Some philosophers, such as Kuhn (1970), do not see science as a rational activity. He emphasises the importance of groups of scientists with shared ideas to which their members are committed and which they do their best to defend. When individuals or groups switch from one set of beliefs to another it is because there have been changes in social forces. Thus the competing perspectives discussed in this book represent groups of economists with similar beliefs who seek to justify their ideas. Changes in these ideas only occur when there have been significant social and economic changes. Kuhn's ideas highlight a problem. If knowledge is shaped by social forces and defended by groups of scientists, how can we distinguish between genuine knowledge and mere belief? This problem of 'cultural relativism' as it is called, has no easy solution. One answer is to accept that economic perspectives are value laden and that what is needed is a clarification of the values of disputing parties. If these are made explicit then readers are in a position to make better judgements about policies. However, in practice it is often difficult to do this. One reason is that many people take most note of facts and theories which support their own values. In addition, economists often conceal their values and present their work as impartial and authoritative.

Conclusion

Economists often claim to use scientific methods of investigation. These involve the use of models which can be tested against the evidence. When the evidence contradicts a theory, then the theory is abandoned or modified. However, some critics say that this is too simplistic. They claim that impartial investigation is impossible and that economists are often concerned to defend perspectives which reflect their values. The reader should try to ascertain these values in order to be able to judge the policies which are advocated.

Data questions

A

B

Question 1

Examine the photographs.

1. (i) Prepare two competing hypotheses for photograph A.

(ii) Prepare two competing hypotheses for the photographs under B.

2. In each case, suggest what type of evidence could be put forward to support these conflicting hypotheses and the perspectives which lie behind them.

Theorising in science

Admittedly, science suffers from our human fallibility, like every other human enterprise. And although we are doing all we can to find our mistakes, our results cannot be certain. But we learn from our mistakes: scientists turn our fallibility into objectively testable conjectural knowledge. They are continuing to do so this very moment. And I trust they will continue to do so, for many years to come.

Ladies and Gentlemen, all I have said so far has been an attempt to introduce myself to you as a valiant lover of science who has the greatest admiration for the marvellous and often true results of science, without believing these results to be certain. The results of science remain hypotheses, which may have been well tested, but not established: not shown to be true. Of course, they may be true. And, at any rate, they are splendid hypotheses, showing the way to still better ones. Our theories, our hypotheses, are our adventurous trials. Admittedly, most of these turn out to be errors: under the impact of our tests they turn out to be false. Those theories that we cannot refute by the severest tests, we hope to be true. And indeed, they may well be true. But new tests may still falsify them.

This method of bold, adventurous theorising, followed by exposure to severe testing, is the method of life itself as it evolves to higher forms. Just as life conquers new worlds, new lands, the ocean, the air, space; so science conquers new worlds: new lands, the ocean, air and space. What we aim to know, to understand, is the world, the cosmos. All science is cosmology: it is an attempt to learn more about the world: about atoms, about molecules; about living organisms, about the riddles of the origin of life on earth.

Source: Sir Karl Popper, *The Guardian,* August 29, 1988.

Question 2

1. What conclusions does the article draw about theory? What implications do these conclusions have for economists?

2. How would the values of an investigator influence the choice of hypotheses to be tested and the way in which the results were presented?

References

Aaronovitch, S. *et al* (1981), *The Political Economy of British Capitalism,* Pluto, London.

Atkinson, G.B.J. ed. (annual), *Developments in Economics,* Causeway Press, Ormskirk.

Bain, J. (1958), *Barriers to New Competition,* Harvard University Press, USA.

Bauer, P.T. & Yamey, B. (1957), *The Economics of Underdeveloped Countries,* Cambridge University Press, Cambridge.

Bauer, P.T. (1982), *Equality, the Third World and Economic Delusion,* Methuen, London.

Baumol, W.J. (1959), *Business Behaviour, Value and Growth,* Macmillan, New York.

Brandt Commission (1983), *Common Crisis,* Pan, London.

Brown, C.V. (1983), *Taxation and the Incentive to Work,* Oxford University Press, Oxford.

Baumol, W.J. (1958), 'On the Theory of Oligopoly', *Economica.*

Coase, R.H. (1937), 'The Nature of the Firm', *Economica.*

Curry, B. & George, K.D. (1983), 'Industrial Concentration - a Survey', *Journal of Industrial Economics.*

Friedman, M. (1966), *The Optimum Quantity of Money,* Macmillan, London.

Friedman, M. & R. (1980), *Free to Choose,* Harcourt Brace Jovanovich, USA.

Gaitskell, H. (1956), *Socialism & Nationalisation,* Labour Party, London.

Galbraith, J.K. (1952), *American Capitalism,* Penguin, London.

Galbraith, J.K. (1983), *A Life in our Times,* Corgi, London.

Gowland, D. (1979), *Modern Economic Analysis,* Butterworth, London.

Greenhalgh, C.A., Layard, R. & Oswald A.J. eds. (1983), *The Causes of Unemployment,* Clarenden, Oxford.

Hattersley, R. (1987), *Choose Freedom,* Michael Joseph, London.

Hayek, F.A. (1984), *1980s Unemployment and the Unions,* Institute of Economic Affairs, London.

Heckscher, E. (1919), 'The Effects of Foreign Trade on the Distribution of Income', reprinted in A.E.A. (1949), *Readings in the Theory of International Trade,* Blakiston, Philadelphia.

Hendry, D.F. & Ericsson, N.R. (1983), *Assertion without Empirical Basis: An Economic Appraisal of Friedman & Schwartz,* Bank of England, London.

Howells, P.G. & Bain, K. (1985), *Introduction to Monetary Economics,* Longman, Harlow.

Junankar, P. & Price, S. (1983), 'The Dynamics of Unemployment', *Economic Journal.*

Kay, J.A. & Silberston, Z.A. (1984), 'The New Industrial Policy - Privatisation and Competition', *Midland Bank Review.*

Keynes, J.M. (1936), *General Theory of Employment, Interest and Money,* Macmillan, London.

Kuhn, T.S. (1970), *The Structure of Scientific Revolutions,* University of Chicago, Chicago.

Laffer, A. (1983), Letter to the Los Angeles Times, USA.

Layard, R. & Nickell, S. (1985), *The Causes of British Unemployment,* National Institute Economic Review.

Layard, R. (1986), *How to beat Unemployment,* Oxford University Press, Oxford.

Lewis, M.J. (1985), 'Money and the Control of Inflation in the UK', *Midland Bank Review.*

Leontief, W. (1954), 'Domestic Production and Foreign Trade: The American Capital Position Re-examined', reprinted in A.E.A. (1968), *Readings in International Economics,* Irwin, Homewood, Illinois.

Marx, K. & Engels, F. (1848), *The Communist Manifesto,* various editions.

Marx, K. (3 vols. 1867), *Capital,* various editions.

Maude, A. (1977), *The Right Approach to the Economy,* Conservative Party, London.

Meade, J. (1984), *Wage Fixing Re-visited,* Institute of Economic Affairs, London.

Minford, P. (1985), *The Causes of Unemployment in the UK,* Blackwood, Edinburgh.

Nickell, S.J. & Andrews M. (1983), 'Unions and Unemployment in Britain', in Greenhalgh *et al,* op cit.

Ohlin, B. (1933), *Inter-regional and International Trade,* Harvard University Press, USA.

Phillips, A.W. (1958), 'The Relationship between Unemployment and the Rate of Change of Money Wage Rates in the UK, 1861-1957', *Economica.*

Powell, J.E. (1969), *Freedom and Reality,* Elliot Right Way, Tadworth.

Pratten, C. (1971), *Economies of Scale in Manufacturing Industry,* Cambridge University Press, Cambridge.

Prest, A.R. & Turvey, R. (1965), 'Cost-Benefit Analysis: A Survey', *Economic Journal.*

Rawthorn, R. (1977), 'Conflict, Inflation and Money', *Cambridge Journal of Economics.*

Ricardo, D. (1817), *On the Principles of Political Economy and Taxation* (various editions).

Robinson, J. (1974), *Reflections on the Theory of International Trade,* Manchester Unviersity Press, Manchester.

Rowley, C.K. (1978), *Liberalism and Collective Choice: A Return to Reality?,* Manchester School.

Savas, E.V. (1983), 'Private and Public: the Record' in Shenfield A. ed., *Public Services and the Private Alternative,* Adam Smith Institute, London.

Scherer, F.M. (1980), *Industrial Market Structure and Economic Performance,* Rand McNally, USA.

Schumacher, E.F. (1974), *Small is Beautiful,* Sphere, London.

Schumpeter, J. (1943), *Capitalism, Socialism & Democracy,* Allen & Unwin, London.

Skinner, R.C. (1970), 'The Development of Selling Prices', *Journal of Industrial Economics.*

Smith, A. (1776), *The Wealth of Nations* (various editions).

Stewart, M. (1981), *Relative Earnings and Individual Union Membership in the UK,* London School of Economics.

Stuckley, J.A. (1983), *Vertical Integration and Joint Ventures in the Aluminium Industry,* Harvard University Press, USA.

Taylor, J. (1988), 'Unemployment: Causes and Policies' in *Developments in Economics* vol. 4, Atkinson, G.B.J., ed.

Taylor, J. & Armstrong, H. (1988), 'Regional Policy and the North-South Divide' in Atkinson G.B.J. (ed.) *Developments in Economics* op cit.

White, M. (1983), *Long Term Unemployment and the Labour Market,* Policy Studies Institute.

Whittington, G. (1976), 'Rate of Return on Assets for Large Firms' in Meeks, G. & Whitton, *The Financing of Quoted Companies in the UK,* Royal Commission on the Distribution of Income and Wealth, London.

Yarrow, G. (1985), 'Privatisation in Theory and Practice', *Economic Policy.*

Index